History of Scotland

P Hume Brown

BIBLIOLIFE

HISTORY

OF

SCOTLAND

VOL. I.

TO THE

ACCESSION OF MARY STEWART

BY

P. HUME BROWN, M.A., LL.D.,

AUTHOR OF "THE LIFE OF GEORGE BUCHANAN,"
"THE LIFE OF JOHN KNOX," ETC

WITH SEVEN MAPS.

CAMBRIDGE:
AT THE UNIVERSITY PRESS.
1899

GENERAL PREFACE.

The general aim of this Series is to sketch the History of Modern Europe, with that of its chief colonies and conquests, from about the end of the fifteenth century down to the present time. In one or two cases the story will commence at an earlier date: in the case of the colonies it will usually begin later. The histories of the different countries will be described, as a general rule, separately, for it is believed that, except in epochs like that of the French Revolution and Napoleon I, the connection of events will thus be better understood and the continuity of historical development more clearly displayed.

The Series is intended for the use of all persons anxious to understand the nature of existing political conditions. "The roots of the present lie deep in the past," and the real significance of contemporary events cannot be grasped unless the historical causes which have led to them are known. The plan adopted makes it possible to treat the history of the last four centuries in considerable detail, and to embody the most important results of modern research. It is hoped therefore that the Series will be useful not only to beginners but to students who have already acquired some general knowledge of European History. For those who wish to carry their studies further, the bibliography appended to each volume will act as a guide to original sources of information and works more detailed and authoritative

Considerable attention will be paid to Political Geography, and each volume will be furnished with such maps and plans as may be requisite for the illustration of the text.

G. W. PROTHERO

PREFACE.

IN accordance with the plan of the Series to which this book belongs, it should have dealt with Scottish history mainly during the last four centuries. In the case of Scotland, however, there was a special reason for departing from this plan. There is not in existence a compendious history of Scotland which at once supplies a consecutive narrative of events, and seeks to trace the gradual consolidation of the various elements that have gone to the making of the Scottish people. It is as an attempt to meet this want that this book was conceived and written.

But there was another reason which seemed to justify a preliminary volume exclusively devoted to early and mediæval Scottish history. Since the publication of the works of Dr Hill Burton and Dr Skene considerable additions have been made to our knowledge regarding various periods dealt with in the present volume. On many points, also, the latest critical opinion constrains us to reject or modify conclusions accepted even by such recent authorities as Burton and Skene. To adduce a single instance, though an important one—Dr Skene's elaborate account of the Roman occupation is largely rejected by the highest modern authorities. On the other hand, the researches of Dr Skene have superseded the portion of Burton's History which treats of the centuries that followed the Roman occupation; and the same remark applies in a considerable degree to the period between the coming of the Saxon Margaret and the death of Alexander III. In my own account of Celtic Scotland I have availed myself of the original authorities brought together by Dr Skene in his *Chronicles of the Picts and Scots* and his *Collectanea de*

Rebus Albanicis, as well as of other sources, and have endeavoured to construct a narrative as intelligible as the scanty materials would permit. So scanty, indeed, are the materials for Scottish history from the invasion of Agricola to the death of Alexander III that, if authorities be critically construed and theories be set aside, the following narrative is nearly as full as is justified by ascertained facts.

During recent years our knowledge of the period of the War of Independence has been both corrected and extended; but even with the fresh material at our disposal, a detailed and trustworthy narrative is still impossible. Though the number of contemporary documents is considerable, they are inadequate to form the basis of a comprehensive history of the period; while the Scottish and English Chronicles are at once so conflicting, meagre, and untrustworthy, that the work of reconciling them is probably beyond the ingenuity of criticism. In consistency with the nature and aim of the present work I have confined myself to what seems to be indisputable fact.

It is from the middle of the reign of David II onwards that the following narrative will be found to differ most materially from previous histories of Scotland. It is not too much to say, indeed, that from the materials that have come to hand in recent years this period of the national history had virtually to be rewritten. Yet even with regard to this period we experience, though in a less degree, the same difficulty as in the case of the earlier times while at certain points our information is surprisingly full, at others it is so fragmentary that it is difficult to follow the mere sequence of events. It is necessary to emphasize this fact, as it explains why the events of one reign are, for no apparent reason, related with so much greater fulness than the events of another. The reign of James I, alike from its importance and from the personality of James himself, is one of the most interesting in Scottish history, yet from the information we possess we are unable to treat it on the scale which it would demand. On the other hand, it is with increasing amplitude that we can recount the reigns of his immediate successors—those of James IV and James V supplying materials of special abundance and value. It has been my endeavour to guard as far as possible against the misconceptions likely to arise from this unavoidable disproportion of treatment.

It should perhaps be added that the bibliography at the end of the volume is not meant to be exhaustive. Such as it is, however, the list of authorities given may be of service both to the general reader and to the student who may wish to investigate a particular period. The copious table of contents will to a large extent supply the place of an index which is reserved for the concluding volume.

I here take the opportunity of thanking Dr James Macdonald, Rhind Lecturer for 1897, for his invaluable assistance in connection with the chapter on the Roman occupation of North Britain. To Sheriff Mackay and Professor Mackinnon, of the University of Edinburgh, I am also indebted for information on points regarding which they are recognized authorities. Through the great kindness of Mr Matthew Livingstone, Deputy Keeper of the Records, I was enabled to examine a mass of unpublished Charters, extending from the reign of Malcolm IV, which he has been engaged in transcribing for some years past; and by the courtesy of the Rev. John Anderson, of the Register House, Edinburgh, I had the privilege of inspecting the Laing Collection of Charters, a calendar of which is about to be published under his supervision. Finally, I have to express my great obligation to Professor Prothero, the Editor of the Series, to whose wide knowledge and experience I am indebted for valuable suggestions in the course of his revision of my proofs.

P. H. B.

December, 1898.

b 2

CONTENTS.

BOOK I.

THE BEGINNINGS OF SCOTLAND. FROM THE INVASION OF AGRICOLA TO THE BATTLE OF CARHAM (A.D. 80—1018.)

CHAPTER I

THE ROMAN OCCUPATION. (A.D. 80—410.)

CHAPTER II

SCOT, PICT, BRITON, AND ANGLE (A.D. 449—844.)

CHAPTER III.

Scot, Briton, and Angle. (A D. 844—1018.)

BOOK II.

The Consolidation of Scotland. (A.D. 1018—1286)

CHAPTER I.

Celt and Saxon

CHAPTER II.

CELT AND NORMAN.

CHAPTER III

The Consolidation of the Kingdom.

BOOK III.

The Struggle with England. (A.D. 1286—1371.)

CHAPTER I.

Beginnings of the Struggle.

CHAPTER II.

JOHN BALLIOL. (A.D. 1292—1296.)

CHAPTER III.

SIR WILLIAM WALLACE. (A.D. 1296—1305.)

CHAPTER IV.

ROBERT BRUCE. (A.D 1306—1329.)

CHAPTER III.

REGENCY OF THE DUKES OF ALBANY. (A.D. 1406—1424.)

CHAPTER IV.

JAMES I. (A D. 1424—1437.)

CHAPTER V.

JAMES II. (A.D. 1437—1460.)

CHAPTER VI.

JAMES III. (A.D. 1460—1488.)

CHAPTER VII.

JAMES IV (A.D. 1488—1513)

CHAPTER VIII.

JAMES V. (A.D. 1513—1542.)

MAPS.

BOOK I.

The Beginnings of Scotland. From the Invasion of Agricola to the Battle of Carham. A.D. 80—1018.

CHAPTER I.

THE ROMAN OCCUPATION. A.D. 80—410.

In its present territorial limits Scotland dates its corporate existence from the year 1266[1]. In that year the King of Norway, the successor of the famous Haco, ceded the Western Islands to Alexander III, thus closing a long struggle which more than once had threatened to prevent the emergence of a Scottish nation and to make the history of North Britain that of another Ireland. While its territory was thus consolidated, the country was still far from forming an organic whole. At various periods of its subsequent history this was to be signally proved. Even into the 14th century "the men of Galloway" remained a hostile and formidable section among the subjects of the Kings of the Scots, and it was a still later day before the Celts of the Highlands and Islands entered into the real life of the main body of the nation. To understand the conflicting interests of the different sections of the Scottish

---

[1] The Orkney and Shetland Islands were not acquired by Scotland till 1468.

people, with their different characters and ideals, it is necessary to go beyond the date of Alexander III. It is in the long process of consolidation that those affinities and antipathies are to be traced which eventually gave its distinctiveness to the national history and the national character When during the reign of David I (1124—1153) the Eastern Lowlands became the heart of his dominion, the future course of Scotland may be said to have been determined, for it was then finally assured that the Teutonic races were to be the predominating force in fashioning the destinies of the country. Thenceforward Scotland only followed the same main lines of development as the other countries of Christendom, and under the institutions of feudalism and the Roman Church her consolidation was completed in the course of a single century. In the stage that preceded the reign of David the process bore a different character. The issue then decided was which of several peoples should eventually be the leading power in the region north of the Tweed. The struggle lasted for many centuries, but happily for the future of all the peoples concerned the predominance of one among them was assured at the fitting time. Of Scot, Briton, Pict, and Angle, the first prevailed in the person of Malcolm I (942—954); and with power thus concentrated his successors were enabled to achieve the task of assimilating the new civilization from the south and of stamping it with a character of their own.

It is with the year 80 A.D, when Agricola entered the region of North Britain, that the history of Scotland as a traceable sequence of cause and effect may be said to begin. When the Romans first came in contact with them, the inhabitants of that region had long passed the stage of mere barbarism. Various remains that have been found prove that they had attained considerable knowledge of many of the arts of life; and from something like direct evidence we

80 A.D

know that they possessed an organized society with civil and religious institutions of some complexity. Yet with the knowledge we possess we are unable to trace such causal relations in that earlier time as would bring it within the domain of history in the ordinary acceptation of the word. On the other hand, from the invasion of Agricola onward, materials, however scanty and intermittent, are never wholly wanting to mark the action of the internal and external forces that eventually moulded Northern Britain into modern Scotland.

It was in the interest of the Roman power in South Britain that Agricola led his forces into the region of the north. Experience had proved that so long as a tribe was left unsubdued in the whole island the Roman colony could never be counted safe; and in six successive campaigns Agricola attempted the task of subduing the northern Britons. From the vague terms of his biographer, Tacitus, it is impossible to trace with precision the course of these various campaigns. In the summer of 80 he entered North Britain, probably by the East coast, and laid waste the country as ***80 A D*** far north as a tidal water which Tacitus calls the Tanaus[1]. The following summer he spent in securing the ground he had won by constructing a chain of forts between the Firths of Forth and Clyde. In 82 he carried his arms into the west and south, and apparently with such ***82 A D.*** effect that in the following year he was able to begin operations against the tribes beyond the Forth. During three successive years he carried on this work, bringing his wars to a close by a great victory over the Caledonians at a place called Mons Graupius, the exact site of which still remains uncertain. Of his line of march, of the positions of his camps and his battles, it is impossible to speak with certainty from any indications that have yet come to hand. To this account if we add that Agricola gave orders to the commander of his

---

[1] This water has been variously identified with the Northumberland Tyne, with the Tweed, and with the Haddingtonshire Tyne.

fleet to sail round the island—orders which appear to have been only partially obeyed—we have before us the main facts that are known regarding Agricola's northern expedition.

On the precise value of Agricola's conquests we have an emphatic comment some forty years later. In 120 A.D. the Emperor Hadrian visited Britain, and built a rampart between the Tyne and the Solway[1]—thus, in keeping with his general policy, abandoning territory which had never been an integral part of the Empire. But during the next twenty years it was seen that Agricola's policy of conquest had been well considered Hadrian's rampart proved no barrier against the tribes to the north, whose inroads left little peace to the inhabitants of the Province. To strike at the head of this evil, Lollius Urbicus was commissioned (140 A.D.) by Antoninus Pius to repeat the work of Agricola as a necessary condition for the peace of Britain. Of the achievements of Urbicus we know still less than of those of Agricola. He must, however, have fought many battles, and he must have virtually subdued all the country south of the Firths of Forth and Clyde, since between these estuaries he built the earthen rampart known as the Wall or Vallum of Antoninus Pius.

120 A D

140 (?) A D

The conquests of Urbicus were not more permanent in their results than those of Agricola During the last half of the second century we have but one or two casual references to the state of North Britain; but from these we gather that the inroads into the Province went on as before, and every year assumed a more formidable character. At the accession of Severus to the Empire (197 A D) two great tribes, the Maeatae somewhere near the one or the other dividing wall, and the Caledonians conterminous with them[2], were specially prominent by their dangerous activity

197 A.D

---

[1] It should be said that what Hadrian's rampart precisely was is still under dispute.

[2] Authorities differ as to the position of these tribes.

For the third time North Britain was to feel the weight of the Roman arm.   In 208 A.D Severus, though confined to a litter by old age and gout, marched   208 A D
northwards in person at the head of a punitive expedition.   On his passing the boundaries of the Roman province, a vigilant foe beset his march at every turn and, without risking a decisive engagement, cut off his men in such numbers that his loss was set down at 50,000.   From the vague accounts that have been preserved nothing can be determined either as to his various fortunes with the enemy or his line of march or his places of encampment.   He is said to have reached "the extremity of the island", but this may be a mere random expression to which no definite meaning can be attached   Like his prede-cessors Severus gained at least a temporary triumph, and forced the Caledonians to terms by which they conceded a considerable portion of their territory.   Like Agricola and Urbicus, also, he is said to have constructed a line of defence which ran from sea to sea, but more probably he only repaired one of those already existing[1].

Severus had hardly turned his back before Caledonians and Maeatae were again at their old work; and
only his death at York in 211 prevented his re-   211 A D.
newing his efforts against them.   For the next century and a half North Britain passes entirely out of sight, and again it is the insubordination of the northern tribes that brings it into notice   Under the general name of Picts these tribes are now reported as ravaging at will the territory south of the Tyne and the Solway—a work in which they were effectually aided by Scots on the western and by Saxons on the eastern shore.   So persistent and general were these combined assaults that the very existence of the Province was now at stake, and to delay the inevitable end Theodosius, father of the Emperor of

---

[1] Some authorities place the wall of Severus between the Tyne and the Solway; while others question its existence as an independent structure.

the same name, was despatched by Valentinian (368 A D) to

the help of the wretched provincials. In two campaigns Theodosius broke the power of the Picts, and recovered certain territories, to a part of which, whose position is not certainly known, the name of Valentia was given in honour of the Emperor. But the evil day had merely been postponed. Rome required all her resources to defend herself against the destroyers who were gathering round her. Twice the great Stilicho, the minister of the Emperor Honorius,

sent a force to the help of the British provincials (396, 406); but with the fall of Rome before Alaric (410) foreign assistance was finally cut off, and henceforward the inhabitants of Britain in all its length and breadth had their own destinies in their hands.

To this account of the Romans in North Britain should be added a passing reference to the geographical description by the famous Ptolemy of Alexandria. From Ptolemy's tables in his great Geography and from the maps that were constructed for them either by himself or by a later hand we gain a view of the whole island with the "towns" and the various tribes that inhabited it. To the region north of the Cheviots he assigns at least seventeen tribes and nineteen towns, thus corroborating other evidence as to the numerous subdivisions of the northern Britons. Yet as far as North Britain is concerned, the work of Ptolemy can be regarded only as an interesting antiquarian relic, offering a wide field of conjecture as to the precise amount of knowledge he really possessed, and the sources from which it was obtained.

For above three hundred years the Romans had thus come and gone in Northern Britain, and at different periods of more or less duration had held as their own at least one half of the country. What determining influence did they exert on the peoples with whom they were thus in such long and close contact? For Scotland these influences were of necessity far less permanent and pervasive than in the case of England.

The greater part of England had been a Roman province in every sense of the word. Its upper classes had become Roman in speech, in dress, in ways of life; and when the country was left to itself, the mere material impress of the conquerors determined to an appreciable degree the direction of its future growth. By their many roads they partly directed the special developments of certain districts; and from many of their settlements sprang great English towns whose names preserve their unmistakeable origin. In Scotland, if we may judge from the meagre accounts that have come down to us, the Roman dominion hardly passed the stage of a military occupation, held by an intermittent and precarious tenure. From the remains of their presence in the country much may one day be learned of the extent and the character of their occupation[1]; yet the tendency of present investigation goes to prove that their influence has been exaggerated rather than underestimated. Roads and mounds, confidently set down as Roman, have yet to stand the tests of the stricter methods of modern investigators. Meanwhile it can be said that the name of but one Roman station in Scotland has been preserved—Blatum- or Blato-Bulgium, identified with Birrens in the district of Annandale[2]. In the case of no Scottish town has its origin been satisfactorily traced to the Roman occupation[3];

---

[1] The elaborate account of the Roman occupation of Northern Britain given by Skene in his *Celtic Scotland* is largely rejected by more recent authorities, as based either on conjecture or insufficient data.

[2] In 1895 the Roman station at Birrens was excavated under the auspices of the Society of Antiquaries of Scotland, which has published in its *Proceedings* a full account of the discoveries made and of the inferences that may be drawn from them. Only one date (158 A.D.) was found in the course of the investigation, and it is uncertain whether this marks the period of the construction of the station. The same Society carried out (1896-7) a similar investigation of the famous camp at Ardoch in Perthshire with the result that it was proved to be indubitably Roman. Unfortunately no date was found to indicate when the "camp" was formed or how long it was under occupation.

[3] Inveresk near Musselburgh may be of Roman origin; but, at least, it

and no place-name in Scotland has yet been shown to be of indubitably Roman origin[1]. While all this may be true, it is impossible to doubt that in many ways Rome exercised a deep and lasting influence on the country which it yet made so imperfectly its own. The very presence of such a power, embodying all the resources of a great civilization, was an experience that could not be forgotten. Moreover, in the very effort to beat back the invader political and social forces were brought into play, which powerfully affected the mutual relations of the various tribes, and introduced a new spirit and new aims and endeavours, which constitute a new departure in the life of a people. Of these internal revolutions we have only vague information from really trustworthy sources; yet when North Britain first comes clearly before us subsequent to the departure of the Romans, its inhabitants are no longer a loose aggregate of tribes, but a few well-compacted bodies with the possibility of one day merging into a united people.

It is to the closing years of the Roman dominion that tradition has assigned the labours of the first Christian missionary in Northern Britain. Of the labours of St Ninian (*circa* 397), however, we know even less than of the campaigns of Lollius Urbicus or Theodosius. A few words of Bede (673—735), themselves only based on tradition, tell us almost all that we know of him; yet one indubitable fact is of some significance in the history of the period. On the shore of Wigton Bay Ninian built a church for Christian worship, known as Candida Casa, the White House, from its being constructed of stone. Besides founding his church, Ninian, also according to Bede, preached to the Southern Picts and converted them to Christianity. Who these Picts were and what is implied in this vague notice of their conversion will

has not preserved its Roman name. A Roman origin is claimed for Cramond, but the name Alaterva sometimes assigned to it is merely an unwarranted inference from an inscription.

[1] The name "Chesters" in Scotland is not derived from *castra*.

probably never be determined; and, as a matter of fact, all traces of Ninian's labours disappear during the centuries that followed the withdrawal of the legions[1]. Yet whatever the sphere and extent of Ninian's labours may have been, it was to Rome that he owed his religion and it was through the influence of Rome that the opportunity was made for him to become the first Christian apostle to Northern Britain.

NOTE.—Inscribed stones or other undoubted antiquities proving or indicating a Roman occupation have been found in or near the various stations on the Vallum of Antonine; at Birrens in Dumfriesshire; at Newstead near Melrose; at Cappuck, near Jedburgh; at Inveresk; at Cramond; at Ardoch in Perthshire; and, as it would seem, at Camelon in Stirlingshire. Lyne in Peeblesshire and Strageth in Perthshire are sites of earthworks similar to those of Birrens and Ardoch. In the south and centre of Scotland and on the east coast as far north as Aberdeenshire are also found what seem to be Roman temporary camps. Coins and other portable objects are more widely distributed.

---

[1] The existence of a monastic school at Whithorn, within a century after Ninian's death, is only a probability.

CHAPTER II.

SCOT, PICT, BRITON, AND ANGLE (449—844).

WITH the departure of the Romans, North Britain enters on a stage of development, which in its broad features was that of all the countries of Western Europe. In general terms, it may be described as a conflict of different races or different peoples, themselves often torn by internal dissensions, for the mastery within a well-defined area. In the case of North Britain the authorities for the story of this struggle are at once so vague and so fragmentary that it is only in the most general terms that it can be told. Yet in its broad outlines the story is sufficiently clear: from certain outstanding events we can gather at once the main drift and the specific character of the forces that eventually transformed Northern Britain into Scotland.

Not till a century and a half after the withdrawal of the legions do we gain a clear glimpse of the state of things north of the Tweed. As we then see it, the country is in the hands of the four peoples who were to settle its future between them. In the latter half of the 6th century, the four nations of the Picts, the Britons, the Scots, and the Angles, were in full rivalry for the possession of the land. Of these four nations, the Picts and the Britons had been settled there from a period which has not been ascertained; while the Scots and the Angles were comparatively new-comers. From the union of these four peoples the Scottish nation was to emerge, though

I.

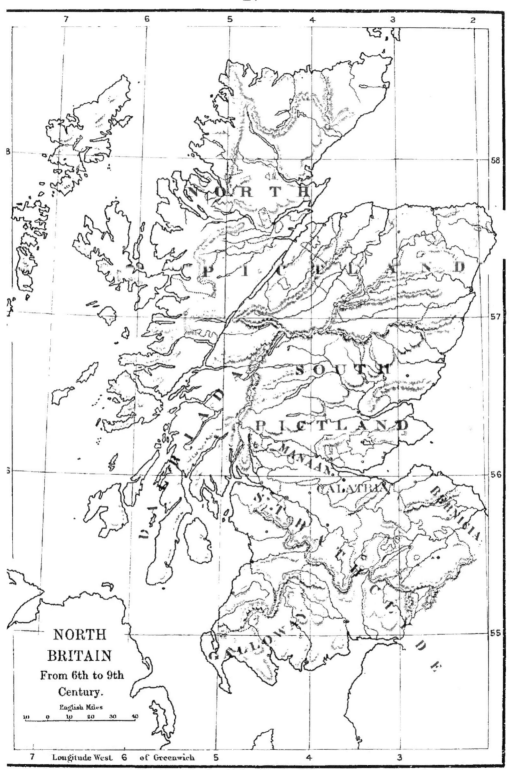

NORTH
BRITAIN
From 6th to 9th
Century.

English Miles

NORTH

P I C T L A N D

D A L R I A D A

SOUTH

P I C T L A N D

MANAAN

CALATRIA

BERNICIA

S T R A T H C L Y D E

GALLOWAY

blended with other elements that appreciably affected its character and destiny.

At the close of the 6th century the nation of the Picts occupied the country to the north of the Firths of Forth and Clyde, with the exception of the modern Argyleshire[1]. They were themselves divided into the Northern and the Southern Picts—the latter occupying the territory corresponding to the counties of Perth, Fife, Forfar, and Kincardine. At the moment when they first come clearly before us, one king appears to have ruled both sections, and even to have extended his sway to the Orkney Islands. As in the case of Ireland, the country was probably divided into provinces, of which seven was the constant number. Like Ireland, also, Pictland was subdivided among a series of greater and lesser tribes, which acknowledged the king or kings who in turn made good their sovereignty. At different periods of their history, as will be seen, there were not only separate kings of the Northern and Southern Picts, but also sub-kings who survived the separate existence of the main Pictish monarchy. In all probability, the large majority of the inhabitants of Pictland were of Celtic origin, more or less mixed towards its northern and southern extremities. In the north there may have been a remnant of a pre-Celtic people whose influence has been detected in certain customs that prevailed among their Pictish conquerors. The main body of the Picts themselves appear to have been Goidelic Celts, and kindred, therefore, with the Celts of Ireland and of the Isle of Man[2]. On their southern limit there was a blending of these Goidels with the Brythonic Celts whose present representatives are to be found in Cornwall, Wales, and Brittany. Whence or at what period the Picts found their way into North Britain has not been determined.

The second people in possession of the country were

[1] As will afterwards be seen, this statement requires some modification.

[2] This point is still under discussion, and I have only adopted the view which seems most consonant with the subsequent course of Scottish history.

Brythonic Celts, a remnant of the race who had formed the main population of Britain at the coming of the Romans   By the English invaders the bulk of this people had been gradually driven westwards into Wales and the territory along the west coast as far north as the Firth of Clyde.   Though of common race and bound by common misfortune, they formed at least two distinct kingdoms under separate princes.   Not even their threatened extinction by the English invaders sufficed to save them from internal dissensions   In 573, at the battle of Arderydd (supposed by some to be Arthuret, near Carlisle), the northern section of these Britons made a new departure in their history, which is of real significance in their relations to the other peoples of Northern Britain.   Hitherto, their chief seat had been Carlisle, but thenceforward it was the rock of Alcluyd, subsequently known as Dumbarton, "the fortress of the Britons" Another incident in their history bears directly on the development of North Britain   From the Bristol Channel to the Firth of Clyde there still existed a solid body of Britons, who by laying aside their rivalries might have made a successful stand against the common enemy.   By the victory of Chester (613) the Northumbrian King Æthelfrith cleft the Britons in twain, and from that date each section was thrown on its own resources against its respective foes.   About the period when we take up their history, therefore, the dominion of these Northern Britons, known as Strathclyde, extended along the valley of the Clyde from Dumbarton at one extremity to the Derwent in Cumberland at the other—the modern counties of Wigton and Kirkcudbright lying outside its limits in the possession of another people.   In the long struggle that was to ensue for the supremacy in North Britain their past history had put them at serious disadvantage.   Under the Roman dominion, intermittent as it had been, they had in some degree lost the ferocity and hardihood of an unconquered race.   Partly Romanized and Christianized, when left to themselves they gradually lost ground before the untamed vigour of Pict, Scot, and Angle.

Of the three it was the English from whom they had suffered most in the past, and from whom they had most to fear in the future. From the shores of the German Ocean the English had beaten them back within their present limits, and for a long period to come they were never to know peace from a foe whose unremitting hate is reflected even in the genial pages of the Anglian Bede.

Of the new-comers to North Britain, the Scots appear to have been the first to form a definite settlement. Between 498 and 503 a colony of them, led by Fergus Mor and his two brothers, made their home in the district that came to be known as Dalriada[1]. By race these colonists were Goidelic Celts; and in Ireland, whence they came, they had received a tincture of the Christianity which had recently been planted there by St Patrick. For the first half century the fortunes of the colony do not appear to have been prosperous. Divided into four tribes, representing the descendants of the three brothers, the Scots failed to make a united stand against the Picts whom they had sought to dislodge. At a critical period of their affairs, however, they were reinforced by all the influence and prestige of one whose figure presents itself at the threshold of Scottish history. Here it is sufficient to say that Dalriada in its fullest extent included the modern county of Argyle, together with the islands of Islay and Jura, and that its chief seat was Dunadd, at the head of Loch Crinan.

Even before 449, the date of the supposed landing of Hengest and Horsa in Kent, Teutonic strangers had found a footing on the coast of Northumbria to the south of the Firth of Forth. To that Firth itself, indeed, a settlement of Frisians appear to have given the name of the Frisian Sea. It is in the year 547, however, that these Teutonic settlements first come clearly before us. In that year an Anglian leader,

---

[1] From analogy we may conjecture that this was only the most important of many bodies of Scots who made their home in the same neighbourhood.

named Ida, succeeded in founding a kingdom, the northern portion of which was to form the heart of the future Scotland. Under the name of Bernicia, and with the fort of Bamborough as its chief seat, this kingdom eventually extended from the Tees to the Firth of Forth. To Bernicia before the close of the century (588) was added the kingdom of Deira, reaching from the Tees to the Humber. At various times these kingdoms became partially consolidated; but for protracted periods their arms were as often turned against each other as against their enemies. But for this disunion the history of North Britain must have been different from what it has actually been. Northumbria, united and fortunate, would have dominated the whole island, and the name of England would have been co-extensive with the limits of Britain. Yet, changing as its fortunes were, Northumbria, at certain periods of its history, was the virtual master of Strathclyde and Dalriada, and even exercised supremacy over the Southern Picts.

Besides these four main divisions of North Britain, there were three other districts which played a subordinate, but still an important, part in its history. These were Calatria, Manann, and Galloway. Calatria corresponded with what is now known as the Carse of Falkirk, extending from the town of that name to the Forth. Immediately to the west of it was Manann, a name still preserved in Clackmannan and Slamannan. In these two districts, comprised in the counties of Stirling and Linlithgow, there was a mixed population of Picts, Angles, and Britons; and from this circumstance they derived such importance as they possessed, since they were long the battle-ground of the contending peoples. The names of Calatria and Manann passed out of history with the consolidation of these peoples; but it has been otherwise with the third district, Galloway. At the period of which we are speaking, the name was given to the region now covered by the shires of Wigton and Kirkcudbright. Of its inhabitants we have only vague and contradictory accounts; but they are usually spoken

of as the "Picts of Galloway," though their connection with
the other Picts has not been clearly made out.   In the rivalries
of the four kingdoms Galloway played a part of its own, but
it was at a later period, when it had extended to far wider
limits, that it rose to an importance which threatened the
existence of a united Scotland.

Scottish history may be emphatically said to begin with
Columba's landing in Iona about the year 563.
It is not only that his biography by Adamnan   563 A D
is its first consecutive chapter : by the great work he achieved
Columba fairly takes his place with the founders of nations
who have a niche apart in the annals of mankind   What
precise motive led him to leave Ireland cannot be ascertained
As far as his motives were religious, however, they came of his
own initiative; for unlike Augustine of Canterbury he conceived
and carried out his work absolutely without reference to the
Church of Rome.   In Ireland he had been one of the notable
personages of his nation, for to royal descent he added a
reputation for learning and sanctity which doubtless preceded
him in his new home.   By his previous training he was specially
fitted for the mission to which he addressed himself.   His high
rank had made him a statesman and even a warrior; and as
the founder of many monasteries he might be called an
experienced ecclesiastic.

Landing in Iona with twelve companions, Columba surrounded himself with a community which was to be the basis
and model of his future operations.   A church constructed of
wattles and clay, with huts of the same materials for the monks,
and an earthen rampart for defence—such was the external
appearance of the settlement.   To the members of the community different functions were respectively assigned.   One
class consisted of novices in training for the spiritual life, a
second performed the round of religious duties, and a third—
the largest class—did all the manual labour requisite to supply
the physical wants of the brethren.   In Ireland this form of

Christian society had grown out of the conditions of its tribal arrangements; and for the Picts, therefore, a people with kindred institutions, it was expressly fitted as the most effective means of winning them to the new faith.

About two years after his arrival in Iona, Columba set forth on his apostolic journey to the Picts. It is hardly necessary to say that he bore other arms besides those of pure truth. As he appears in the pages of Adamnan, Columba is in fact half Druid magician, half Christian missionary, ready, as occasion arises, to fight his adversaries with their own weapons. Nor were his followers the typical apostles of the Founder of Christianity. *Milites Christi* they called themselves; and the designation was more than a mere figure of speech. Columba himself is known to have been engaged in at least three battles; the various monastic settlements not unfrequently had recourse to the arm of flesh, and on the occasion of great ecclesiastical assemblies the brethren regularly carried arms till as late as the days of Adamnan. Moreover, the saint had doubtless other words to speak to King Brude than the simple statement of the principles of the Christian religion. To the close of his career he was deep in all the politics of his time, and, if not at this moment, he was at a later date the powerful intermediary between the kings of Ireland, Dalriada, and Pictland.

Columba found Brude in his palace on the banks of the Ness. His reception was discouraging; but, as it happened, this proved the means of his immediate success. King Brude refused to open his gate; but on the saint's making the sign of the Cross, it flew open of its own accord, to admit him. On this convincing sanction of the saint's mission Brude appears to have been overcome, and to have lent a willing ear to the new teaching. A subsequent thaumaturgic contest between Columba and the ministers of the old religion incontestably proved the superiority of the former, and thenceforward the King took his side by the new teacher. But by the very nature of the tribal system, the religion of the King necessarily became the religion of his people, and within Columba's own lifetime the Christianity of Iona took such deep root among the Picts that not till its own decay did it yield place to a new and more vigorous form of the same faith.

This conversion of the Picts may fairly be regarded as the governing fact in Scottish history. Happening at the time it did, it determined those subsequent turns in affairs which gradually led up to a consolidated Scotland and a united Scottish people. From the scanty materials that have come down to us it is impossible to say to what extent the change of faith affected the structure of the Pictish nation. There is no reason to suppose, however, that any great breach was made with the past either in social or political conditions. The new faith did its work by insinuating itself into the old order, by elevating the national consciousness, and by setting before it an ideal of well-being that was inconceivable under the old nature-religion. But the acceptance of the new faith brought an immediate good to the Pictish kingdom, which was likewise of the most far-reaching consequence. Through a common religion it was brought into direct relations with Ireland, by whose higher civilization it was influenced for at least a century and a half. Shortly after their conversion, also, the Picts seem to have concluded a stable peace with the Scots of Dalriada—themselves nominally a Christian people. Under different conditions, with the Dalriadic Scots and the Bernician Angles as their united foes, the kingdom of the Picts might have collapsed before completing the work needed to make a national union possible.

Next to Columba's work in evangelizing the Picts must be reckoned his success in restoring and consolidating the kingdom of Dalriada. A few years before his arrival in Iona, King Brude had driven the Scots into Kintyre, and seemed on the point of destroying their kingdom. Himself of the royal family of the Dalriadic Scots, Columba strove with

all his might to restore their fortunes.   By his advice and through his authority, Aidan was chosen as their king, though not the rightful heir by the Scottish law of succession. A further exercise of his great influence placed the Dalriadic kingdom on a firm basis.   At a great synod,
575   held in **575** at Drumceatt in Londonderry, Columba secured the recognition of Aidan as a king independent of Ireland; and he crowned his work by extracting a similar acknowledgement from the King of the Picts.   What we know of Aidan proves that he was a ruler fitted to mend the fortunes of a kingdom.   So strong was his position in his last years that he carried his arms far beyond the bounds of his own territory. At peace with the Picts, he gave his aid to the Britons of Strathclyde in repelling the encroachments of the Angles of Bernicia, whom he drove from the debateable land of Manann. Of the four battles he is recorded to have fought, the last is the most significant of the general drift of things to the north of
594   the Tweed.   In 594 Æthelfrith, grandson of Ida, became King of Bernicia, and proved one of the most powerful rulers of his time.   According to Bede, no king before him had done such harm to the Britons in subjecting them to his sway, in driving them from their lands, and in planting Angles in their places.   But if the Britons should be completely broken, the subjection of Dalriada must soon follow, as at a later date was actually seen.   With a great army
603   Aidan met Æthelfrith (603) at a place called Degsastan, perhaps identical with Dawstane near Jedburgh, close to the boundaries of Strathclyde and Bernicia. So complete was the overthrow of Aidan that till Bede's day, more than a century later, no Scottish king dared to carry arms against the Angle.   In spite of this great reverse, however, at his death three years later, after a reign of thirty-seven years, Aidan left Dalriada a compact kingdom ruled by one prince, who was recognised as their head by the separate tribes that composed it.

The work of Columba in evangelizing the Picts was in a partial degree done by St Mungo, or Kentigern, in Strathclyde. Of St Mungo's labours, however, we have no such trustworthy account as in the case of Columba ; and he must be regarded as a legendary rather than as a historical personage. As in the case of Ninian, it is the tradition of a church that assures us that he is not wholly the creation of the popular fancy. Some five hundred years after his death a bishopric was revived in Glasgow on the strength of evidence that its church had been founded by St Mungo, and was the centre of his see. Of his immediate successors in office no memorial has been preserved ; and there is good reason to believe that in the centuries that followed St Mungo's labours the Christianity of Strathclyde was little more than nominal.

In different degrees the Britons, Scots, and Picts had thus been Christianized, and Bernicia alone remained wholly Pagan. But within a few years Northumbria also found its apostle. By a victory over the great Æthelfrith, Edwin of Deira gained the throne of Northumbria, and attained a predominance beyond even that of his predecessor. Among the Britons he made his power more strongly felt, and the outpost of Edwinesburg, which preserves his name, indicates the extent of his dominion towards the north. Like his predecessors, Edwin had been reared in Paganism, and during the first part of his reign had ruled as a Pagan king In 627, however, Paullinus, Bishop of **627** York, appeared at the Northumbrian court, and presented the claims of his religion with such effect that Edwin made public profession of his change of faith. He had six years before him to give proof of his devotion, and from the zeal he displayed we may conclude that Bernicia, like the rest of his dominions, profited by the mission of Paullinus. The triumph of the new faith was shortlived. In 633 Edwin was defeated and **633** slain at the battle of Heathfield (Hatfield in Yorkshire); and

2—2

his conqueror, Penda, the heathen king of Mercia, reduced Northumbria to temporary anarchy. When next Christianity was introduced into the country of the Angles, it was not through the medium of the Latin church: by a notable coincidence it was the inheritors of the work of Columba who were to do for Northumbria what he had so effectually done in the land of the Picts.

After a year's anarchy Northumbria regained its unity under a king whose reign is perhaps the most notable epoch in its history. With Penda of Mercia, in his wars against Northumbria, had been associated Cædwalla, one of the kings of the Britons of Wales, who, after the battle of Heathfield, wreaked vengeance on the masterless country for all the inherited wrongs of his race. His course of devastation was effectually checked from an unexpected quarter. On the overthrow of Æthelfrith by Edwin, his two sons, Eanfrid and Oswald, had been driven to seek safety in exile—the one among the Picts, the other among the Scots of Dalriada or in Ireland. In this crisis of his country's fortunes, Oswald now appeared to make good his hereditary claims, and at the battle of Heavenfield, some eight miles north of Hexham, utterly broke the power of the British king. In the reign of nine years, which Bede assigns to him, Oswald made Northumbria once more what it had been under his father and under Edwin. Bernicia and Deira were again united, and their ascendancy was asserted over Strathclyde, Dalriada, and Pictland. But the chief glory of Oswald's reign was the final settlement of Christianity in his dominion. On this occasion the new faith came not from Rome, but from the centre of Columban Christianity, Iona. During his exile Oswald had himself become a convert to that form of faith; and one of his first acts, on finding himself king, was to send to Iona for a preacher. One brother, who was sent in response to the request, returned from his mission in despair at the hopelessness of his task, but his successors more than fulfilled all the hopes of Oswald. Through the labours of Aidan from

his see in Lindisfarne Northumbria passed finally from
Paganism to Christianity   In Bernicia, the monastery of
Melrose founded by Aidan was a centre of influence, whence
somewhat later in the century St Cuthbert achieved the work
which constitutes him the true apostle of Lothian.   Thus
Christianized and consolidated, Northumbria appeared destined
to predominance both in Northern and Southern Britain.   A
succession of kings equal in capacity to Oswald must in the
end have prevailed over Scot, Briton, and Pict alike.   But the
reign of Oswald, like those of his father and of Edwin, closed
in shame and disaster   The heathen King Penda, the inveterate enemy of Northumbria, was again the instrument of
its misfortunes.   In 642 at the battle of Maserfield, a place probably in Shropshire, Penda   642
overthrew Oswald, who himself died on the field; and for the
next twelve years Northumbria had to struggle for bare existence against the Mercian king.

The very year of the overthrow of Oswald a similar misfortune overtook the kingdom of Dalriada.   At his death in
606 Aidan, we have seen, had left that kingdom so compact
and vigorous that his successors even made attempts to extend
their territory.   On the debateable land between the Avon and
the Pentland Hills they appear to have had some claim, and
in this district we find them in frequent strife with the Angles.
The third king from Aidan, Donald Breac, seems to have been
specially energetic in his endeavours to gain the disputed
territory.   Three battles with the Angles are recorded of him,
in all of which he was unfortunate, the last (642)
proving fatal to himself and disastrous to his   642
country.   For the remainder of the century Dalriada ceases to
be a rival to the other three kingdoms.   Broken into its old
tribal divisions, it fell under the dominion of the Britons and
the Picts, though it was again to recover its position, and
eventually to give a king to Pictland itself.

It is again in Northumbria that we have to seek the significant events in the development of Northern Britain, and again it is a change of religion that has to be emphasized. On the death of Oswald at the battle of Maserfield he was succeeded by his brother Oswiu, whose rule for the first twelve years was distracted by the invasions of the indefatigable Penda. At length, by the banks of the Winwæd, near Leeds, Oswiu rid himself of his enemy by a great victory (655), in which Penda himself perished on the field. To Oswiu Bede ascribes even greater power than to Æthelfrith, or Edwin, or Oswald. In his later years, he, like them, united Deira and Bernicia, and was virtual master of Dalriada, Strathclyde, and parts of the land of the Picts. With the Picts his relation was peculiar. In Talorcan, a contemporary Pictish king, grandson of Æthelfrith, the Angles gave a king to their northern neighbours, who may have recognized Oswiu as his superior. Over all three kingdoms, however, Northumbria for nearly thirty years must have exercised an effective suzerainty.

655

But the great work of Oswiu was the displacement of Irish Christianity by the religion of Rome. The rivalry between the two systems was bound to come to an issue sooner or later; and at the period of which we are speaking the two parties were fairly matched both in influence and zeal. The representatives of Rome had now made nearly all England their own with the exception of Northumbria; and in Northumbria they had ardent champions, notably Wilfrid of York, who were bent on adding that kingdom to their conquests. In Dalriada, Pictland, and partially in Strathclyde, the system of Columba prevailed; and in Northumbria it had likewise attained a predominance, which Bede, himself a follower of Rome, declares to have been the natural result of the high character and devotion of its preachers. It was mainly round two points that the battle between the respective parties was waged—the shape of the tonsure[1] and the proper time for

[1] Bishop Dowden (*Celtic Church in Scotland*, pp. 241-2) seems to

holding Easter. In reality, the two systems differed fundamentally alike in spirit, method, and aims. While Roman Christianity had fitted itself into the mould of the municipal institutions of the empire, Celtic Christianity had grown out of the tribal system of the peoples who had embraced it. Thus by the very conditions of their development the spirit and aims of the two parties were in essential opposition. As to how the issue must be decided, there could be little doubt from the very nature of the opposing forces. With no ecclesiastical capital, with no prestige of a great empire behind it, the ill-regulated enthusiasm of Irish Christianity could only break its strength against the highly organized system of Rome, which every year was bringing to a higher perfection. In Northumbria the question was decided as to which party was to have Britain and Ireland for its own. At the Synod of Whitby (664) Oswiu gave his decree for Rome,
and so effectual was his mandate that, with   **664**
Colman their bishop at their head, the Columban clergy in a body left Northumbria for ever. On the future of North Britain this revolution had a determining influence which marks it as one of the turning-points in its history. Through the zeal of the now dominant church all Bernicia and part of Southern Pictland were speedily won to Rome; and before the middle of the eighth century all North Britain, with apparently the exception of Strathclyde, had followed their example. In North as in South Britain the church thus became one of the most potent influences in hastening that national unity towards which both countries were unconsciously tending.

Northumbria now seemed in a fair way to become the paramount power to the north of the Tweed; but she had attained the height of her fortunes, and she was on the point of a series of disasters which gave a new turn to the development

prove that an erroneous view has prevailed regarding the form of the Celtic tonsure.

of the four kingdoms. On the death of Oswiu in 670 her
troubles began. In the second year of his successor, Ecgfrith,
the Picts made a strenuous but unsuccessful attempt to throw
off the yoke of the Angles. Apparently, however, their strength
was not broken, for in 685 Ecgfrith led a great
army beyond the Forth with the intention of
dealing them a final blow. At Nectan's Mere, identified with
Dunnichen in Forfarshire, he was met by the Pictish king,
Brude, and in a great battle defeated and slain with the bulk
of his army. The defeat was a disastrous one for his nation.
From that day, according to Bede, the hopes and strength of
Northumbria began to abate; the Picts recovered their
territory, and Strathclyde and Dalriada regained their independence So far as North Britain is concerned, one fact is
sufficient to indicate the significance of the battle of Nectan's
Mere. From that defeat till the year 844, when Kenneth
MacAlpin united the Scottish and Pictish peoples, it is no
longer Northumbria that plays the most important part in the
history of the northern kingdoms Henceforward, it is on the
relations of the Picts and Scots that the future of these peoples
seems to depend till the day of their union, when they were
able to present a united front against the Angles of Bernicia
and the Britons of Strathclyde.

By their long relations with Northumbria, the Picts were
subjected to influences hostile in many ways to Iona and
Columba. In one great matter this was to be seen in a notable degree. A king of the Picts, Nectan or Naitan by name,
appears to have had searchings of conscience as to the vext
questions between the Roman and the Irish church—the
form of the tonsure and the time of observing Easter. In
Northumbria, as we have seen, the Roman rule in both these
points had been universally adopted. To Ceolfrid, Abbot of
Jarrow on Tyne, therefore, Naitan applied for light on the
two disputed points; and, in a long letter in reply, Ceolfrid
expounded the mind of his church. Convinced by the reasoning

of Ceolfrid, Naitan not only became a convert himself,
but enforced the Roman system on all his
clergy (710), who according to Bede universally   710
submitted to the royal decree[1]. Seven[2] years later Rome
triumphed in the very stronghold of the rival system Iona
itself abandoned the rule of its founder, and Dalriada, we
may suppose, must speedily have followed her example. Thus,
with the exception of Strathclyde, the whole of North Britain
had definitively broken with the church whence it had derived
its original faith From the Church of Ireland she had received an impulse towards a higher civil and religious life,
which, when the opportunity came, enabled her to take her
place among the nations of Christendom. But the Irish
Church had not grown with the consciousness of the peoples while socially and politically there was a prevailing
tendency towards unity, in religion the tendency was towards
segregation and disintegration. The revolution effected by
Naitan, therefore, was an event of the first importance in the
development of Scotland and its people. Not only did that
revolution place the three northern kingdoms in line with the
advancing civilization of Europe it raised them indubitably
to a higher plane of endeavour. In rejecting Iona for Rome,
they entered a world at once ethically and intellectually superior to that which they left. To realize this superiority we
have but to compare the life of Columba by his successor
Adamnan with the work of Bede, born only half a century
later. The difference between the two men is not merely

---

[1] On the strength of a passage in the Irish annalist Tighernac (ob. 1088)
it is usually stated that the Pictish clergy, rather than submit to Naitan's
decree, left his dominions in a body. On this point, however, it seems
more reasonable to follow Bede He was in Northumbria when Ceolfrid's
answer to Naitan was sent, and his narrative of all the circumstances is
specially minute and precise. In the subsequent history of the Pictish
church there is nothing that decisively confirms the statement of Tighernac.

[2] Bede leads us to believe that it was about 714 that Iona embraced the
Roman rule · Tighernac gives the date 717.

one of relative intellectual force : it is a difference of mental and moral atmosphere.   In his keener sense of truth and of the relations of things, Bede represents a general movement of mind of which Adamnan, with his childlike taste for the wonderful and the miraculous, had no conception.

From the overthrow and death of Donald Breac in 642, Dalriada had almost continuously been torn by dissensions between its different tribes.   In the beginning of the 8th century, however, three kings in succession, Sealbach, Dungal, and Alpin, seem to have made good their claims to the throne of Dalriada.   But this union was of short duration

731   In 731 a king began to reign among the Picts, whose exploits, even from the scanty notices we have of them, give him an important place in the history of his people.   From his repeated attacks on his neighbours we may infer that Angus MacFergus was master in his own country beyond most of his predecessors.   In the sixth year of his reign he subdued Dalriada, whose nominal king, Alpin, fell in battle five years later, to be followed by no successor for the interval of a century.   In the strife of the kingdoms of South Britain Angus also found his opportunity, and made himself so dreaded that an English chronicler speaks of him as "a bloody tyrant throughout his whole reign."   In concert with Mercia he first made war on Northumbria, inflicting heavy losses on that kingdom, which was no longer the formidable power it had been   More important in the history of the northern kingdoms, however, was his subsequent alliance with Northumbria against Strathclyde.   In 756,

756   uniting his arms with King Eadberct, he attacked the British kingdom and, seizing the chief seat of Alclyde, reduced it to complete submission.   As two years later Eadberct, weary of being a king, adopted the religious life, it was Angus who derived the chief profit from this con-

761   quest.   After a reign of thirty years, Angus died in 761, virtual master of Dalriada and Strath-

clyde, as well as king of the Picts[1]. Of no one before him could it be said that he came so near being overlord of North Britain; and had his work been continued by his immediate successors, North Britain might have been consolidated before any country of Western Europe. But a century was still to elapse before Bernicia should be added to round the limits of modern Scotland.

Of the immediate successors of Angus, or of their contemporaries in the other three kingdoms, no event of importance is recorded. Divided against itself, Dalriada made ineffectual attempts to recover the position it had maintained under Aidan; Northumbria, harassed alike by the Picts and its southern neighbours, was growing weaker every day, and Strathclyde, though apparently it had once more recovered its independence, still invited attack rather than asserted itself against its rivals. With the reign of Constantin I, who succeeded his father Angus in 789, we enter on a new epoch in the history of the four northern peoples. In this reign North Britain received its first visits from the race that in different ways was to leave its mark so deep on the future of the British Islands. In 793 the Northmen began their work of havoc in Northumbria, which effectually crippled that kingdom, and reduced it to a subsidiary place in relation both to Northern and Southern Britain. A year later they made their first appearance in the Western Islands, which their successors made their own till past the middle of the 13th century. In 802 they burnt the buildings of Iona, and, repeating their visit four years later, slaughtered as many as sixty-eight persons. On the fortunes of North Britain the result of this visitation was at once immediate and lasting. By their permanent hold on Ireland, which they first touched in 795, as well as on the Western Islands, the

789

793

802

---

[1] On somewhat doubtful authority the foundation of the Church of St Andrews has been assigned to Angus MacFergus.

Northmen sundered for several centuries the connection between the two divisions of the Scottish race. Even before the coming of the terrible strangers Iona had lost something of its prestige by the triumph of the Church of Rome. As it also, however, had adopted the Roman rule regarding the tonsure and the observance of Easter, it had maintained the first place among the churches of the two northern kingdoms. Its late disaster and its precarious situation now made this supremacy impossible, and Constantin I took a step that in itself was sufficient to signalize his reign. He transferred the religious centre from Iona to Dunkeld, and thus set up in his own kingdom an ecclesiastical capital for Scots and Picts alike. As a movement towards that union of the two peoples which was now imminent, this act of Constantin I may be fairly regarded as one of the significant events in the history of Scotland.

820

844

On the death of Constantin I in 820 there follows one of the obscurest periods in Scottish history, closing in an event of the highest interest and importance. In 844, Kenneth, son of Alpin, king of Dalriada, became ruler of the united Picts and Scots, who were never again to exist as separate nations. Of the precise and immediate causes of this fusion no satisfactory account has come down to us. What is singular is, that the smaller kingdom, at a time when apparently its own resources were not most flourishing, should have given a ruler to its more powerful neighbour[1]. From the scanty materials that exist we may conjecture that Kenneth made good by force a plausible claim to the Pictish crown. Taking advantage of an invasion of Pictland by the Northmen, or possibly acting in concert with them, Kenneth attacked the Picts and forced them into submission. In all the circumstances his dominion could not be regarded as that of a

---

[1] We have a parallel case in the union of the Scottish and English crowns in 1603.

foreign tyrant. During the preceding half-century not only had kings passed from the one people to the other, but for brief periods a Pictish or a Scottish king had occasionally ruled over both peoples. Moreover, by their own law of succession, Kenneth had a right to rule over the Picts, which circumstances compelled them to acknowledge with special approval. In Pictland it was the sons of the mother who inherited the crown; and, by the maternal descent of his father, Kenneth could make this claim. But besides these special grounds for the acceptance of a common ruler, there were general forces at work which must have commended the union as in the highest interest of both peoples. For more than three centuries they had waged mutual war, and wasted their strength in futile attempts at annexation. Originally of kindred blood and language, a common faith also urged them to united counsels and united action. As late events had shown, they must now count on the systematic attacks of an enemy who would not rest till he had made himself master of both. For these various reasons Kenneth the Scot may not have been an unacceptable ruler to his Pictish subjects; and the best proof of the expediency of this union of the two peoples is the fact that thenceforward no disruptive forces were strong enough to prevail against it. Of the four northern kingdoms, therefore, only three now remained; and among the three it is that of the united Scots and Picts with whose fortunes we are mainly concerned in tracing the development of modern Scotland. In less than two centuries, it will be seen, the united kingdom succeeded in annexing both Strathclyde and Bernicia, to be itself in turn brought down from the primary place it seemed to have finally made its own.

CHAPTER III.

SCOT, BRITON, AND ANGLE. (844—1018.)

OF the four kingdoms of North Britain three now remained to work out the problem of their eventual coalescence; and among the three it was that of the united Picts and Scots which was to be the principal factor in the process   From the time of Bede, Northumbria had steadily declined from its ancient greatness, and during the period now before us she met with a succession of disasters that effectually stayed her from further interference with her northern rivals.   In her various contests with Scots, Picts, and Angles, Strathclyde had suffered so much that she was hardly a match for the new power to the north of her.   It was in this weakness of its neighbours that the new kingdom found its opportunity; for in itself there were sources of weakness which a powerful neighbour might have turned to decisive advantage.   What had been known as Pictland had never been really consolidated, and the immediate successors of Kenneth MacAlpin found a constant source of trouble in a district on the east coast, known as the land of Moerne, corresponding with the modern county of Kincardine or the Mearns.   By frequent wars of succession, also, the new kingdom was threatened with a disruption which might have delayed for centuries the consolidation of the peoples north of the Tweed.   Of the violence of the time one fact yields us signal proof. out of fifteen kings who reigned during the hundred and ninety years that followed

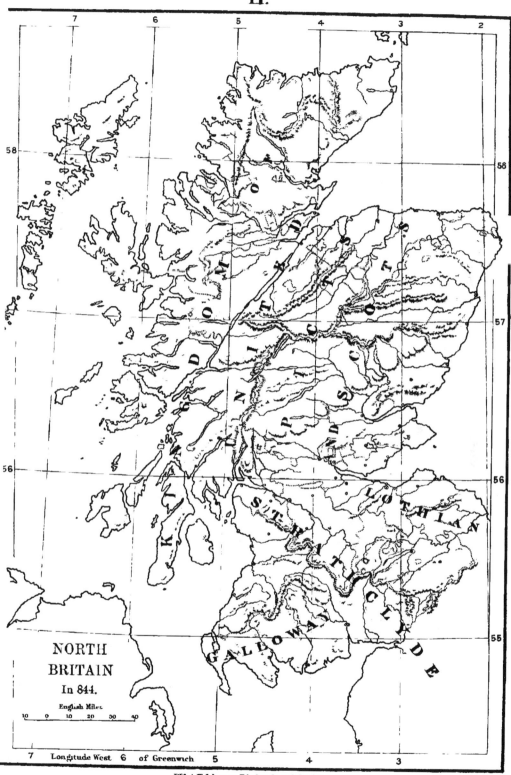

NORTH
BRITAIN
In 844.

English Miles

10   0   10   20   30   40

W. & A. K. Johnston Edinburgh and London

the union of Scot and Pict, ten are said to have died by assassination or on the field of battle.

As in the case of the period that has been described, the development of North Britain still keeps pace with that of other contemporary peoples. The beginnings of a strictly French power date from past the middle of the 9th century, and Hugh Capet became first king of the French in 987. In the 9th century, Norway, Sweden, and Denmark each attained a corporate existence by the ascendancy of one king over his many rivals. In Ecberght of Wessex (802–839) England found her first overlord, whose work, soon undone, had to be completed under a foreign race of kings some two centuries later. Ireland, the country to which North Britain owed most, was less fortunate than her neighbours. Elsewhere the in-roads of the Northmen healed the enmities of rival princes, and evoked a national feeling which eventually led to national union; but in Ireland the presence of a foreign enemy only added another element of strife. With all these countries North Britain was more or less directly concerned during the period now before us; but it was the growing force of South Britain that was the most notable external influence in determining the course of her future development. By hostile invasion or by politic concession successive rulers south of the Tweed gave an impetus to the creation of a northern kingdom which a united England was subsequently unable to bend to its own purpose.

Of the reigns of Kenneth and the kings who followed him we have somewhat fuller indications than in the case of their predecessors in the four kingdoms. Even in this later period, however, it is only of the general trend of events that we can speak with any degree of certainty. From the scanty and conflicting accounts of the different chroniclers it is often impossible to determine either the precise date or the precise nature of the occurrences to which they refer. As in the previous period, therefore, we have to be satisfied with noting the relative importance of the different reigns, and the special significance of certain events in the general movement towards the consolidation of North Britain.

In his reign of sixteen years (844–860) Kenneth MacAlpin gave proof that he was one of those rulers of men who make an era in the history of kingdoms. In addition to his difficulties at home, he had three enemies against whom he had to make head, if he were to hold the new kingdom together—the Britons, the Danes, and the inhabitants of northern Bernicia, or Lothian, as it now began to be called. By the first two he appears to have been constantly harassed, as the Britons at one time burned Dunblane, and on another occasion the Danes penetrated the country as far as Dunkeld. But it was with regard to Lothian that Kenneth began that policy, which, persistently carried out by his successors, eventually made that district an integral part of Scotland. On grounds which have not been discovered the Picts laid claim to the territory between the Forth and the Tweed; and to make good this claim appears to have been the leading object of Kenneth's reign. Six times, we are told, he broke into Lothian, and in one or other of his inroads burned Dunbar and Melrose. One other act recorded of Kenneth indicates a deliberate intention of giving consistency and continuity to the power that had come together in his hands. In the invasions of the Northmen Iona had been a special object of their plunderings, and was no longer a fit place for an ecclesiastical centre. By an act dictated alike by policy and necessity Kenneth, carrying on the work of Constantin I, transferred the supremacy of Iona to Dunkeld in the heart of his dominion. Hither, to a church built by his order, he conveyed part of the relics of St Columba, thus giving sanction and prestige to a step of high political importance. As the common apostle of Scot and Pict, Columba was a bond of union between the two peoples, who had many memories that might have tended to hold them apart. Moreover, the

Kenneth MacAlpin, 844–860.

recognition of an ecclesiastical capital was in itself a movement towards that consolidation of his power, at which Kenneth seems to have aimed from the very outset of his career.

Kenneth died a natural death at his palace of Forteviot on the banks of the Earn. By the law of tanistry, which had prevailed among the Scots, he was succeeded by his brother Donald, of whose reign of four years one obscure action is related, the meaning of which we can only conjecture. Even the place and manner of his death are uncertain By the same law of succession Constantin, son of Kenneth, came after Donald, and during a reign of fourteen years (863–877) had to accomplish a

Donald, brother of Kenneth, 860—863

Constantin II, son of Kenneth, 863—877

task resembling in many points that which fell to his contemporary, Alfred the Great. That his kingdom survived the various forces directed against it, is convincing proof of its strength and solidity In the fourth year of his rule Olaf the White, the Norwegian king of Dublin, landing on the west coast, made his way into the heart of Constantin's dominion, and for two months and a half harried the country at large Four years later he again appeared ; but on this occasion Constantin was spared, as Olaf was occupied for four months in capturing Dumbarton, the capital of Strathclyde. With that kingdom Constantin seems also to have been embroiled, as it is specially noted that by his counsel its king was put to death in 872. But on all sides dangers seemed to thicken as his reign proceeded. A son of the terrible Olaf, Thorstein the Red, outdid even his father in his performances in North Britain About 875 Thorstein landed on the north coast, and held such a triumphant course that he actually made himself master of "more than half" of the country beyond the Forth At the end of the year, however, he was taken off by treachery, and his kingdom at once came to an end. Fortunately for Constantin he had no Northmen to contend with on the plains of Lothian. By the Treaty of Chippenham, a year

after Constantin's death, Alfred surrendered territory to the
Danes as far north as the Tees.   Beyond the Tees, however,
the further half of Northumbria was ruled by an English
prince, and possessed by an English people.   With Danes
besetting him on the south, and Norwegians on the north,
Constantin could hardly have maintained his kingdom in its
integrity, and continued the work of his great father, Kenneth.
As the close of his reign proves, his actual dangers strained
all the powers at his command.   In 877 a fresh swarm of
Northmen from Ireland poured into the country, and inflicted
a severe reverse on him at Dollar.   Still pressed by the enemy,
Constantin made a final stand in the parish of Forgan in Fife,
and there fell with a multitude of his followers.

From the death of Constantin till the year 900 reigned four
kings, of whose doings little can be said with
certainty   One of them, Girig or Grig, deserves
a passing mention as having earned the title of "Liberator
of the Scottish Church," an expression which would throw
an interesting light on the period if we could be certain
of its meaning.   On the strength of this reputation, whatever
it may have implied, Girig acquired a posthumous fame far
beyond that of his fellows.   In the narratives of the later
Scottish historians Girig grew into Gregory the Great, a paragon of princes, an Alfred and Charlemagne combined; and
is still commemorated in the familiar name of St Cyrus.   To
the reign of one of these shadowy kings belongs an event of
signal importance in its bearing on Scottish history.   By the
great fight of Hafursfiord, Harald Harfagr had made himself
master of Norway; and about the year 890 he
led a great expedition which took in the Orkneys
and the Sudreys or Western Islands.   In both groups of
islands he found settlements of vikings with whom he dealt
in summary fashion.   To Ketil Flatnose he gave up the
Sudreys, which till the year 1266 remained a Norwegian
possession, and a thorn in the side of every Scottish king till

877—900

890

the day of their acquisition by Scotland. Even more important in its issues was the new dominion established in the Orkneys. Under the rule of Sigurd, the first Norwegian jarl, it soon appeared what part the Orkneys were to play in the affairs of North Britain. In a great invasion of the mainland, Sigurd overran the country as Thorstein the Red had done before him, and his career of conquest was checked only by an untoward accident. Thenceforward the mainland was never secure from the attacks of successive jarls, who for long periods held firm possession of what is now Caithness and Sutherland. As things now went, this was in truth in the interest of the kings of the Scots themselves. To the north of the Grampians, as everything seems to show, they exercised little or no authority; and the people of that district were as often their enemies as their friends. Through the action of the Orkney jarls, therefore, the Scottish kings were at comparative liberty to extend their territory towards the south; and the day came when they found themselves able to crush every hostile element even in the north.

To Constantin III (900–942) the chroniclers assign a larger place than even to Kenneth MacAlpin; and his long reign of forty-two years in itself proves that he must have ruled with prudence and vigour.

Constantin III, 900—942.

Even from the scanty knowledge we have of it, it is clear that all his powers were needed to play the part that fell to him. In his third year the Irish Danes once more made their way into Alba, as the new kingdom now begins to be styled; and, settling down for a year, ravaged the country at their will. A severe defeat inflicted on them by Constantin in 904 drove them from the country, which never

904

again suffered a similar invasion by the same people. To the year 906 belongs an event of special interest and importance. On the Mote Hill near the "Royal

906

City" (*regalis civitas*) of Scone, Constantin along with a certain bishop, Cellach by name, held a great ecclesiastical council, at

which various matters relating to the rule and discipline of the
church were discussed and settled.   Unfortunately we can only
conjecture what was the precise significance of this council, either
in its bearing on the past or the future of the Celtic Church
During the period covered by Bede's History, he occasionally
throws a passing light on the rival church; but from the date
when his work closes we are almost completely in the dark
till the innovations made by the Saxon Margaret.   Of another
event of Constantin's reign we can see more clearly the direct
and important bearing   In Cumbria or Strathclyde the native
line of princes having failed, Constantin's brother, Donald,
was received as king; and henceforward, till its absorption in
Alba a hundred years later, Cumbria was ruled by a branch
of the family of Kenneth MacAlpin.   As we shall see, the
antagonism between the two kingdoms still continued: nevertheless this further triumph of the house of Kenneth was one
more step towards the final union which that house did so
much to hasten.   Constantin needed all the support that
Cumbria could give.   In 918 occurred another
918   invasion of the Danes as formidable as any that
had yet tried the strength of the Scottish kings.   On this
occasion the attack was made from another quarter; and
eventually led to entanglements which brought trouble and
even disaster on the later years of Constantin.   Regnwald, a
leader of the Irish Danes, crossed to the help of his kinsmen
in the Danish kingdom of Northumbria, who were being hard
pressed by the West Saxon king, Edward the Elder.   With united
forces the Danes entered Lothian, then ruled by Eldred, whose
chief seat was still the ancient Bamborough.   The conquest of
Lothian might have involved that of Alba; and Constantin
joined Eldred in making head against the common enemy
From the obscure and conflicting accounts that exist nothing
definite can be affirmed as to the battle that ensued.   Eldred
and Constantin were apparently beaten; but the conquerors
were unable to follow up their advantage; and, so far as

Constantin was concerned, his proper dominion never seems to have been touched. This invasion of Regnwald was the last great attempt made on North Britain by the Danes, though for a long period to come it was often to be threatened by the men of Norway. Through the Danes of Northumbria, however, Constantin was brought face to face with an adversary more formidable than themselves. By the marriage of his daughter with Olaf Sitricson, the nephew of Regnwald, he embroiled himself with the English Æthelstan, the most powerful monarch whom England had yet known. So far did the quarrel go that, with an army and a fleet, Æthelstan invaded Alba (934), and harried it with such effect that he extorted a temporary submission from the Scottish   **934**
king. Three years later, Danes, Scots, and Britons, made a final effort to crush the power of the mighty Æthelstan at the famous fight of Brunanburh ; and among the combatants were Constantin and his kinsman of Cumbria. The triumph of Æthelstan was complete, and his enemies were scattered to the various quarters whence they had come. Constantin left one son on the field; but he himself found his way home to reign for a few years longer. Fortunately, perhaps, for North Britain, Æthelstan died in 940, and his successor Edmund found himself fully occupied in holding his own against his Danish enemies in England. Constantin, that "hoary war-man," as he is called in the Song of the Fight of Brunanburh, did not wait till death should release him from the weight of empire In 942 he abdicated in favour of Mal-colm, the son of Donald II, who, according to the   **942**
law of tanistry, was next heir to the throne. Of the ten years that remained to him Constantin seems to have spent five at St Andrews in the offices of religion, only emerging once on a critical occasion to aid his successor by his valour and experience.

To the reign of Malcolm I (942–954) belongs at least one event that deserves more than a passing mention. At all points of his dominions Malcolm appears to have carried out the policy

Malcolm I,
942-954. of his predecessors, and attempted to enlarge his borders at the expense of his neighbours.

His reign began by his carrying his arms into the district of Moray beyond the Spey; but all we know of his expedition is that he slew a prominent personage, named Cellach, who was possibly the mormaer of the district. But it is in connection with his southern neighbours that Malcolm's reign is chiefly memorable; and, as in the case of Constantin, it is again through the Danes that his policy and his fortunes

944 are largely determined. In the year 944, the fourth year of his reign, Edmund of England triumphed everywhere over his Danish enemies, even mastering Northumbria, and driving their king to take refuge with his kinsmen in Ireland. The following year he pursued his victories a step further. It was through the modern Cumberland, part of the ancient Cumbria, that the Irish Danes usually made their way to Northumbria. In this district, indeed, there came to be a considerable Danish settlement extending to the neighbouring parts of Scotland, where the number of Scandinavian place-names is still expressive evidence of their presence. To stay all further inroads from this quarter Edmund laid waste the whole district, and handed it over to Malcolm on condition that he should become his " fellow-worker[1]." If this transaction really took place, it implies that Malcolm was virtual master of Cumbria, which, as we have seen, was now ruled by a kinsman of the king of Scots. Under Edmund's

---

[1] There are two difficulties regarding this point—Was the cession actually made, and, if so, was it the whole of the ancient Strathclyde, or only the district corresponding to the modern Cumberland that was ceded? The authority for the cession is the Anglo-Saxon Chronicle; but if the transaction really took place, it must have been little more than nominal, since for long afterwards Strathclyde remained in active and even dangerous hostility to the kings of the Scots. Further, if the grant was made, it is more in accordance with the previous and subsequent histories of all the parties to suppose that the modern Cumberland was the territory ceded.

successor, Eadred, the understanding was again renewed, Malcolm pledging himself, in the words of the Anglo-Saxon Chronicle, to do all that the English king would.   Yet three years later we find Malcolm in active hostility against this acknowledged superior.   In 949, Olaf Sitricson, son-in-law of Constantin, made a last attempt to recover his Northumbrian kingdom ; and it was to aid him in this enterprise that Constantin emerged from his retirement. The accounts are somewhat conflicting as to the respective parts played by Malcolm and Constantin.   What is important, however, is that we have again one of those inroads into Lothian which eventually forced the English king to hand over the whole district to the inveterate invader.   The close of Malcolm's career shows him still engaged in defending or advancing his frontier; for in the year 954 he seems to have fallen in battle either with the men of Moerne or the men of Moray.

949

954

Of the three following kings, Indulph (954–962), Dubh (962–967) and Cuilean (967–971), few facts are recorded, yet these are sufficient to indicate the general relations that subsisted between the different powers that now divided North Britain among them.   To the reign of Indulph one notable event is assigned : Dunedin or Edinburgh was abandoned by the English king, and thenceforward was a permanent possession of the Scots.   But the possession of this fortress carried with it the district between the Pentland Hills and the Forth, and from this vantage-ground the territory of Lothian became a still more easy prey to encroaching Alba.   A victory over the Northmen, who had attacked the shores of Buchan, is the one other event recorded of Indulph, regarding the mode of whose death the chroniclers are not agreed.   Dubh's reign was absorbed by a war of succession in which he was eventually overcome and slain by his rival Cuilean.   The manner of Cuilean's own death reminds us that we are still far off from

Indulph, 954–962; Dubh, 962–967; Cuilean, 967–971.

the final consolidation of the northern kingdoms. He and his brother, we are told, both fell in battle against the Britons of Strathclyde—a fact which proves that in spite of all its misfortunes, the British kingdom was still a formidable rival to that of the Scots.

The reign of Kenneth II (971–995), son of Malcolm I, was as crowded with events as that of his namesake, the founder of Alba. It is against the Britons that we first find him displaying his activity— apparently with indifferent success. While engaged on a marauding expedition into their territory, a body of his foot-soldiers was attacked, and worsted with great slaughter. So far from being the aggressive party in the future, Kenneth had at least for a time to defend his own dominion against the Britons by a line of forts at various fords of the river Forth. Against Lothian Kenneth was more successful. The kingdom of Northumbria had lately (966) come to an end, and its southern half, Deira, was now ruled by Oslac, an English earl, subject to the overlord of England. Twice at least Kenneth overran his territory—on the second occasion making prisoner a son of some prince, possibly Earl Oslac himself. According to a somewhat doubtful authority, Edgar, the English king, granted Lothian to Kenneth on condition of being recognized as his superior, and in view of Kenneth's doings in that territory it is not improbable that such a grant was really made. As in the case of Cumberland, however, the cession was a mere nominal transaction; and it was not till three reigns later that Lothian became an integral part of the Scottish kingdom. In the case of his northern frontier, the reign of Kenneth was a period of special activity. We have seen that towards the end of the ninth century a Norwegian jarl, subject to the King of Norway, had established himself in the Orkney Islands, and had for a time even held possession of a part of the mainland. In the time of Kenneth, the jarl of Orkney was Sigurd the Stout, whose exploits show

Marginal notes:

Kenneth II, son of Malcolm I, 971-995.

966

him to have been of the true stock of the vikings. Not content with the dominion of the islands, he apparently set his heart on the mainland. A previous jarl, his own grandfather Thorfinn, the Skull-cleaver, had married the daughter of Duncan, mormaer of Caithness, and it was Sigurd's contention that Caithness was his by right of descent. His claim was not admitted; but for a time he was able to hold forcible possession of a considerable part of the mainland. In a great battle at Duncansness or Dungal's Nœp, fought about 994, he was met by two Scottish mor-   994 maers, named Hundi and Melsnati, and the issue was finally decided. The victory lay with Sigurd; but apparently his loss was so great that he abandoned all further attempts to master the coveted territory. What is noteworthy in connection with the whole struggle is that Kenneth bore no part in it, and that the mormaers acted as independent princes. Within his own dominions, indeed, Kenneth from the first had sufficient work to occupy him. In the beginning of his reign he put to death Olaf, son of Indulph, probably as a rival claimant to the throne. With the Danes, also, he had his own troubles. Though they failed to make way into the interior[1], they still threatened the Western coasts. On Christ-   986 mas Eve of 986 they fell upon Iona, and slaughtered the abbot and fifteen of the clergy. The following year they repeated their attack; but found the brethren better prepared, and were beaten off with heavy loss. Two years later Dalriada was attacked by the Norwegians of the Sudreys, who continued to be as formidable neighbours as their kinsmen in the Orkneys. In one direction Kenneth appears to have added to the power of his predecessors. The men of the Mearns had on various occasions shown their hostility to the family of Kenneth, and had caused the death both of his father and grandfather. Of Kenneth, however, we

---

[1] It is to the reign of Kenneth that Hector Boece assigns the battle of Luncarty, in which the Danes were worsted in so singular a manner.

read that he "gave the great town (*civitas*) of Brechin to the Lord," a phrase which probably implies that he effectively asserted his power over the surrounding country. Yet it was in this neighbourhood that Kenneth, like his two ancestors, was to meet his end. By putting to death her son he had made a mortal enemy of Fenvella, daughter of the mormaer of Angus, and at Fettercairn in the Mearns she at last had her revenge by the treacherous murder of the king.

Of the next two kings, Constantin IV (995–997) and Kenneth III (997–1005), nothing of account is recorded beyond the manner of their deaths Both fell in a war of succession—Constantin at Rathinveramon, near the mouth of the Perthshire Almond, and Kenneth at Monzievaird in the same county. The conqueror of Kenneth was Malcolm II, son of Kenneth II, whose reign (1005–1034) marks an epoch in Scottish history as distinctively as those of Kenneth MacAlpin, David I, Robert I, or James VI. He began his rule with the usual invasion of Lothian, and made his way as far south as Durham, to which he even laid siege Here, however, he sustained so severe a reverse that for twelve years he seems to have left Lothian unmolested But the general course of his reign proves Malcolm to have been a ruler equal to new policies, and capable of directing them to happy conclusions. In his dealing with the Orkney jarls this was signally shown. Sigurd the Stout was still jarl, and still held to his claims on the northern mainland. Shortly after Malcolm's accession a pitched battle with the mormaer of Moray resulted in the decisive victory of Sigurd, and the consequent strengthening of his position as master of Caithness and Sutherland The step that Malcolm now took throws a curious light on the relation of the kings of the Scots to those northern mormaers, over whom they claimed what must have been a merely nominal sovereignty. He gave Sigurd one of his daughters in marriage; and six years later followed up this

Margin notes:
Constantin IV, 995–997;
Kenneth III, 997–1005

Malcolm II, 1005—1034

step by an act which indicates at what end he was aiming.   In
1014 Sigurd fell at the great battle of Clontarf
in Ireland; and Malcolm conferred on Thorfinn,   1014
his son, a boy of five, both Caithness and Sutherland, thus
securing, as he doubtless hoped, a future ruler, who would be
better affected to himself than any of the native mormaers...
Not till the memorable year 1018, do we come
upon another noteworthy event in Malcolm's   1018
reign.   In that year he again led his forces into the plain of
Lothian, and on this occasion with far different result.   For
thirty nights before his coming a comet had portended to the
people of Northumbria the approach of some great disaster.
Aided by his kinsman, Owen, the king of Cumbria, Malcolm
met the Northumbrians at Carham on the Tweed, and inflicted
on them such a defeat as realized their worst forebodings.
Nearly the whole male population between the Tweed and
the Tees was cut off, and the Northumbrian leaders were in
no condition to dictate terms to an inveterate enemy in the
hour of his triumph.   By a definite transaction, they ceded
the territory north of the Tweed to the king of the Scots, who
thus at last saw himself master of the prize for which his predecessors had so long vainly striven[1].

As will afterwards be seen, this final cession of Lothian
is second in importance to no event in Scottish history.   The
great results that issued from it did not immediately appear;
yet in the end these results involved nothing less than the
transference to another race of the main destinies of a united
Scottish people.   Had Lothian remained in the possession of
England the history of North Britain must have been so
different that it is with Hastings rather than Bannockburn that
Carham must be reckoned in the list of British battles.

From the foregoing chapters it will have appeared that in
its general features the history of North Britain differs little
from that of Southern Britain throughout the same period.   In

---

[1] King Cnut confirmed the cession of Lothian to Malcolm.

the case of both there had been the same struggle between rival princes, the same gradual movement towards national unity. At the moment we have reached, it seemed as if Northern Britain were to be the first to attain the goal at which both were aiming. Under Malcolm II she had attained a degree of cohesion and an extent of territory that promised a future advantage over her southern neighbour. As it happened, a succession of foreign kings, Danish and Norman, achieved for England what had been beyond the power of her native princes; and by the close of the 11th century she had gained that permanent superiority which was assured to her by a more numerous people and a more extensive territory. To the Danish and Norman conquests it was due that Scotland did not eventually become the predominating power in the British Islands.

Of the general process by which there came to be a Scottish people in possession of a definite territory we can form a sufficiently clear idea from such materials as have come down to us. Of the growing consciousness of its different elements, however, of the political, social, and religious conditions under which that consciousness developed, we can speak only in the vaguest terms. In the case of England a continuous literature reveals the mind and heart of the various Teutonic tribes who fashioned the nation among them. In the poems associated with the name of Cædmon, in the work of Bede and King Alfred, we have the expression of the interests and the desires of the men for whom they spoke. From other sources also, we have definite information regarding the social and domestic life in Mercia, or Wessex, or Northumbria. For North Britain throughout the same period such materials do not exist. Not a line of literature has been preserved, nor a historical document which might enable us to fill up the bald outline of its general history[1].

Of Strathclyde we may venture to make a few vague state-

---

[1] The Book of Deer throws little light on the obscurity.

ments, which apply to the period described in the preceding chapters. Differently from Alba, one prince seems to have been uniformly recognised as master of the country; and from the analogy of other Celtic peoples we may infer that his territory was subdivided among tribes of varying degrees of strength and importance. The country was nominally Christian, and from the testimony of Bede we are led to believe that the people were so stubbornly attached to Celtic religious ideas that these may have prevailed even to the date at which we have arrived. In whatever form it existed there is evidence that as late as the 12th century Christianity could hardly have been a living force in the life of the people.

Regarding Alba our information is somewhat fuller and more precise. From casual statements in the different chroniclers and from the reflected light derived from the changes introduced under Saxon and Norman influences, we may form some notion of the general framework of the Alban kingdom. From the time of Kenneth MacAlpin one king claimed sovereignty over the whole country to the north of the Forth. Yet in many ways his power was limited, and his claim merely nominal. As late as the reign of Malcolm II we find King Cnut, during his invasion of Alba, dealing with two other kings besides Malcolm himself. These were doubtless sub-kings, owing allegiance to the head of Alba; but their importance is proved by the mere fact that Malcolm did not represent them in the arrangement made by the English king. In the course of the preceding sketch certain personages known as *mormaers* have occasionally been mentioned as playing an important part in the affairs of the northern kingdom. Of these mormaers seven appears to have been the fixed number, and under the designation of the "seven earls" they may have survived till the close of the 13th century[1]. In their origin they were probably hereditary officials, representing the authority of the king in the respective provinces assigned to them. As

---

[1] But see below, p. 88.

we have seen, however, certain mormaers, such as those of
Moerne, Moray, and Caithness, were practically independent
princes; and it was long after Malcolm II before the Scottish
kings succeeded in breaking the power of these dangerous
subjects.   Under the mormaers were certain officials known as
toisechs, of whose precise character we know even less   The
word is equivalent to the Latin *dux*; and it may be inferred
that the toisech's duties were chiefly militaiy; though at a later
period he appears to have been a kind of "ground-officer" and
"sheriff-officer" in one.   By analogy and conjecture we may
fill up this general framework; but of the precise conditions,
political and social, under which king and mormaer discharged
their respective functions, no contemporary authority enables
us to speak with certainty.

From the year 731 when Bede closes his History till the
coming of the Saxon Margaret about the year 1070, we have
only a few vague hints regarding the state of religion to the north
of the Tweed.   Its history south of the Forth may be briefly
told.   Under Oswiu of Northumbria Roman Christianity
triumphed at the Synod of Whitby in 664, and as long as Oswiu
reigned the see of Wilfrid extended beyond the Forth, and
his authority may have been felt even in Dalriada and Strathclyde.   By Ecgfrith's defeat at Nectansmere in 685 the church
in Bernicia received a blow from which it did not recover till
the days of Margaret.   In Galloway the church had a similar
history.   Around Candida Casa, the foundation of Ninian,
Christianity had made such way that about 730 a bishopric
was erected in connection with the northern church at Lindisfarne.   In the decline of Northumbria, however, the see
became untenable, and after some seventy years the fiercest
people in North Britain weie left to their own devices.

A few isolated facts make up our knowledge of the church
to the north of the Forth.   In 710 King Naitan, we have seen,
imposed on his subjects the Roman rule regarding Easter and
the tonsure, and Angus MacFergus (731–761) is credited

with having founded the monastery of St Andrews From reasons that may at once have been political and religious, Constantin I transferred the primacy of the northern church from Iona to Dunkeld, and Kenneth MacAlpin emphasized this step by transferring part of Columba's relics to the same centre[1]. To what extent the Columban Church now became Romanized it is impossible to say, but the process was doubtless delayed by the chronic hostilities between Alba and Northumbria. In one matter, at least, we mark a decisive departure from the polity of Columba. In the monastic families on the model of Iona the bishop was subordinate to the abbot, and differed from the presbyter only by possessing the privilege of ordination. But under the year 865 the death is noted of Tuathal "first bishop of Fortrenn," by which may be meant the southern half of the kingdom of Alba. Whether this implied first in time or first in dignity, the bishop must now have possessed that diocesan authority which is assigned to him in the Church of Rome. In 906, also, we have seen that Constantin along with a bishop Cellach[2] held an assembly on the Mote Hill of Scone for the express purpose of dealing with the affairs of the church. The Roman order of bishops was thus distinctly recognized by the church which had sprung from the monastic system of Columba; and now that Alba had mastered Lothian, and was brought into immediate and constant relations with Roman Christendom, the triumph of the new system in its entirety could not be far off.

In connection with the Church of Alba, but apart from its main development, arose during this period the mysterious body called Keledei, and popularly known as Culdees. Of the origin and real character of the Keledei we have only

---

[1] There is no satisfactory proof that Abernethy was ever the seat of the primacy.

[2] As this Cellach seems to have been bishop of St Andrews, this would prove that the primacy had by the time of Constantin been changed from Dunkeld to that town.

the vaguest hints. "Friends of God," "servants of God," "worshippers of God," are different interpretations that have been put upon their name. That they were an offshoot from the Columban Church seems probable from the general facts of their history. Every place where they are found in Scotland is to the north of the river Forth. The earliest notice of them dates before the year 710, when Naitan issued his decree that opened the way to Northumbrian influences. At a later date in their history, also, they stood before the world as the champions of the Celtic race and of the Celtic Church against the political and ecclesiastical innovations of Saxonized and Normanized Scottish kings. As they then come before us—at least three hundred years after the date when we first hear of them—they must have lost something of their original character, regarding which, indeed, we have but a single sentence in the Chartulary of St Andrews. There we read that Brude, "the last king of the Picts[1]" (died 706), granted "the Isle of Lochleven" to the Keledei hermits living and serving God in that place. From this isolated statement little can be inferred as to their origin and peculiar doctrines and practices. In this hermit life, however, we note a departure from the condition of the Columban monastery, which was but a village where the practices of religion constituted the chief business of the community[2]. It is possible, therefore, that the Keledei hermits, dissatisfied with the secular distractions of the Columban monastery, chose their mode of life as a better way for those who had given themselves to Heaven—thus but following the developments of Christianity elsewhere. In course of time, as we shall see, they came to make such terms with the world that in the interests of church and state alike they appear to have met a deserved fate.

---

[1] He was not, in fact, the last king of the Picts.

[2] In the Columban Church there was from the beginning a tendency towards the solitary life.

BOOK II.

The Consolidation of Scotland 1018—1286.

CHAPTER I.

CELT AND SAXON.

Scottish Kings.			English Kings	
Malcolm II	1005		Cnut	1016
Duncan I	1034		Sons of Cnut	1035
Macbeth	1040		Edward the Confessor	1042
Malcolm III	1057		Harold	1066
Donald Bane ...	1093		William I	1066
Duncan II	1094		William II	1087
Donald Bane ...	1094		Henry I	1100
Edgar	1097			
Alexander I	1107			

By the acquisition of Lothian Malcolm II became nominal master of the country from the Tweed to the Pentland Firth. More than two hundred years were to pass, however, before there was to be a king of Scotland in reality as well as in name; and this time of consolidation is divided into two well-marked periods which have a character and a tendency of their own. From the reign of Malcolm to the accession of David I (1124) the central fact in the history of North Britain is the conflict between Celt and Saxon for the first

place in the direction of the affairs of the kingdom. The
superior wealth and natural advantages of Lothian inevitably
drew the political centre from its ancient place beyond the
Forth; and through the various turns of English history Lothian
steadily grew in importance after Malcolm's victory at Carham
Through the troubles in England consequent on the Danish
and Norman invasions, also, a succession of Saxon settlers
crossed the Tweed in search of the peace they could not find
at home. In itself this immigration must powerfully have
affected the course of Scottish history, but under the Saxon
Margaret and her sons the southern influence was directed
and concentrated with a deliberate persistence that eventually
reduced the Celtic element to a subsidiary place in the development of the Scottish nation

Compared with the contemporary kings of the English or
French, Malcolm II was relatively in advance
of both, at once in the security of his throne
and in the degree of his authority over those
who owed him allegiance. Altogether he impressed his contemporaries as the greatest prince who had yet reigned in
Alba. In the very year that he won Lothian by the victory
of Carham he became the real master of the troublesome
territory of Strathclyde In that year Owen, its last independent king, died, and Malcolm was able to appoint as his
successor his own grandson, Duncan, whom he meant to be
the heir of his whole dominion. Thenceforward Strathclyde
ceased to be a separate kingdom, and became an appanage
of the Scottish crown. In the northern section of his dominions Malcolm's authority was apparently held as light as
that of his predecessors, and the bare facts recorded by the
different chroniclers exhibit a state of things which shows
little advance from the days of Kenneth MacAlpin. In
1020 the son of a mormaer, who is styled "King of Alba,"
was slain by his own people; in 1027 Dunkeld was burnt
to ashes, and in 1032 a son of the mormaer of Moray was

*Malcolm II
(1005–1034).*

burnt with fifty of his men. In 1031 Malcolm received one
of those periodical visits, which warned the
Scottish kings that they had a dangerous neigh-   1031
bour to reckon with in their efforts to create a strong and
independent people.   In that year, from what immediate cause
is uncertain, Cnut invaded Alba, and extorted from Malcolm
and two other kings an admission of his superiority—an acknowledgement, adds our only authority, which lasted only
"a little while."   Of the details of the transaction nothing
is known, and it must remain uncertain whether Malcolm's
acknowledgement was made for the newly-acquired Lothian
or for his whole kingdom.   One other event marks off the
reign of Malcolm from those of his predecessors.   According
to the law of alternate succession, which had hitherto held
in Alba, a member of the family of Kenneth, Malcolm's
predecessor, should have inherited the throne.   Who this
heir was cannot be ascertained; but it is laid to Malcolm's
account that he had him removed by violence, and thus
secured the transmission of the crown to his own family.
The following year (1034) Malcolm died—by
a natural death according to early accounts, by   1034
violence according to those of later date.   Two early notices
of his death emphasize the significance of Malcolm's reign in
the history of his country.   In one he is termed "King of
Scotia," the territorial name being thus decisively transferred
from Ireland to the country now ruled by the successors of
the Scottish kings of Dalriada.   The other notice marks the
authority and prestige of Malcolm himself, styling him in
somewhat vague and hyperbolical phrase "the head of the
nobility of the west of Europe."

Malcolm was succeeded by his grandson Duncan, whose
father, it is worthy of note, was Crinan, abbot
of Dunkeld.   In the Shakspearian Duncan and   **Duncan,**
Macbeth creative fancy has probably outdone   **1034-1040**
all its feats in the sheer transformation of historical characters

and incidents. What little we know of the real character and deeds of both is so curiously inconsistent with the creations of the poet that the bare facts acquire an adventitious interest from the mere suggestion of contrast. Duncan's reign was as unfortunate as it was brief. During the reign of his grandfather he had been set over Strathclyde on the death of Owen, the last of its independent kings. On his accession to the Scottish throne, the hereditary enemy of his house, Aldred, Earl of Northumbria, seized the opportunity of the youth and possibly the weakness of Duncan, and devastated Strathclyde "with sufficient atrocity." On another occasion Duncan suffered a cruel reverse from the same enemy. Either before or after this invasion of Strathclyde, Duncan made an expedition beyond the Tweed and, like so many of his predecessors, laid siege to the town of Durham. Though he commanded a great army of foot and cavalry, he was beaten back with heavy loss—the infantry being cut off to a man, and their heads placed on stakes in the market-place of the town

But it was in the northern portion of his dominions that Duncan found the chief call for his exertions; and here he was attended by equal ill-fortune. It will be remembered that Malcolm II had given a daughter in marriage to Sigurd the Stout, and that he had conferred on their son both Sutherland and Caithness. The object of Malcolm had doubtless been to strengthen himself and his successors against the refractory northern mormaers, but so far as Duncan was concerned, this policy issued in the unhappiest of results. The son of Sigurd by Malcolm's daughter, Thorfinn by name, had now grown up, and proved one of the most formidable personages with whom the Scottish kings had ever had to cope. In the words of the Saga he was "one of the largest men in point of stature, ugly of aspect, black-haired, sharp-featured, and somewhat tawny, and the most martial-looking man." As ambitious as he was terrible, Thorfinn did not rest till he had secured a footing in the Orkneys, which his father had bequeathed to three sons by a previous marriage. Confident in his strength, he refused to acknowledge the Scottish king as his superior, and was in all respects a dangerous rival rather than a subject, as was now to be fatally proved. In the endeavour to place a nephew, named Moddan, in Thorfinn's earldoms, Duncan had to try his strength against the redoubtable Norwegian. Moddan himself was first beaten by Thorfinn, who added Ross to his dominions, "and made war far and wide in Scotland." Duncan now organized an attack which is a signal testimony to the strength of his enemy. He himself sailed with a fleet to the Pentland Firth, while Moddan led an army against Thorfinn by land. Thorfinn proved invincible. Duncan's fleet was scattered by the enemy, he himself making a narrow escape with his life. The king thus disposed of, Thorfinn turned against Moddan, whom he surprised in Thurso, and slew with his own hand, after setting fire to the house in which he found him. Once more Duncan collected an army, which was even strengthened by a contingent from Ireland; and met Thorfinn at Torness, a place identified with Burghead on the Moray Firth. Again the victory lay with Thorfinn, who, driving the fugitive Scots before him, made his way as far south as Fife. Such is the account of Duncan's wars as related in the Norwegian Saga, and in its main outlines it may not be far from the truth, as the condition in which it leaves Duncan satisfactorily explains the closing event of his reign. From another authority we learn that Duncan met his end at the hand of one whose name does not even appear in the Saga. Macbeth, son of Finnlaec, was mormaer of Moray, and chief leader of the royal forces, and to the authority which these high offices gave him, he added a claim which made him a dangerous subject of the unhappy Duncan. His wife Gruoch was the grand-daughter of Kenneth III and, in default of another representative, had a claim on the throne by the old law of alternate succession. The claim was a sufficiently slight one; but the men of Moray had all along been jealous of the southern royal house, and Macbeth could count on their faithful support. Apparently the broken fortunes of Duncan brought to Macbeth the opportunity he sought; for, under circumstances imperfectly known, he slew him (1040) at Bothgouanan[1] near Elgin, and at once took possession of the kingdom which he was to hold for seventeen years.

From the comparative length of Macbeth's reign and from what little we know of it, we may infer that he ruled at once with vigour and acceptance. The first attempt to unseat him was made by Crinan, abbot of Dunkeld, the father of the late king; but in a decisive battle Crinan was slain with "nine times twenty heroes," and not till his last year was Macbeth again troubled by internal tumult. The eleventh century was marked by an outburst of pious feeling which was confined to no class or nation of Christendom. The year 1000 had come and gone, and the anticipated end of all things seemed to have been indefinitely postponed. In gratitude for the unexpected respite, kings and other great persons gave proof of their devotion by lavish gifts to the church. In Scotland, we shall see, a succession of princes were so profuse in their bounty that in the end it proved a snare to the institution it was meant to benefit Usurper as he might be called, Macbeth showed either his policy or his piety in his generosity to the church.

Macbeth, 1040–1057.

1050

In 1050 he distributed sums of money among the poor of Rome, and he may even himself have made a pilgrimage for the purpose. At home, also, we have at least two instances of his liberality. In the name of himself and his wife Gruoch the lands of Kyrkness were granted to the Culdees of Lochleven; and to the same body he himself made a gift of the lands of Bolgyne "with the deepest veneration and devotion." By the general character

---

[1] Said to mean "the smith's bothy or hut."

of his rule, indeed, Macbeth appears to have gained the
support of all parts of his kingdom. In 1054
the strength and solidity of his dominion was   1054
put to a test which it could not otherwise have stood. In
that year Siward, Earl of Northumbria, possibly in the interest
of Malcolm, the son of Duncan, invaded Scotland by land and
sea, with a force meant to carry all before it. A general rising
against the usurper could not have failed to effect his ruin,
but no such defection took place. Macbeth met the enemy in
the open field and, though he appears to have been worsted,
Siward himself was so crippled that he led back his force
without accomplishing any definite object. Three years later
Macbeth had to encounter Malcolm himself, now old enough
to make good his own claims. Of the details of the contest
no word has come down to us. In the year
1057, however, Macbeth was slain by his enemy   1057
—probably in open fight at Lumphanan in Aberdeenshire.
Such are the facts that may be regarded as authentic concerning
the historical Macbeth. Of the defamatory legend that supplied
the materials of the poet the explanation is at once simple and
satisfactory. With the Scottish historians who followed the
War of Independence it was a prime concern to produce an
unbroken line of Scottish kings stretching to the fathers of the
human race. As an interloper in this series Macbeth was a
monster, whose origin and whose actions must alike have been
contrary to nature. In the hands of Wyntoun, therefore,
improved by Hector Boece, Macbeth was transmuted into the
diabolic personage whom Holinshed presented to the genius
of Shakspeare.

Malcolm III, known as Canmore (Bighead), had as his
contemporaries in England, Edward the Confessor, Harold, William the Conqueror and   Malcolm III,
William Rufus. To Scottish history during his   1057–1093.
reign belong no events of such prime importance as the Battle
of Hastings and the Norman Conquest; yet, regarded as a

whole, the reign of Malcolm is one of the most important in Scottish history A continuous narrative of his achievements cannot be constructed from such materials as have been preserved; nevertheless, as compared with the best known of his predecessors he is a figure of well-marked lineaments in a recognisable environment. The interest that attaches to him is found in his relations to that English element which now threatened to absorb and transform the old Celtic kingdom that had come together through the union of Pict and Scot under Kenneth MacAlpin. Under Malcolm it is already evident that the centre of the kingdom is no longer beyond the Forth. With the exception of one expedition against a rebellious northern mormaer, his whole energies were turned towards his southern frontier. For this there were various reasons, all of which doubtless went to form the persistent policy of his reign. During his long residence at the court of Edward the Confessor he must have seen that with England consolidated as far as the Tweed his own country must lead a precarious existence. To extend his frontier, at least as far as the Tees, therefore, seems to have been his deliberate object from the beginning of his reign His marriage with the Saxon Margaret was assuredly an alliance of policy as well as of love, falling in as it did with his personal ambition and the interests of his kingdom Only a succession of able monarchs could have saved England from the efforts of Malcolm and his successors to press beyond the Tweed as their ancestors had passed the Forth. Five times Malcolm crossed the border with fire and sword ; at different periods four castles, Carlisle, Durham, Newcastle, and Norham, were built or repaired to check his inroads ; and twice during Malcolm's reign an English king sought his restless enemy in his own country. As it happened, in spite of all his endeavours, Malcolm at his death left his kingdom with diminished limits and a divided people.

On the fall of Macbeth the men of Moray set up as his successor, Lulach, the son of their mormaer ; but within a year he was slain at Strathbogie, and Malcolm became undisputed master of the kingdom. To strengthen his position in the north he married Ingibiorg, the widow of that Thorfinn who had brought such disaster on Duncan. The step seems to have been a politic one, for only once, so far as is known, had Malcolm any further trouble with the men of Moray. Owing to other circumstances Malcolm's position was stronger than that of any king who preceded him. As the grandson of Crinan, abbot of Dunkeld, he inherited the great influence that must have pertained to the family of that dignitary. On his mother's side he was connected with the Danes of Northumbria, whose late earl, Siward, had proved his power and perhaps his willingness to do him service. By his father's rule in Strathclyde Malcolm inherited a standing in that district such as had belonged to no king before him. Thus secure at home, Malcolm found himself free to do his utmost at the expense of his southern neighbours. It was apparently in 1061 that he made his first expedition into Northumberland, which was so often to know the 					1061 terror of his presence. Tostig, brother of Harold, afterwards King of England, was now its earl, but had gone on pilgrimage to Rome. No reason is assigned for Malcolm's inroad, and it is specially mentioned that he and Tostig were pledged to mutual friendship. Whatever may have been his motive, he left his mark deep on the country, not even sparing the sacred island of Lindisfarne. Yet, except as proving his capacity to do mischief, no ostensible result seems to have come of his raid.

Directly and indirectly the Norman Conquest influenced Scotland only less profoundly than England itself. In the case of Scotland it was less immediate and obtrusive, yet in its totality it is a fact of the first importance in the national history. In its full measure, however, that influence will appear only in the gradual modification of Scottish society and Scottish institutions throughout the reigns of Malcolm and his

successors. On Malcolm's personal fortunes the Conquest had
a direct and lasting effect. In 1068[1] Edgar the
1068   Atheling, and his two sisters, Margaret and Chris-
tina, attended by certain persons of high rank, sought refuge
in Scotland from the Conqueror. Gratitude and policy alike
would prompt Malcolm to give a welcome to the exiles. He
had himself been an exile at the court of Edward the Confessor,
and naturally sympathized with the English against the Norman.
Moreover, if the foreigner were but master of England, he
would lose no time in adding Lothian to his conquest. His
marriage with Margaret may thus have been a maturely
considered action on the part of Malcolm. The conquest was
as yet far from being complete, and a united England, supported
by foreign aid, might yet succeed in expelling the stranger. In
that event Malcolm's alliance with the English royal family
must be altogether in the interest of the Scottish kingdom;
and in any case it would strengthen his hands against Norman
encroachments. Brother-in-law of the English heir-apparent,
Malcolm had now a plausible pretext for that line of action
which he had already adopted.

Of all Malcolm's southern raids the second seems to have
been the most lamentable for its unfortunate victims. As it
took place in 1070, it could not have been long
1070   subsequent to his marriage with Margaret[2]. In
the previous year the Atheling Edgar, assisted by Cospatric,
now Earl of Northumbria, had made a desperate endeavour to
recover Yorkshire from the Conqueror. The attempt had
failed utterly, and William had made himself master of the
country as far as the Tweed. The enemy had thus touched
his own border; and it was doubtless in self-defence, as well
as in the interest of Edgar, that Malcolm carried fire and

[1] The precise date cannot be determined. The years 1067, 1068, and
1070, are given by different authorities.

[2] The date of Margaret's marriage with Malcolm is involved in the
same difficulty as that of her arrival in Scotland.

sword into what was now an enemy's country. Entering England through his own district of Cumberland, he struck eastwards, and overran the district between the Tees and the Tyne. While in the midst of these doings, news came to Malcolm that Earl Cospatric, lately the friend of himself and the Atheling, was harrying Cumberland in the interest of the Norman. The news threw Malcolm into one of those rages to which he was apparently subject, and he addressed himself anew to the work of destruction. The chronicler who tells the story of Malcolm's vengeance doubtless exaggerates the havoc done—otherwise there would have been little need for the successive repetitions of the same performance. In one statement, however, he probably only exaggerates an actual fact After this visitation, he says, there was no village or even cottage in Scotland where some English slave or hand-maid was not to be found. Two years later Malcolm was called to account by the mighty William himself.

In 1072, having triumphed over his last great   **1072** adversary, Hereward, the Norman king led a fleet and an army against Scotland. Crossing the Tweed, "he found nothing to reward his pains", and apparently without previous fighting met the Scottish king at Abernethy on the Tay In the chronicler's vague phrase Malcolm became William's man, giving in pledge his son Duncan by his first wife Ingibiorg. On the reality of this engagement Malcolm's subsequent conduct is the sufficient comment

In 1077 a disturbance in the district of Moray was effectually suppressed by Malcolm, who hence-   **1077** forwards seems to have given all his thoughts to strengthening himself on his southern frontier. The absence of William in Normandy in 1079 was an oppor-   **1079** tunity which Malcolm could not neglect In this third incursion he went over the same ground, and repeated the same atrocities, ravaging at will the country between the Tweed and the Tyne In the autumn of the following year Malcolm himself was the sufferer; but already the Scots had learned the art of dealing with the English invader. When Robert, the son of the Conqueror, crossed the Tweed, and made his way as far north as the river Carron, he found no enemy to meet him, and was forced to retreat "with nothing accomplished" What is significant, however, is that on his southward march, Robert founded a new castle on the banks of the Tyne (Newcastle)—a signal testimony to the alarm inspired by the king of the Scots.

When next we hear of Malcolm's dealings with the English, it is William Rufus whom he has for an adversary. With freer hands than his father, Rufus came into closer relations with the Scottish king, who like all who crossed his path, was to learn his force and lack of scruple, and to be worsted in their trial of strength A pretext and an opportunity for renewing hostilities was offered to Malcolm in 1091.

1091 Fleeing from Normandy, where he had been dispossessed of certain lands that had been granted to him, Edgar the Atheling once more sought refuge and support from his brother-in-law. At this moment Rufus was in Normandy, hampered by his difficulties with his brother Robert. Again, therefore, Malcolm entered England on his old errand; but on this occasion, though he did his usual mischief, he was met and beaten back by a force specially entrusted with the defence of the country. The news of this invasion brought Rufus home at the earliest opportunity, and with a fleet and an army, and accompanied by his brother Robert, he proceeded to bring his enemy to terms Broken by a violent storm, the fleet proved useless; but with his army William entered Lothian, where through the mediation of Robert and the Atheling the two kings met without striking a blow. The arrangement made between them was based on the compact that had been struck between Malcolm and the Conqueror. Malcolm was to retain the lands granted by previous English kings, was to become Rufus's man, and to repair to him on occasions when his feudal superior should lawfully demand his presence

The good understanding between the two kings was of short duration. The very next year Rufus broke into Cumberland, part of the Scottish Cumbria, with the evident intention of making it his own. So thoroughly did he do his work that he repaired and garrisoned the castle of Carlisle, and planted a colony of English families in the district. The following year Malcolm had still another proof of Rufus's real mind towards himself. Stricken at Gloucester by what seemed a mortal sickness, Rufus hastened to make his peace with Heaven by lavish promises of future amendment. Hearing apparently of his favourable state of mind, Malcolm sent to demand the fulfilment of the late treaty. At the suggestion of his advisers Rufus invited the Scottish king to Gloucester, offering hostages as a pledge for his safety. Travelling south by way of Durham, where, it is worth noting, he was present at the foundation of a new church, Malcolm was met by the Atheling and other important persons and conducted with much honour to Gloucester. Here his treatment was such as could never be forgiven. Rufus refused even to see him, and gave him to understand that he was in all respects but an English subject. His whole history proves that Malcolm was not the person to sit down tamely under an insult. Returning to Scotland, he gathered an army, and before the year was out, let loose his vengeance on the country to the south of the Tweed. His wife Margaret, then in her last illness, had with a foreboding of evil besought him to remain by her side. Her fears were too well justified. Somewhere on the banks of the Alne, Malcolm and his eldest son were treacherously cut off, the king dying by the hand of one who had been his most intimate friend. Deprived of their leader, the Scots were driven northwards in confusion, many being slain by the enemy, and still more perishing in the rivers, then swollen by the winter rains. Two Northumbrian peasants conveyed the body of the king to Tynemouth in a cart, and not till some twenty years later was Malcolm laid beside his wife in the new church they had founded at Dunfermline.

The news of the national disaster was brought to Margaret, already at the point of death. On the fourth day her son Edgar, having escaped the slaughter, entered the sick-room with the terrible tidings; and almost immediately she passed away with all the manifestations of the Christian saint. By a curious accident it is her name rather than that of her husband that has made his reign notable above that of most Scottish kings. Her biography, written by her confessor Turgot[1], has put her at advantage over every other character in early Scottish history. After St Columba she is the first person we really know alike in her daily walk and in the general tenor of her life and character. As in the case of Columba, a difficulty arises regarding the fidelity of the portrait. A biography of a queen, produced at the command of that queen's daughter, herself a queen, by one who had known the bounty of both, must manifestly be taken with large reserves. And, as a matter of fact, the biographer did not feel himself at liberty to suggest a single flaw in his portrait. Through the haze of panegyric we can discern that Margaret was an able and ambitious woman, bent on the aggrandizement of her own family and the predominance of the English interest. It is a significant fact that not one of her six sons bore the name of a Scottish king. She understood the art of imposing on the popular mind by a fitting display of ceremony and show. She herself dressed with magnificence, and loved to surround herself with gorgeous furnishings. Through her influence the abode of the Scottish king became a court with some pretensions to luxury and refinement. Over her husband she appears to have exercised considerable influence, though her biographer doubtless exaggerates on this point as on others.

---

[1] It seems almost certain that Turgot was the author of the book.

Even her dying wish had not availed to stay him from his last
fatal expedition , and, saint as she was, she could hardly have
approved of those previous inroads in which he wrought such
havoc among her own people.   Yet in public affairs she
undoubtedly took an important part, which her husband's
military undertakings may have rendered necessary.   With
these worldly propensities Margaret displayed even in the
prime of life a feverish asceticism and a tendency to ostentatious works of piety which was a characteristic of the time.
She wore herself away by the excess of her self-mortification.
Each morning during the forty days of Lent and the forty days
before Christmas she went through a round of pious acts
which only a devout mind could have converted into a custom.
Assisted by the king, she first washed the feet of six poor
persons, nine little orphans were next brought to be fed by her
own hand   again with the aid of the king she served food and
drink to three hundred poor people, specially gathered for the
purpose , and lastly she did, unassisted, a similar service to
twenty-four others, whom she supported during the rest of the
year.   Traits of more rational piety were her liberal alms-
giving, and her efforts to mend the lot of her own countrymen
who had been brought as captives into Scotland   Like other
great persons of her time, Margaret was as eager in affairs of
church as of state.   The church at Dunfermline probably
owed its origin more to her than to her husband , and to the
clergy in general she was a munificent patroness.   She even
set herself to reform certain practices which were contrary to
her own notions of apostolical purity.   Among many councils
she summoned with this object one is specially noted in which
for three days she almost single-handed did battle against the
representatives of the Scottish customs.   The changes she
proposed were of comparatively slight importance, and with the
application of some pressure readily applied by the king, they
were apparently adopted by the country at large.   The points
she thus carried were five in number : the beginning of Lent

on Ash-Wednesday, reception of the Eucharist on Easter-Day, a reformed ritual of the Mass, a stricter observance of the Lord's Day, and the suppression of marriage with a step-mother or with a deceased husband's brother. In connection with the work of Malcolm and Margaret two questions arise, neither of which can be answered with fulness or precision. To what extent during their reign did English settlers become owners of land in different parts of the country, and how far did English influence affect the people at large? The events that followed the death of Malcolm and his queen are perhaps the most satisfactory answer to both questions. From these events we gather that their policy had divided the country in twain, and that it was in the immediate possibilities of things that the Forth should again be a line of separation between Lothian and Alba, between Saxon and Celt

A story sufficiently well-vouched is a remarkable comment on the tendencies of the late reign. Immediately on the news of the death of Malcolm, his brother, Donald Bane, with a formidable force, laid siege to Edinburgh Castle, where the body of Margaret still lay. Under cover of an opportune mist, however, her sons stole out by a west postern with their mother's corpse, and conveyed it to Dunfermline. Taken with the events that were to follow, this incident proves that only the firm hand of Malcolm had held together the heterogeneous elements in his kingdom. No one man, it now appeared, combined at once the vigour of character and the requisite claims to compel his recognition as master of the whole country Edward, the eldest son of Margaret, had been designated as his successor by Malcolm, but he had fallen with his father on the banks of the Alne. So strong was the feeling against the late queen, however, that her surviving sons had to flee the country to save their lives. In these circumstances Donald

Donald Bane, 1093-1094

Bane had a clear field for his ambition. By the old law of tanistry which had regulated the succession to the north of the Forth, he was the rightful heir of his brother Malcolm. Moreover, the intense hatred of the Saxon gave a force to this claim, which brought to his side the whole Celtic portion of the kingdom. To what extent his authority extended it is impossible to say, but it is specially recorded among his acts that he drove all the English out of his kingdom. Donald had reigned only six months (1093—1094) when a rival appeared on the scene. This was Duncan, son of Malcolm by his first wife Ingibiorg, who had been given to the Conqueror as a hostage in 1072. By his long residence in England, therefore, he was virtually a Norman knight and could have little patriotic scruple in the step he now took. With the countenance of Rufus, to whom he appears to have pledged unconditional allegiance, he gathered a force of Normans and English with the intention of winning his father's crown. Of the details of the struggle nothing is known; but its immediate result shows the complete unsettlement of the country. Donald at once went down before his adversary, who now in his turn became nominal king for the next six months.

Two charters in which he makes grants of land to the churches of Dunfermline and Durham **Duncan, 1094.** are the only records of Duncan's acts that have been preserved. Even during his short reign there was another attempt at a revolution. In a rising of the men of Alba his army was all but cut off, he himself escaping from the field with a handful of followers. To Duncan as the son of his father his Celtic subjects had no objections; and on his agreeing to dismiss all his Norman and English supporters he was permitted to retain the kingdom for a short time longer. Eventually Duncan fell a victim to the machinations of three powerful personages all of whom had an interest in his end. Donald Bane found an ally in an unexpected quarter. Edmund, the only unworthy son of Margaret, agreed with Donald that if Duncan were taken off, they should divide the kingdom between them—Donald to reign to the north and himself to the south of the

Forth. In the mormaer (or, as under southern influences the
office now begins to be styled, the *Comes* or Earl) of Mearns,
Malpeder MacLoen, they secured a valuable coadjutor. At
Monachedin, now Mondynes, on the banks of the Bervie, in
Kincardineshire, Duncan appears to have met the united forces
of Donald and the mormaer. Whether by treachery or in fair
fight, Duncan here met his end; and a great stone still standing
is said to mark the spot where he fell.

For three years Donald and Edmund governed the country

**Donald Bane
and Edmund,
(1094-1097)** between them, and it seemed that Scotland was
about to revert to the position in which it had
been left by Kenneth MacAlpin An unex-
pected champion, however, appeared in Edgar the Atheling,
now living at the English court, and apparently on excellent
terms with its king. With the help of an army supplied by
Rufus he entered Scotland, worsted both usurpers, and set up
as king his nephew Edgar, another of the sons of Margaret
and Malcolm Edmund and Donald were effectually prevented
from working further mischief. The former was at once
caught and doomed to perpetual imprisonment; and two years
later Donald Bane shared the same fate.

Edgar was a pious and amiable monarch who reminded his

**Edgar,
(1097-1107).** contemporaries of Edward the Confessor His
reign of ten years, indeed, presents a singular
contrast to that of his warlike father Not a
single battle or disturbance of any kind seems to have followed
the contest which placed him on the throne Yet, if we may
judge by the manner in which he settled the succession, he
must have felt the difficulty of ruling two peoples, by race and
by past relations each the natural enemy of the other It was
on the English portion of his kingdom that he placed his
dependence, and it was in its interest that he chiefly reigned
While his father Malcolm had made Dunfermline his chief
seat, it was at Edinburgh that Edgar seems mainly to have
resided From his charters that have been preserved a few

facts emerge which indicate his relations to the different elements of his people. He speaks of himself as "King of the Scots"; but he addresses his subjects as Scots and English. From the names of the witnesses to his charters we also gather that he was surrounded by men of English extraction. Like a true son of Margaret, he was generous to the church, and one of his pious acts was to refound the monastery of Coldingham, and make a gift of it to the monks of Durham. In connection with this grant we have probably the explanation of the peace and security of his rule, alike over Scot and Saxon. He could securely count on the support of the two English kings who were his contemporaries—Rufus, who died in 1100, and Henry I who succeeded him. In granting the lands of Coldingham Edgar expressly states that the grant is made after consulting his lord King William; and a charter of King William himself confirms the grant that had been made by his feudal inferior. Standing in this relation to the English king, Edgar had a powerful ally behind him, should his Scottish subjects prove refractory. But through the most interesting event of his reign he found himself in still closer relations to Henry I. Owing to the necessities of his position a son of the Conqueror found it a politic step to marry Edgar's sister, Eadgyth, known in English history as Matilda or Maud. In the eyes of his English subjects the children of Malcolm and Margaret were the rightful heirs to the English crown. By this marriage, therefore, Henry at once strengthened his own claims, and gained the support of the English at a time when the Norman barons as a body were actively hostile to him. In Scotland the marriage had its own results. By the recognition of the political importance of the children of Malcolm and Margaret, the prestige of Edgar and his two brothers who succeeded him was materially increased; and specially in the acts of the youngest, David, we trace the distinct consciousness of the greatness of his claims.

Thus, supported by the alliance of two successive English

kings, Edgar was comparatively safe from those formidable risings which had shaken the power of his predecessors. Against another enemy, however, if he had chosen to do his worst, even Rufus or Henry might have been unable

1098 to protect him In 1098 Magnus Barefoot, King of Norway, came on an expedition similar to that of Harald Harfagr at the close of the 9th century Having compelled both the Orkneys and the Sudreys to recognise him as their superior, he returned to Norway under the impression that the work had been done once for all. But the Gallgaels, as the mixed population of the Sudreys was called, were the most restless and ungovernable of peoples. A king, Ingemund, whom Magnus had sent to reign over them, was massacred with all his following.

1102 Magnus took a terrible revenge Touching first at the Orkneys (1102), he seized the sons of that Earl Thorfinn who had distinguished himself in the days of Macbeth and Duncan, and set his own son, Sigurd, a mere boy, over the islands. Proceeding southwards, he carried fire and sword into the Sudreys, driving their inhabitants before him in all directions, and completed his triumphal course by the conquest of the Isle of Man. It was on his return northwards that he appears to have made his notable transaction with Edgar. Magnus claimed as his own all the western islands "between which and the mainland a helm-carrying ship should pass." At no time could these islands have been more than a mere nominal possession of the kings of the Scots, and Edgar might consider himself well rid of a formidable enemy by readily acknowledging Magnus's claim. What the terms of the treaty were cannot be ascertained. The mainland of Scotland, however, was left unmolested, and till past the middle of the 13th century the Western Islands acknowledged the King of Norway as their superior.

Dreading the recurrence of the confusion that had followed the death of his father, Edgar sought to make an arrangement which would ensure a peaceful succession to his own government. He desired that his brother Alexander should rule with the title of King of the Scots over the country to the north of the Forth, inclusive of Lothian as far as Edinburgh. To his younger brother, David, he proposed to give Cumbria and the greater part of Lothian with the title of *comes* or earl. There were two reasons which justified this division as in the best interest of the country at large. In the case of Lothian and Strathclyde the King of Scots was the feudal inferior of the King of England, and this relation inevitably led to misunderstandings between the two parties. To prevent such misunderstanding the most effective step was to hold no fief of his brother of England. But a second and stronger reason for the division was the fact that no single ruler was likely to be acceptable to the peoples north and south of the Forth. The course of events between the death of Malcolm and the accession of Edgar had made this abundantly clear; and that Edgar desired to make a final separation proves that he himself had felt the impossibility of uniting the two peoples.

Alexander I, surnamed the Fierce, had something of the spirit of his warlike father. His first act would have been to set aside his younger brother, and to make himself master of the whole kingdom.

Alexander I, 1107–1124.

But, as his subsequent reign was to show, David was not a person to be trifled with, and he was firmly supported by the English king and a considerable body of Norman barons, who made the chief following at his court. During the whole of Alexander's reign there is no indication of trouble between the two brothers—a proof of their mutual respect for each other's resources. With England, also, neither had any serious misunderstanding—Alexander, indeed, becoming son-in-law of Henry by marrying his natural daughter Sibylla. It would appear, however, that the English king had profited by the late divisions in the northern kingdom. In

the reign of the Conqueror, a castle had been built on the
Tyne to check the invasions of the Scots, but
1121   in 1121 Norham Castle on the Tweed was
founded by Henry for the same purpose—a proof that Northumberland was now a part of English territory, in spite of all
the efforts of Canmore.

From the charters of David and Alexander we have an
interesting glimpse of the chief personages from whom they
sought advice and support. In those of David we find the
names of Moreville, Somerville, Lindsay, Umphraville, Bruce,
and Fitz-Alan (ancestor of the Stewarts), all of them among the
most distinguished in the history of Scotland. On the other
hand, Alexander acts with the consent of seven earls, six of
whom were the representatives of the old Celtic mormaers.
Further, we learn of Alexander that Invergowrie, near Dundee,
was his favourite residence, and that he reckoned as his chief
towns, Edinburgh, Stirling, Inverkeithing, Perth, and Aberdeen.

Though his most powerful subjects were Celtic earls or
mormaers, Alexander did his utmost to anglicise both church
and state to the north of the Forth. Little is known of what
he actually accomplished, but his work indubitably simplified
the policy so effectually carried out by his successor David.
One rising of the men of the north is recorded, though
the accounts of it are somewhat contradictory. All authorities
agree, however, that he suppressed it with such vigour and
effect as justified his cognomen of the Fierce. In gratitude
for his victory, it is said, he founded the famous monastery
of Scone, planting in it a body of Augustinian canons brought
from Nastley, near Pontefract, in Yorkshire. In the matter
of pious gifts and active concern for the interests of the
church, Alexander was indeed a true son of his mother.
An Augustinian priory on an island in Loch Tay, and a
monastery on Inchcolm in the Firth of Forth, are other examples of his munificence. More notable than such foundations
was his effort to establish diocesan episcopacy as an effective

form of church government throughout his dominions. The bishoprics of Moray and Dunkeld date from this reign, though it was not till a later day that any real authority could have pertained to the former. But the outstanding event of Alexander's reign, and that which at once illustrates his personal character and the direction of his policy, was his conduct with reference to the see of St Andrews. Before the time of Alexander St Andrews was the only diocesan episcopate beyond the Forth, and it had been held by a succession of Celtic bishops—the last of the line, Fothudh or Modach, having died in 1093. In consequence of the confusions that had followed the death of Malcolm, the see had remained vacant till the death of Edgar. With the decision that distinguished him, Alexander, in the first year of his reign, appointed Turgot to the see, thus placing an Englishman at the head of a church which was Celtic in speech, and still largely Celtic in its customs and its polity. But not even his respect for his mother's confessor held Alexander back when he believed the interests of his kingdom were at stake. Turgot was disposed to recognise the Archbishop of York as his ecclesiastical superior, but Alexander saw in this acknowledgement the implication of the English king's superiority over himself. Rather than yield the point he parted with Turgot, and had a new bishop, Eadmer by name, sent from Canterbury. Eadmer was as little to Alexander's mind as Turgot, insisting, as he did, on the primacy of Canterbury over the whole length and breadth of Britain. With Eadmer, therefore, Alexander likewise quarrelled, and the unfortunate diocese was again without a resident bishop. The death of   1124
Eadmer in 1124 gave the king the opportunity of choosing a bishop on whose dispositions he could securely count—Robert, the prior of his own monastery of Scone. Alexander gave further substantial proof of his genuine interest in the prosperity of the see. In the last year of his reign he made a grant of land in the neighbourhood of St Andrews, known as

the *Cursus Apri* or Boar's Raik. In other cases, in which he made gifts of lands, Alexander confirmed them by charters, but for some reason unknown he reverted to Celtic custom in his grant to the bishops of St Andrews. In presence of his lords the king ordered his Arabian charger, equipped with all its trappings, to be led up to the altar, "in wytnes and taknyng[1]" of the gift he proposed to bestow on the diocese.

While Alexander thus showed his goodwill to the church, his brother David gave no less decided proof of similar leanings. Even while in his subsidiary position as earl, he took an important step in that policy which he was afterwards to carry out with such memorable results. He restored the see of Glasgow, which, as originally founded by Kentigern, was co-extensive with the district of Cumbria. Underlying the ecclesiastical policy of all the sons of Margaret, there was undoubtedly a political intention, which the representatives of the old order were not slow to discern. Through the means of an organised church, attached to the crown by gratitude and interest, the Scoto-Saxon kings gained a hold on the country at large which could hardly have been acquired by direct political action. Yet, when in the prime of life, Alexander died in 1124, it was still doubtful what were to be the future relations of the two peoples to the north and the south of the Forth. Had the division made by Edgar continued, Lothian and Cumbria must inevitably have gone to England as a far more formidable power than a divided Alba. Two circumstances, it may be, determined the emergence of a united Scotland. Alexander died without an heir, and his brother David proved to be a king whose ability and good fortune were equal to the task of consolidating the entire extent of the country committed to his charge. In effecting this great work, as we shall see, he introduced new factors into his policy which mark his reign as one of the notable periods of Scottish history.

[1] Token

CHAPTER II.

CELT AND NORMAN.

Scottish Kings.		English Kings.	
David I ... ... 1124—1153		Henry I ... ... 1100—1135	
Malcolm IV (the		Stephen ... ... 1135—1154	
Maiden) ... ... 1153—1165		Henry II ... 1154—1189	
William I (the Lyon) 1165—1214		Richard I ... ... 1189—1199	
		John .. .. 1199—1216	

WITH the reign of David I begins the second period of the consolidation of Scotland. It is distinguished from the first by the fact that it is by Norman rather than Saxon influence that the process is now carried on. Before the accession of David, Normans had already played an important part in the affairs of Scotland. It was with the help of a Norman force that the Atheling had placed his nephew Edgar on the throne, and Normans had secured David in his earldom against his brother Alexander. But it was during David's own reign that the Norman element attained such a predominance as to become the great formative influence in the Scottish kingdom. Many circumstances combined to make David a strong and fortunate monarch, yet the most potent influence that sustained him in all his undertakings was the disciplined strength of the Norman knights and barons behind him. At one crisis, indeed, it will be seen that

David I, 1124-1153

only with their aid was he able to quell a rising in the north and maintain his seat on the throne.

Of all the reigns of Scottish kings that of David is undoubtedly the most memorable in every aspect of the life of a people. In its radical breach with the past it has its only parallel in the sixteenth century, when a new religion changed the destinies of the nation. But in the extent of its civic, political, and ecclesiastical changes it surpasses in importance the religious revolution which gave the country to Protestantism. Like that revolution the transformation wrought by David placed the country in new relations to the other countries of Christendom. But besides remoulding the church, he recast the social condition of the people in such degree as makes his reign an epoch in the national development. At no period of its history has Scotland ever stood relatively so high in the scale of nations. By a fortunate combination of circumstances, the country profited beyond its neighbours in the great awakening of Christendom throughout the 11th century. It was the age of St Bernard, whose name is associated with three of the great movements that absorbed the heart and mind of the time—of the religious revival, which under his direction took one of its shapes in the great Cistercian order; of scholasticism, in whose developments in the hands of Abelard he saw and crushed the spirit of scepticism and denial; and of the mighty third crusade, due to him beyond every other single person, which in the greatness of its disaster tarnished his own fame and shook the faith of Christendom. It was the age, also, when in all the great countries of Europe free towns sprang up with a rapidity which transformed the policy of kings. In these tendencies and aspirations Scotland had her full share during the reign of David, and embodied them in practical results which have no parallel elsewhere. While the king of the French was struggling for bare existence against refractory barons as powerful as himself, while England was distracted by the wars of Stephen and Maud so that men said that " Christ and his saints were asleep," Scotland enjoyed a peace and prosperity which made her a refuge for exiles and a mart for foreign countries.

David, "the beld¹ off all hys kyn," as he is styled by the chronicler Wyntoun, came to the throne with advantages beyond those of any Scottish king before him. He had reached middle age, and by his long residence in England and by his experience as Earl of Cumbria and Lothian had received a training that specially fitted him for the work he was to accomplish. As the brother and sole heir of the late king, his accession met the conditions both of feudal law and the law of tanistry. By a politic marriage he gained an influence and a prestige beyond the border which for a time made him arbiter of the fortunes of England. His wife, Matilda, granddaughter of Siward of Northumbria, brought him the Honour of Huntingdon, with lands in at least six English counties, the earldom of Northampton during her lifetime, and a claim to the earldom of Northumberland, which David practically made good during the latter half of his reign. Strong in all these advantages, David was enabled in a large degree to accomplish the two great objects which had determined the policy of his father Malcolm. He extended the Scottish frontier to the Eden and the Tees; and by creating new political conditions advanced the consolidation of the country far beyond the point where he found it.

Till the death in 1135 of his brother-in-law, Henry I, David had only friendly relations with England. As Earl of Northampton, he was one of the English barons who in 1127 took oath to acknowledge Henry's daughter Maud as his successor on the throne. During another friendly visit to the English court in 1130 occurred the first of two attempts to dispossess him of the country beyond the Forth. In each case it was in the interest of the rival house of Moray that the attempt

1127

1130

¹ Paragon.

was made. Two men now represented that house, Angus, mormaer or earl of Moray, and his brother Malcolm, both grandsons of that Lulach who had been put up as the successor of Macbeth. Taking advantage of David's absence, the brothers raised a force, which by its formidable numbers proved the widespread detestation of the policy of the sons of Margaret. Fortunately the affairs of the kingdom had been left in competent hands. Edward, constable of the kingdom, met the brothers at Stracathro in Forfarshire, and defeated them with a loss of 4,000 men, Angus the earl being among the slain. But the danger was not at an end. For five years, Malcolm, "the heir of his fathers' hate and of English wrongs," held David at bay, and refused to give in his submission. Unable of himself to bring Malcolm to terms, David took a step which proved a turning-point in the history of Moray. He appealed to the barons of the north of England to aid him in suppressing his Celtic subjects. By interest and affection these barons were attached to David, and they readily responded to his invitation. Under Walter l'Espec, a Yorkshire baron of great possessions, a numerous body of them met at Carlisle, and with the help of a fleet prepared to support the Scottish king. But their actual presence was hardly needed. The rumoured coming of these formidable warriors struck terror into the adherents of Malcolm, who of their own accord gave him into the hands of David, to remain a prisoner in Roxburgh Castle for the next twenty-three years. So complete was the victory that the district of Moray was definitively attached to the crown, and its lands divided among Normans and such of the natives as the king could trust. On more than one occasion Moray was still to give trouble, but never again did it attain its former importance; and this action of David is one of the events of his reign that mark its pre-eminence in the development of the country.

By the death of Henry I, December, 1135, David's relations to England were fundamentally changed. Before the

year was out, Stephen, Earl of Blois, seized the crown in
express violation of his own oath and of the late king's desire
for the succession of his daughter, the Empress Maud.   But,
alike by interest and predilection, David was bound to support his niece, and during the remainder of his reign he lost
no opportunity of defending her interest whenever it did not
clash with his own.   He was not long in showing Stephen
what policy he meant to follow.   In the beginning of the year 1136 he led an army across the   1136
border, and made himself master of every castle in Cumberland and Northumberland except Bamborough, penetrating as
far as Durham   As was proved on subsequent occasions, the
barons and common people of these districts hardly regarded
him as an enemy, and they readily pledged their allegiance
in favour of Maud.   In the beginning of February Stephen
marched northwards to repel the invader, and on his approach to Durham David retired to Newcastle.   After facing
each other for a fortnight, the two kings came to a settlement which was hardly to the credit of David's magnanimity
Ignoring the ostensible object of his invasion, he made no
stipulation in favour of his niece, but gained considerable
concessions to himself.   His son Henry received the Honour
of Huntingdon with the castles of Carlisle and Doncaster,
with a promise that his maternal claim to the earldom of
Northumberland should receive due consideration   In con-
firmation of this settlement Henry took the oath of allegiance
to Stephen at York, and became for a time an attendant on
his court.   His father, with excellent reasons for satisfaction,
recrossed the frontier, surrendering the various castles he had
taken, with the exception of Carlisle

The peace between the two kings was of short duration
On the Easter following their treaty a trifling incident again
placed them in strained relations, and again David hardly
appears in a favourable light   On the occasion of a great
festival Stephen gave young Henry precedence over all the

leading personages about the court, and thus specially offended the Earl of Chester and the Archbishop of Canterbury. So far did their feelings go that they publicly insulted the Scottish prince, and left the court in indignation. When the incident was reported to David, he immediately recalled his son, and would not listen to Stephen's demand that he should return.

1138　　The following year David had an opportunity of showing what his real feeling was towards the English king. During Stephen's absence in Normandy he collected a great army, and prepared to repeat his former invasion of Northumberland. Before he crossed the border, however, he was met at Roxburgh by Thurstan, Archbishop of York, who persuaded him to delay hostilities till the return of Stephen before Christmas. As it happened, the delay effected nothing. Stephen refused David's demand that the earldom of Northumberland should be given to his son Henry in right of his maternal descent. As his army was still at his back, David now determined to make good his claim by the strong hand. In two divisions he led his forces across the Tweed, and after an unsuccessful siege of Wark castle ravaged Northumberland and part of Durham. In the horrors perpetrated by his wild followers, this invasion of David rivalled those of his father Malcolm, though of the son it is recorded that he did his best to protect all sacred places But on this occasion nothing was gained by these atrocities. Civil war had not yet broken out between the supporters of Stephen and Maud, and the English king was still free to meet his enemy In the beginning

1138　　of February Stephen appeared at the border with the intention of offering battle to the Scots. But David, who had friends in the enemy's camp, had plans of his own for taking Stephen at advantage. Retreating to Roxburgh, he quartered a few soldiers in the town, and concealed his main body in the neighbouring woods and marshes. Stephen, he supposed, would on entering Scotland be certain to pass a night in that town, and might be cut off by a nocturnal assault. Whether from accident or from knowledge of David's design, Stephen avoided the train set for him, and, after laying waste a great part of Lothian, led his army southwards without coming to an engagement.

It was the difficulties of Stephen's position that had hurried him southward, leaving his enemy still on his border. Aware of his present advantage, David only waited till the close of Lent to re-enter England on his former errand. Of the many Scottish invasions of England, this third one of David is among the most memorable. In the words of the Saxon Chronicle he came as if he thought to win the land. Entering Northumberland, he took the castle of Norham and blockaded Wark, and completed his previous work of devastation. In the north of Lancashire and the neighbouring districts of Yorkshire a section of the Scottish army under the king's nephew, William Fitz-Duncan, wrought similar havoc and defeated an English force at Clitheroe on the Ribble. But David was bent on more important achievements. Uniting all his forces, which now amounted to more than 26,000 men, he marched to the Tees with the intention of continuing his course into the heart of England. Here, however, he was to be brought to a stand. Thurstan, the venerable Archbishop of York, drew the barons of Yorkshire together and sent them to meet the Scots with the enthusiasm of men fighting for their altars and their homes. Yet many of the English barons had strong reasons for not bearing arms against the King of Scots. Some of them were his personal friends, and not a few had received large grants of land from him beyond the Tweed. In their dilemma they made an effort to avert the impending battle. Two of them, both owning lands in Scotland, and bearing names notable in Scottish history—Robert de Brus and Bernard de Balliol— went to the camp of David, and besought him to desist from his present purpose, pledging themselves that the earldom of Northumberland should be bestowed on his son Henry. Either distrusting their pledge or because he aimed at greater things, David rejected their proposal; and the two barons, disclaiming their feudal allegiance, returned to the English camp.

A battle was now inevitable, and, crossing the Tees, David faced the English army near the village of Northallerton. In numbers he had greatly the advantage, but in arms and discipline the superiority was all with the enemy. The bulk of the English army were trained men-at-arms, and were led by the veteran Walter l'Espec, who on another occasion had done the Scottish king so great a service. The presence of a bishop and many priests also gave a sacred sanction to their cause, while in the centre of their host a trebly consecrated standard seemed to assure victory to those who fought under its shadow. The mast of a ship, fixed in a waggon, bore aloft the sacred host together with the banners of St Peter of York, St John of Beverley and St Wilfrid of Ripon, "so that Jesus Christ was bodily present as commander in the battle." The various elements that made up David's army afforded a curious illustration of the composite nature of his dominions. Norwegians from Orkney, Scots from Alba, Angles from Lothian, Norman knights, and apparently even mercenaries from Germany, formed his motley following. One other element, however, deserves special mention, as from this time forward it was to play a noticeable part in the general history of Scotland. From the beginning of David's doings in England, the Galwegians, or Picts, as they are otherwise styled by the contemporary chroniclers, had played a prominent part in all his operations. By their fierce insubordination and their savage treatment of the conquered English, they had distinguished themselves among the rest of David's host. Their wild spirit was now to bring disaster on an enterprise which, if it had succeeded, might have changed the course of British history. By an ancient privilege, of whose origin we know nothing, their leaders claimed the right of forming the van of the Scottish army. Against the mailed Norman knights David knew that their undisciplined followers, without defensive armour, could have little chance in pitched battle, but so fierce was the clamour that, to stop inopportune dissensions, David granted their demand. The result was what he had feared. All that native strength and valour could do was done by the men of Galloway, but they were unable to break the Norman line, and showers of English arrows rapidly thinned their ranks. In another part of the field Prince Henry showed how different the issue might have been had other counsels prevailed. With his Scoto-Norman knights he bore down the force opposed to him, but by an error of judgment pursued a section of the enemy many miles from the field. For two hours the Galwegians fought with desperate fury, but the fall of their last chieftain at length broke their courage; and when a cry went round that the king was slain they turned their backs, and the flight of the Scots became general. In the arrangement of the battle David commanded a reserve force consisting of the men of Moray and his own body-guard of knights, and with this detachment he was able to leave the field and to check all dangerous pursuit. Considering his late dealings in Durham and Northumberland, he could hardly have ventured to make his way through these counties; and, as his nearest place of safety, he led his broken host to his own town of Carlisle. For two days no tidings came of the fate of Prince Henry, but on the third he appeared in Carlisle attended by nineteen knights out of the two hundred who had formed his body-guard.

In the existing state of England the Battle of the Standard, as it came to be called, was not the crushing blow for the Scots which it might otherwise have been. Stephen was now fully occupied in holding his own against the supporters of Maud, and the war which had at last broken out taxed all the resources at his disposal　Far from fleeing across the border with his broken host, therefore, David prepared to recommence the operations which had been so summarily checked by the late battle　Leading his army across to Northumberland, he laid siege to the castle of Wark, which had so often baffled his attempts to master it, but whose garrison was now starved into surrender　While engaged in this siege, he received a visit which was indirectly the means of effecting a temporary peace between the two countries. Orderic, bishop of Ostia, had just come in the capacity of legate to look after the interests of his church both north and south of the Tweed.　Seeing everywhere the disastrous results of the recent wars, the legate earnestly besought the Scottish king to consent to a truce with a view to an eventual understanding with Stephen　David consented; and Orderic, during his sojourn in London, did his best to dispose Stephen and his advisers to peace　A more influential intermediary, Maud, the cousin of David and wife of Stephen, at length succeeded in effecting a reconciliation between the two kings;

1139　and at Durham, on the 9th of April, 1139, peace was finally concluded.　Its terms were more advantageous for David than the treaty of 1136, and again the interests of his niece, the other Maud, were sacrificed to his own.　The earldom of Northumberland, with the English fiefs he already held, were to be conferred on Prince Henry, Stephen retaining the castles of Newcastle and Bamborough　At Nottingham the treaty was confirmed by Stephen, and till the close of the summer Henry made his home in England, assisting the king in his contest with Maud.

David's subsequent relations to England may be briefly told.　In 1141 Stephen was taken prisoner at

1141　Lincoln, and for a time the party of Maud triumphed.　Though by the treaty of Durham David had bound himself to support Stephen, he lost no time in proceeding to London and offering his services to Maud But through her own faults of temper and policy her success was of short duration, and at Winchester her supporters sustained a decisive defeat, in which David narrowly escaped being made prisoner. For eight years the struggle went on between the two parties, but David does not seem again to have interfered. In 1148 Maud gave up the struggle and left the country. Her claims, however, were taken up by her son, afterwards Henry II, who put himself in communication with his grand-uncle David. In 1149 they met at Carlisle and came to an understanding as to their future relations. In the event of Henry's securing the English throne, he was to confirm David and his heirs in all their English fiefs which they claimed in right of their descent from Earl Waltheof; and, meanwhile, the Scottish king was to do his utmost to break the power of Stephen. In accordance with this arrangement, David, accompanied by Henry, led an army to Lancaster with the intention of giving battle to Stephen, who was now at York. Through the treachery of a third party, however, the expedition came to nothing. In the negotiations at Carlisle, Ranulph, Earl of Chester, the same baron who had publicly insulted Henry of Scotland at the English court, had pledged himself to support the cause of the son of Maud. Claiming Carlisle as his by right, he had long borne a grudge against David and his son. In the late arrangement, however, he had agreed to accept the fief of Lancaster in return for Carlisle, and had promised to join forces with David and Henry. The place of meeting was Lancaster, whence all three were to march against the English king. At the appointed time Ranulph failed to make his appearance; and fearing treachery, Henry deemed it prudent to leave the country, and David retraced his steps without striking a blow. Such was David's last interference in the affairs of England. Through all his relations with that country he had never lost sight of the policy of his father

1149

Malcolm. For the safety of Scotland he was convinced that Carlisle and Newcastle must be his frontier towns, and, in point of fact, throughout the entire reign of Stephen, the Eden and the Tees were the boundaries of the two countries.

From the battle of the Standard onwards David was mainly occupied in effecting those internal changes which have given his reign its special character and importance. One strange episode, however, can hardly be passed over, as another evidence of the wild elements out of which the kingdom of Scotland was being formed. At some period during the last years of David a personage appeared in the Western Islands, giving himself out as a son of the Earl of Moray who had been slain at Stracathro. From the vague and confused accounts of him we learn that his real name was Wimund, and that he had been a monk in the abbey of Furness, in Lancashire. When next we hear of him it is in the Isle of Man, where he gained such ascendency over the inhabitants that they resolved to have him for their bishop. In explanation of their choice we are only told that his gifts of mind and person made him a natural leader of men. The diocese of Man included the Sudreys, and in the population of these islands he found a ready response when he made known his claims and proposed to carry fire and sword against the king of Scots. Of the details of the contest that followed little is known. From the time that it lasted, however, we may infer that Wimund had a formidable force behind him, and that he had the skill and resolution to turn it to account. His tactics were to avoid the royal forces sent against him, and to betake himself to his ships or seek hiding in inaccessible parts of the country. One of his adventures is specially noted, which appears to have struck himself as an irony of Providence. A certain bishop, rather than pay tribute to the impostor, put himself at the head of his flock, and went forth to meet him in battle. To put heart into his followers he threw a light battle-axe at Wimund, and

with so sure an aim that it struck him on the forehead and
brought him to the ground.　Though his followers at once
gave way, they contrived to save their leader, who continued
to be as formidable as ever　Hopeless of putting him down
by force, David was at length constrained to buy him off by
a grant of the lands and abbey of Furness.　Here Wimund's
fierce and restless temper finally wrought his ruin.　Rendered desperate by his tyrannous exactions, the people of
the neighbourhood rose against him, and depriving him of
his sight, had him confined in the monastery of Biland in
Yorkshire.　To the last his spirit remained unbroken, and
words fell from him that prove his contempt for the faith
of the men around him.　Even Providence, he said, had
been able to overthrow him only through the faith of a
silly bishop ; and he declared that, had his enemies left him
the eye of a sparrow, they would have had little ground for
exultation[1].

After his deliverance from Wimund David had no further
trouble on either side of the Tweed　But the greatest trial of
his life came to him at the last.　In 1152
Prince Henry, his only son and heir, died, to the　　1152
grief of the whole nation, to which he was endeared by all the
qualities that commend a prince to his people.　Even in his
old age and sorrow, however, David did not forget the interests
of his kingdom and his house.　Malcolm, the eldest son of
Prince Henry, was now heir to the throne ; and David at once
took steps to ensure his accession.　Accompanied by a strong
force, Duncan, Earl of Fife, conducted him through the different
parts of the kingdom, and had him publicly acknowledged as
the rightful heir to the throne　Similarly Henry's second son,
William, was taken to Newcastle, to receive the homage of the
English barons for the earldom of Northumberland.　David
did not long survive his son. · At Carlisle, on the 20th May of

---

[1] The story of Wimund is full of obscurities and contradictions, and I
can profess only to have told it in the way that seems to me most probable.

the following year, he was stricken by mortal sickness, and
with all the piety of his mother he prepared to
meet his end During the three days that remained to him he displayed the same spirit of prudence and
devotion that had characterized him all through life.   On the
morning of Sunday the 24th he passed away so quietly that
his attendants did not even perceive his end ; and from the
posture in which they found him it appeared that his last act
had been one of devotion.

1153

Like his mother Margaret David was fortunate in finding a
eulogist who has ensured him a good name with posterity.
With Ailred of Rievaulx, however, we have the same difficulty
as with the biographer of Margaret.   Through the emotional
rhetoric of the "Lament" it is difficult to perceive the distinctive traits that marked David as a man and a king.   In
the eyes of Ailred David's almost reckless bounty to the church
covered a multitude of sins.   From his own words, also, we
gather that he disliked and despised David's Scottish subjects,
and could see no injustice in the high-handed fashion in which
their interests and their rights were set aside by a Normanized
king.   From Ailred's panegyric, therefore, large abatement is
necessary, as in the case of Turgot's portrait of Margaret.   As
of certain other kings, we hear that David would sit at his
palace gate and administer justice to all the poor old women
who had complaints to lodge   So sweet was his natural temper
that he would hold an argument with the poorest suppliant,
and endeavour to show him that his poverty did not necessarily
put him in the right.   Ailred had even seen him emulate the
famous action of the emperor Trajan.   When on the point of
riding to hunt, he would return to the court at the prayer of
an unfortunate suitor, and give up his pleasure till he was
assured that justice was done.   When we turn from such
conventional eulogies to the general policy of David's reign, we
receive a somewhat different impression at once of his public
and private character.   Of the one half of that policy—his

relations to England—we have seen the drift and ultimate aim
In the interests of Scotland it was possibly the wisest that could
have been adopted; but of the highmindedness of a St Louis,
with whom he has sometimes been compared, there is little
trace. From first to last his conduct was purely selfish, and
on more than one occasion he had recourse to methods which
place him precisely on the level of the average ruler of his
time

In the sweeping changes by which he transformed his
kingdom David only carried out movements which had been in
action possibly even before the reign of his father Malcolm. In
church and state alike there are indications that by the first
half of the 11th century Scotland was already touched by the
general influences at work throughout Christendom. The
decay of institutions north of the Forth was due at once to
internal developments and to European forces which were
moulding the modern societies through the agencies of feudalism and the organization of the Church of Rome. In the
inadequacy of the Celtic institutions to meet the growing needs
of the people, Malcolm and his successors found the opportunity they needed of making themselves feudal monarchs like
the other princes of Europe

But beyond every Scottish king before him, David had
the power and the opportunity of giving effect to the policy
which he approved The way had in part been prepared for
him: England was too much occupied with its own affairs to
give him uneasiness; and with his formidable Norman following
he was independent of the most powerful of the native chieftains.
In carrying out his various schemes, he was supported by
no body that bore the slightest resemblance to a parliament.
In Celtic Scotland the king had taken counsel with the hereditary
seven mormaers, and till as late as the reign of Alexander III
these personages, under the changed name of the seven Earls,
claimed a nominal right to advise the king. What was the
precise extent of their original function it is impossible to

say[1]; but from the time of Malcolm it is with another body that we find the Scottish kings holding council and taking action. It is with the consent of the bishops, earls, and barons, of his kingdom that they grant their charters and exercise the general functions of government.   But in the time of David this body possessed no defined powers giving it a precise constitutional authority.   Its influence varied with the king whom it advised; and in the case of David it must have done little else than countersign what he approved.   From the documents of his reign we learn that the great majority of the leading persons in the country were those Normans who owed him their fortunes, and would be little disposed to thwart him in a policy which strengthened their own position as aliens and inter-lopers   In the list of the great feudal officials now found at the Scottish court we have a curious proof of Norman pre-dominance   During the reign of Alexander I the feudal dignitaries—the Constable, the Justiciary, and the Chancellor—already existed, and under David we find, in addition, the Chamberlain, the Seneschal, and the Marshal.   In the beginning of David's reign Constantin, Earl of Fife, held the office of Justiciary, but all the other great dignities were in the hands of foreigners; and even in David's lifetime the de Morevilles and the Fitzalans were appointed the hereditary Constables and Seneschals of the realm.

The dominating fact of the period is the extensive assign-ment of lands within the bounds of Scotland to men of Norman, Saxon, or Danish extraction.   Wherever these strangers settled they formed centres of force, compelling acceptance of the new order in church and state by the reluctant natives.   Materials do not exist for tracing this gradual apportionment of lands by successive kings   It had begun at least in the reign of Malcolm Canmore; but it was David who performed it on a scale which converted it into a revolution   Three examples

---

[1] So imperfect is our information regarding the "Seven Earls," that their existence as a body with definite functions may even be doubted.

will suffice to show the extent to which the invasion proceeded. While he was still only Earl, David granted Annandale to de Bruce, Cunningham in Ayrshire to de Moreville, and Renfrew with part of Kyle to Fitzalan. We have no certain knowledge of the manner in which this transference was carried out by David or other kings. South of the Forth, at least, there appears to have been no occasion for forfeiture on a large scale, and in that part of the country, therefore, there must have been other grounds for the wholesale appropriation of territory in favour of the newcomers. From all we know of Strathclyde and Galloway previous to the time of the Saxonized and Normanized kings, extensive districts must have consisted of waste land, which could be alienated without great injustice being done to existing rights. Moreover, in Strathclyde and Galloway the idea of property in a precise feudal sense must still have been comparatively strange to the great body of their inhabitants. When a stranger was introduced among them, therefore, it was not as in the case of the Normans dispossessing the Saxons in England In many cases, indeed, the Norman baron, with his definite notions regarding his lands and his tenants, must have been a welcome change from the savage chiefs whose atrocities disgraced the English raids of Malcolm and David In the case of Moray we have seen that there was an immediate reason for the importation of a new element. The formidable rising of Earl Angus and the subsequent exploits of the impostor Wimund made urgent occasion for reorganizing a district which again and again had endangered the unity of the kingdom.

Only the subsequent course of Scottish history enables us fully to realize the transformation wrought by these "plantations" of foreigners Certain parts of the country, indeed, were little affected by the new influence As the future was to show, neither Galloway nor the Highlands underwent any such radical change as that which transformed Strathclyde, Lothian, or the east country to the north of the Forth. In the case of these

three districts the revolution was at once rapid and far-reaching.
Following the example of his fellows elsewhere, the southern
baron planted a castle on the most advantageous site on his
new estate With him he brought a body of retainers, by
whose aid he at once secured his own position, and wrought
such changes in his neighbourhood as were consistent with the
conditions on which his fief had been granted In the *vill* or
town which grew up beside his castle were found not only his
own people, but natives of the neighbourhood who by the
feudal law went to the lord with the lands on which they
resided.   What had been the previous condition of these
natives can only be conjectured, but in becoming the property
of a southern master they probably changed a harsher for a
milder form of bondage.   In the east country to the north
of the Forth a change in nomenclature is a significant indication
of the breach that was made with the old order   The titles of
mormaer and toisech passed into those of earl and thane;
and the changed titles implied nothing less than the fact that
the land had passed from tribal or private ownership to that
of the king.   By the close of David's reign the most valuable
part of his dominion was held by vassals and sub-vassals who
looked to him as their feudal head.   For the time this changed
relation between the king and his great subjects gave new
strength to the royal authority.   As the recent recipients of
their bounty, the great feudatories gave their loyal support to
David and his immediate successors; but the day came when
the descendants of these barons occasioned as much trouble to
the kings of the Scots as the Celtic mormaers and toisechs
whose existence was now so summarily cut short

In another matter the general European development is
seen at work in raising the level of thought and feeling in
Scotland. Before the revolution effected by Malcolm Canmore
and his successors there existed a body of law in the country
—*assiza terrae*—of which traces are found in the oldest
written legislation that has been preserved. For the protection

of life and repute there existed the two systems of compensation and compurgation, both of which remained in force till a period much later than the reign of David By the system of compensation a value was set upon life according to the rank of the person slain Thus a king was valued at a thousand cows, his son at a hundred and fifty, and an earl at the same rate Under the same old Scottish law those charged with crime might clear themselves either by compurgation or by the ordeal, in accordance with what had been the general practice of Christendom. But among the Christian nations there was now growing up a strong feeling against every form of the ordeal; and in 1216 the Council of the Lateran only gave expression to the highest public opinion when it abolished the whole system In Scotland under David there were already misgivings as to the adequacy and justice of compurgation and ordeal. The system known as *voisinage, visnet,* or *jugement del pais,* "the verdict of the good men of the country," was possibly introduced before the reign of David, but under him it received a prominence which eventually led to the abrogation of the ancient methods of administering justice.

Under the firm and settled government of David the towns of the kingdom naturally grew in prosperity and influence Free towns in considerable numbers must already have existed both to the north and the south of the Tweed. Before the time of David, indeed, certain towns beyond the Mounth[1] had actually formed a *hanse* or league for the advancement and defence of their common interests. South of the Forth, also, at the same early period, is found a similar combination, whose history is better known, and which eventually filled a great place in the national life. This was the association of the Four Burghs, which originally consisted of Berwick, Roxburgh, Edinburgh, and Stirling, and in time grew into the Convention

---

[1] This was the name given to the mountain-chain extending from near Aberdeen to Fort-William. It should be said, however, that the early Scottish writers use the term somewhat loosely.

of Burghs, which exists to the present day. Like their contemporaries in other countries, the immediate predecessors of David had doubtless found it their interest to foster the growth of towns within their kingdom. The towns were found to be a counterpoise to the power of the great territorial magnates, and they ministered, moreover, to the growing desire for greater comfort and convenience of living. Not till the reign of William I are charters to be found definitely constituting what were known as royal burghs; but even before the reign of David such burghs must already have been in existence. The date cannot be determined when the Scottish burghs received the privilege of electing their own magistrates; but in this all-important advantage they appear to have preceded England and even the continental countries. In carrying on their trade the free burghs enjoyed two privileges from the earliest period when we hear of them—the monopoly of traffic within a fixed area, and freedom from imposts in the transfer of their goods. Besides the burghs which looked to the king as their patron and protector, others now began to rise under favour of the bishops and the greater and lesser barons who had recently settled in the country and who followed the example of their king. The creation of free towns in Scotland was by no means the special work of David ; but by his deliberate policy and by his settled government he gave an impulse to their development which marks his reign as an epoch in their history.

From the deliberations of the Four Burghs issued a code of municipal laws and regulations which afford us our only glimpse of the social life of Scotland in the time of David. At stated periods commissioners from the Four Burghs met at Haddington under the presidency of the Lord Chamberlain, and settled such questions as arose between the intervals of assembly. On certain occasions, also, the Chamberlain held an *ayre* or court in each royal burgh, as representative of the interests of the king. At these ayres every burgess " as well foreigners as denizens " had to be present under pain of a fine.

Their object was mainly twofold—to see that the king was defrauded of none of his dues, and that on the part of the burgesses there was no breach of privilege, either in the separate trades or in their general commercial relations. The possession of property within the burgh was the indispensable condition to the enjoyment of its liberties and privileges. One law, at least as old as the reign of David, is of special interest as throwing light on the state of society within and without the privileged townships. By purchasing a holding in the burgh and occupying it unclaimed for a year and a day, a knight's or baron's thrall at once became a freeman and a privileged burgess. In immediate proximity to the burgh was the castle under whose shadow it may have grown up, and where resided the *ballivus* or king's baillie, who had the double duty of protecting the burgh and representing the king's interests in its commercial transactions. One other building noted in the laws is the Spittal or Hospital for lepers, regarding whom the strictest, yet by no means callous, legislation existed from the earliest period. The laws regulating the community itself were thoroughly socialistic in their character. Twelve burgesses, chosen by the mayor or aldermen, were entrusted with the duty of seeing that honest dealing reigned in the various trades. Bakers and butchers had to expose their goods in the window under the penalty of a fine and the confiscation of their wares to the poor; and other industries were carried on under similar stringent regulations. Every adult in the town took his turn in keeping watch from curfew till daybreak. A sharp distinction was evidently made between the various trades in point of dignity. No magistrate was allowed to bake bread or brew ale except for his private consumption; and butchers, dyers, and shoemakers must abjure their special craft before they could receive burghership. Every fortnight a court of law was held for the punishment of evildoers, and thrice in the year—at Michaelmas, Christmas, and Easter—a great moot assembled to deliberate on the general interests of the burgh Every burgh had its annual fair, when pleasure and business went hand-in-hand in curious fashion. Originally started to commemorate some saint, the fair brought immunity to all law-breakers except those whose crimes did not admit of sanctuary. If any one broke "the peace of the fair" he was tried by a temporary tribunal known as the Court of *Pies-poudrees* [Dusty-feet] or pedlars From the stringent laws by which it was protected, cloth appears to have been the most lucrative article of trade—only burgesses being allowed to buy and sell it, or to purchase and to dye wool The list of commodities that came under toll and custom indicates a standard of living for which we are hardly prepared by the general history of the time Rice, figs, raisins, almonds, pepper, alum, and ginger, are among the foreign articles of consumption, and the number of domestic utensils that are casually specified similarly suggest comfort and even luxury. Thus in these communities, at once numerous and energetic, Scotland was following the lead of the great cities of southern Europe. Directly and indirectly the Scottish burghs owed impulse and energy to foreign example; their laws and privileges were largely copied from English models, and English and Flemings were in many cases their leading citizens Nevertheless, through the policy and good fortune of David, Scotland had now entered on her commercial development under fairer auspices than any other country in Europe.

Beyond all David's achievements it was what he did for the church that gave him his great name among the kings of Scotland. In the words of Wyntoun.—

> "He illumynyd in his dayis
> "His landys wyth kyrkys and wyth abbayis"

In this work also he was no initiator, but by the extent of the changes he wrought, he definitively made the Church of Rome the national Church of Scotland. Before his accession

there were but four bishoprics—St Andrews, Glasgow, Dunkeld, and Moray, and to these he added five—Ross, Aberdeen,
Caithness, Dunblane, and Brechin.   In the insecurity of the
preceding reigns episcopal jurisdiction had been at once precarious and inefficient, but except in the case of Caithness, the
powers of each bishop now became adequate to his claims.
In the various dioceses, therefore, parishes are now first heard
of, and, what seems never to have found favour with the
Scottish people, tithes were for the first time enforced for the
settled maintenance of the church.   More palpable memorials
of David's munificence are the great abbeys he founded for the
various orders who came to divide the country among them—
Kelso, Melrose, Newbattle, Dundrennan, Kynloss, Cambuskenneth, Holyrood, and Jedburgh

In the political and ecclesiastical revolution the representatives of the ancient Celtic church could only be an obstacle
in David's way.   They represented a national tradition and
ideas of church order that ran counter to all that he had at
heart for converting his kingdom into a Romanized and feu-
dalized power like the other countries of Christendom   At
St Andrews and Lochleven, the chief seats of the Keledei,
such pressure was brought to bear on them, that their eventual
suppression was virtually assured.   Of their spiritual condition
at this time we have only the evidence of their enemies; yet
one fact suggests that the Keledei may not have been behind
the new clergy themselves in the culture of the age.   In a
library of sixteen books at Lochleven there was a copy of
the Sentences of St Bernard—a curious proof that the great
new movement known as scholasticism was not unknown to
these doomed Keledei hermits   That in his dealings with
the two churches David proceeded with a certain reckless-
ness, the subsequent history of the country was decisively to
show.   As in the case of his mother, indeed, there was in
him a strain of superstition which distorted his vision in all
matters concerned with the church.   In the excess of his

zeal he enriched the clergy beyond the relative wealth of the country; and in the end the very greatness of their posses-sions sapped their spiritual energy and invited the hand of the spoiler. In James I's saying that David was "a sore saint to the crown," we have the testimony of one of the ablest of the Scottish kings. From the first the people resented the burdens imposed on them for the support of an alien clergy; and when another religious revolution came their conduct be-trayed what little affection they had inherited towards the church established by David. To the class of the nobles, who now imitated the king in his pious bounty, the possessions of the church before long became an object of permanent cupidity which was eventually gratified to the fulness of their desires.

One glory alone was wanting to put the seal on David's reign as the greatest in Scottish history. In contemporary France, so much less prosperous than Scotland, a literature had sprung out of feudalism and the Christian Church. In England there was no such corresponding movement; but the civil confusion of the reign of Stephen sufficiently explains its absence. On the other hand, the state of Scotland under David seemed specially favourable for one of those literary outbursts which come of the sudden expansion of a people. A double oppor-tunity seemed now to be created for the expression of poetic genius. A Celtic people was face to face with an enemy bent on their suppression, and if they possessed the adequate ex-ponents of their wrongs, this was the time to make their voices heard. On their side, also, the victorious Saxon and Norman, in township and feudal castle, had grounds for an exaltation of feeling which might naturally have found vent in song or tale. From neither the conqueror nor the conquered, however, has a line come down to us; and alike in the interest of Scottish literature and history it must be regretted that the most interesting period of the national development has left no imaginative expression of that sanguine energy which was its special characteristic.

Great as had been the work of David in knitting the bonds between the different parts of the kingdom, the reign of his successor proved how much yet **Malcolm IV, 1153—1165.** remained to be done in the same direction. In accordance with David's desire he was succeeded by his grandson, Malcolm IV, known as the Maiden on account of his effeminate appearance. Malcolm was but twelve years old at his accession, and to his youth and inexperience was added uncertain health which crippled his action to the end of his brief reign. In the very first year of his rule the country had reason to know how much of its late prosperity had depended on the life of David. The district of Moray, we have seen had been largely colonized by Norman settlers, who acted as a check on the insubordination of its native people. The great house of Moray, however, still possessed a head, Donald Mac-Heth, son of that Malcolm MacHeth who was still a prisoner in Roxburgh Castle. In his own strength Donald could probably have done little mischief, but he had formed an alliance with a personage of truly formidable resources. This was Somerled, King of Argyle, nominally a dependent of the Scottish kings, but who by his conduct showed in what light he regarded his obligation. Having given his daughter in marriage to Donald, Somerled naturally desired to see his son-in-law on the throne of Scotland. With their united forces, therefore, Somerled and Donald for three years carried on a war of revolt in various parts of the kingdom.
At length (1156), Donald was taken prisoner at **1156** Whithorn, and sent to join his father in Roxburgh Castle. Even now Somerled was disposed to continue the struggle, had his attention not been called elsewhere. With the unfortunate Malcolm MacHeth, who for twenty-three years had been a captive, an arrangement was made by which he was allowed to go free and to take his place among the great nobles who surrounded the king; and during the remainder of Malcolm's reign we hear nothing of the house of Moray.

B. S.   7

On the side of England the Scots had to pay a similar penalty for the weakness of their king. The relative condition of the two countries was now the reverse of what it had been in the days of Stephen and David. It was now Scotland that suffered from internal dissensions, and it was England that possessed in Henry II a king who knew how to profit by all his advantages. In 1157 the two kings met at Chester, when Henry gave Malcolm to understand on what conditions he could retain his friendship. Malcolm, it must be remembered, was a boy of sixteen, and the experience of the last three years must have shown him that he was not in a position to defy the English king. It would appear, moreover, that certain of his leading counsellors, probably Norman barons owning lands in both countries, urged the young king to make the concessions demanded of him Under these circumstances the arrangement made at Chester was the surrender of all the advantages that had been gained by the policy of David. At Carlisle, in 1149, Henry had taken oath that on attaining the English throne he would cede to Scotland the district between the Tyne and the Tweed Disregarding his pledge, he now demanded the surrender of all the three English counties—Durham, Northumberland, and Westmoreland, which had been in the hands of the Scots at David's death. The Honour of Huntingdon alone was granted to Malcolm as an English fief; and to his brother William Henry left Tynedale as a substitute for the earldom of Northumberland which he had received from his father David. Malcolm's further relations with Henry were hardly more satisfactory to his subjects In 1158 the two kings met at Carlisle, when Malcolm took deep offence at Henry's refusal to confer on him the honour of knighthood; but in the following year we find him fighting in the English army in an expedition against Toulouse. On this occasion he received the knighthood which had been previously refused, though from the condition of

1157

1158

affairs in Scotland it seemed that the honour had been dearly bought

While still in France, news reached Malcolm which demanded his immediate presence in his own kingdom. Of the events that followed on his return we have only the most meagre account, but enough is known to prove that in the Celtic portions of the country there was still widespread discontent with Southern influences, and that only a strong ruler was as yet able to hold its incongruous elements together. While he was residing at Perth during the year 1160, the town was beset by a force 1160 led by Ferteth, Earl of Strathearn, and five other earls of whom we know nothing beyond their connection with this incident. The object of the revolt was to gain possession of Malcolm, doubtless with the view of effecting a revolution in the kingdom. How the scheme miscarried we are not clearly told, but a reconciliation seems to have been effected by the clergy, and the revolt came to nothing. This danger was scarcely over when trouble arose in another Celtic portion of Malcolm's dominions. It is in the English invasions that led up to the Battle of the Standard that Galloway first enters the main stream of Scottish history. As he then appears, Fergus, lord of Galloway, was a dependent of King David, furnishing his own contingent to the Scottish army. Of the origin of this dependence no record has been preserved; but from the moment we hear of it Galloway becomes the most troublesome portion of the Scottish kingdom It was there that, in the beginning of Malcolm's reign, Donald MacHeth found his last refuge, and now it was the scene of a revolt which evidently strained all the resources of the young king. Twice he attacked the district to no purpose; but a third expedition seems to have been completely successful. Surrendering his son Uchtred as a hostage, Fergus himself retired to the monastery of Holyrood, and spent the rest of his days in the duties of a canon-regular.

Two more events complete our knowledge of the reign of Malcolm. In 1163 he visited the English king at Woodstock to do homage to the infant Henry, the heir to the English throne. A year later his power was threatened by a danger as formidable as any he had yet encountered. His old enemy, Somerled, now more powerful than ever, landed on the coast of Renfrew with an army reinforced from Ireland and the Western Islands. Supported by a fleet, he was preparing to advance against the King of Scots. Fortunately for Malcolm he was saved another trial of strength against the fierce old king. Hardly had Somerled landed when he and his son were slain by some act of treachery, the details of which are not recorded[1].

At Jedburgh the following year Malcolm himself died, leaving as his heir his brother William, in whose favour the sympathies of the people were already enlisted. As far as had lain in his power, Malcolm had only carried out the policy of his immediate predecessors. Like them he had sought to conciliate England at the risk of alienating his Celtic subjects; and it was probably expedient to make large concessions rather than provoke the enmity of such a powerful king as Henry. What the reign of Malcolm showed was that the relative strength of the two countries was to depend on the ability and good fortune of their respective kings. Another minority and another inexperienced ruler might reduce Scotland to its ancient limits beyond the Forth, and might undo all the work of her kings from the days of Kenneth MacAlpin.

The reign of William the Lyon (the longest in Scottish

---

[1] All that history and tradition have to relate of Somerled will be found in "The Clan Donald," by the Rev. A. Macdonald, minister of Killearnan, and the Rev. A. Macdonald, minister of Kiltarlity (Inverness, the Northern Counties Publishing Company, 1896).—Vol. I. p. 38 et seq. Somerled is described by the authors as "probably the greatest hero that his race has produced." Vol. I. p. 54.

history) was a further illustration of what has been said of his predecessors. Under a weaker king than William—himself not among the most judicious of Scottish monarchs—Scotland would have been in serious risk of relapsing into its original elements, and of being eventually absorbed in the growing power of England. Against England without or rebel subjects within, William was more or less in an attitude of defence throughout his reign of forty-nine years During its first eleven years it was with England that he had his chief concern. Like his predecessors he desired to add Cumberland and Northumberland to the Scottish kingdom, but Henry II was the last ruler in the world to quit his hold on any portion of his territory. At first, the relations of the two kings were sufficiently friendly. In 1166 William accompanied Henry on one of his expeditions to France; but all that he succeeded in gaining was the Honour of Huntingdon which had been held by Malcolm before him In his youth William must have been impetuous even to imprudence; and, as events were to show, he was determined at all costs to recover his rightful inheritance. In council with Henry's many enemies he sent envoys to Louis VII of France—the beginning of a policy that was to be of such importance in the subsequent relation of all three countries Yet no open breach occurred between the two kings. During Easter of 1170 William and his brother David, with the leading Scottish barons, took oath of homage to the young king, whom his father in one of his few imprudent actions crowned as his successor to the English throne. At length an opportunity came which promised to William the fulfilment of all his desires. In 1173 young Henry, in a widespread conspiracy against his father, was desirous of attaching the King of Scots as a powerful ally. On condition of his support William was to receive the whole of Northumberland as far as the Tyne, and his brother David the fiefs of

(marginal notes:)
William I (The Lyon), 1165–1214

1166

1170

1173

Huntingdon and Cambridge. In accordance with this arrangement William led an army into Northumberland, where his Galwegians repeated their old work of pillage and butchery. Stayed from proceeding further southwards, he crossed into Cumberland, laid siege to Carlisle, and made himself master of several castles. Of his subsequent exploits the contemporary accounts are at once confused and conflicting. In July of 1174 he was engaged in the siege of Alnwick, and had sent the main body of his army to ravage the surrounding country. As at the Battle of the Standard, it was the barons of Yorkshire who were to punish the invader. With a small but well-armed force they marched northwards against the Scottish hosts, which, however, had no wish to risk the chance of another Northallerton. Pursuing the retreating enemy, the English leaders met with a piece of good fortune which changed for a time the relations of the two countries. As they approached the walls of Alnwick, they came on a small band of Scottish knights engaged in the amusement of tilting. The knights were no other than the bodyguard of the King of Scots, who, little dreaming of an enemy so near, mistook the English force for a part of his own following. Perceiving his mistake, William dashed against the enemy with his handful of attendants, and was immediately overpowered and made prisoner. As he was now to learn, William had played his game and lost. Conveyed to Northampton, he was presented to the triumphant Henry, who shortly afterwards made his captive safe in the castle of Falaise in Normandy. In December of the same year, a treaty was there extorted from him, which at one stroke undid the work of all his predecessors he became the vassal of the English king for the entire extent of his dominion, north as well as south of the Forth. The guarantees given for the observance of the treaty completed William's ignominy. The castles of Berwick, Edinburgh, Jedburgh, Roxburgh, and Stirling were to receive English garrisons, and as a pledge for

1174

their surrender, the king's brother David and twenty-one of the leading Scottish barons were meanwhile given up as hostages.

During the remainder of Henry's reign William was never allowed to forget his humiliating position. Again and again he was summoned to England and even to Normandy on matters connected with his own kingdom; and before lifting his hand against a rebel subject he had first to receive the consent of Henry. In the year following the Treaty of Falaise, William and David, together with the chief clergy and nobles of Scotland, did homage to Henry and his son at York. In 1176 he was summoned on an errand of special importance. In the Treaty of Falaise the rela- 1176 tions of the English and Scottish churches had been imper- fectly defined; and one of the objects of the Council at Northampton was to establish the ecclesiastical as well as the political supremacy of England. As on previous occasions the rivalries of York and Canterbury extricated the Scottish bishops from their strait. Each of these sees claiming the supremacy over the northern church, the council broke up without settling the question; and twelve years later (1188) Pope Clement III definitively decreed that the Scottish Church was directly subject to the Apostolic See. On another occasion the affairs of the church constrained William to appear before his feudal superior, then sojourning in Normandy. All his humiliations had not broken William's spirit, and he was now at feud with the pope himself. Against the will of pope Alexander III, whose own nominee was a learned ecclesiastic, known as John the Scot, William insisted that his chaplain, Hugh, should be bishop of St Andrews. So far did the quarrel go that in 1181 William was excommunicated and his kingdom laid under an interdict. The visit to Normandy 1181 settled nothing; but the death of Pope Alexander cleared the way for an amicable settlement; and the following year William received the Golden 1182

Rose from the new pope, Lucius III, in token of perfect reconciliation.

During all these years William had been in incessant trouble from his refractory subjects in Galloway and the North. His capture at Alnwick had been the occasion of a general revolt among the Celtic peoples, who wreaked their vengeance on the various new-comers settled in the country—Norman and English barons, as well as the English and Flemish burghers. After the Treaty of Falaise William was a discredited king, whose authority was set at defiance in one insurrection after another. Galloway, we have seen, had been temporarily subdued by Malcolm IV; but the captivity of William again evoked all its hostility to the Scottish Kingdom. By the murder of his brother Uchtred, who had been given as a hostage to Malcolm, Gilbert and his son Malcolm made themselves virtually independent for eleven years; and only the death of Gilbert in 1185 opened the way for a peaceful settlement. With the assistance of William, Roland, the son of the murdered Uchtred, became lord of Galloway. During an exile of ten years at William's court, Roland had married the daughter of Richard de Moreville, hereditary constable of the kingdom, and had become a Scoto-Norman more than a Galwegian. The fidelity of Roland was of the first importance to William, who soon had reason to know the value of such an ally.

While Galloway had been in rebellion, the northern parts of the kingdom were in a chronic state of disaffection. In 1179 William found it necessary to lead an army into the district of Ross between the Dornoch and Moray Firths, and to build two castles to keep the inhabitants in check But it was in 1181 that William's most formidable enemy arose. This was Donald Bane or Mac-William, who claimed descent from Ingibiorg, the first wife of Malcolm Canmore. For seven years MacWilliam was virtually a rival sovereign, being master of Ross and Moray, and so confident in his strength that, in the words of Fordun, he aimed at the whole kingdom.   In 1187 William made a desperate effort to rid himself of his enemy.   With as great a force as he could muster, he entered Moray, dividing his army into two detachments   On a moor near Inverness, Roland of Galloway, at the head of one of the detachments, came unexpectedly upon MacWilliam, who was defeated and slain in the battle that followed.   For a time Scotland was at peace from the Pentland Firth to the Solway, but before his work was done William had still battles to fight with enemies if not as formidable as MacWilliam and Gilbert, yet sufficiently troublesome to harass his last years and to retard the peaceful development of the country.

1187

With the death of Henry II in 1189 began a new phase in the relations between England and Scotland   Richard I was in character and aims a very different personage from his father, and he readily made an arrangement with William, which, as the subsequent history of the two countries showed, was in the best interest of both.   Bent on achieving the conquest of Jerusalem, it was the immediate interest of Richard to find money to defray the costs of his expedition, and at the same time to secure the friendship of the Scots during his absence from his own kingdom   For 10,000 marks he restored the independence of Scotland, and gave up the castles of Roxburgh and Berwick, the only two in the hands of Henry at his death The wisdom of this arrangement was proved by the fact that for more than a hundred years there did not occur one serious quarrel between the two countries

1189

With Richard's successor, John, William had difficulties which more than once threatened hostilities; but in his last years William was not the rash knight-errant who had given himself away under the walls of Alnwick   From the friendly Richard William had in vain endeavoured to recover Northumberland and Cumberland, and he repeated the attempt on the accession of John. John, however, also evaded the demand, and for the second time William made overtures to France The contemporary French king was the aspiring Philip Augustus, whom John had already such good reason to fear At John's invitation, therefore, William appeared at Leicester (1200) on the double errand of paying homage "saving his own right," and of considering the question of the two northern counties. The interview settled nothing, and the tension between the two kings became greater than ever To command the town of Berwick the English king made several attempts to erect a fortress at the mouth of the Tweed; but on each occasion the attempt was baffled by the Scots. Again the two kings met (1204)—on this occasion at Norham on the banks of the Tweed; and again their meeting led to no satisfactory result. At length, in 1209, the standing quarrel between them was settled for the remainder of their respective reigns. In that year John marched northwards with a great army to punish the Scots for their interference with his fortress at Tweedmouth In a strong position near Roxburgh William prepared to stay his progress through Scottish territory. A battle now seemed inevitable; but neither king was in a warlike temper, and by the mediation of their barons a contest was averted, and peaceful messages were interchanged. As appeared from the result of the negotiations, William had been intimidated by the greatness of the force with which John had threatened him. By the treaty as finally concluded at Northampton no castle was to be erected at Tweedmouth; but, on the other hand, William agreed to pay a sum of 15,000 marks as an equivalent for what injuries he might have inflicted, and as the price of John's goodwill to himself

William's timid policy towards England had all along been a source of weakness at home. Galloway, Ross, and Moray, had in turn disturbed the peace of his kingdom; and still another district demanded the strong hand before it could be brought to acknowledge his authority. Even in the days of King David the earldom of Caithness owed little more than a nominal dependence on the Scottish crown To the man who now held it the successive troubles of William offered the opportunity of making himself an independent sovereign. Half a Scot and half a Norwegian, Earl Harald was a personage of the stamp of Sigurd the Stout and Thorfin the Ugly, who had both in their day proved themselves more than a match for the kings of the Scots. Times were now changed, however, and William was master of resources far beyond those of his unfortunate ancestor Duncan. When the real trial of strength came, it was found that Harald, abetted though he was by John of England, had little chance of success against the full strength of the king of Scots. In 1196 William led a force into Caithness, and after inflicting a decisive defeat on Harald, left a garrison to hold the country. His enemy, however, was not yet subdued. In the following year the rebel forces penetrated as far as Inverness; but there they sustained a complete overthrow—a son of Harald being among the slain. A third campaign brought the struggle to an end Again making his way into Caithness, William at length secured the person of Harald himself, whom he detained in the castle of Roxburgh till a settlement was assured with his refractory people.

1196

One last attempt was made to unseat William, now broken with sickness and old age. His new adversary was Guthred, son of Donald MacWilliam, and therefore possessing a certain claim to the throne and representing the anti-Norman feeling of the Celtic people. By the invitation of the thanes of Ross, Guthred came from Ireland at the beginning of the year 1211, and speedily overran a great part of the country. In the end the power of William once more prevailed. Leading a force into the district of Ross, he defeated Guthred, and pacified the country. Though still

1211

at large Guthred was no longer able to make head against the
king; and the following year he was betrayed by his own
supporters and put to death with all the barbarities of the
age.

William died at Stirling in his 74th year, and was buried
in the abbey of Arbroath, which had been
founded by himself in honour of St Thomas
of Canterbury. Judged by the events of his long reign, William
must have had grave defects both as a man and as a king. As
the country had been left by David, a ruler of firmness and
capacity should have had less trouble in maintaining the peace
of the kingdom. From first to last, however, William showed
himself unable to master the unruly elements in his dominion
with which his grandfather had so successfully coped. Fortunately for the unity of Scotland, he was followed by two kings
superior to himself in the qualities of a successful ruler; and
under them the country attained a degree of strength and
cohesion which enabled it to survive the terrible ordeal that
awaited it.

1214

As far as had lain in his power, William carried out the
internal policy of David. His munificence was not on the
scale of his grandfather's; but he founded the great abbey of
Arbroath, and he insisted on the payment of tithes and dues
in all the districts where his authority prevailed. It is in his
patronage of the burghs, however, that William shows to most
advantage. To this reign belong the first charters granting the
various privileges which favoured their development. Ruther-
glen, Perth, Inverness, and Ayr, all possess charters from
William—that of Ayr being the oldest document of the kind
that has been preserved. The reign of William also marks a
growth in the constitutional development of the country. We
are still far from anything like a definite body representing
the various interests of the people; yet the King's Court had
evidently acquired functions at once more extended and better
defined. The persons who composed it were as before, the

prelates, earls, barons, and free tenants; but from two sources we learn for the first time that this body exercised the power of imposing taxes. According to a contemporary English chronicler, Benedictus Abbas, Henry II demanded of William a grant of tithes for the crusade against Saladin. William readily agreed if his subjects would consent; but a great assembly held at Brigham, consisting of his bishops, earls, barons, and "an infinite multitude of his subjects," unanimously refused to pay the tithe. Similarly, according to Fordun, an assembly met at Holyrood to impose a tax to purchase the independence of the kingdom from Richard I; and we learn from other sources that the money was raised by a general assessment of the country. Though no account of them has been preserved, such aids may date from an earlier period than the reign of William; but never before had they been granted on so great a scale. In meeting the debts incurred by the folly or misfortunes of William, therefore, a machinery must have been called into play which gave a distinct impulse to the constitutional development of his kingdom.

CHAPTER III.

CONSOLIDATION OF THE KINGDOM.

Scottish Kings.		English Kings.		
Alexander II ...1214—1249		John	...	1199—1216
Alexander III...1249—1286		Henry III	...	1216—1272
		Edward I	...	1272—1307

THE period of seventy-two years, covered by the reigns of Alexander II and Alexander III, is the golden age of Scottish history. It was a period of almost unbroken peace, for the few revolts in remote districts of the country never seriously disturbed the public order. In these years the revolution begun by Malcolm Canmore and accomplished by David bore its full effects in a steady progress towards national feeling and territorial unity. Though the Celtic elements of the country still on occasion gave ominous proof of their presence, they were no longer a standing menace to the stability of the throne. Through the efficacy of the feudal institutions and the organization of the Church Scotland had become a consolidated kingdom which only some unforeseen catastrophe could avail to break up. While the new institutions gave consistency to the various classes that made up the nation, the intermarriage between Scot and Norman and Saxon tended to obliterate those racial antipathies which had hitherto endangered the unity of the kingdom. During the reigns of the two Alexanders there is little indication of that jealousy between the Celtic and the Norman barons which had been a constant source of trouble to David and Malcolm and William. If any danger now threatened the royal authority, it was the selfish interests of the baronage as a whole, which at a later day was to prove so disastrous to king and people alike. During these reigns, however, this danger assumed no formidable shape; and once more it was the good fortune of the country to be blessed beyond its neighbours in all the conditions that make the welfare of a people. While the great countries of Christendom —England notably among the rest—were distracted by foreign wars or internal revolutions, Scotland pursued her peaceful development with such profit that at the death of Alexander III she was relatively to her resources the most prosperous country in Europe.

Alexander II was only in his 17th year when he came to the throne; but whether from his own discretion or the prudence of his advisers, the beginnings of his reign were marked by no errors or mis-fortunes. To ensure his peaceful succession he was crowned at Scone the day after his father's death in the presence of seven earls and the bishop of St Andrews. He had reigned little more than a year when the old enemies of his house made one more effort to make good their claims. Donald Bane or MacWilliam, a son of the person of that name who had risen against his father, appeared in Moray with auxiliaries from Ireland. The speedy suppression of this revolt shows that the work of preceding kings in Moray had broken the strength of that formidable district. In one campaign Donald was completely crushed by Ferquhard Macintagart, the Earl of Ross.

Alexander II, 1214—1249.

But during the first years of Alexander's reign it was his relations with England that mainly occupied his attention. Like David I he was fortunate in ruling at a period when that country was weakened by internal dissensions and by the folly of two successive sovereigns. During his first three years

Alexander's contemporary was the faithless John, now in the thick of the struggle connected with the Great Charter. To strengthen themselves against their king the English barons made an offer to Alexander with which he readily closed. On condition of his coming to their aid they promised to make him master of the three northern counties. Twice Alexander led an army southwards in the interest of the barons, when the death of John (1216) changed the conditions of the struggle. In the new turn of affairs the Scottish king found himself in a predicament which tested both his prudence and his vigour. On the accession of Henry III, a boy of nine years, the majority of the English barons returned to their allegiance, and the new king was further strengthened by the support of the pope, who by the abject submission of John was overlord of the kingdom. But there was still an ally with whom Alexander might work in concert, and win from England the territory which had so often eluded the grasp of his predecessors. Along with himself the English barons had invited Louis, the eldest son of Philip Augustus, to assist them in their revolt against John. Bent on the possession of the English domains, therefore, Alexander once more entered England with the intention of uniting his forces with those of Louis—the immediate result being the excommunication of himself and all his subjects. The defeat of Louis at Lincoln left Alexander no choice but to come to terms with the English king and the pope At Berwick (1217) he received absolution for himself, and did homage for the earldom of Huntingdon and his other English fiefs, at the same time abandoning all claims to the northern counties. But this arrangement at Berwick settled neither his relations to the pope nor to Henry. He had himself been relieved from his excommunication; but his clergy and his people were still under the ban, and it was only by a special embassy to Rome that the country was reconciled to the Roman see. With Henry, also, an arrangement was at length concluded which proved the basis of a permanent peace between the two countries.   In 1221 Alexander married Joanna, the sister of Henry, and gave his own sister Margaret to Hubert de Burgh, then the most powerful personage in England, and thus a valuable ally for the King of Scots

1221

At peace with England, Alexander was now at leisure to bestow his attention on affairs at home ; and his first act was to accomplish a work which had been left undone by all his predecessors.   The district of Argyle, part of which had formed the ancient Dalriada, whence Kenneth MacAlpin had issued to the conquest of the Picts, had never been thoroughly subject to the Scottish crown   It had played little part in the development of the country subsequent to the union of the Picts and Scots , but on different occasions it had given support to the enemies of the Scottish kings   What was the immediate occasion of his enterprise is not known ; but in the autumn of 1221 Alexander sailed against Argyle with an army gathered from his subjects in Lothian and Galloway   Owing to a great storm, however, the expedition came to nothing , but in the following summer Alexander repeated his attempt with signal success.   Without out striking a blow he reduced the country to submission, and as a security for its further allegiance, expelled all such persons as were likely to prove troublesome, and distributed their lands among his own followers

1221

1222

Successive disturbances in various parts of his dominions demanded all the alertness and prudence which were Alexander's characteristics as a king   In 1222, when on his way to England after his expedition to Argyle, news was brought to him of an atrocious deed in the diocese of Caithness.   Its bishop, Adam, by his excessive exactions, had driven his people to desperation, and they had taken the law into their own hands   Three hundred of them had on a certain Sunday seized their bishop, handled him

1222

B. S.   8 with great violence, and finally roasted him alive in his own kitchen On hearing the ghastly story, Alexander delayed his English journey, and led an army northwards to punish the malefactors. In previous reigns this would not have been an easy task, but even Caithness was now amenable to the royal authority, and Alexander had little trouble in avenging the death of his bishop

Two successive revolts in Moray served also to prove the strength of the crown. In each case the leader of the revolt was a member of the family of MacWilliam, but both were put down with a celerity which proves the great authority of Alexander as compared with that of his father A rising in Galloway, however, called for greater exertions before it was

1234   finally suppressed. In 1234 Alan, the lord of the country, died, leaving three daughters as his heirs. To have been thus subdivided would once for all have broken their power, and the Galwegians, rather than see themselves rendered impotent, offered the lordship to the king himself Whether from policy or a sense of justice, Alexander refused the offer, and the Galwegians followed their usual fierce instincts Placing a natural son of Alan at their head, they broke into the neighbouring territories, plundering and massacring at will In two campaigns Alexander brought them to submission; but both in his own reign and those of his successors the inhabitants of Galloway were still to prove their unconquerable love of independence and their fierce hatred of Norman kings and Norman institutions.

The fall of his brother-in-law, Hubert de Burgh, brought a change in Alexander's relations to England The occasion of the change was the desire on the part of Henry to assert those claims which had been yielded by William the Lyon at the treaty of Falaise. So bent was Henry on his design that he persuaded Pope Gregory IX to bring his authority to bear on the Scottish king. Alexander not only rejected the demand, but renewed his own claim on the northern English counties, and prepared to support them with the sword. To avert hostilities the two kings met at Newcastle in 1236, and, on the strong representations of the English barons, they agreed to defer the settlement of their quarrel. At York the following year the long dispute between the two countries was settled by a compromise which held good till the misfortunes of Scotland tempted the ambition of Edward I. Alexander abandoned all claims to the southern English fiefs, but received a grant of lands in Northumberland and Cumberland equal to the annual value of 200 pounds.

1236

In 1242 the good understanding between the two countries was endangered by one of those sensational incidents of which Scottish history is so full. At a tournament held near Haddington, Patrick of Galloway, Earl of Athol, unhorsed a Scoto-Norman baron, Walter Bisset, of a great family in Mar and Moray. The following night the house in which Athol slept was burnt to the ground, himself and two of his followers perishing in the flames. As a feud existed between the families of Bisset and Athol, the friends of the latter accused the Bissets of murdering their kinsman, and cried for revenge. In the events that followed we have the first example of what was so often to be seen in Scottish history—the king coerced by his barons into a course of action which he himself disapproved. The Bissets loudly asserted their innocence, and the queen offered to swear that they knew nothing of the crime. But the strength of their enemies rendered a fair trial impossible; and against the wish of the king the estates of Bisset were forfeited, and himself banished from the kingdom. Alexander had done his best to protect Bisset; but he had good reason to wish that he had given him up to his enemies. Proceeding to the English court, Bisset did his utmost to embroil the two countries. The king of Scots, he told Henry, was unable to protect his own subjects, but he had given harbour to a rebel who had escaped from an English prison. At this

1242

8—2

time Henry was disposed to regard the Scottish king with suspicion In 1239 Alexander had married Mary de Coucy, a daughter of Ingelram de Coucy, one of the greatest barons of France; and Henry was jealous of the connection between the two countries. On both sides preparations were now made for the contest that seemed imminent With an army of 100,000 foot and 1000 horsemen[1], Alexander advanced to the frontier of Northumberland A French contingent from his brother-in-law was to have joined him, but it was intercepted by the vigilance of the English king. On an equal scale Henry led an army to Newcastle with the intention of carrying war into Scotland But again the English barons succeeded in averting a contest. Their own king was not governing according to their desires, and they were not disposed to abet his ambition. On the other hand, Alexander was as popular in England as in Scotland; and, as in the days of John, the barons might find him a useful ally against their own king. The compact now made did not alter the conditions of the treaty of York—the sole agreement being that neither king was in any way to attack or injure the other except in self-defence.

As we have seen, the most important achievement of Alexander's reign had been the subjugation of Argyle; and in his last years he sought to crown this work by still further extending his authority. The Scottish kings had always regarded the Sudreys as part of their dominions, though at no time had they been able to make good their claims. To bring these islands under his power, therefore, Alexander seems to have bent all his energies. At first, his efforts were entirely peaceful. An embassy of two bishops, despatched by him to Haco of Norway, demanded the islands as the rightful possession of the Scottish kings. The claim being repudiated, Alexander made an offer of purchase, but this

---

[1] As in so many other cases these numbers must be taken for what they are worth.

also was refused As further negotiations led to no result, Alexander determined to gain his end by the strong hand. In 1249, under circumstances 1249 which are not satisfactorily explained, he sailed with a fleet to take possession of the coveted islands But it was not to be Alexander's fortune to give the Sudreys to Scotland On the voyage he was seized with a severe illness, and died in the island of Kerrera off the coast of Lorn, his body being conveyed to Melrose according to his own wish.

The reign of Alexander is marked by no great constitutional change. The great council, consisting of barons, the great ecclesiastics, and freeholders, often met to deliberate on the business of the country; but its powers were still undefined, and no burgher element as yet had a share in its proceedings. From such of its enactments as have been preserved we may gather that, in industrial progress as in moral tone, the country was steadily rising to a higher level of well-being To agriculture Alexander appears to have paid special attention, and one of his statutes curiously illustrates how he sought at once to benefit a class of his subjects and to bring the country under cultivation Whoever was the owner of four cows had to take land from his lord, and to plough and sow it for his own sustenance. The owners of less than five cows, dwelling on land that could not be tilled by oxen, must till it with their feet and hands—the reason assigned being that, in accordance with the precept of the apostle, every man "through his own wit and reason" was bound to support himself and those dependent on him

The work of Alexander in consolidating the country was reinforced by the increasing power and prestige of the Scottish Church. In 1218 Honorius III confirmed its independence of the jurisdiction of England, and in 1225 granted it a privilege of the first importance for its future development. Hitherto the dignitaries of the Scottish Church could not hold a Synodal Council without the intervention of a papal legate. This privilege was now granted, and henceforward these councils regularly met under a president of their own choosing, and known as the "Conservator of the Privileges of the Scottish Church." Like the other countries of Christendom, Scotland profited by the zeal of the two great religious orders which overran Western Europe in the 13th century. Both Dominicans and Franciscans, but especially the former, were welcomed by Alexander, and they speedily obtained foundations in every part of the country It was, therefore, with borders extended, with increased solidarity, and with every promise of developing resources, that Alexander passed on the crown to his son and successor, a child in his eighth year.

According to the chronicler Wyntoun, Alexander III was known among his countrymen as "the peaceable king." His reign of thirty-seven years did not pass without some actual fighting, but of foreign or domestic war it was absolutely free. Yet, in its beginnings, Alexander's reign promised no such happy immunity At its very outset two parties made their appearance, whose divided aims kept the country in a state of unrest during the whole of the king's minority. From the inadequate materials that have been preserved it is impossible to conclude what was the real character of the leaders of either party, or what was the precise policy they respectively followed The division was not one of race, as Celt and Norman are found equally on either side To a certain extent, however, the relation of Scotland to England seems to have determined the aims of the two parties Many of the leading Scottish nobles owned lands in both countries, and found themselves in difficulties between their two liege lords A certain section of them would willingly have seen the King of Scots reduced to the position of the English king's feudatory, as by this arrangement their lands in both countries would have been safe, and they themselves would have escaped

Alexander III, 1249-1286

an embarrassing position. On the other hand, another section, composed also of Norman and Celt, resented all English interference, and in time grew into that national party which eventually saved the independence of Scotland. As yet, however, there was no clear line of demarcation between the two parties, which followed with shifting allegiance the leadership of the two most powerful barons then living in Scotland—Alan Durward and Walter Comyn. As High Justiciary, Durward was the first councillor of the king, and to his great position he added a claim which made him a dangerous subject. He had married a natural daughter of the late king, and, with a view to future contingencies, he was said to have made interest at Rome to have her legitimatized. His rival, Comyn, was the Earl of Menteith and the head of a family which numbered two earls and thirty knights For the first nine years of Alexander's reign the rivalries of these two nobles absorbed the public interest, and produced a confusion and unsettlement which seriously affected the prosperity of the country.

The conflict of the two parties began with the coronation. For reasons of his own Durward wished the ceremony postponed, while Menteith and his followers were eager that it should take place at once. The counsel of the latter prevailed; and, with a degree of splendour beyond that of any of his predecessors, Alexander was crowned at Scone on the famous Stone of Destiny, on which another King of Scots was never again to sit. One incident of the ceremony deserves a passing mention, as symbolising that union of Celt and Norman and Saxon which had created the kingdom of Scotland After the forms prescribed by feudalism and the Church of Rome, a Highland Sennachy knelt before the king and recited the list of his Gaelic ancestors. Alexander was to be the last of the Celtic kings; and the incident, if authentic, has a pathos of its own in view of the past and the future of the Celtic race in Scotland

During the first years of the new reign it was the party
of Menteith that contrived to possess themselves of the chief
power According to Fordun, to whom, however, the name
of Menteith was one of sinister suggestion, the use they made
of their power was not in the interest of the people. The
king's councillors, he says, were so many kings, and the text
was realized to the full: "Woe unto the kingdom whose
king is a child." Whatever may be the truth of Fordun's
statement, the ancestor of the reputed betrayer of Wallace
was at least unpleasing to the English king Fortunately for
Scotland, it was Henry III who was then king in England.
Ineffective in himself and with his own many troubles at
home, Henry was unable to take full advantage of the minority of Alexander and of the dissensions of the Scottish
nobles. That he had the wish to profit by his opportunity,
his actions made sufficiently clear. Alexander had not long
been crowned when he applied to the pope to have the
Scottish king declared his feudal inferior The reply of the
pope was an emphatic negative; but Henry had another
opportunity of attempting to gain his end. In accordance
with the treaty made during the late reign,
1251   Alexander appeared at York (1251) to be married to Henry's daughter, Margaret. Like his predecessors,
Alexander did homage for his possessions in England. In a
spirit which was not royal, however, Henry demanded of the
boy of ten that he should likewise do homage for his own
kingdom of Scotland. The demand had probably been anticipated, for the young king was ready with his answer. He
had come, he said, on another errand; on the point now
raised he must first consult his council. Apparently Henry
did not take the reply in ill part, for he now performed two
good offices in the interest of the King of Scots. He informed his councillors that a plot had been formed by Alan
Durward to overthrow their authority. In view of Durward's
subsequent line of conduct, it is difficult to understand why

Henry should have given this warning. Meanwhile, however, his warning had the direct result of attaching Durward to Henry, whom he shortly afterwards followed to France. Henry's other service was to supply Alexander with a confidant and adviser who might work in concert with his other councillors. The person chosen was Geoffrey de Langley, a noble detested in England, and who speedily made himself so obnoxious in Scotland that he was forced to leave the country.

For the next four years the family of the Comyns maintained their authority, and whatever may have been the faults of their government, they had the good opinion of the people. Their adversaries, however, were many and powerful. In 1255 Alan Durward was again in Scotland, and he was associated with the Earls of 1255 March, Strathearn, and Carrick, Robert de Brus, and Alexander the Steward of Scotland. On the side of Durward's party, also, the English king threw his interest and his authority. In 1254 he had despatched the famous Simon de Montfort on a secret mission to Scotland, and the following year took the further step of sending the Earl of Gloucester and a special confidant of his own, John Maunsel, to give actual aid to the enemies of the government. Setting the example so often followed in later days, the English party seized the king and queen in Edinburgh Castle, and the revolution was complete. Meanwhile, Henry had led an army to the borders to support, if necessary, the enterprise of his friends. The late regents, however, had been taken at advantage, and no fighting was needed. With the king in their keeping the victorious party at once proceeded to meet Henry, whom they conducted with much pomp from Roxburgh to Kelso. In the abbey of that town an arrangement was effected that virtually made Henry the dictator of Scotland. The whole body of the former regents were removed from their office, and twenty-one successors appointed, chief among whom were Durward and the leading earls and barons who had acted along with him.   In the terms of the treaty the independence of Scotland was in no way compromised, but, as the nominees of the English king, the new councillors were hardly free to govern the country in its own interests.   By a modest euphemism Henry veiled his real power under the title of "Principal Counsellor to the illustrious king of Scotland."

The compact made at Kelso was to hold for seven years; but public opinion was against the new councillors, and the great family of the Comyns with their supporters never ceased to plot for their overthrow.   Two men, the Earl of Menteith and Gamelyn, elect bishop of St Andrews, were specially dangerous enemies   Gamelyn, like Menteith, had refused to sign the treaty of Kelso, and the new regents did their best to prevent his appointment to the see of St Andrews.   Eventually the triumph of Gamelyn was complete.   Not only did the pope confirm his election, but he excommunicated all who had taken part in opposing it   Other circumstances, also, tended to strengthen the party of the Comyns   The English king was so occupied by his own affairs that he had little leisure to attend to Scotland; and the appearance of the Queen-Mother, Mary de Coucy, always the enemy of England, gave a further impulse to the schemes of Gamelyn and Menteith.   At length, in the autumn of 1257, the national party, as it may be

1257

fairly called, took action with decisive effect In Cambuskenneth Abbey, the councillors of the king were solemnly excommunicated by the Bishop of Dunblane and the Abbots of Jedburgh and Melrose   Menteith lost no time in profiting by this advantage.   On the plea that excommunicated persons could not be fit advisers of a king, a party of the supporters of Comyn made their way through the king's guards at Kinross, seized him in his sleep, and bore him to the castle of Stirling.   The collapse of the late regency was now complete, and Durward himself fled to the English court.   The victorious Comyns acted both with prudence and decision   With the king in their keeping, they collected a force at Jedburgh that they might be prepared to face whatever might come from the side of England One step they also took which deserves a passing mention At this period, Llewelyn, the Prince of Wales, was in active hostility against the English king, and thus was an ally whom it was politic for the new regents to conciliate. In March, 1259, therefore, a treaty was concluded between the Comyns and the Welsh, by which they bound themselves to mutual defence and exchanged certain privileges of trade.

1259

Meanwhile the late councillors were urging the English king to exert his influence for the recovery of their authority. But Henry was in no position to compel Scotland to act against her will What steps he took, however, sufficiently prove that he deeply resented the overthrow of the men whom he had himself been the main instrument in setting up. In the autumn of 1259 the Earls of Hereford and Albemarle, accompanied by the Scoto-Norman John de Balliol, appeared at Melrose with the ostensible object of coming to terms with the governors of the king In reality, their desire was to get possession of Alexander, and with the aid of a force which was stationed at Norham to effect a counter-revolution. The design, however, was fully known to the Scottish Council, and they proposed that a conference should be held at Jedburgh to settle the government of the kingdom If they were to hold their own at the conference, it must be proved that they had the strength of the country behind them. Issuing from the forest of Jedburgh, one body of spearmen after another surrounded the place of meeting, and by their imposing numbers decided the result of the conference. Ostensibly the result was a compromise, for of the ten new regents four were members of the English party, in reality, however, the triumph of the Comyns was complete, and not even the death of Menteith in the year of the treaty sufficed to turn the scale in favour of their opponents.

1259

On the death of his leading opponent in Scotland Henry made one more effort to recover his authority in that country. A monk of St Albans, William Horton, was despatched to the Scottish Court with letters to Alexander and his leading councillors.   His real mission was a secret one, and its object has not been discovered ; but his letters conveyed an invitation to Alexander to visit England on important business.   At the time of Horton's arrival the great council was sitting, so that he received his answer from the king's assembled advisers.   It proves their suspicion of Henry that they flatly refused to allow their king to accept his invitation   Nevertheless, a secret embassy of their own to the English court was followed the next year by the visit of Alexander and his queen to Henry in London.   Only, however, after the most specific stipulations did Alexander's advisers allow the visit to take place.   There was to be no talk of affairs of state during the visit ; and as the queen was on the point of becoming a mother, neither she nor her child was to be detained in England.   Under these conditions the young king and queen proceeded to London, and were received with a splendour which Henry's subjects had occasion to remember.   In February, 1262, the queen gave birth to Margaret, afterwards Queen of Norway, Alexander in the meantime having returned to his own kingdom.

1261

1262

Alexander had now attained his twenty-first year, and thenceforward it was himself who took the leading part in the affairs of his country   He had still twenty-four years to reign ; but it is mainly with one outstanding event that his name is associated in Scottish history.   His father had made Argyle an integral part of Scotland : it remained for him to add the Hebrides to Scottish territory   Since the conquest of these islands by the Norwegians, they had never ceased to be a thorn in the side of Alexander's predecessors, and as long as they owned allegiance to a foreign king, Scotland could never be safe from annoyance and even from invasion.   It is in

1262 that we first hear of Alexander's endeavours to compass his end. In that year he sent an embassy to Haco of Norway with the view of acquiring the islands by negotiation. Haco, however, was in no humour to listen to any overtures. From his subjects in the Hebrides he had received grievous complaints against the Earl of Ross, who had carried war into Skye and the adjacent islands. Instead of giving an answer to Alexander's envoys, therefore, he refused to let them leave the country; and it was only on the representation of Henry of England that he permitted them to return

1262

In reply to Henry, Haco had declared that he had no hostile intention against the king of Scots. The next year was to show what truth was in his promise. Collecting a mighty fleet, he sailed for the Orkneys, and proceeding southwards through the Hebrides received the homage of the King of Man and other island chieftains. Of the events that followed it is impossible to speak with certainty, as the Norwegian and Scottish narratives are in many points at variance. Entering the Firth of Clyde, Haco took his station off the coast of Arran with the intention of bringing Alexander to terms. But it was already late in the season, and a protracted storm told heavily on the Norwegian galleys, many of which were driven ashore near the village of Largs on the Scottish mainland. Attacked by a body of Scots, the Norwegians were driven to their ships, with what loss is variously told by the chroniclers of the two nations. Five days later, according to the Saga, Haco drew together his shattered armament, and sailed northwards to Kirkwall. Here it was his intention to pass the winter; but, broken by age and sickness and mortification, he died on the 15th of December in the palace of the jarls of Orkney.

1263

On this disaster of Haco Alexander lost no time in following up his advantage. His first intention was to chastise Magnus, King of Man, who had assisted the Norwegian king in the late invasion. Collecting an army, Alexander proposed

to sail for Man and to bring the island to submission.   In
his own strength, however, Magnus was no match for the
King of Scots; and, presenting himself at the town of Dumfries,
he agreed to accept Alexander as his liege lord.   Against the
Hebrides, also, similar action was taken ; and a force, under
Alan Durward and the Earls of Buchan and Mar, subdued
them in the name of the King of Scots.   Three
years later (July, 1266) the Western Islands were
definitively united to the Crown of Scotland.   In that year
Haco's successor, Eric, ceded the islands to Alexander for
the sum of 4,000 marks and the annual payment of 100 marks
in perpetuity.   The Isle of Man was included in the treaty ;
but at a later period Alexander had once more to make good
his claim to it by the strong hand.

     1266

Like all his contemporaries, Alexander had his disagree-
ments with the church on the ground of its excessive exactions;
but, more fortunate than they, he was able to save his people
from extortion.   In a contest that extended over three years he
carried out the policy of his predecessors in maintaining the
independence of the Scottish Church.   To compose the quarrels
between Henry III and his barons, the Cardinal-Legate, Ottobone dei Fieschi, had been sent to England, and during his
sojourn there he made the following demand
(1267) of the bishops of Scotland.   Every
cathedral church was to send him six marks, and every parish
church four, to pay the expenses of his visitation.   With one
accord the Scottish king and clergy refused to listen to the
demand, and appealed to the pope in support of the justice of
their cause.   The following year Ottobone summoned the
whole body of Scottish bishops with two abbots or two
priors to meet him in council at whatever place he might
appoint.   Instead of obeying his order they sent two bishops
with one abbot and one prior; but only with the purpose of
guarding the interests of the Scottish Church.   Ottobone, however, was not yet baffled.   It was the time of the great crusade

     1267

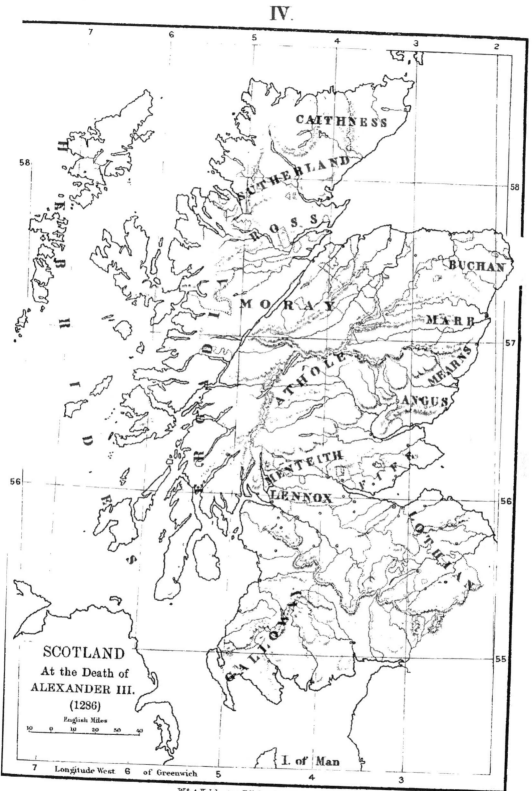

SCOTLAND
At the Death of
ALEXANDER III.
(1286)

English Miles

Longitude West 6 of Greenwich

I. of Man

W.& A.K.Johnston, Edinburgh and London

associated with the name of St Louis, and he persuaded the pope to grant the tenths of the Scottish kingdom to the English king Again Alexander and his clergy refused to submit to the exaction, affirming that they would see to it that Scotland should equip crusaders of its own.

Another attempt at exaction on the part of the pope was more successful. In 1275 Scotland received a visit from a personage whose name is one of the most familiar in the national history. This was Benemund or Baiamund (or, in the corrupted form it assumed in Scotland, Bagimont) de Vicci, who came to collect a tax for another attempt to recover the Holy Sepulchre At a great Council in Perth he told the assembled clergy that they must either pay a tithe on all their benefices or be laid under the ban of the church On this occasion the Scots had no good grounds for refusal, as the tax was to be paid directly to the pope and not to any foreign king. Against one condition, however, they protested with much earnestness. According to Baiamund's instructions the tithe was to be raised on the *true value* of goods and benefices ; but the clergy besought that it should be proportioned to the *auld extent*, or ancient valuation. So eagerly did they press their plea that Baiamund consented to submit the question to the pope The pope proved inexorable, and the tax had to be paid on the *true value* ; and from this time the detested Bagimont's Roll became the basis of taxation on the property of the church.

It is emphatic testimony to the wisdom of Alexander's rule that his last years were unbroken either by foreign or domestic disturbance. In 1278 he paid a visit to England which in view of what was to follow after his death has a special significance. Before the English Parliament at Westminster he took the oath of homage to the king who was to prove the deadliest enemy whom Scotland had yet encountered. In the proceedings that accompanied the ceremony there was ominous suggestion of that policy which the

1275

1278

first Edward was to carry out in the teeth of a nation's will
When Alexander declared that he was liegeman to Edward,
saving only his own kingdom, the Bishop of Norwich inter-
posed "And saving also the right of my lord King Edward to
homage for your kingdom." "To that," was Alexander's reply,
"none has a right save God alone."

In the light of subsequent events the last years of
Alexander assumed a lurid gloom in the popular imagination
to which there is no parallel in Scottish history.   One
calamity after another seemed to portend the storm that was
about to burst on the devoted people.   Of Alexander's
children one after another passed away before
him.   In 1281 died his youngest son David—
"the beginning," says Fordun, "of Scotland's sorrows to
come."   In 1283, within a few weeks of each
other, he was followed by his sister, Margaret,
wife of Eric of Norway, and by his elder brother Alexander,
married to Margaret of Flanders.   Only the infant daughter of
the Queen of Norway now represented the male line of the
ancient Kings of Scotland ; and within a week after his eldest
son's death, Alexander summoned a council at Scone to settle
the succession on the child on whose life the nation's destiny
depended   In the great assembly that met we have signal
proof of the anxiety of the public mind   Thirteen earls,
eleven bishops, and twenty-five barons, as representatives of
the nation, recognized the Maid of Norway as heiress of
Scotland, the Hebrides, Man, Tynedale, and Penrith—for
such was now the full extent of the Scottish kingdom.   Of the
earls it is worthy of note that four at least were Norman, and
of the barons not fewer than eighteen

Alexander was still only in his 44th year, and other heirs
might yet come to him.   In 1285 he married
Joleta, daughter of the Count de Dreux ; but
even this auspicious event did not relieve the nation from its
fatal forebodings   At the marriage-feast in Jedburgh Abbey,

Marginal dates:
1281
1283
1285

according to Bower, a pageant was enacted, apparently strange in Scotland, but familiar in the late Middle Age as the Dance of Death. While a band of maskers danced before the king and queen, Death in the form of a skeleton appeared in their midst and struck terror into spectators and performers alike[1] In the gloomy apprehensions of the time, it was believed that Death himself had appeared to warn the king and his people of his approaching doom. As his end drew near, terrible prodigies occurred "which in the judgment of the wise announce the falls of princes" In the month of December thunderings and lightnings filled men with consternation, and in the following March their worst fears were more than realized

On the 19th of that month Alexander held a 1286 council in the castle of Edinburgh; and though the day was tempestuous, and it was evening before he could take horse, he insisted on returning to his queen at Kinghorn. By the time he had crossed the ferry and had reached Inverkeithing the night was so dark that the riders could distinguish each other only by their voices. With the assistance of two guides the king pursued his journey, but so dark was the night that the party could only trust to the instinct of their horses They were now approaching Kinghorn, but before the journey was completed the horse of the king stumbled over a cliff, and his rider was killed on the spot.

Alexander left Scotland a prosperous and consolidated kingdom With the exception of England, indeed, no country in Christendom had in the same degree filled out its limits and welded its people Spain had still Granada to conquer, and was as yet made up of five independent kingdoms, France had scarcely attained the half of its present extent, in the decline of the Holy Roman Empire Germany was distracted by the rivalries of its petty princes, and Italy was divided among contending cities and factious parties. England and Scotland

---

[1] This appears to be the earliest instance of the pageant on record

alone had reached their final limits; and in both about the same period, Saxon and Norman in the one, and Celt, Norman, and Saxon in the other, had been fashioned into one nation. In Scotland the fusion was not so complete as in England; but the War of Independence was to prove that a Scottish nation had really been formed in the long process in which the first step had been taken by Kenneth MacAlpin.

To the reign of Alexander III, as to that of his father, no constitutional change can be referred. For the administration of justice he erected four Justiciaries instead of the original two—namely for Galloway, Lothian, and the districts north and south of the Mounth respectively. Of Alexander as of his predecessors it is recorded that, accompanied by his Justiciar and his chief nobles, he made an annual progress through his dominion to see that the law was justly administered. Besides the Royal Court, presided over by the Justiciar, there were the courts of Regality and Barony, whose judges represented the jurisdiction of the greater and lesser barons and church-men—each within its limits possessing the right of capital punishment[1].

To the commercial progress of the country during this reign there is emphatic testimony, though the means taken to promote it appear singular in the present day. Stringent laws enacted that no goods should be exported from the country, the reason adduced being that the land would be impoverished through the destruction of export ships by storms and pirates. One interesting proof of the prosperity of the country is related by Bower, the continuator of Fordun. A numerous body of Lombards arriving in Scotland offered to erect factories near Queensferry and on the island of Lenery near Cramond in the Firth of Forth; but for reasons which are not recorded the proposal was not accepted. Among the towns of Scotland

---

[1] By the time of Alexander III the greater part of Scotland had been divided into sheriffdoms—the Sheriffs discharging the functions of the Earls. Cf. *Exchequer Rolls*, vol. I. p. xliii.

none as yet could be considered the capital, though far before all the rest Berwick-on-Tweed led the way in wealth and enterprise. There is no contemporary description of the general aspect of the country; but in the Lowlands both north and south of the Firth we may believe that arable land was largely under cultivation[1]. From the legislation of later date it would appear that timber was a scarce commodity even in the district of Lothian. By this period, however, the rapid increase of abbeys and churches must have done much to soften the general appearance of the country. Simultaneously with ecclesiastical buildings numerous castles had arisen in consequence of the introduction of southern influences. In 1292 twenty-three castles were in possession of the crown, and it is recorded of Robert Bruce that within six years of the death of Edward I he had dismantled one hundred and thirty-seven strong places of various descriptions. Of the nation itself it may be said that the Teutonic element had now the preponderating influence in directing its affairs. The most valuable parts of the country were in the hands of men of Norman and Saxon descent, and the towns owed their prosperity to the same peoples. The languages spoken throughout the country curiously illustrate the various sources from which its people had sprung. In 1212 the Scottish kings could be described as "French [Norman] in manners, speech, and religion"; and French continued to be the language of the court till about the period when it was displaced in England. In Lothian and the east country to the north of the Forth English had superseded the Celtic dialects, which still, however, remained the speech of Galloway, extending to Ayr on the one hand and to Dumfries on the other.

In the course of the preceding narrative the greater and lesser barons, churchmen, and burghers have frequently been mentioned; but of the mass of the people we know little except

[1] The rent of the Crown lands was largely paid in oats, wheat, barley, malt, fodder, cattle, swine, and poultry. *Ibid.* p. lm.

from casual references in charters and acts of the royal council
It would appear, however, that they belonged to one of two
classes, the relative numbers of which we have no means of
determining.   The first comprised the free tenants, who were
themselves divided into two clearly-defined orders   In the
case of the one, land was held for a term of years, or even for
one or more lives.   The other order, whose position two
hundred years later moved the commiseration of John Major,
were annual tenants removable at their landlord's will.   Under
these were the serfs or bondmen bought and sold with the
land, and forbidden at the risk of their lives to remove from
the place of their birth.

As in the case of the reign of David, the prosperous period
of the Alexanders is illustrated by no form of literature, poetry
or prose.   In England work was being produced which prepared the way for the great achievement of Chaucer, but of
Scottish literature no authentic specimen has been preserved.
A casual remark of Barbour, however, proves what all analogy
would lead us to believe, that there was a popular literature of
ballad and song in Scotland as elsewhere.   The lament written
on the death of Alexander, preserved by Wyntoun, is the
oldest fragment of Scottish literature that has survived ; and as
the expression of popular feeling when fate was about to turn
the gloomiest page in the nation's destinies it is an appropriate
comment on what has here been said of the period that had
now closed

Quhen Alysandyr oure Kyng wes dede,
    That Scotland led in luve and lé[1],
Away wes sons[2] off ale and brede,
    Off wyne and wax[3], off gamyn and glé,
Oure gold was changyd in to lede
    Cryst, borne in to Virgynytie,
Succoure Scotland and remede,
    That stad in hir pirplexyté

[1] Love and Law   [2] Abundance.   [3] Wassail cake

BOOK III.

The Struggle with England (1286—1371).

CHAPTER I.

BEGINNINGS OF THE STRUGGLE.

Scottish Sovereigns.	English King.	French King.
Margaret, 1286—1290.	Edward I,	Philip IV, 1285—1314.
Interregnum, 1290—1292	1272—1307.	

ALEXANDER III was killed on the 19th of March, 1286; and on the 11th of the following month an assembly met at Scone to adjust the affairs of the kingdom. The only legitimate descendant of the late king was his granddaughter, Margaret; and, as she was an infant and in a foreign country, a regency of six was appointed to carry on the administration. In this arrangement it is interesting to note that the dividing line of the Forth was still a practical consideration: of the six regents three were respectively assigned to the north and south of that river. From the first it appeared that their task was not to be a light one. Not since the death of Malcolm Canmore, indeed, had a new reign opened with such a gloomy prospect. An infant sovereign, a band of competitors eager to profit by her death, a neighbouring monarch bent on availing himself of the inevitable dissensions—in these circumstances all that happened could easily be foreseen. Trouble first came from one of the most powerful barons in the kingdom—Robert Bruce, Lord of Annandale. In 1238 Alexander II, before the birth of Alexander III, had designated him as his successor, and in the present juncture the designation seemed not unlikely to take effect. Bruce himself was now in advanced age; but his claims were supported by his son, Robert, Earl of Carrick by right of his wife, the representative of the Earls of Galloway. From his castle of Turnberry the earl and his father became the centre of a confederacy which for two years seriously broke the peace of the country. The

1289

death in 1289 of two of the northern regents, one of them by assassination, further disturbed the balance of interests which had determined the formation of the regency.

It is in 1289 that the interest and importance of the period begins. In that year Eric of Norway despatched

1289

commissioners to England concerning the affairs of his daughter, the Scottish queen. As Eric was deep in Edward's debt, he was hardly free to act apart from his own special interests, and was constrained to defer to the English king. At the request of Edward, and apparently with perfect willingness on their own part, the Scottish guardians sent four representatives to Salisbury to settle the future of their country. The four men chosen were Bruce, Lord of Annandale, and three of the guardians themselves—Fraser, Bishop of St Andrews, Wishart, Bishop of Glasgow, and Comyn, Lord of Badenoch. "Saving always the liberty and honour of Scotland," the Scottish commissioners were instructed to assent to whatever was proposed by the representatives of Eric. In the vagueness of its important provisions the treaty now concluded left all the advantage with the strongest party. The Scots were to receive their queen only on condition of establishing order in their country, and their guardians were virtually to be the nominees of the English king. Before they married their

queen, also, they must receive Edward's advice as well as the
consent of her father

The significance of this last clause soon became apparent.
Though no hint of it was dropped at Salisbury Edward had
determined that his own son should be the husband of the
Scottish Queen. The children were within the forbidden
degrees, but Edward had already sought a papal dispensation,
and shortly after the meeting at Salisbury it came into his
hands. Still he made no formal overture to Scotland or
Norway, but in the beginning of 1290 the Scots
had tidings of his intention, and were not slow
to express their eager desire for its fulfilment. A great
assembly of the nobles, clergy, and "community" of the
country, which met at Brigham in the month of March, took
energetic steps to bring about the desired result. To the
English king they sent a communication in which they gave
their hearty approval of his rumoured desire; and to Eric they
wrote urging him to send his daughter to England at the
earliest possible date. Eric, however, was in no haste to part
with his daughter, but meanwhile no time was lost in settling
her destinies. In June the English king appointed his commissioners; and in July, at Brigham, the Scottish Estates met
to arrange terms with them In the number and precision of
its clauses the marriage-treaty bears signal testimony to the
sensitive patriotism of the Scots As far as detailed definition
could ensure the result, Scotland by the conditions of the
treaty was to remain a free and independent country Yet the
treaty was essentially a compromise; for, while Scotland was
to preserve its ancient liberties, it was expressly stated that this
was always "saving the right of the King of England in the
marches or elsewhere"—a clause which virtually left open the
whole question of the supremacy.

Two steps which Edward took immediately after the signing of the treaty proved to the Scots how widely it could be
interpreted By the conditions of the treaty Edward had

1290

taken oath to defend the laws of Scotland, and on this plea he appointed the Bishop of Durham as his lieutenant in that country As two of the four guardians were supporters of the English interest, the presence of the bishop gave Edward a decisive predominance in the councils of Scotland. His next step was even more significant of his deliberate purpose. On the ground of certain rumours that had reached him he demanded that all the strong places should at once be put in his hands. To this demand the Scots refused to listen · they would place their castles at the discretion of their own king and queen, but they would give them up to no other. Edward apparently took the rebuff in good part; but an event now happened which necessitated a fresh departure in the relations of the two countries. In the month of September the Maid of Norway at length sailed for England, but died at one of the Orkneys on the voyage.

The nation had now to face a disputed succession in its most aggravated form. Out of the many

1290

claimants who were to make a show of right to the crown, two were so equal in their claims and their resources that a contest between them must have been the temporary ruin of the country Troubles were not slow to develop: on the news of the queen's death Bruce of Annandale appeared at Perth, and, supported by the Earls of Mar and Athol, let it be known what he considered was his right. A few days later (October 7), Fraser, bishop of St Andrews, the only guardian beyond the Forth, wrote a letter to the English king in which he described the gloomy prospects of the country. As the best means for its good, he urges Edward to intervene with all speed, and recommends as a serviceable instrument the other powerful claimant to the Scottish crown—the unhappy John Balliol. By the death of Margaret Edward had lost his special position with regard to the affairs of Scotland; but in his heart he considered himself the rightful master of the country, and as such he had

determined to prove himself.   Meanwhile the death of his wife
Eleanor postponed the course of action which he meant to
follow.

There is no evidence that the Scots as a nation invited the
interference of Edward in the affairs of their country; but he
must have known that his intervention would not be rejected
by certain of its leading personages.   Acting on this conviction, he desired the Scottish barons and clergy to meet him
at Norham on the 10th of May, 1291.   To
guard against contingencies and to give reality   1291
to his function, virtually self-assumed, he also summoned the
barons of the northern English counties to appear in arms at
the same place.   With politic adroitness, however, he ordered
them not to present themselves till three weeks after his meeting with the Scots.   At the outset of the proceedings Edward
plainly announced in what capacity he was present it was as
Superior and Lord Paramount of Scotland that he was there to
settle the affairs of the country According to two English
chroniclers, the Scots were staggered by this announcement,
and they asked for time to consider it.   Edward granted them
till the following day; but when they met they were as far off
as ever from a conclusion; and again at their request, Edward
granted them three weeks to make up their minds During
the interval the Scottish "Communitas" (a term of somewhat
vague import) made a representation on the subject of the
superiority, which significantly enough was suppressed in the
English official account.   On the 2nd of June, the day
before the appearance of the English army, Edward again
met the Scots to settle the point in question—on this occasion
not at Norham, but in a field on the north bank of the Tweed,
and therefore in Scottish territory Among the Scots present
were eight of the claimants to the throne, and the whole
eight formally acknowledged the English king as Lord Paramount of Scotland.   At a meeting on the following day
John Balliol made a similar acknowledgement, and it only

remained to settle the preliminaries towards the final award of the crown. To assist the arbiter in coming to a decision a hundred and four commissioners were to be appointed—forty of whom were to be named by Balliol and Comyn, forty by Bruce, and twenty-four by Edward himself. A further arrangement made Edward in reality as well as in name the absolute master of the situation. By the 11th of June every castle in Scotland was placed in his hands, to be held by him till two months after the final award. As the state of Scotland necessitated an early decision, the Commissioners were to meet the claimants at Berwick on the 3rd of August; and in the meantime Edward made a progress through Scotland as far as Perth, rigorously exacting homage from every class in the country.

On the 2nd of August Edward met the Commissioners and the claimants in the chapel of the Castle of Berwick. Of claimants there were no fewer than twelve, though only three could be seriously considered—John Balliol, Robert Bruce, and Henry Hastings. Balliol was the grandson of the eldest daughter of David, Earl of Huntingdon, brother of William the Lyon; Bruce was the son of the second daughter, and Hastings the son of the third. The contention of Hastings was that the Scottish kingdom was divisible, and that in right of his descent a third of the kingdom should fall to himself. In any event Edward could make good his own claims with the strong hand, but three sub-kings could not all have proved as feeble persons as Balliol; and the proposal of Hastings was eventually rejected. On the present occasion, however, no decision was taken: the claims of the competitors having been heard, Edward desired the Commissioners to meet him at Berwick in the following year, when their report would be laid before himself and his Parliament.

The English Parliament met on the 2nd of June, 1292, and the Commissioners gave in their report. When asked for advice, they declared that they had

1292

none to give. There was no precedent in Scotland, they said, for settling the question at issue, and they requested the assistance of their English colleagues. Their united councils advanced the question no further; and again Edward postponed proceedings, declaring that he would consult continental opinion before their next meeting. On the 15th of October the English Parliament again met at Berwick, when a preliminary difficulty was decisively settled. If no law existed by which the case might be judged, Edward was advised to make a new one with the assistance of his own wise men. The claims of Balliol and Bruce were then heard once more; and Edward put this question to the assembly—the kingdom of Scotland and its revenues, were they divisible or not? It was unanimously answered that they were not. On the 17th of November, in the hall of the castle of Berwick, the award was at last pronounced in presence of the competitors. In his capacity of Lord Superior Edward declared that the kingdom of Scotland was indivisible, and that by the laws both of England and Scotland John Balliol was its lawful head. In token of the superiority of England the great seal that had been used by the Scottish regents was broken in pieces and deposited in the English treasury. On the following day Balliol swore fealty to Edward, and by a special mandate was crowned at Scone on the last day of November.

Such was the termination of a series of proceedings in which the judge had even more at stake than the parties at the bar. All through his career Edward professed a careful regard for the letter of the law, and it was professedly in accordance with law that he gave the preference to Balliol over his rival competitors. But Edward's reverence for justice was not unfrequently tempered by other considerations, and, as events were to show, John Balliol was a person peculiarly adapted to serve his further purposes regarding the devoted land.

CHAPTER II.

JOHN BALLIOL (1292—1296)

EDWARD'S real intention with regard to Scotland soon became apparent. Before Balliol had reigned a month, he found himself in trouble with his imperious master. One Roger Bartholomew, a citizen of Berwick, complained directly to Edward of some injustice that had been done to him during the late interregnum. By the treaty of Brigham Edward had bound himself to allow all Scottish cases to be decided in Scotland, and Balliol reminded him of the contract. The reply made convincingly clear to the vassal-king on what terms he held his office. His superior, he was told, held himself at liberty to judge every Scottish case that was brought before him, and to summon his vassal when the case required it.

1292

Another, but far more important, case of appeal eventually led to the overthrow and ruin of the "Toom Tabard," as the Scots sarcastically styled their king. The case arose in connection with certain lands in the earldom of Fife. Malcolm, Earl of Fife, had died in 1266, and his representative was now an infant. The brother of this Malcolm, known to us only as Macduff, claiming part of the earldom, appealed to Edward on being dispossessed by the bishop of St Andrews. By the order of Edward Macduff's claims were tried by the Scottish regents, who gave decision in his favour. At a council held

by Balliol at Scone, however, Macduff was not only deprived
of his lands, but thrown into prison for having broken the law
of the kingdom.   On his release Macduff was not slow to
carry his tale where he knew he was safe of a favourable
hearing.   He appealed to the Lord Paramount, who promptly
summoned his vassal to appear before him by the 25th of
March, 1293.   On this occasion, however, Balliol
was recalcitrant, and failed to appear on the   1293
appointed day   But Edward was not to be balked, and a more
imperative order was sent that he should present himself on
the 14th October of the same year.   To have declined a second
time to appear would have been a challenge to war, and for this
extremity Balliol was not yet prepared   Humiliation was not
spared him by his haughty superior, but he bore himself with
a firmness and dignity which proved that he was not destitute
of a due sense of his office.   When called to justify himself for
his dealings with Macduff, he replied that he was king of
Scotland, and could speak only with the advice of his people.
The result, however, was his complete effacement as an independent king.   He was to pay damages to Macduff for his
imprisonment, to commit the whole case to Edward for re-
judgment, and as a penalty for his disobedience to place in
Edward's hands his three principal castles with the towns in
which they stood   On a mild protest from Balliol, however,
Edward consented to postpone further proceedings till the
following year.

In 1294 Balliol made his last appearance before Edward
in his official capacity.   In May of that year
Edward had summoned a Parliament to advise   1294
with him on a contemplated expedition against Gascony.   To
carry out this expedition he was driven to desperate means to
find money, and his own subjects bitterly resented the impositions that were laid upon them.   With the Scots he
proceeded in the same high-handed fashion, and Balliol was
sent north with orders to see that money and troops were

forthcoming for his lord's need. On his arrival in Scotland, however, Balliol found his subjects in no mood to defer to the English demands. In a council held at Scone decisive measures were taken which could have only one end All Englishmen were to be expelled from the court, and their Scottish estates forfeited—an important step towards national unity which is of special significance in the light of what was to follow. When it is said that Annandale now passed from the hands of Bruce into those of Comyn, it will be seen that the measure was charged with great results for the future of Scotland. Another measure showed the determination of the Scots to put their country on a different footing, as it also showed their distrust of Balliol: for the direction of public affairs a standing committee was appointed from the ranks of bishops, earls, and barons.

These proceedings naturally roused the suspicions of Edward; and Balliol as a pledge of his innocent intentions delivered the castles of Berwick, Roxburgh, and Jedburgh to the bishop of Carlisle. In truth, however, the Scots were bent on shaking themselves free of England; and at that particular period a special opportunity presented itself The English king had now on his hands a war with France and trouble in Wales, and was, moreover, on ill terms with every class of his own subjects. With the advice of his committee Balliol now took a step of which no one could see the far-reaching importance He concluded (1295) a defensive

1295

alliance with France against the king of England. There had been previous understandings between the French and Scottish kings, but it was this treaty made by Balliol which established the tradition of a Scoto-French alliance. The immediate consequences of the new league were sufficiently disastrous In 1296 the Scots made

1296

an expedition into Cumberland and another into Northumberland; but though they wrought some mischief, both inroads resulted in failure. Meanwhile Edward prepared to take a terrible revenge. By sea and land he laid siege to Berwick-on-Tweed, and on the capture of the town gave up its inhabitants to an indiscriminate butchery which was of evil example in that international war which had now fairly begun, and which for more than half a century was to evoke the worst passions of two kindred peoples.

Before he had approached Berwick Edward had summoned Balliol to meet him; but Balliol had already gone too far to expect a pleasant reception. By the advice of his council, indeed, he had determined to renounce his allegiance, and shortly after the fall of Berwick their decision was formally conveyed to Edward. This proceeding of Balliol was precisely what Edward would have wished, and he prepared to carry out his easy task. The Scottish king, he knew, was in no position to offer him any serious resistance. His barons were divided among themselves, and the committee of government had given mortal offence to the family of Bruce by depriving them of the district of Annandale. A battle at Dunbar, whose details are variously related, placed its castle in the hands of the English; and the fall of the castles of Roxburgh, Edinburgh, and Stirling, soon followed. In his now hopeless case Balliol sent in his submission to the conqueror and begged for reconciliation. Within fifteen days, he was told, Edward would come to him in person and settle his affairs. The details of the interview appear to have made a deep impression on the Scots who were present. As described by Fordun, Balliol appeared with a white rod in his hand, and stripped of all kingly ornaments. Surrendering   **1296** his baton and staff of office, he then formally renounced all claims to the kingdom of Scotland[1]

---

[1] The place of Balliol's abdication is variously stated as Montrose, Brechin, and Kincardine, and its date as the 2nd and 10th of July, 1296. A document printed by the Rev. Joseph Stevenson proves that July 7 was the date, and the churchyard of Stracathro the place.—*Illustrations of the History of Scotland*, II. 59—77.

CHAPTER III

SIR WILLIAM WALLACE (1296—1305).

HAVING humiliated the king, Edward had now to complete
his conquest of the people. With this object
1296
he pursued his march as far north as Elgin,
the Scottish barons crowding in upon him to offer their homage
and to forswear the French alliance. Even its symbols of
independence were removed from the prostrate land. On his
southward march he bore off from Scone the immemorial
"Stone of Destiny" and certain charters which he thought
were better in his own keeping; and at Edinburgh he laid
hands on the Holy Rood, the most sacred relic in Scotland,
whither it had been brought by the sainted Margaret. In a
Parliament held at Berwick (August 28) he made his final
arrangements for the government of the country. Henceforth
there was to be no sub-king to hamper whatever policy he
might choose to adopt. Three Englishmen were appointed to
carry out his plans—John de Warenne, Earl of Surrey, as
governor; Hugh de Cressingham as treasurer; and William
Ormsby as justiciary In other respects he left things as they
were, doubtless in the hope that the nation would take little to
heart a mere change in its rulers. To put the seal to his
conquest, the Scottish clergy and laity gave in their allegiance
as a body—notably among the rest, Robert Bruce, Earl of
Carrick, and his son, afterwards Robert I, who now recovered

the district of Annandale of which their house had lately been dispossessed.

Before a year was gone Edward was to learn that his triumph was as empty as it had been cheap. In Scotland, as elsewhere, his representatives showed little of his own prudence and self-control. Warenne, the governor, was prevented by ill-health from doing his duty; Cressingham was a headstrong and sensual churchman; and Ormsby alienated all classes by his tyrannical ways. Most exasperating of all to a free people, a foreign soldiery was everywhere the standing proof of their humiliation. The general discontent came rapidly to a head, and a champion appeared with the special gifts of a popular hero. From his den, as it were, says Fordun, William Wallace now lifted up his head. It is but the scantiest authentic knowledge we possess of Wallace's achievements; but enough is known to prove that in capacity and aims he was of a different order from the mere guerilla chief. Of the various exploits which brought him prominently before his country-men little can be said with certainty. Two, however, are vouched on excellent authority. In May, 1297, for some reason unknown, he fell upon the English quarters in Lanark, and slew an English official of the name of Hazelrig. The same month he was engaged in a bolder enterprise. While Ormsby was holding his court at Scone, Cressingham and Warenne being both absent in England, Wallace and his band broke into the place, gained a large booty, and as nearly as possible seized the justiciar himself.

In the summer of 1297 certain Scottish barons resolved to strike a blow for their country. The deeds of Wallace had doubtless shown to them what might be done by a strenuous effort; and at this time, moreover, the English king was in bitter strife with his own barons and clergy. The result of their enterprise was a further lamentable proof of the conflicting interests of the natural leaders of the Scottish people. When at Irvine in Ayrshire they found themselves face to face with an English force, their jealousies broke forth, and placed them at the mercy of the enemy. In the circumstances nothing was left but submission, and once more the Scottish barons who were present acknowledged themselves the subjects of the king of England.

With the submission of the barons it might have seemed that the hope of the country was again cut off. But in the transaction at Irvine Wallace had no part; and with one prominent ally, Andrew de Moray, he pursued his heroic labour of freeing his people. So formidable had his power now grown that Warenne and Cressingham determined to make a special effort to crush him. Wallace was busy with the siege of the castle of Dundee when the news reached him that the English army was approaching Stirling. His strength was now so considerable that he apparently thought himself, aided by skill and good fortune, to be a match for the force that was meant to annihilate him[1]. As told by the English chroniclers themselves, the battle that now ensued was as signal a proof of the folly of the English commanders as of the skill of Wallace. Across a narrow wooden bridge, which spanned the Forth near Cambuskenneth Abbey, the English troops were allowed to defile in the face of an enemy strongly posted on the other side of the river At the fitting moment the Scots took the fullest advantage of the strange blunder, and a brief struggle was followed by the total rout of the English host, Cressingham himself being among the slain.

1297

The results of the victory at Stirling were at once immediate and decisive. A document, which has been preserved, written a month after the battle, brings this vividly before us. It is a letter addressed by William Wallace and Andrew de Moray[2], to

---

[1] The army of Surrey is said to have numbered 50,000, and that of Wallace 40,000 men ; but these numbers are incredible

[2] It is uncertain who this Andrew de Moray was. The Andrew de Moray previously mentioned is said to have fallen at Stirling Bridge, and

the magistrates and commons of the Hanseatic cities, Lubeck and Hamburg. Styling themselves "the leaders of the army of the Kingdom of Scotland," they thank their correspondents for their past favour and goodwill, and invite them to continue their commerce with Scotland, as the country is now "recovered by war from the power of the English." That this was not an idle assertion was proved by the immediate proceedings of the Scots. Urged by famine in their own country as well as by the sense of recent injuries, Wallace and Moray broke into Northumberland and Cumberland and for three months harried the country at their will. A document granting protection to the monastery of Hexham, in the name of "the leaders of the army of Scotland," is another of the authentic memorials of the national hero.

For a few months longer Wallace was to maintain his ground against the great enemy. On his return from his English expedition his name and influence were so great that he was appointed "guardian of Scotland and leader of its armies in the name of the illustrious King John." Of the circumstances under which the office was conferred we have no precise knowledge. One fact, however, would seem to prove that he had raised the hopes of his country and put heart even into the nobles themselves. The English king had crossed to Flanders before the battle of Stirling Bridge, and had returned in March of 1298. To a parliament which he at once assembled at York he summoned the 1298 Scotch as well as the English barons, but of the former not one put in an appearance—a signal evidence of the change that had been wrought by the achievements of Wallace. Edward lost little time, however, in reminding them that he was still the same personage whom by this time they should have known so well. In June he led a strong force along the east of Scotland, the castle of Dirleton alone placing an

his son was at this time but a child.—Bain, *Calendar of Documents relating to Scotland*, vol. II. pp. xxix—xxx.

obstacle in his march At first, it seemed as if his usual good fortune were about to desert him. Reviving the old Scottish tactics, Wallace kept out of the enemy's way and made a desert of the district through which he had to pass Edward had sent a provision-fleet to the Firth of Clyde ; but none of its stores had reached him, and his army began to suffer from famine. To add to his anxieties actual fighting broke out between the English and the Welsh soldiers in his camp. At length, while lying at Kirkliston, he received news that Wallace with his army was encamped in the neighbourhood of Falkirk. Near that town he found the Scots, numerically far inferior to his own force, but strongly posted on sloping ground with a morass in front of them Wallace had arranged his troops in "schiltrons" or circular bodies, armed with spears, to receive the charge of the formidable English cavalry. Unfortunately, he made no provision against another part of the enemy's force The English archers pouring their arrows into the Scottish ranks, opened a way for the English horse, and the battle was lost[1].

With his defeat at Falkirk the public career of Wallace came to a close For reasons unexplained he now demitted the office of Guardian, though, as we shall see, he never despaired of his country. His work, moreover, lived after him, for he had taught his countrymen that resistance even against the mighty Edward was not hopeless. After his victory at Falkirk, Edward did all the mischief he could in the richest parts of the country, but eventually he withdrew with his main purpose unaccomplished. With no recognition of Edward's authority John Comyn the younger, John de Soulis, and at a

---

[1] It is affirmed that at Falkirk Edward began those tactics with the English archers which had such splendid results in the Hundred Years' War with France.—*Eng Hist. Review* (July, 1897), pp. 427 *et seq.* Wallace, we are also told, "was a born soldier" ; and his schiltrons "were, in truth, an important advance in the art of war."—Hereford George, *Battles of English History*, pp 42, 43 (3rd edit)

later date Robert Bruce, Earl of Carrick, and Lamberton, bishop
of St Andrews, were chosen as Guardians of the country. Even
with greater resources behind it such a government was ill-
fitted to carry the country through the present crisis. Various
circumstances, however, enabled the guardians to keep the
enemy at bay for still a few years longer. Edward was
occupied in holding his own against his refractory barons and
clergy, twice the French king secured a truce for his allies
the Scots; and in 1300 a doughty champion arose in their
defence. This was no less a personage than Pope Boniface
VIII, who claimed to be the authentic Lord Superior of
Scotland on the ground that the country had been gained to
Christianity by the relics of St Andrew. But Edward's
knowledge of history was as intimate as that of Boniface,
and he was able to reply that Scotland had been subject to
England since the days of Brutus the Trojan, who gave his
name to Britain. In 1302 Boniface found it prudent to conciliate Edward, and waived the apostolic claims on the unhappy country. In 1303 the Scots were deserted even by
their ally Philip of France, and had now in their own strength
to bear the brunt of the whole might of England. Since
the battle of Falkirk, except during 1299, an English army
had in each successive year penetrated Scotland. In 1300
Annandale had been wasted, and Galloway subdued; in 1301
Edward built a castle at Linlithgow, and passed the winter
there, though in the following year his troops received a
severe check at Roslin But it was in the year
1303 that Edward found himself free to bear   1303
down on the Scots with undivided resources The country
south of the Forth had already been subdued, and the north-
eastern lowlands were now added to the English conquests
The castle of Stirling still held out, but so desperate had
affairs now become that Comyn the chief guardian gave in his
submission to the conqueror From the conditions of the
capitulation only one person was excepted—Sir William

Wallace, who, it was proclaimed, must surrender at the will and mercy of his lord. The following year the castle of

1305   Stirling fell, and at length in 1305 it seemed that Scotland was at the feet of her immitigable foe. Every stronghold in the country was now in his hands, and as the crown and seal of his triumph Wallace was given up to his mercy through the agency of a Scotsman, Sir John Menteith[1] Of the doings of Wallace from the battle of Falkirk we have only the most casual glimpse. To the end, it would appear, his one thought was the deliverance of his country. In this cause we find him in France apparently on the fruitless errand of gaining the support of Philip IV, who supplied him with credentials to the court of Rome; and as late as 1304 he was still fighting against the English. Once in the hands of Edward his fate was assured. With his usual severe regard to law when its decisions lay with himself, Edward found him guilty of high treason, and to the terror of future imitators had him disembowelled and quartered—the various portions of him being assigned respectively to Newcastle, Berwick, Stirling, and Perth.

[1] Menteith, it should be said, was a supporter of England.

CHAPTER IV.

ROBERT BRUCE, 1306—1329.

English Kings		French Kings.	
Edward I	... 1272—1307	Philip IV	... 1292—1314
Edward II	... 1307—1327	Louis X	... 1314—1316
Edward III	... 1327—1377	Philip V	... 1316—1322
		Charles IV	... 1322—1328

SCOTLAND being now apparently at his feet, Edward took upon himself to supply the country with a constitution. In accordance with his order, ten Scotch and ten English commissioners drew up an "Ordinance for the Government of Scotland." So far as was consistent with its dependence on England, the laws and institutions of the country were to remain what they had been. Instead of four justiciars, eight were now to be appointed, and the number of sheriffs was to be similarly increased. So far as they were contrary to reason and the law of God, the customs of the Picts and Scots[1] were to be abolished with the assistance of "the good men of the country." There was to be no vassal-king to give further trouble—Edward's nephew, John of Brittany, being made lieutenant or guardian of the country. The plan was prudent and well-intentioned; but the day had passed when the Scots would accept anything that came from England. In less than six months the new constitution existed only on paper, and

[1] See above pp. 90, 91.

Edward had virtually to recommence the work of conquest. By twelve years of harsh and imperious dealing he had evoked a truly national hate; and at length a man arose with the prudence and the resolution to direct it. With the opening of the year 1306 a new phase of the long struggle begins, though with little promise of a happier day for Scotland.

On February 10, 1306, Robert Bruce, the grandson of the claimant, slew John Comyn, the late regent, in the chapel of the Minorite Convent at Dumfries. From the position and the relation of the two parties this deed involved the national fortunes. In virtue of his alleged descent from Donald Bane, and as nephew of John Balliol, the Red Comyn, as he was called, could advance a strong claim to the Scottish throne. As the grandson of the rival of Balliol, Bruce also had hereditary pretensions of his own, for his father had died in 1304. Alike by their claims, their possessions, and their family influence, Comyn and Bruce were thus the two most powerful men in Scotland. Of the circumstances that led up to the quarrel between the two nobles and even of the tragic deed itself we have but the vaguest information. The results, however, were at once immediate and momentous. Since 1303 Comyn had been acting in the interest of Edward, who therefore regarded his death as a direct blow against his own authority. Only one course was thus open to Bruce—to strike out for himself a career, which, as his immediate action showed, he had long maturely considered.

The deliverance of the country could hardly have begun under less promising circumstances. The antecedents of the future deliverer himself were not such as to inspire a nation with confidence or enthusiasm. He had changed sides so often that it is difficult to follow his devious career. For two reasons, however, this does not necessarily imply that he was of a shifty character or specially doubtful honour. Holding large dominions both in Scotland and England, he belonged as much to the one country as the other, and if he had changed sides often, Edward also had changed his policy towards himself. As for the breaking of pledges, it was common to the highest personages of every country in Christendom; and the clergy themselves were not the least frequent and flagrant sinners. King Edward plumed himself on his good faith, and took as his motto "keep troth," but in point of fact he was specially observant of treaties only so long as they served his personal interests.

Not only had Bruce done little to win the confidence of the nation: the difficulties in front of him might well have seemed insurmountable. The enmity of the Comyns meant that half the country would be leagued against him. At this moment, moreover, every strong place was in the hands of the English. The people, indeed, had come to hate their English conquerors; but, as Barbour has said, they would fight only for one who proved that he was able to protect them. To crown all his difficulties, the wild deed with which he began his career put him outside the pale of Christendom, and made his extinction a duty to God and man. But in spite of his passionate act in slaying Comyn, Bruce, as his subsequent career was to show, was preeminently gifted with the prudent courage which does not exaggerate obstacles. In one direction he could not but see the prospect of a happy result for himself and the Scottish people. Edward, the great enemy, was now in his sixty-eighth year, and so infirm that he could not long be dangerous. Moreover, the character of his son and heir was such that all the world already foreboded what his reign should bring to pass[1]. But if England should come to be distracted by the follies of its king, Bruce might have a reasonable confidence that he would be able to make good his cause against his enemies in Scotland.

---

[1] Bruce is said to have declared that he was more afraid of the bones of Edward I than of his living son; and that it would be greater glory to have won a foot of land from the one than a kingdom from the other.—*Annales Paulini* (Chronicles of Edward I and Edward II, 1 265. Rolls Series).

The first step of Bruce let the world know what he meant:
six weeks (March 27) after the murder of Comyn
he had himself crowned at Scone   On the
significance of the ceremony one fact is the striking commentary of all the great personages in the country two earls,
three bishops, and one abbot, were the new king's only supporters   Nor did success at first attend these small beginnings
The English king, in a paroxysm of rage at Bruce's doings, at
once despatched Aymer de Valence, Earl of Pembroke, to put
down the revolt.   A lucky accident promised to make Pembroke's task an easy one.   In June, at Methven in Perthshire,
he fell unexpectedly on Bruce's small force, dispersing it so
effectually that with a handful of followers the king had to seek
safety among the mountains   Approaching the borders of
Argyle, he was attacked by another enemy, the lord of Lorn,
uncle of the slaughtered Comyn, and with forces still further
reduced, and the winter approaching, Bruce found it unsafe to
abide on the mainland.   In the full intention of renewing his
enterprise the following year, with a few personal attendants he
withdrew during the winter months to the island of Rathlin,
off the north coast of Ireland[1].   To complete the first chapter
of his misfortunes, during his sojourn in Rathlin his wife and
daughter were taken by the English, and his brother Nigel and
many of his supporters executed as traitors

In February, 1307, Bruce landed at Turnberry, in his own
Earldom of Carrick, with the resolution of once
more trying his fortunes.   It was but a scanty
band he could muster with all his efforts; but he was aided by
two men specially fitted to advance a desperate cause—his
own brother Edward, and the "Good" Sir James Douglas,
second only to himself in the traditions of their country.   The

_1306_

_1307_

[1] As Bruce was not safe from Edward even in Rathlin it has been con-
jectured that he could not have spent the winter in that island, and may
possibly have gone to Norway.   Bain, *Calendar of Documents relating to
Scotland*, vol. II. p xlix, note.

steady prudence of the king himself and the enterprising courage of these two champions slowly but surely carried the conviction to the Scottish people that their day of deliverance at length had dawned. But their first great advantage they did not owe to any merits of their king. On the 6th of July Edward I died at Burgh-on-Sands, in the very act of leading an army into Scotland, which was to crush all resistance. The circumstances of his death might have satisfied the most ardent Scot. Baffled in one of the dearest schemes of his life, in his impotent rage he besought his son to have his bones borne at the head of the invading army; and yet his bitterest feeling must have been that his worthless son was incapable of entering into his labours and carrying them to a fair conclusion. But, in truth, national prejudices apart, in regard to the relations of the Scotch and English peoples Edward is not an inviting figure in British history. He found two kindred nations, which for a full century had been involved in no serious quarrel; and by the time he had done his work he had evoked international antagonisms which bore immediate fruit in incessant wars that lasted for two centuries and a half, and which can never be wholly effaced from the memories of the two peoples. Edward II so far obeyed the wishes of his father that he led his army as far as Cumnock in Ayrshire; but the inglorious result of the expedition was a significant indication that the destinies of England were now in other hands. Returning to his own country, he was there to reign with such miserable folly that Scotland found the opportunity to which her king had doubtless looked from the beginning. The year 1308 brought important successes to the Scottish king. He himself gained Aberdeen with its surrounding district, and later in the year he overran the land of Lorn, and captured the castle of Dunstaffnage. An even more important achievement was Edward Bruce's conquest of Galloway, which had all along been fiercely hostile to the slayer of Comyn. In Tweeddale Douglas gained further

1308

ground at the expense of the English, notably bringing to
the side of Bruce Sir Thomas Randolph, the third of the
daring paladins associated in story with the war of Scottish
independence   Though every year did not bring equal good
fortune, the cause of the Scots went steadily forward   During

1309
1309 Philip IV of France endeavoured, though
with little success, to effect a truce between the
two countries, and even addressed Bruce secretly as king of
Scotland.   But a more important recognition strengthened

1310
Bruce's hands in February, 1310.   In a Pro-
vincial Council held at Dundee, the clergy of
Scotland declared to all the world that Robert Bruce was the
lawful king of their country   To the cause of Bruce, an excommunicated man, this testimony from the national church gave a
sanction which materially reinforced the vigour of his own action.

During all these doings in Scotland Edward II was in
continual strife with the chief men of his kingdom   In the

1310
autumn of 1310, however, he found an opportunity of trying the effect of his own presence
in the revolted country   From Roxburgh he led an army to
Biggar, and from Biggar to Renfrew, returning by Linlithgow
to Berwick.   Not an enemy appeared to encounter him ; the
season was late and inclement , and a severe famine in the
land completed his discomfiture   The following year he
would have repeated the enterprise ; but his own difficulties
interfered, and Bruce turned the tables on him by a merciless
inroad into the bishopric of Durham   Such being now the
relative position of the two countries, the expulsion of the

1311
English went on apace   In 1311 the castle
of Linlithgow was taken, and in the same year
Bruce again broke into Durham.   The capture of Perth and,
in rapid succession, of the castles of Roxburgh, Dumfries,
and Edinburgh[1], and others of less importance, made Bruce

---

[1] The capture of Edinburgh and Roxburgh castles is assigned to 1314
in *Chronicles of the Reigns of Edward I and Edward II* —ii. 199.

the master of his kingdom in reality as well as in name[1]. By the year 1313 he was so confident in his resources that, making his way through Cumberland, he landed on the Isle of Man and recovered it to the Scottish crown.

But the crowning stroke for freedom was now to be struck. The only stronghold of importance now in the hands of the English was Stirling castle; and in November of 1313 it was being hard pressed by the king's brother, Edward Bruce. A proposal made by its governor, Sir Philip de Mowbray, was rashly accepted in the spirit of a knight-errant rather than of a responsible commander. The castle was to be surrendered to the besiegers if it were not relieved by June 24th of the following year. The conditions involved a pitched battle between the two nations; and, in spite of his late successes, Bruce of his own accord would never have chosen to risk the chances of the unequal encounter. As it happened, the event was to exceed his most sanguine hopes, and to make him the hero of the proudest day in the history of his country.

In spite of his difficulties at home, the English king appeared on the appointed day with an army which, in point of numbers and equipment, surpassed every force that had as yet been led against Scotland. Its exact numbers are not known[2]; but a contemporary English chronicler assures us that it was the mightiest host that had been seen in England in his generation; and he adds that its war-carriages extended in a line would have stretched to twenty leagues[3]. Owing to delay in the muster, it was only by forced marches

---

[1] A treaty with Haco V, King of Norway (Oct. 29, 1312), confirmed the cession of the Western Isles of Scotland.—*Acts of Parl. of Scot.*, I. 481.

[2] The numbers assigned to the English and Scottish armies were respectively 100,000 and 40,000; but in both cases these numbers are incredible. The English were at least two to one.

[3] *Chronicles of the Reigns of Edward I and Edward II*, II. 201—2.

that Edward found himself face to face with the Scots on the Eve of St John, Sunday, the 23rd of June. Well aware of the immense superiority of the enemy, Bruce had chosen his ground of battle with admirable skill in the Royal Park between the Bannock Burn and the castle of Stirling. The appearance of the approaching host was as grand as it was terrible, and might well have struck panic into less tried troops than those of the patriot-king. But the omens were with the Scots from the beginning. Two incidents of the evening before the battle must have given them fresh heart for the work before them on the morrow. Under circumstances which are variously described, Bruce slew with his own hand the English knight, Sir Henry de Bohun, who had thought to end the national quarrel by riding down the Scottish leader. Equally decisive in favour of the Scots was a second event of the same momentous evening. In an attempt to carry succour to Stirling castle, an English troop commanded by Lord Clifford and the Earl of Gloucester was met by Randolph and thrown into headlong rout. The manner in which the opposing armies spent the night showed the different spirit with which they looked to the coming issue. Inspired by the insolent confidence of their king[1], the English spent it in uproarious revelry; while the Scots, though carefully supplied with food and wine, passed it in silence and devotion[2].

Of the details of the battle that followed (June 24) it is impossible to speak with confidence[3]. Even the position and

---

[1] An English chronicler tells us that Edward had marched as confidently to the battle as a pilgrim to Compostella.—*Chron. of Ed. I and II*, ii 202.

[2] *Ib.* 299—300. It is an English chronicler who contrasts the behaviour of the Scots and English on the night before the battle. But the same story is told in connection with Agincourt and other battles.

[3] A detailed account of the battle could consist only of a balancing of authorities, and these authorities themselves are both brief and obscure, and, in general, entitled to no implicit faith. In the main result all are agreed.

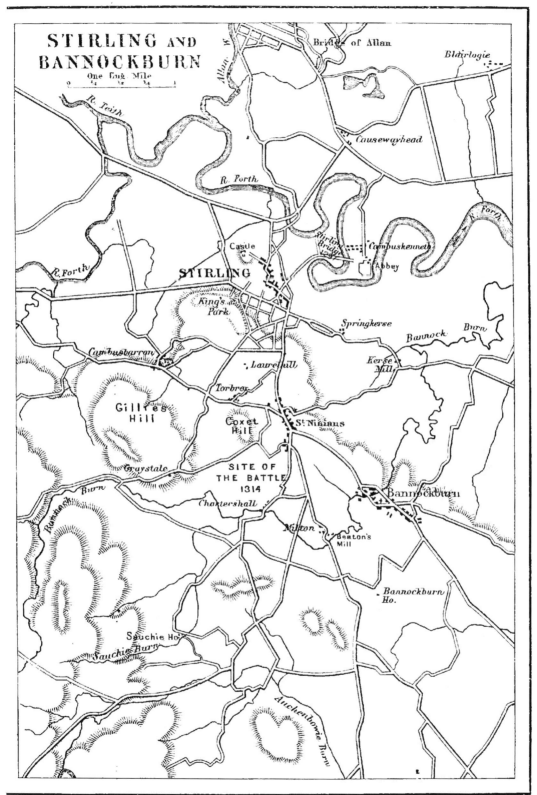

STIRLING AND BANNOCKBURN

One Eng. Mile

Bridge of Allan

Blairlogie

R. Teith

Causewayhead

R. Forth

R. Forth

R. Forth

Castle

Stirling Bridge

Cambuskenneth

STIRLING

Abbey

King's Park

Springkerse

Bannock Burn

Cambusbarron

Laurelhill

Kerse Mill

Torbrex

Gillies Hill

Coxet Hill

St Ninians

Graystale

SITE OF THE BATTLE 1314

Bannockburn

Bannock Burn

Chartershall

Milton

Beaton's Mill

Bannockburn Ho.

Sauchie Ho.

Sauchie Burn

Auchenbowie Burn

W. & A.K. Johnston, Edinburgh

arrangements of the Scottish army must remain matter of dispute. It seems most probable, however, that Bruce drew up his men facing the north bank of the Bannock, and that he arranged them in four divisions, himself commanding the reserve, the others being entrusted to his brother Edward, to Randolph, and to Sir James Douglas and Walter the Steward. Though the channel of the Bannock presents no formidable obstacle, it would yet weaken the force of the English attack in front; and at other points of his position Bruce brought strategy to the aid of nature. To break the ranks of the English horse he constructed covered pits— though what was their nature or in what parts of the field they were relatively placed, the conflicting authorities do not enable us to decide. In approaching the Scots from the south bank of the Bannock, the English army had difficulties to overcome which proved disastrous in the hour of action. It was only in front of the Scottish position that the banks of the stream offered an easy passage to bodies of horse, so that the English had no choice but to attack the Scots at that point. But the ground to be traversed in approaching this point put the English at further disadvantage. The position of certain bogs broke up their immense host, dis- ordered its ranks, and effectually crippled the action of their cavalry.

From the confused and conflicting accounts of the battle, only a few of its more striking incidents emerge with clear- ness. Charging straight on the Scottish front, the English men-at-arms became at once entangled in the concealed pits that had been prepared for them, and their broken ranks threw the advancing masses into hopeless disorder. On this day, also, the terrible English archers did little to retrieve the field. Where they were placed it is impossible to say, but, with a foresight which the Scots strangely neglected to follow in subsequent contests with the same enemy, Bruce had set apart a special detachment of cavalry to deal with them, and at the fitting moment the whole body of English bowmen were cut to pieces. Another notable incident of the battle may perhaps be attributed to the prudence of the Scottish leader. On an eminence behind the Scottish right, afterwards known as the Gillies' Hill, a promiscuous mob with raised banners appeared to the English to be another army about to join the enemy At whatever juncture this event may have happened it decided the fortunes of the day. The English host was thrown into a panic rout which was the last result of a succession of disasters and of lost confidence in its leaders. From the appalling carnage that followed, the English king, with a folly in keeping with his whole conduct of the day, rode to Stirling castle as the nearest place of safety With prudent hospitality the governor Mowbray bade him seek an asylum elsewhere ; and, as fast as their horses could carry them, Edward and his body-guard made for the town of Dunbar, pursued to the very gates by the Good Sir James. Embarking in a boat provided by the Earl of March, Edward made haste to his own kingdom with a tale to tell unparalleled in its annals

The defeat at Bannockburn was the greatest disgrace that ever befel the English arms , and it was regarded at the time as a special visitation of Heaven for the sins of the nation. The overthrow of Xerxes by the Greeks and of Israel by Benjamin seemed the only fitting parallels for the ruin of the mighty English host by so pitiful a people as the Scots[1] The number of the English who fell can only be matter of conjecture ; but among them were forty-two knights and twenty greater and lesser barons—the Earl of Gloucester, Sir Giles de Argentine, Sir Edward de Mauley, the Marshal of England, being the most notable. The multitude of prisoners included twenty-two greater and lesser barons—the Earls of Hereford and Angus, and Sir Ingelram de Umphraville among the

---

[1] *Chron. of Ed I and Ed. II*, ii. 207.

rest   In ransoms and spoils the booty acquired by the Scots was enormous, and it permanently contributed to the wealth of their country   Alike from the point of view of glory and interest, therefore, the fight at Bannockburn legitimately holds the first place among the triumphant actions of the Scottish people.

As the result of the battle of Bannockburn a state of things recurred which more than once had been seen before, and which was the true justification of the policy of Edward I. Scotland with a strong king became a truly formidable enemy to England with a weak one   What had happened in the times of David I and Stephen was now repeated in the relations of Bruce and Edward II.   His defeat at Bannockburn and his own incurable folly crippled the English king till the tragic close of his reign in 1327.   The Scots, on the other hand, rendered audacious by their successive triumphs, repaid with interest the long suffering of their country at the hands of the English soldiery   Down to the close of Bruce's reign one inroad after another into the north of England was the lamentable proof of the evil policy of the first Edward

In Scotland Bruce was now acknowledged master[1], and it only remained to wring from the English king the formal recognition of Scottish independence.   During the years that followed Bannockburn it was to this object that Bruce devoted himself with the same steady purpose which had already triumphed over so many adverse circumstances   In September of 1314 he made overtures to Edward, but the elation of the one country and the irritation of the other were not favourable to a peaceful understanding, and nothing came of the proposals.   An assembly held at Ayr in the following year (April 26) at least   1315

---

[1] In a Parliament which met at Cambuskenneth on Nov 6, 1314, sentence of forfeiture was passed against all who would not acknowledge Bruce's authority.   The number of charters granted by Bruce indicates the large extent to which lands changed their owners in his reign

settled the affairs of the kingdom as far as lay in its own power. To avert the disastrous results that had followed the death of Alexander III, the succession to the crown was defined with a careful regard to all possible contingencies. If Bruce died without male heirs, with his own consent and that of his daughter Marjory, he was to be succeeded by his brother Edward and his male heirs. In the event of a minority Randolph, now Earl of Moray, was to administer the kingdom.

It was mainly by invasions of England that Bruce sought to bring Edward to terms; but in the same year as the assembly at Ayr a proposal was made to him which directly fell in with his own policy. The Irish of Ulster, hearing of his victorious course, besought him to come to their aid against the common enemy. There was a double reason why he should accede to the request. It was an opportunity of wounding the enemy in another part[1]; and, moreover, it would rid him of a difficulty which was already a stumbling-block. Edward Bruce, in the words of Barbour, found Scotland too small for himself and his brother. Accordingly in May, 1315, Edward, with a force

1315

of 6000 men, landed at Carrickfergus, and addressed himself to the conquest of Ireland. It was agreed that, if he won the country, he was to be its king. Over three years he fought with varying success, and was actually crowned king in May, 1316[2]. But the rashness

- 1316

which had carried him through so many exploits proved his ruin at the last. Against the advice of all the other leaders, he engaged with the English at Dundalk (October, 1318), and was there defeated and

1318

slain. But, though Edward Bruce had thus

[1] It was rumoured in England that should Edward Bruce be successful in Ireland, Wales would be the next point of attack.—*Chron. of Ed I and Ed. II*, II. 211.

[2] During 1316 and 1317 the king of Scots was in Ireland assisting his brother.

failed in his main object, the enterprise had not been fruitless in the interest of Scotland. It broke the power of the English nobles in Ireland, and for a time confined the English dominion to the neighbourhood of Dublin, and thus gave one other proof of the mischief which the Scots could inflict on their powerful neighbour

Meanwhile the king of Scots was strengthening his position year by year We have seen that he had already subdued Galloway and Argyle: and in 1315 he made himself master of the Western Islands[1], so that his kingdom was now coextensive with the Scotland of Alexander III. King of a united country and strong in the support of the national clergy, Bruce was emboldened even to hold his own with the pope, who now intervened in Scottish affairs in the interest of England. In 1317 John XXII sent two cardinals to England to proclaim a truce between the two hostile nations. If Bruce should prove refractory, he was to be excommunicated along with such other persons as were troublesome. Two messengers despatched by the cardinals to the king of Scots made known to him the desires of the head of the church. In the letters they bore, however, he was not addressed as king, and he ironically informed the envoys that he could not be the person they were seeking. Not to be thwarted, the cardinals next sent a Minorite Friar to proclaim the papal truce in Scotland. But again the Scottish king showed that he was not to be beaten from his ground. On hearing that the pope's bull did not recognize his title he refused to see the friar, who, on his way back to Berwick-on-Tweed, was waylaid and robbed of every document with which he had been furnished.

The capture of Berwick in 1318 was, after Bannockburn, the severest blow that Bruce inflicted on England;

---

[1] It should be said that Angus Og, the head of the Clan Donald, was on friendly terms with Bruce, and lent valuable assistance at Bannockburn. *The Clan Donald*, I. 96.

and an attempt (**1319**) on the part of Edward to recover

it led only to his fresh discomfiture. To relieve the town when hard pressed by the English army, Douglas and Randolph led a force into Yorkshire with the intention of seizing the English queen, then living near the town of York. The adventure miscarried; but they succeeded in striking a blow which effectually relieved the garrison of Berwick. At Mytton-on-Swale they were opposed by a motley force of clergy and country-folk, led by the archbishop of York, doubtless in the hope of repeating the triumph of his predecessor at the Battle of the Standard. On this occasion the result was far different. The English force was completely routed, and so many of the clergy were among the slain that the battle was known among the Scots as the Chapter of Mytton[1].

Still the English king was unwilling to treat with Scotland as an independent country, and, as Scotland now stood, it was only on this condition that her king would agree to a permanent peace. At length the Scots took a step which, seconding their successes in war, seems to have hastened the accomplishment of their desires. If the pope could be gained over, they seem to have felt that Edward must succumb to the double pressure of ecclesiastical authority and chronic invasion. At Arbroath, therefore, in 1320, a

great assembly of the nation drew up a document in which they put before the pope their case against England. From time immemorial, they declared, Scotland had been a free country till Edward I, "in the guise of a friend and ally," had made himself its tyrant and oppressor. Now they had a lawful king, by whom they would stand against all his enemies. Should even he, however, propose to subject them to England, they would refuse to obey him

---

[1] It was known in England as *The White Battle.* The fullest account of the battle is given by the Bridlington canon.—*Chron. of Ed. I and Ed. II*, ii. 57—8.

though only a hundred of them were left. Such being their rights as a free people, they called upon the pope as the father of Christendom to support what is reasonable and just[1].

The success of the appeal was not immediate; for more than two years later Edward led an army into Scotland, and made his way as far north as Edinburgh. But the expedition was attended by Edward's usual ill-fortune. From a wasted country he led back his baffled army, pursued by the Scots as far as Biland in Yorkshire, where he escaped their hands only by abandoning his baggage and his personal possessions. A discovery made by Edward in the beginning of the following year further showed him how hopeless was his present policy towards the Scots. His warden of the West Marches, Andrew Hartcla, Earl of Carlisle, was found to be aiding and abetting the enemy in their inroads into the northern English counties. Hartcla was put to death as a traitor; but Edward at length found himself forced to come to terms with the Scots. On March 30, 1323, a truce was concluded which was to last till 1336. In the proceedings that led up to this arrangement Bruce uniformly assumed the title of King of Scots; but Edward never formally acknowledged it. Nothing short of this formal acknowledgment, however, would satisfy the Scottish king, and the very year that the truce was signed he despatched Randolph to Rome to submit his cause to the pope. At first the mission of Randolph promised all that was desired, for the pope was persuaded to recognize Bruce's title. The displeasure of the English king, however, gave another turn to the pope's mind, and he was effectually restrained from showing further favour to the Scots. When in the following year they besought him to remove the ban of excommunication under which they still lay, they were informed that their prayer

1323

---

[1] To the year 1320 belongs the conspiracy of Sir William de Soulis. A Parliament which met in August at Scone dealt so severely with those concerned in it that it came to be known as "The Black Parliament."

could be granted only on condition of restoring the town of Berwick. Rather than give up the town which they considered the key of Scotland, they preferred to continue under the pope's displeasure.

The year 1326 is a memorable one in the constitutional history of Scotland. In that year, on July 15, the first Scottish Parliament in name and reality met in Cambuskenneth Abbey. The name had been applied to the Scottish assembly which negotiated the treaty of Brigham in 1289; but the first Scottish assembly to call itself a Parliament was that held by John Balliol at Scone in 1292. What distinguishes the assembly at Cambuskenneth from all those that preceded it is the fact that for the first time, as far as is known, representatives from the burghs took part in its proceedings. The special object for which the assembly was summoned explains the presence of the new element. To meet the heavy expenses of his wars with England, Bruce found it necessary to appeal to the country for an extraordinary contribution. The Parliament readily responded to his demand, and granted him the tenth penny of all rents according to the old extent[1]. It was in 1295 that Edward I convoked a similar assembly in England, and in this as in other political adjustments the Scottish king followed the example of his great enemy.

The reign of Bruce was now nearing its close; but before the end he was to see the triumph of all his endeavours. It was the ill-fortune of England that again brought him his opportunity. In 1327 Edward II was deposed, and his son, a boy in his fifteenth year, took his place. The truce between the two countries was confirmed at the beginning of the new reign; but neither was in the temper to observe it, and in the month of June the Scots under Douglas and Randolph were at their old game in the north of England.

1326

[1] See above, p. 127.

As described by Froissart and Barbour, this new raid was the most brilliant and successful that was achieved even by these two heroes. With a mighty force young Edward made desperate efforts to come up with the enemy; but after a month's exertions he was forced to disband his army, leaving the Scots to return to their own country unpunished and laden with booty[1]. With difficulties at home and an intractable enemy on his frontier, the advisers of the young king felt that only one course was possible to them. In December they opened negotiations with the Scots, which resulted in the Treaty of Northampton in April, 1328. By this treaty the Scots gained every   1328 point for which they had striven since the death of Edward I. They were recognized as an independent people, and their king as an independent sovereign; and, as a pledge of co-equality, Joanna the sister of Edward was to marry the son and heir of Robert Bruce.

The settlement had not come much too soon; for, on the 7th of June in the following year, King Robert died at Cardross of a disease which is described   1329 as leprosy. He was only in his 56th year; but, in the conditions in which men then lived, this was in reality an advanced age. So thoroughly had he done his work, however, that not even the weakness of his immediate successors could undo it. In view of the work he accomplished, it may be confidently said that he was the greatest king that ever sat on the Scottish throne. David I is the only other who may dispute the preeminence; but while David built up and improved Scotland, of Bruce it can be affirmed that he saved it. At the beginning of his great enterprise the probability is that he was prompted solely by the desire of making good the claims of his own house. But as his work grew and prospered, he rose to the conception of a

[1] It appears that Bruce conducted a military expedition into the north of Ireland in the summer of 1327.—Bain, III. 127, 167.

true patriot-king   From the great Edward himself he doubtless learned to conceive the kingly function in a large and
disinterested sense; and, aided by good fortune, his higher
prudence and more winning personal qualities assured to him
a far happier destiny in the enthusiastic regard of his country.
Of his personal traits we can speak with some confidence, for
tradition is in certain points supported by authentic facts
As a mere knight, he ranked with the first in Christendom—
in this point also resembling his enemy king Edward.   In
spite of the passionate deed with which he began his career,
the qualities he subsequently showed were precisely those
of prudence and self-control.   From Barbour we learn that
these qualities were lightened by unfailing spirits and good
humour; and from an authentic document which has come
down to us it appears that, when crossed or opposed, his
usual weapon was good-natured irony[1].

The great achievement of Bruce was the deliverance of
his kingdom from the ambition of England; but his career
gave abundant proof that he possessed other high qualities
besides those of an accomplished knight and a prudent soldier.
When he definitively gave a place to the burghs in the Scottish
estates, he showed that he possessed the instincts and the foresight of the best kings of the Middle Age.   By this act his
reign is, after that of David I, the most important in the
constitutional history of Scotland; and, moreover, his general
legislation had this advantage over that of his immediate
successors, that he had the power and the will to see that
it was enforced   By the conditions under which he had won
and continued to hold his kingdom, his legislative acts were
largely directed towards the strengthening of his fighting
power.   Thus, it was enacted that wapinschaws should be
held every Easter, that every layman worth ten pounds
should provide himself with armour; that all who owned the

---

[1] Lord Hailes, *Annals of Scotland*, II. 94.

value of a cow should possess a spear, or a bow with twenty-four arrows.   With the same object of strengthening the defences of his kingdom, he formed the beginnings of a Scottish navy—a policy, however, which was not consistently followed up till the reign of James IV.   As the future of the country was to show, he might be charged with one grave error of policy.   In achieving the mastery of his kingdom he had many and powerful barons to crush, and he had as many supporters to reward.   But by his extensive assignment of forfeited lands to Douglas, Randolph, and, in less degree, to many others, he gave a power to the Scottish baronage of which his immediate successors were to know the woeful result.   Yet, in the conditions of his own reign, his action had its sufficient justification.   Its first necessity was the independence and consolidation of the kingdom, and the work could hardly have been consummated without a lavish and unsuspicious generosity towards those who were his indispensable instruments.

CHAPTER V.

DAVID II, 1329—1371

English King	French Kings
Edward III .. 1327—1377	Philip VI . . 1328—1350
	John ... ... 1350—1364
	Charles V ... 1364—1380

LIKE Edward I, King Robert had expressed a dying wish that his heart should be borne in war against the infidels ; and Sir James Douglas undertook to carry out his desire. With a company of Scottish knights Douglas set out the year following the king's death, and fell in battle with the Moors on the frontiers of Andalusia. As was to be lamentably proved, there could not have been a heavier loss to Scotland in the new conditions on which she had now entered.

On the 24th November 1331 David II was crowned at Scone, being the first Scottish king to receive
1331 anointment. David was only in his eighth year, and in accordance with the arrangement made during the late reign, Randolph, Earl of Moray, was appointed Regent. It soon appeared that there were troubles ahead that would have tasked the great Robert himself. By the treaty of Northampton a number of barons, known as "The Disinherited," were to be restored to their estates which they had forfeited in Scotland. As certain of these barons were attached to England by special ties, Randolph refused to carry out the

terms of the treaty in their favour. At this time, moreover, the English king had already made it plain that he was resolved to take advantage of the changed state of affairs in Scotland. With this object in view he found a convenient tool in Edward Balliol, son of John Balliol, whom he could cast aside when he had attained his end. Accompanied by the disinherited barons and a considerable force, Balliol landed in Fife and prepared to make good his claim to the throne of his father[1]. The English king had professed to forbid the enterprise, but the sequel showed that he was at least ready to take advantage of it. Balliol was successful beyond what he could have hoped. At the head of an army collected to repel the invader, the Regent Randolph died at Musselburgh, July 20, 1332; and his successor, Donald, earl of Mar, appointed a few weeks later, soon gave **1332** proof that he could not fill his place[2]. The months of August and September saw the temporary triumph of Balliol in Scotland. He defeated and slew the new regent at Dupplin Moor, captured Perth, and was crowned at Scone by the earl of Fife and the bishop of Dunkeld. Having achieved all these triumphs, he had now to acknowledge in whose interest he had acted, and on November 23rd, at Roxburgh, he formally recognized the English king as his lord and master. But the Scots had now recovered from their temporary confusion, and prepared to deal with the invader. They chose as their third regent, Sir Andrew Moray of Bothwell, and a force was brought together by the second son of Randolph, now earl of Moray, and Archibald Douglas, brother of Sir James. Falling upon Balliol, carelessly quartered at Annan, they cut off his following, slew his younger brother, and drove himself across the border in a state of destitution.

---

[1] The fullest account of the doings of Edward Balliol in Scotland is given by the canon of Bridlington (*Chron. of Ed. I and Ed II*, II. 102 *et seq*).

[2] The invaders expected Mar to support them. *Ib.* p. 104.

The two nations were thus again at war. In the spring
of 1333 Balliol re-entered Scotland with a
numerous body of English barons and their
followers, and fixing his quarters at Roxburgh prepared to lay
siege to Berwick. It was not till later in the year, however,
that the place was really endangered, but meanwhile a double
disaster befell the Scots. Sir William Douglas, known as the
Knight of Liddesdale, one of the most distinguished Scottish
soldiers of the time, and the Regent, Sir Andrew Moray,
were captured by the English in separate engagements. The
loss of these two leaders told heavily against the Scots in
the crisis that now awaited them. In spite of the protests of
France the English king in person joined forces with Balliol
and attacked Berwick by sea and land. To relieve the town
the new regent, Sir Archibald Douglas, led an army into
Northumberland, but the stratagem was unsuccessful, and if
the town was to be saved the Regent found that he must
fight. In the battle (July 19) that ensued, the foolhardiness
of the Scots can be explained only by their long career of
success during the reign of Bruce. The English were encamped on the slope of Halidon Hill immediately to the west
of Berwick, and their position was still further strengthened
by a marsh in front of them. Through the marsh and up the
slopes of the hill the Scots made their way to the enemy with
the result that their rashness ensured. Their rout was complete—the Regent, six earls, and many other persons of distinction being among the slain.

The defeat of Halidon Hill undid for a time the whole
work of Bruce in Scotland, and it was only the memory and
inspiration of his example that eventually saved her. Only
five places of strength remained to the supporters of David II,
who along with his queen was sent for safety to
France in 1334. As there was no authority to
oppose them, Balliol and the English king proceeded to
arrange the country between them. In an assembly held at

Edinburgh (Feb. 10, 1334) Balliol acknowledged Edward as his Lord Paramount, and surrendered Berwick for ever as a possession of the English crown. Later in the year, however, he made a more notable gift. In June, at Newcastle, he gave up to Edward nearly the whole tract of country between the Tweed and the Forth; and within a fortnight a justiciary, a chamberlain, and a body of sheriffs were appointed to govern the district as a part of English territory.

In June, 1334, the arrangement made by Edward and his vassal appeared to have settled the fate of Scotland; but before the year was out they were again reminded of the character of the people with whom they were dealing. The disinherited barons, who had been the origin and cause of the disaster of the Scots, fell out among themselves, some taking the side of Balliol, and others of David II. About the same period, also, Sir Andrew Moray of Bothwell returned from his captivity in England, and the earl of Moray from his exile in France. Moreover, the French king, Philip VI, was giving Edward to understand that the interests of Scotland were bound up with his own. So strong, indeed, had the patriotic party now become that Balliol was forced to flee from the country, and Edward had to lead an army into Lothian to reassert his authority. Left to himself, Balliol was no longer able to hold his own against the lawful king, and it was only the presence of an English force that enabled him to live in the country. On two other occasions the English king led a great army through Scotland; but as soon as his back was turned the struggle recommenced with the result that the supporters of David gained ground every day.

The work that had been accomplished in the early years of Bruce had now to be laboriously repeated by the Regent, Sir Andrew Moray, and the leaders who stood by his side. The castles in the hands of the English had to be retaken one by one; and though we are no longer in the heroic period of the Scottish wars of independence, exploits were frequently performed that were worthy of the companions of Bruce. The Regent himself, Alexander Ramsay, and the Knight of Liddesdale, made themselves specially conspicuous by their activity and daring. Yet even by the admission of Wyntoun, it was fortunate for Scotland that the energies of the English king were now distracted by another enterprise on which he came

1337　　　specially to set his heart. In 1337 Edward declared himself King of France, and the Hundred Years' War began. Thenceforward it was only with intermittent efforts that he intervened in Scotland, and though the war between the two countries still went on, it was no longer the life-and-death struggle of the days of the first Edward.

By a succession of exploits the Scots now cleared the country of the invader. The defence of the castle of Dunbar is specially notable in Scottish tradition. Attacked by the English under Lord Salisbury, it was defended by the Countess of March, daughter of the famous Randolph, and known as "Black Agnes" from her dark complexion. For nineteen

1338　　　weeks (1338), the siege was carried on both by sea and land; but the resolution of the countess, seconded by the opportune aid of Alexander Ramsay, baffled the assailants. The year of the siege of Dunbar the Regent, Sir Andrew Moray, died, and Robert, the Steward of Scotland, was appointed his successor. The town of Perth still remained in the hands of the English, and the new regent addressed himself to recover it. It was in this town that Balliol had made his head-quarters, and if any town could then claim to be the capital it was Perth. For reasons of his own Edward, before the siege began, recalled Balliol to England, and placed the town in charge of one Thomas Ughtred. According to the ideas of the time, Perth was a strongly fortified place, but the Scots, reinforced by a body of French auxiliaries, appear to have had little difficulty in bringing

1339　　　the garrison to terms. In August 1339 Ughtred capitulated, and was permitted to lead his forces across the border. The capture of the castles of Stirling and Edinburgh followed the taking of Perth, and by 1341 the country was deemed safe for the return of the king and queen from France.

1341

The years that immediately followed the king's return saw a succession of wars and truces which only further illustrate the bitterness of the hate that had grown up between the two countries. As his character began to show itself, it appeared that David had little of the prudence and self-control that had brought success to his father. "Young, stout and jolly" (so his contemporary Wyntoun describes him), he appears to have been equally devoid of the qualities that inspire respect or affection. In the first notable action recorded of him he displayed a lack of temper and prudence which his subsequent career proved to be the essential trait of his character. In 1346, in the interests of France rather than of his own country, he led an army into England as far south as Durham. The English king was now in France, engaged in the siege of Calais; but as the event showed, his affairs were in competent hands. The archbishop of York with Ralph Neville and Henry Percy gathered a force and met the Scots within sight of the town of Durham. David fought with the courage of his race; but he had chosen his ground ill, and as at Halidon the English archers threw his ranks into confusion. The defeat of Neville's Cross, as the battle came to be called, ranks among the national disasters of Scotland. Not only was the rout complete, but David himself was taken together with four of his earls and the archbishop of St Andrews (Oct. 17).

1346

For eleven years David remained a prisoner in England, though more than one attempt was made to compound for his liberation. In Scotland he was not greatly missed; for though Robert the Steward was not an able ruler, he contrived to save his country even after the disaster of Neville's Cross. Nevertheless, the times were not happy; and two calamities were long remembered in the traditions of the country. In 1350 the

1350

Black Death, having done its work on the Continent and in England, at length appeared in Scotland, which had begun to consider itself protected by a special Providence In Scotland it was known as "the first pestilence"[1], and it raged in the land for more than a year, and slew a full third of the people. The second calamity was of another character, and was apparently due to the imprudence of the men responsible for the management of the country

1354

In 1354 an arrangement had been made with England by which the Scottish king was to regain his liberty. But the arrangement was displeasing to the French, who to prevent its conclusion despatched to Scotland a considerable body of soldiers and a large sum of money. The Scots, who, according to Fordun, "often lose a shilling to save a penny," chose to accept the overtures of France, and

1355

in fulfilment of their bargain made war upon England. In 1355 they took the town of Berwick, but it did not remain long in their hands The

1356

following year the English king marched north with an army which swept all before it. Berwick immediately opened its gates, and proceeding to Roxburgh Edward received from Balliol the surrender of the Scottish crown and all his private estates to the north of the Tweed As Edward had always professed to regard Balliol as the lawful King of Scots, he now considered himself as his successor and acted accordingly. At Roxburgh he waited some days for the Scottish barons to give in their submission; but, as they did not appear, he invaded the country as far as Edinburgh As usual the Scots had removed every form of sustenance from the course of the enemy, whom they likewise harassed at every point of his march. Baffled in his purpose, Edward took a terrible revenge. Every town, village, and

---

[1] The Scots spoke of the pestilence as "the foul death of the English."

hamlet, that came in his way, he burnt to the ground; not even sparing the sacred buildings, among which is specially noted a beautiful church in Haddington, known as the "Lamp of Lothian." In Scottish tradition this visitation came to be known as "the Burnt Candlemas."

By attacking England in the interests of France, the Scots had prolonged the captivity of their king. Henceforward, therefore, David manifested a leaning towards England, which was to show itself in a singular manner before the close of his reign. His subjects never knew the worst, but we have it on authentic evidence that David was ready to give away his country at any moment if his own freedom were to be the return. At last (October 3, 1357) a treaty was concluded at Berwick, by which the King **1357** of Scots was restored to his country. In the state to which Scotland had been reduced by her protracted calamities, the bargain was a hard one. As a ransom for their king, they were to pay in ten yearly instalments 100,000 marks, and in pledge of payment they were to place certain of the leading men of the country in the hands of Edward.

David reigned for fourteen years after his return to his kingdom; but he was not the ruler to mend the broken fortunes of a people. The task that awaited him, indeed, would have tried a ruler of the highest capacity. To pay 100,000 marks in ten years was a strain beyond what his people could bear. His first step on his return was to summon a parliament at Scone (Nov. 1357) to con- **1357** sider the ways and means of paying his ransom to the English king. The stringent proposals adopted brought vividly home to his subjects what burden had been laid upon them. The king was empowered to buy up all the wools and fleeces in the kingdom at the rate of four marks for every sack of wool; the great customs were to be raised to twice their previous amount; all the crown property which had been alienated was to be at once resumed; and with a view to increased taxation all lands and rents were at once to be revalued. In one Parliament after another the payment of the ransom absorbed the attention of David and his counsellors; yet, in spite of every effort, the debt was but half paid at the end of fourteen years.

In the troubles connected with excessive taxation we have the explanation of the leading events of the last years of David's reign. So intolerable did the nation find their burden that, in 1359, proposals were made to France to renew the war with England; but by the Peace of Bretigny in 1360 every hope in that direction was cut off. David's own folly aggravated the evils of the time. As if the English debt were not enough for his people to bear, by his own lavish habits and his frequent visits to England he tried their patience beyond endurance.

1363

At length, in 1363, affairs came to a crisis. In that year, on the plea of the misdirection of the public money, the Earl of Douglas broke into rebellion. He found allies in the two leading persons in the country, Robert the Steward and the Earl of March. David, however, wanted neither courage nor decision, and, having surprised Douglas as he lay at Lanark, forced him and his allies to give in their submission. This revolt had been crushed only a few months when David took a step which shows to what straits he was driven. Proceeding to the English court in October, 1363, he entered into a secret arrangement with Edward III. On condition of being relieved from his ransom, he agreed to recognize Edward as his successor, should he himself leave no male heir[1]. When, in March 1364, however, David

1364

---

[1] On the same occasion another strange agreement was made between the English and Scottish kings. According to this agreement the Scots were to assist the King of England in his Flemish wars; not only "the Disinherited Barons," but other Scotsmen who had thrown off their allegi-

ventured to make this proposal to his parliament, he was met with such a peremptory refusal that the subject was not brought up again. To the end, therefore, David had his English debt to face; and, though an actual rebellion did not again occur, there were whole years during which the king's writ did not run in the Islands and the northern mainland. A foolish marriage added to the troubles of his last years. His first wife, Joanna of England, died in 1362; and by the beginning of 1364 he had married a Margaret Logie, the aunt of Annabella Drummond, queen of Robert III. Of Margaret's connections and doings little is known; but it is certain that she did not contribute to her consort's happiness. For reasons which have not been ascertained he eventually divorced her; but, having carried her case to Rome, Margaret prevailed on the pope to repeal the decree. Before this result was obtained, however, David himself was dead (February 22, 1371)[1].

1362

1364

1371

In spite of the desires and endeavours of David II, Scotland found itself a free and independent kingdom at the time of his death; and for a long period to come the condition of England was such that she never found the opportunity of renewing the work of Edward I and Edward III. It has been constantly said that, through their long struggle with England, the Scots were fashioned into national unity: it would be nearer the truth to say that, had not Scotland been a nation before, it must inevitably have

---

ance, were to be reinstated in their lands; there was to be a thousand years' peace between the two countries; and David was to be succeeded by any son of Edward III except the heir to the English crown. See Bain, *Calendar of Documents relating to Scotland*, vol. IV. pp. xiii, 21.

[1] This account of the last fourteen years of David's reign differs materially from those of such recent historians as Tytler and Hill Burton, and is based on Mr Burnett's Introduction to the second volume of the Exchequer Rolls of Scotland (1878).

gone to pieces in the ordeal through which it had passed.
At the death of Alexander III in 1286 she was in every sense
a greater and more prosperous nation than at the death of
David in 1371. In the modern significance of the word,
indeed, a nation could not then exist. A truly national consciousness was impossible while self-expression in literature,
in art, in religion was so imperfect, and when intercommuni-
cation was so inadequate. But in comparison with the other
countries of Christendom, Scotland under Alexander III was
as really a nation as any of them—England alone excepted.
She had a dynasty of centuries' standing, a national church,
a national council, and national laws; and to the north and
south of the Forth her leading towns were bound in a confederacy which was based on national interest and policy
The Celtic portions of her territory, indeed, were imperfectly
incorporated with the main kingdom, but this is as true of
the close of David's reign as of the close of Alexander's
In truth, the hold of Alexander on the outlying parts of his
kingdom was firmer than that of David or of his immediate
successors   That Scotland had beaten off a power so much
stronger than herself was undoubtedly a great triumph for
her people, and the memory of her triumph was a great
formative influence in her future development.   But the
triumph had been won at a terrible cost   Yet in her
miserable history during the 14th century, Scotland was
not alone among the countries of Europe.   In the closing
years of Edward III England herself, exhausted by her wars
with Scotland and France, and distracted by internal divisions, had reached a pitch of misery which was to issue in
the national disasters of the times that followed   At the
beginning of the same century France had been the first
power in Europe ; but misgovernment, the English invasions,
and her own brutal soldiery, had brought her to a state compared with which the state of Scotland was happy.   In the
whole chapter of her woes Scotland has no such page as that

which records the uprising and suppression of the Jacquerie of France[1].

Of internal development in any direction there is little to record regarding Scotland during the 14th century. In 1326 we have seen that the national assembly became a veritable Parliament by the admission of the representatives of burghs into its councils. Under David II, as under his contemporary Edward III, the Parliament made large encroachments on the royal prerogative. What had not been seen before, Parliament now regulated the coinage and currency, settled the terms of peace and war, controlled the revenue, and even the personal expenditure of the sovereign. But if the powers of Parliament were thus extended, a change in its mode of conducting business, introduced in this reign, eventually wrought in another direction. To many of the small freeholders, poor at the best, and now impoverished by the miseries of the country, it was an actual burden to attend the meetings of Parliament, held at all seasons and in no fixed locality. Thus, in 1368, the inconvenience of the seasons and the dearness of provisions were urged in excuse for the absence of freeholders. Another difficulty also suggested a change in the conduct of Parliamentary business. In the case of certain questions it was found to be against the interests of the country that they should be publicly discussed in full assembly. For these two reasons—the easing of the freeholders and forwarding of debate—the plan was adopted of appointing committees "to hold the Parliament." From this arrangement sprang two institutions famous in Scottish history—the "Committee of Articles" and the Committee for Causes, out of which and other judicial bodies James V evolved the Court of Session. The arrangement served its immediate purpose; but in the end it left little but the name of repre-

---

[1] Wyntoun, the contemporary Scottish chronicler, it is worth noting, speaks of the Jacquerie as "felon carles."

sentative government, since the standing committees inevitably passed into mere nominees of the crown.

In the prolonged agony of her struggle with England social progress in Scotland was impossible. If her towns were not burnt by the enemy, she had to burn them of her own accord in mere self-defence. At one time or other, it would seem, all her leading towns were given to the flames. The insignificance of the greatest of them is attested by Froissart, who spent six months in the country during the reign of David. Edinburgh, he tells us, was regarded as the capital[1]; but, far from being equal to Paris, was inferior to Tournai or Valenciennes, and had not more than four hundred houses[2]. What the majority of the houses were like he has also casually told us. With five or six stakes and boughs to cover them, the Scots boasted that they could build a house in the space of three days. Yet, in spite of this humble scale of living, one fact appears to have arrested Froissart's attention: the peasantry of Scotland were not as the peasantry of France. When the French knights rode carelessly through their crops, the Scottish peasants signified their displeasure with such emphasis that the strangers became eager to leave the country. Such being the poverty of the people, the arts which at an earlier period had promised so fair could only wither at the root. During the occupation of the country by Edward I it is supposed that many feudal castles were erected; but in the case of churches and abbeys it was a time rather of burning than of building them[3].

In the reigns of David II and his successor flourished

---

[1] In the history of the time, as has been said above, Perth played a more important part than Edinburgh. Aberdeen, Perth, Inverness, and Stirling were richer towns than Edinburgh.

[2] In the best MSS. of Froissart, 400, and not 4000, houses, appears to be the reading.

[3] In the last years of David II there appears to have been a considerable amount of building. Cf. Exchequer Rolls, vol. II. p. cv.

the first two authentic Scottish authors—John Barbour and Andrew of Wyntoun. "The Bruce" of Barbour may be regarded as the national epic of Scotland; and, though as literature it cannot rank high, it has all the interest of expressing the popular feeling of the generation that succeeded the War of Independence. Of Wyntoun's "Original Chronicle" the same can hardly be said Beginning with the Creation, he plods through universal history till he arrives at his own country, whose annals he relates in conscientious detail, but with no poetic attractiveness and little of the enthusiasm that animates certain pages of Barbour. What is notable in both is that neither appears to have profited by the best vernacular literature which had been produced in other countries As representatives of the highest culture and intelligence of their time in Scotland, they afford fresh evidence of the fact that the energies of their countrymen had been absorbed in the struggle for bare existence Neither Barbour nor Wyntoun appears to come in sight of that "central view of life" which received expression in Dante and Petrarch and Chaucer.

BOOK IV.

The Crown and the Barons, 1371—1513.

CHAPTER I.

ROBERT II, 1371—1390.

English Kings		French Kings	
Edward III .. 1327—1377		Charles V ... 1364 —1380	
Richard II .. 1377—1399.		Charles VI ... 1380—1422	

THE period of Scottish history from the accession of the House of Stewart till the battle of Flodden has a specific character of its own What now absorbed the energies of the country was not the consolidation of its peoples nor the struggle for existence against another nation . it was a contest between a succession of Scottish kings and their great vassals for the ruling power in the direction of the national destinies. In other countries, and notably in England and France, the same conflict proceeded, in similar fashion and throughout the same period In England the bands of retainers kept by the great nobles were a standing trouble and menace to the sovereign , and in France as late as 1464 a confederacy of the great barons shook the throne of Louis XI. With the battle of Flodden in 1513 the long struggle which had distracted

Scotland was practically closed Long after that disaster, indeed, the Scottish nobles continued to disturb the peace of the kingdom; but other aims and other motives now shaped their counsels and determined their action. At one stroke the fatal day of Flodden effected, in a large degree, for Scotland what her Wars of the Roses had effected for England. the slaughter of so many of her first nobles broke the power of their order and altered the relative position of the crown.

The period of the first Stewarts has usually been regarded as one of chronic misery and arrested national development; and if we look only to the record of events it is difficult to avoid this conclusion. Open rebellions, private feuds, border raids, and English invasions, make the main part of the narrative, and it is hard to see how under such conditions a people could know the repose requisite to the cultivation of the arts of life. Yet compared with the history of England and France throughout the same period, that of Scotland has no special pre-eminence in misfortune. She has no tale to tell like that of the Wars of the Roses in England, and she knew no such bloody and protracted feud as that between the Burgundians and the Armagnacs in France. If she has incidents to relate like the murder of James I and the exploits of the Wolf of Badenoch, it would be easy to find a parallel to them in any other country in Christendom But apart from the sensational record of events there are many indications that the nation did not spend its life in misery, and that after the danger from England had ceased there was a steady expansion of the people along every line of social progress In the fifteenth century three of the four Scottish universities were founded; a succession of poets testify to the existence of an educated opinion, numerous Acts of Parliament as well as other records prove that there was a prosperous burgher class both north and south of the Forth; and we have the testimony of foreigners to the fact that the country was largely under cultivation and that the peasant class of Scotland lived on better terms than their fellows elsewhere. It is only with such facts before us that we can attach their due significance to the wild deeds of king and noble which are apt to determine our judgment regarding every past age.

In accordance with an Act of 1318, David II, dying without legitimate male issue, was succeeded by his nephew, Robert the High Steward. By his possessions and his family connections, as well as by his office, the new king had been the first subject in the country. He was the ninth in descent of the Fitzalans who had held the hereditary office of High Steward; his family possessions included the shire of Renfrew and the island of Bute; and through his father Walter's union with Marjory, the daughter of Robert Bruce, he now attained to the kingdom. An incident which has not been satisfactorily explained at first seemed to threaten an unfortunate beginning of his reign. William, Earl of Douglas, the nephew and representative of the "good Sir James," claimed to be the rightful heir to the throne. On what grounds he urged his claim it is difficult to say[1]; but apparently he was not disposed to push it to extremes. Robert's daughter, Isabella, was pledged in marriage to his eldest son, and he himself was made Warden of the East Marches and Justiciar south of the Forth. The dispute being thus compromised, Robert the Steward was crowned at Scone on the 26th of March, 1371—his son John, Earl of Carrick, being named as his successor on the same occasion.

1371

In Robert II the famous line of Stewart made no very brilliant commencement. He was in his fifty-fifth year—an age which then implied that the main work of life was done; and even in his prime, though he had given proof of firmness and prudence, he had never displayed the qualities of a great

---

[1] According to Bower Douglas claimed the crown in virtue of his descent from the Comyns and the Balliols. As a matter of fact, he could boast no such descent.

statesman or commander. As described in his later years
by Froissart, he was of stately presence but with inflamed eyes,
and of a disposition that led him to peace and retirement.
Fortunately, the circumstances under which he reigned were
not such as to call for the highest qualities of a ruler. At
home his position was strengthened by a progeny which formed
a solid phalanx round his throne. By his first and second
wives[1] he had six sons and eight daughters ; and to these were
added at least eight natural sons, all recognized among the
nobles of the land. While within his own kingdom his hands
were thus strengthened, he had not like his immediate predecessors to live in constant dread of the ambition of England.
During his reign of nineteen years he had, as his English
contemporaries, Edward III and Richard II. But the closing
years of Edward III were such that he had neither heart nor
leisure to prosecute his old aims against the independence of
Scotland. During the reign of Richard II the two countries
were more than once in strained relations, and Richard himself led an army into the heart of Scotland ; but his own
personal character and the condition of his own kingdom
effectually prevented his being a really formidable enemy.

It was fortunate for Robert that England was not in a
position to direct her full strength against his kingdom. Even
as it was, his relation to the English king was sufficiently
embarrassing. Little more than half of David II's ransom was
paid, and the towns of Berwick and Roxburgh, the castle of
Lochmaben and much of the surrounding districts, were still
in the hands of the English. Moreover, his hands were tied
by the fourteen years' truce which had been concluded in 1369.
In these circumstances, he followed what had
now become the traditional policy of the country.   1372
In the second year of his reign he made a comprehensive

---

[1] His first wife was Elizabeth Mure, daughter of Sir Adam Mure of
Rowallan ; his second, Euphemia, daughter of the Earl of Ross.

treaty with France which bound the two countries to mutual action against England.

In spite of the fourteen years' truce there never was real peace between the two sides of the Border; and on the death

1377

of Edward III (1377) certain English and Scottish nobles, setting their respective governments at naught, began what was practically open war. At Roxburgh Fair a retainer of the Earl of March, grandson of the famous Randolph, was slain in a tumult, and the earl in vain demanded redress. Taking the law into his own hands, he fell suddenly on the town, gave it to the flames, and made a general massacre of the English. Reprisals immediately followed. In a three days' invasion, known as "the Warden's Raid," Henry Percy, Earl of Northumberland, laid waste the district surrounding Dunse, which belonged to the Earl of March. In the petty warfare that followed the Scots had the

1378

decided advantage. In 1378 they recovered Berwick, though only for a brief period; and they gradually drove the English within the limits of their own territory. Another incident of the same time further embittered the feelings of the two peoples. A famous Scot, named Andrew Mercer, half merchant and half pirate, at the head of a strong squadron of French, Spanish, and Scottish vessels, had attacked and plundered the town of Scarborough, in revenge for the ill-treatment of his father. His triumph, however, was shortlived. A London merchant, named Philpot, of the same stamp as himself, met him with an armament more powerful than his own, and in a decisive victory took Mercer captive with the whole of his fleet.

On the Border there was still continuous fighting. Berwick was regained by the English, and the Earls of Northumberland and Nottingham made a fresh raid into Scottish territory. At

1380

length, in 1380, the government of Richard II determined on decisive measures for bringing the two countries to a better understanding. With a great

army, John of Gaunt, Duke of Lancaster, marched towards the
Border, bringing with him the offer of peace or war. The King
of Scots himself was all for peace, and on this occasion his
desires were seconded by his most powerful barons. At
Berwick John of Gaunt was met by the Bishops of Dunkeld
and Glasgow, the Earls of Douglas and March, and Sir
Archibald Douglas, lord of Galloway; and the existing treaty
was confirmed for the next three years, the date originally fixed
for its expiry. From the truce which he had thus effected John
of Gaunt himself was to reap substantial benefit. In the
following year occurred the Peasants' Revolt under Wat Tyler,
when Lancaster found it necessary to be out of England for a
time. Proceeding to Scotland, he there received a hospitable
reception which he was to pay back on another day.

With the year 1384 begins what may be considered the
second period of Robert's reign of nineteen
years. The fourteen years' truce with England   1384
expired at the beginning of February; and it seemed that the
Scots had been holding themselves in readiness for the event.
Two days after the expiry of the truce (February 4), the lord
of Galloway and the Earl of March gained possession of
Lochmaben Castle, and with it the district of Annandale in
which it stands. Other events of the year 1384 mark it as the
most notable of Robert II's reign. On January 26 a truce was
concluded between England and France in which Scotland was
to have the option of sharing; and an embassy from Charles
VI was despatched by way of England to make known the
arrangement to Robert. But the late doings of the Scots had
incensed the English king and his advisers, and they determined to have their revenge before the Scots could claim the
benefit of the new truce. Accordingly, before the French
ambassadors arrived a strong force was led into Scotland
with the object of effecting all the mischief it could. Fortunately for the Scots the commander of the expedition was John
of Gaunt, whose late experience of their hospitality now stood

them in good stead Conducting his force as far as Edinburgh, he dealt as gently with the country as lay in his power; and as the result of his invasion his own soldiers were greater sufferers than the Scots themselves Scarcely, moreover, had he recrossed the border when the Earl of Douglas recovered his family possessions of Teviotdale, with the exception of Roxburgh and Jedburgh castles.

At length, about the middle of April, the French embassy arrived The circumstances of their visit throw a curious light on the extent of Robert's authority in his own kingdom What that authority implied had been signally illustrated by an event that had happened in 1381. The king's own son-in-law and High Chamberlain, Sir John Lyon, had been slaughtered by Sir Patrick Lyndsay, who only a short time before had been Justiciar or Guardian of the law to the north of the Forth Affection and justice alike urged Robert to punish the murderer, but he was powerless to do more than to effect Lyndsay's temporary disgrace at his own court The king's impotence was now to be further shown in connection with the embassy from France. Disposed for peace as he always was, Robert received the envoys with the utmost cordiality , but his leading nobles were on this occasion of a different mind from his own. About the very time when the French envoys arrived another band of their countrymen made their appearance in Scotland. A party of thirty knights and esquires landed at Montrose, and making their way to Edinburgh, announced their desire of proving their prowess against England. In defiance of the king's wish, a meeting of barons in the church of St Giles decided that the desire of the adventurers should be gratified. There was no delay in carrying out their determination. A foray into the territories of the Earls of Northumberland and Nottingham, resulting in an immense booty, gave the strangers a taste of a mode of warfare which appears to have impressed them favourably. All that the King of Scots could do he immediately did. He sent a herald to the English court with the strange message that the raid had taken place in his own despite, and prayed that he might have the benefit of the truce between England and France. The request was granted; but as the truce expired in October it opened up no great prospect of permanent peace. But the late raid did not go unavenged. In the month of March the two earls who had been its victims led an army into Scotland which behaved very differently from that of John of Gaunt. Far and wide throughout the Lothians and even Dumfries it wrought devastation—the town of Edinburgh being demolished and the town of Haddington burned to the ground. The capture of Berwick by the Scots and its recovery by the Earl of Northumberland close the record of hostilities for the year 1384.

To the year 1385 belongs one of the best-known episodes of Scottish history. The truce with England
had been extended from October, 1384, till May   **1385**
of the following year; but the prospects of peace were so uncertain that Robert and his advisers took a decided step. An embassy despatched to France (1384) besought Charles VI to send a force to Scotland for the purpose of making war on the common enemy. There was a ready response on the part of the French king or those who represented him. In the beginning of the summer of 1385 Sir John de Vienne, Admiral of France, appeared with a body of 2000 men, bearing also the acceptable presents of 1400 suits of armour and 50,000 francs of gold. In support of Vienne, a French fleet was also to attack England on the south; but this part of the plan was never carried out. In no respect indeed was the French visit to Scotland a success. On both sides there was dissatisfaction from the beginning. On the part of the Scots it was felt that the presence of so many luxurious strangers was as great an evil as an English invasion; and the French were equally displeased at their poor entertainment and the general coldness of their reception. Nor did the campaign that followed improve their relations. The French leader and his knights

had looked for brilliant pitched battles; but what they saw
was an ordinary border raid.   With an army of 30,000 Scots,
reinforced by their French allies, the Earls of Douglas and
Moray, and other leading barons, invaded Northumberland,
and penetrated half-way between Berwick and Newcastle
Here, however, the news came that the Duke of Lancaster and
the Earls of Nottingham and Northumberland were on the way
to offer them battle.   Greatly to the disgust of Vienne and his
companions, the Scottish leaders retreated before the enemy,
contenting themselves with leaving a desert behind them.   But
the union of the French and Scots had seemed so formidable
that the English king himself appeared at the head of an army,
which along with the force that had been raised by Lancaster
entered Scotland along the east coast   Supported by his fleet,
Richard was able to spend some time in the country and to
leave memorable traces of his visit.   What had never happened
before, he gave the Abbey of Melrose to the flames; and he
successively burned the towns of Edinburgh, Perth, and
Dundee   To the amazement of the French the Scottish
commanders made no attempt to defend their country.   Avoiding the English king, they broke into Cumberland and
Westmoreland, and secured a booty which left them easily the
winners in the game they had played.   As the English king
retired by the way he had come, and the Scots for the time
had had enough of fighting, there was no longer any occasion
for the continued sojourn of the French   So uncomfortable,
indeed, was their stay now made that they themselves were in
haste to be gone.   But on one condition only their leaders
were at length allowed to depart: the expense of maintaining
their bands in Scotland must either be paid or pledges be
given for payment   De Vienne himself undertook to discharge
the debt; and with no very pleasant memories of their visit, he
and his companions made their way home in the autumn of the
year in which they had come

The Scots did not long discontinue their efforts against

England The state of that country, indeed, brought opportunities that were not to be neglected. Richard II was in the midst of his troubles with the Lords Appellant, and on the Border the great families of Neville and Percy were at feud. During the two years that followed the departure of the French no special achievement of the Scots is recorded; but the year 1388 is notable in border history In that year, Sir William Douglas, natural son of Sir Archibald of Galloway, led an expedition to Ireland, burnt the town of Carlingford, and laid waste the Isle of Man on his voyage home. Landing at Loch Ryan, he made haste to join a body of his countrymen who were on the point of crossing the English border. The exploits of this party were to make their expedition the most notable of border raids.

1388

In revenge for the late invasion of Richard the leading Scottish nobles had determined to achieve something beyond an ordinary raid. Unknown to the king, they met at Aberdeen and carefully planned the details of their enterprise. An army of over 40,000 men was to be brought together, and it was to be led by the king's second son, Robert, Earl of Fife, assisted by the leading nobles of Scotland The details of the expedition are variously told; but in the story of its main events all the chroniclers are agreed. Arrived at the Border, the army separated into two divisions, the main body under the Earl of Fife crossing the western border, the lesser under James, Earl of Douglas, crossing by the east It was the detachment of Douglas that was to win for itself the chief honour. Having carried destruction as far as Durham, they had retraced their steps to Otterbourne, about twenty miles from the Border. Here in a moonlight autumn evening they were surprised by Hotspur, son of the Earl of Northumberland, and a fight ensued, which according to Froissart was the hardest fought that had ever come to his knowledge The victory remained with the Scots, Hotspur being among the captives and Douglas among the slain. Embellished by the genius of Froissart,

idealized and transformed in the ballad of Chevy Chase, the
fight at Otterbourne ranks among the feats of Scottish arms;
but in its bearing on the national history its significance lies in
the fact that in all the circumstances which led up to it, it
was the irresponsible act of the leading men in the kingdom.

Robert II had now passed his seventieth year, and his
bodily and mental feebleness alike disposed him to retire
from the cares of government. As his eldest son, John, Earl
of Carrick, was hardly more vigorous than himself, his third[1]
son, Robert, Earl of Fife, was appointed Regent at a meeting
of the Estates in 1389. Two more events close
the record of the reign of Robert. In the year
of his appointment as Regent, the Earl of Fife led a force
against the English border,—but with no results to signalize his
vigour or skill. The second event fitly terminated the career
of the peaceful Robert. By a treaty concluded at Boulogne in
1389 a truce of three years was arranged between Scotland,
England, and France. The following year Robert died at the
Castle of Dundonald in Ayrshire at the age of seventy-four and
in the twentieth year of his reign. "A tenderare hart mycht
na man have," is the character given of him by a contemporary,
and so far as they are known to us his actions do not belie it.

1389

---

[1] His second son, Walter, was dead.

CHAPTER II.

ROBERT III, 1390—1406.

English Kings.		French King.	
Richard II ..	1377—1399.	Charles VI ...	1380—1422.
Henry IV ...	1399—1413		

ROBERT II was succeeded by his son, John, Earl of Carrick, who had already passed his fiftieth year. During his father's lifetime he had been effaced by his younger brother, Robert, Earl of Fife; and his promotion to the throne added little to his actual importance. Even in greater degree than his father he was the passive agent of his councillors, and in the whole course of his reign it is hard to find an instance of his individual action. By way of happy omen he was crowned under the name of Robert III, his own name John having sinister suggestions alike in England, Scotland, and France Unlike his father he had not around him a phalanx of sons who might be a safeguard against the ambition of his nobles. He had long been married to Anabella Drummond, niece of the famous Margaret Logie, and he had as yet but one son—David, afterwards the unfortunate Duke of Rothesay. One fact shows in what estimation the new king was held by his countrymen In 1388 Robert, Earl of Fife, had been appointed the Guardian of the Realm; and now at the beginning of a new reign he was continued in his office. Yet among his subjects at large Robert was a popular king. His personal appearance had that picturesqueness which the people look for in royal personages. He had been lamed in youth by the kick of a horse; but his stature was majestic, and his long, snow-white beard and his benignant expression gave him the aspect of a true father of his people. Nor did his appearance belie his character. Authentic incidents prove that he had the welfare of his people at heart, and that he had a genuine zeal for justice in the administration of his office. In this reign—says Bower, who continued the History of Fordun—in this reign there was great abundance of victual, but very great discord among the leading men of the nation.

The reign of Robert III falls into two well-marked periods. During the first eight years the country was governed by the Earl of Fife, and the chief events of the time belong to the internal history of the country. In 1398, however, the king's eldest son, David, displaced his uncle, with consequences that embroiled the leading Scottish nobles, and involved the country in war with England. In the latter half of Robert's reign it was the feud of the uncle and the nephew that determined the course of events in Scotland.

Ever on their guard against England, one of the first acts of the Scots was to renew the treaty with France which had been concluded in the second year of the preceding reign. With England, also, a truce of eight years was arranged which, though imperfectly kept on the Borders, averted serious war for a time. But if there was peace with England there was sufficient trouble at home, though apparently it was confined to the country north of the Forth. A few incidents that have been recorded afford signal proof of the lawlessness of that region. In the first year of Robert's reign his own brother Alexander, Earl of Buchan, known under the significant name of the "Wolf of Badenoch," gave the town and the cathedral of Elgin to the flames: his only punishment was to do penance in the Dominican church at Perth. Two

1390

1392

years later the illegitimate sons of the same earl broke into Angus at the head of a body of katerans, and defeated the force led against them by Sir Walter Ogilvy, the sheriff of the district. In 1395 Robert Keith, "a mychty man be lineage," besieged his own aunt, the 1395 wife of Sir David Lyndsay, in her castle of Fyvie in Buchan, and was subsequently defeated by her husband, who had made haste to her rescue. But to the year 1396 belongs one of the most singular inci- 1396 dents in the history of the Scottish Highlands. Two clans, vaguely known as Chattan and Kay, had long been at feud, and by their quarrels had been a permanent source of disturbance in the country. With the approval, and apparently at the suggestion of the government, the leaders of the hostile clans were offered an opportunity of finally settling their disputes. Thirty men, chosen from either clan, should fight to the death with bow, sword, knife and axe. The proposal was accepted, and on the north Inch of Perth the combatants met in the presence of the king and a vast number of spectators[1]. So fierce was the fight which ensued that, out of the sixty champions engaged, only twelve survived. As the result of the barbarous show, we are told, the Highlands had peace for many years to come.

Meanwhile the king's eldest son David, Earl of Carrick, was approaching manhood, and was already giving proofs of a spirit and capacity which he had not derived from his father. In the year of the fight of the two clans he was appointed, though only sixteen, to the charge of the northern parts of the country. In 1398, for reasons which are not on record, the title of Duke, 1398 now for the first time known in Scotland, was conferred on

---

[1] When the combatants were arrayed, it was found that one of the Clan Kay was missing; but his place was taken by a mechanic of Perth, known in tradition as Hal o' the Wynd, or Henry Gow.

the prince and his uncle, the Earl of Fife[1]. While the prince, however, took his new title merely from the town of Rothesay, the earl received the ambitious designation of Duke of Albany, the ancient name of the whole country to the north of the Forth. Yet it would appear that Rothesay was more than able to hold his own against his uncle. Supported by his mother and two of the most influential men in the country, Archibald the Grim, the third Earl of Douglas, and Walter Traill, bishop of St Andrews, he was in 1399 appointed Guardian of the Realm in place of the Duke of Albany. Thenceforward Rothesay had to reckon with his uncle as his undisguised enemy, and the imprudence of his own conduct, public and private, placed him at increasing disadvantage in their rivalry. An event of the following year laid the train for all the consequences that followed. Though he had been betrothed to the daughter of the Earl of March, Rothesay, on the promise of a larger dowry, married the daughter of the Earl of Douglas. In deep indignation at the affront put upon his house, and doubtless for other reasons which are unknown, March betook himself to England to seek the means of revenge. As it happened, the relations of the two countries at this moment were specially favourable to his schemes. In 1399 had occurred the Lancastrian revolution which had placed Henry IV on the throne of England; and in the same year one of the many temporary truces had expired. The new king made peaceful overtures to the government of Robert; but there was no ready response, and the Scots began the usual work on the Border. Finding his advances thus coldly received, Henry made preparations for the invasion of Scotland, and it was on his way north with his army that he was met by the fugitive Earl of March. March had already done

1399

---

[1] The title may have been given to enable them to treat on equal terms with the English Dukes of York, Albemarle, Exeter, and others.—Bain, Vol. IV. p. xxvi.

mischief by harrying his own lands in East Lothian, and now at Newcastle he formally renounced his allegiance to the King of Scots, and received the grant of a castle and lands from Henry

It was the last time that an English king in person conducted an invasion of Scotland; and the expedition was honourably distinguished from most invasions of the kind. Few English invasions of Scotland were accompanied with less suffering to the people of the invaded districts. For the Scots, indeed, it was fortunate that Henry's own affairs prevented his carrying the war to extremities, since the divisions of their own leaders placed them at special disadvantage Having duly summoned Robert and his barons to render him homage in Edinburgh, Henry crossed the Border and led his army against that town The castle of Edinburgh was defended by the Duke of Rothesay, and fifteen miles off, on Calder Moor, an army was posted under the command of Albany But between the two leaders there was no communication and no concerted action. For three days Henry lay before the castle, but the prospect of its capture was remote, and troubles in Wales demanded his presence in England. Raising the siege, therefore, he led his army homewards, and recrossed the Border after an invasion which had lasted fifteen days. His retreat was immediately followed by the capture of the castle of Dunbar, the strong fortress of the Earl of March, which, along with the neighbouring lands, was now placed in the hands of Douglas.

Events now followed that brought to a crisis the rivalries of Rothesay and Albany. The deaths of the queen, of the Earl of Douglas, and of Traill, bishop of St Andrews, gave a preponderance to Albany which he was not slow to turn to his advantage The conduct of Rothesay, who had always been dissolute, had now become a public scandal, and with the consent of his father he was removed from the office of Guardian, and apparently placed under a certain restraint.

At length, in 1402, at the suggestion of certain evil counsellors[1], he took a step which was to put a term
to his career. With a few attendants he rode to
St Andrews with the object of seizing the castle now vacant
by the death of Traill. His intention was known, for he was
seized by the way and led to the castle itself, whence he was
conveyed to Falkland Tower by Albany and Archibald, the
young Earl of Douglas. His death shortly afterwards, while
he was still under restraint, naturally gave rise to the suspicion of foul play. Considering the manner of life he had
led, there was nothing remarkable in Rothesay's early death;
but the circumstances that had preceded it could not fail to
raise suspicions in an age familiar with the violent deaths of
princes, and at a meeting of estates it was deemed necessary
to go through the form of an investigation of the case—the
conclusion being that the prince "had departed by divine
Providence and from no other cause." A dark suspicion must
always rest on Albany and Douglas; but no satisfactory proof
of their guilt has as yet been forthcoming[2].

    Hostilities with England still continued—the renegade Earl
of March being now the most determined enemy of the Scots.
In retaliation for his successive inroads they organized counter-
raids into England, in two of which (1402) they
came off worst. In the first a body of 400
Scots was cut off at Nesbit Moor, about three miles to the
south of Dunse, mainly owing to their countryman, March.
In the second the results were on a larger scale and of
national importance. Led by Murdoch Stewart, the eldest
son of Albany, and Archibald, the young Earl of Douglas,

(margin note: 1402)

---

[1] Specially Sir John Ramorgny, familiar to readers of the *Fair Maid of
Perth.*

[2] In Wyntoun there is no hint that Rothesay came by a violent end
Bower's statement is that dysentery was the cause of death, though he hints
at a rumour that the prince had been starved. Without further evidence
later historians converted the rumour into fact.

an army of Scots made their way as far south as Newcastle On their march home, while encamped on Homildon
Hill, some five miles to the north of Wooler, they were
overtaken by the Percies and their ally, the Earl of March.
Their position was all that could be desired ; but the incompetence of their leaders made the day a repetition
of Halidon Hill With hardly an opportunity of striking a
blow, the Scots were shot down in their ranks by the English
bowmen and the rout was complete, Stewart and Douglas
and three other earls being among the prisoners.

The year 1403 was a memorable one in the history of
England ; and in its great events Scotland had
a share of its own. In June of that year the   1403
Percies laid siege to Cocklaws, a tower near the village of
Yetholm ; but so resolute was the defence that Percy came
to terms with the besieged. The place was to be put in
his hands if it were not relieved within the space of six
weeks. At this moment Albany, now at the head of affairs
in Scotland, was in a position of peculiar difficulty. To the
government of Henry IV he was personally hostile , and there
was now in his hands a person given out to be Richard II,
the late king of England, whom he was playing off against
his successor. On the other hand, his own position was such
that he could not afford to run the risk of another invasion
by Henry in person. He determined, however, to carry relief
to Cocklaws , and with this object he led southwards one of
the largest armies that had ever been brought together in
Scotland[1]. On his arrival at the Border he found no enemy
to fight The Percies, strengthened by a body of Scots under
Douglas, were in the midst of the insurrection which closed
so disastrously for them in the battle of Shrewsbury The
news of their defeat reached Albany while he was encamped
beside Cocklaws , and, apparently convinced that it was not

[1] According to Bower, Albany's host consisted of 50,000 cavalry, and
"almost as many foot."

the time to challenge the English king, he at once disbanded his army without striking a blow

Albany was already virtual master of the country; but a succession of events was now to leave him without a rival The king was old and feeble, and public and private troubles hastened the work of disease   The death of Rothesay had been followed by the murder of Robert's brother-in-law, Sir Malcolm Drummond, by a natural son of the Wolf of Badenoch; and in 1406 came the crowning calamity of his life as a father and a king.   For reasons that are not expressly specified, but which may be easily conjectured, he had decided to send his son James, a boy in his twelfth year, to be educated in France.   Every precaution was taken to secure his safe voyage, but, off Flamborough Head, the vessel in which he sailed fell into the hands of the English. It was in February or March of 1406[1] that his son was captured, and on April 4th Robert died in his castle of Dundonald, where his father died before him   In a sentence of the Acts of the most notable Parliament of his reign (1398) we have the final judgment on Robert's capacity as a king   The Act is headed   "The misgovernment of the realm to be imputed to the king and his officers", and the sentence runs as follows   "If it likes our lord the king to excuse his defaults, he may at his liking call his officers to the which he has given commission and accuse them in the presence of his Council."

---

[1] The exact date of James's capture has given rise to much discussion, and has acquired a certain significance in connection with the authorship of the *King's Quhair*.   See *Exchequer Rolls*, vol. IV. p. CXXXIV and App CCIII, Ramsay, *Lancaster and York*, I. 97, J. H. Wylie, *History of England under Henry IV*, Vol. I chap 61; and Brown's *The Authorship of the King's Quhair*.   I have given the date which, in all the circumstances, seems most probable.

CHAPTER III.

REGENCY OF THE DUKES OF ALBANY, 1406—1424.

English Kings.		French Kings.	
Henry IV ..	1399—1413	Charles VI	1380—1422
Henry V ..	1413—1422	Charles VII .	1422—1461
Henry VI ...	1422—1461		

AT a meeting of Estates held in June 1406[1], the second month after the death of Robert III, his son James was proclaimed king and the Duke of Albany appointed regent. Albany was approaching his seventieth year, yet he was to live fourteen years longer and to retain his office to the end. In spite of his advanced age, his government betrayed no decay either in his ambition or his ability. Like no regent either before or after him, he ruled in his own name and not in that of the king. His own income, also, was princely. From his Earldoms of Fife and Menteith he had a revenue estimated at £1200, and the salaries of his various offices raised it to at least £2600[2]. Yet, if we may believe the two contemporary Scottish chroniclers, Wyntoun and Bower, there was no class of his people who had occasion to be dissatisfied with his rule. Peasant, churchman, and noble had

---

[1] Wyntoun is our authority for this meeting. Its proceedings have not been preserved

[2] For the financial year 1421—1422 the gross revenue of Scotland was £3,323 *Exchequer Rolls*, IV. 358—378.

all reason to praise his moderation, his justice and his generosity.   At the very outset of his administration he gave proof
of his tact in managing the great nobility.   In
1408 he contrived to obtain the restoration of
Archibald, Earl of Douglas, who had been taken at the battle
of Shrewsbury[1], and the following year the renegade Earl of
March was induced to return to Scotland, though he had to
leave in the hands of Douglas the lordship of Annandale with
its castle of Lochmaben.

In Albany's relations with England there is no event
of outstanding importance.   The captivity of his own son
Murdoch and of the young king made negotiation more
politic than actual hostilities.   Yet in the interval of the
frequent truces between the two countries the Scots contrived to recover two strongholds which were still in the
hands of the English.   Jedburgh had been in their hands
since the Battle of Neville's Cross (1346); but
in 1409 it was taken by the men of Teviotdale.
In connection with its capture a story is told which explains
Albany's popularity.   So solid was the cement with which the
castle of Jedburgh was built that to demolish it was a work
of unusual labour.   To defray the expense of demolishing
such an important stronghold it was proposed in a Parliament held at Perth that a tax of two pounds should be imposed on every hearth.   But to this proposal Albany would
not listen.   He had never imposed a tax before, he said, and
he would not begin now to make himself a byword with the
poor commons.   The capture of Jedburgh was followed the
next year by the recovery of Fast Castle on St Abb's Head
by Patrick Dunbar, son of the Earl of March.   For this
advantage, however, the Scots had to pay dear.   Sailing up

_____

[1] In an Indenture dated June 20, 1409, Albany and Douglas bound
themselves "to mutual friendship, service, and support against all others,
their allegiance to the King alone excepted."—*Exchequer Rolls*, Vol. IV.
p. CCIX.

the Forth, Sir Robert Umphraville and his nephew, Gilbert, took fourteen Scottish vessels freighted with cloth and grain. In 1415 there were similar reprisals—the Scots burning Penrith and the English the town of Dumfries. To the year 1416[1], however, belongs the most notable attempt of the Scots to inflict injury on their neighbours In that year Albany collected a great army and advanced to the English border. As the expedition was planned, he was himself to lead one portion of his host against Berwick, and the Earl of Douglas was to lead the other against Roxburgh. In neither case was any success achieved, and Albany returned with so little honour that the expedition became currently known as the " Foul Raid." The temporary possession of Wark Castle in 1419 and the burning of Alnwick by the Earl of Douglas in 1420 make up the list of the achievements of the Scots at the expense of England during the rule of Albany.

1415

Three events that belong to Albany's administration are landmarks in the history of Scotland—the burning of the Lollard, James Resby, the battle of Harlaw, and the founding of the University of St Andrews

The teaching of John Wycliffe had speedily made its way into Scotland, and even before a similar Act was passed in England the Scottish Estates had passed a law for the burning of heretics England, however, had led the way in practical example by burning William Sawtry in 1401. It was in 1406 or 1407 that James Resby met the same fate in Perth. According to Bower, Resby was "an English priest of the school of John Wycliffe," who had made himself specially active in disseminating pernicious opinions On no fewer than forty points he was found to be at variance with the Church ; but only two of his heresies are recorded. The pope, according to Resby, was not really the vicar of Christ; and no one could be pope without being personally holy Though taken in hand

[1] Or, 1417.

by the most learned theologian of his day in Scotland, Resby proved refractory, and was burned by due course of law

The battle of Harlaw (1411) ranks with the battle of Carham (1018) in its determining influence on the development of the Scottish nation. At Carham the Celts of Alba overthrew the Saxons of Northumbria, and by the annexation of Lothian made possible the growth of a Teutonic Scotland distinct from a Teutonic England. At Harlaw the victory of the Saxon over the Celt definitively ensured the same result; for never since that day has Teutonic Scotland been in real danger from the Celtic race to whom it originally owed its being. The ambition of a Celtic chieftain, Donald, Lord of the Isles, was the occasion of the great contest between the two races. In right of his wife, Donald demanded of Albany the Earldom of Ross; but Albany himself had a personal interest in the disposition of the earldom. His own granddaughter, Euphemia, was the rightful heir[1], but she had become a nun and had resigned her inheritance in favour of John, Earl of Buchan, the first son of Albany by his second marriage. But Donald was not disposed to accept this arrangement without a protest. The Western Islands over which he ruled had been annexed to Scotland by Alexander III, but during the long struggle with England his predecessors had become independent potentates, making wars and treaties without regard to their nominal sovereigns[2]. At Inverness Donald assembled an army of 10,000 men, and marched to the plunder of Aberdeen. Aberdeen being taken, his intention was to make himself master of the country as far south as the Tay. Luckily for Scotland, he was encountered by one of the most notable men of his time, of a spirit even fiercer than his own—Alexander

[1] She was the daughter and heiress of Alexander de Lesley, Earl of Ross.

[2] "Donald's policy was clearly to set up a Celtic supremacy in the west." *The Clan Donald*, i. 146.

Stewart, son of the Wolf of Badenoch, and now Earl of Mar. Originally a mere kateran like his father, he had forced the widowed countess of Mar to take him as her husband, and under his new title had become a law-abiding subject.   In England he had won honours as an accomplished knight, and had subsequently seen military service in Flanders.   About eighteen miles to the north of Aberdeen, at Harlaw in the district of the Garioch, he checked the course of Donald in one of the bloodiest battles ever fought in Scotland   So heavy was Donald's loss that he had no choice but to retreat to his fastnesses, whither he was soon pursued by Albany himself, who captured the castle of Dingwall and overran the whole of Ross.   The following summer Albany led another expedition against Donald and forced him to make submission and give hostages for his good behaviour.   Of the deliverance that had been wrought at Harlaw the nation was fully aware, and the memory of the battle remained a vivid tradition in districts of Scotland far distant from Aberdeen.   Towards the close of the century in which the battle was fought the boys of East Lothian played at Harlaw in their games[1].

The third event that marked Albany's rule was the foundation of the University of St Andrews in February, 1414[2].   As John Major has said, the wonder is that the foundation had not taken place long before.   From various sources we learn that the Scots students abroad had long been so numerous as to call for the erection of a university at home.   In time of peace there had been a constant stream of them to Oxford and Cambridge   But it was in Paris that the Scottish students found their peculiar home, and where their numbers were so

---

[1] It is John Major who tells us this.   He was born in East Lothian about 1480, and had played at the game himself

[2] Lectures had been read at St Andrews from 1410; but it was in February 1413—4 that the Papal letter of privilege founding the University was brought by Henry Ogilvy   To Henry Wardlaw, bishop of St Andrews, belongs the chief credit of the foundation.

great as to call for special note by the historian of the university. In 1326 the bishop of Moray founded the Scots College in Paris to meet the wants of students from his own diocese[1]. At the close of the 14th century the Scots in Paris appear to have been more numerous than ever. Out of a list of twenty-one suppôsts representing the English nation[2], nine are Scots, all of whom were subsequently bishops in their own country[3].

With the accession of Henry V in 1413 the relations of Albany to England assumed a more friendly character. Negotiations at once began for the restoration of the Scottish king and of Albany's son, Murdoch. In the case of the king the negotiations had no immediate result; but in the beginning of 1416 Murdoch was exchanged for the young Earl of Northumberland, who since the battle of Shrewsbury had resided in St Andrews under the charge of its bishop. Henry V's invasion of France again led to estrangement between the English and Scottish governments. Torn by internal dissensions, and beaten at all points by England, the French appealed to the Scots for assistance in their extremity. The response was at once prompt and generous. Under the command of Albany's son, John, Earl of Buchan, a force of 7000 men was despatched to France, which did effectual service for their allies. In 1420[4] the regent Albany died, having been virtual ruler of Scotland for about fifty years. One of the great figures in Scottish history, the character of Albany is specially difficult to determine. By his contemporaries he was eulogized in terms

1416

1420

---

[1] Subsequently the College was opened to students from all Scotland.

[2] The English nation was drawn from Germany, Scandinavia, and the British Isles. Owing to the Hundred Years' War, English students at Paris could not be numerous.

[3] *Liber Procuratorum Nationis Anglicanae (Alemanniae) in Universitate Parisiensi* (Tom. I. pp. xxxv, xxxvi), ediderunt Henricus Denifle, O.P., Aemilius Chatelain (Paris, 1884).

[4] This is the correct date and not 1419, which is usually given. *Exchequer Rolls*, Vol IV. p. 79.

which raise suspicion as to their good faith. On the other hand, he has been denounced by subsequent historians for motives and acts which can only be matter of conjecture. The death of Rothesay, the capture of the young king and his long detention in England, naturally raise suspicion regarding Albany's conduct, yet in the case of all these three events there is no proof whatever of his complicity. Nothing indeed was more natural than his taking upon himself the government of the country. Robert II and Robert III were imbecile kings, and the heir-apparent Rothesay was incapable of guiding himself. By the force of circumstances, therefore, Albany was thrust into the position which he alone could fill. The manner in which he discharged his trust might seem to justify a severe judgment. It was by humouring the great nobles and overlooking their misdeeds that he retained the regency and preserved the peace of the country. But the heroic policy which cost James I his life would have been impossible for Albany. Had a few discontented nobles acted in concert with the Lord of the Isles, the battle of Harlaw might have had a different ending and the history of Scotland might have followed a different course.

Albany was succeeded in the regency by his son Murdoch, who held the office for four years. Under his feeble rule the great men of the country set law at defiance, Murdoch's own sons being the greatest offenders. But events now led to the restoration of the lawful king to his throne. In 1422 Henry V died, and there were various 1422 reasons why the English government should desire to come to terms with the Scots. The large ransom that must be paid for the surrender of James would be acceptable to the English treasury. Moreover, in their wars with France the English had reason to know the importance of securing the friendship of the Scots. In 1421 the Scottish force, commanded by the Earl of Buchan, had been the chief means of inflicting a severe defeat on the English at Baugé. For these and other reasons

the English government was disposed to make an arrangement with the Scots, and in the spring of 1424
James was at length permitted to return to Scotland. For his ransom, euphemistically styled his "expenses,"
the Scots undertook to pay £40,000 (60,000 marks English)
in six instalments. From this sum, however, 10,000 marks
were deducted by an arrangement which appears to have been
dictated by love[1] and policy. Before returning to his native
country, James was married to Lady Joan Beaufort[2], the "milk-
white dove" of the King's Quhair, and the deducted sum
represented the lady's dowry.

[1] As will afterwards be seen, the motive of love must now be regarded
as questionable.

[2] Daughter of John, Earl of Somerset, fourth son of John of Gaunt, and
grandson of Edward III.

CHAPTER IV.

JAMES I, 1424—1437.

English King.	French King.
Henry VI, 1422—1461.	Charles VII, 1422—1461.

THE well-known saying attributed to James I is at least in keeping with the general character of his government. On the first day of his return to his kingdom some one commented in his hearing on the long misgovernment that had suffered crime to go unpunished. "God granting me life," he is said to have exclaimed, "I will make the key keep the castle and the bracken-bush the cow." All ranks of his people, indeed, soon discovered that in James they were to have a very different master from Robert II and Robert III. He was now in his 30th year, and in full vigour of body and mind. Somewhat below the middle height, he possessed great personal strength, and excelled in all manly sports. During his sojourn in England he had acquired at once the lighter graces of the mind, and the discipline required for the discharge of his kingly duties. In the task which he set himself all these gifts and accomplishments were to be tried to the utmost and to prove inadequate to its achievement.

Even before his coronation James showed the country how he meant to rule. On the 13th of May (1424), within two months after his return, he arrested   1424
Murdoch's eldest son, Sir Walter Stewart; his brother-in-law,

Malcolm Fleming of Cumbernauld; and Thomas Boyd, the younger, of Kilmarnock On the 21st of the same month he was crowned at Scone along with his queen—Murdoch, as representing the ancient Earls of Fife, placing him on the throne. Five days later he held his first Parliament at Perth, and by two of its enactments gave deep offence alike to the barons and the commons. By the first James was empowered to summon his vassals at pleasure and to demand the charters by which they held such lands as they possessed. By the second a tax of twelve pennies in the pound was imposed on all his subjects for the payment of his ransom to England. So great was the popular discontent at this tax that it was exacted only for two years; and not till 1431 did James venture on a similar imposition. The arrest of two more notable persons in the same year gave further proof of the inflexible determination of James to be master in his own kingdom. The one was the aged Duncan, Earl of Lennox, father-in-law of Murdoch; the other, Sir Robert Graham, younger son of Sir Patrick Graham of Kincardine, who was one day to wreak a terrible retribution on the head of James

The following year (1425) saw even sterner measures on the part of James. During the sitting of his

1425 second Parliament at Perth he committed to prison Duke Murdoch himself, his wife the daughter of the Earl of Lennox, and his son Sir Alexander Stewart[1]. An ill-advised act on the part of another of Murdoch's sons gave James the pretext he needed for proceeding to extremities against the house of Albany. Descending on Dumbarton with a strong force, this third son gave the town to the flames, and slew thirty-two persons, including the keeper of the castle, Sir

---

[1] From a misunderstood passage in Bower it was long supposed that on this occasion James also arrested other twenty-six of the leading Scottish barons. The mistake was first pointed out by Sir James Ramsay in the *Scotsman* of July 12, 1883. See also his *Lancaster and York*, Vol. I. p. 490, note

John Stewart of Dundonald. Such a deed could not fail to quicken James's action, and when his adjourned Parliament met again in May, the fate of Murdoch was decided. Before an assize of twenty-one noblemen, Murdoch, his two sons, Walter and Alexander, and the Earl of Lennox, were found guilty on charges which are not recorded. The house of Albany had always been popular, and as the father and sons, all men of majestic appearance, and the aged Earl of Lennox, were led to execution on the Heading Hill at Stirling, the sympathies of the onlookers were not with the king.

Having crushed the house of Albany, James turned with equal vigour to another achievement. In spite of the battle of Harlaw, the Hebrides and the Highlands were still in an unsatisfactory condition; and James prepared to deal with both in more thorough fashion than any of his predecessors. When the Hebrides were ceded to Alexander III, the arrangement was that Scotland should pay 4000 marks, together with an annual sum of 100 marks in perpetuity. As the first step towards his object, James in the year 1426 paid all arrears due to the Norwegian king. Having now only his own subjects to deal with, he proceeded as usual with all the appearance of law. In the spring of 1427 he held a Parliament at Inverness to which he summoned the   1427
Lord of the Isles and other leading men in the Highlands. The Lord of the Isles at this time was Alexander, son of Donald of Harlaw, who with James's consent had taken possession of the Earldom of Ross. In all confidence, therefore, Alexander and the other chieftains appeared at Inverness; but no sooner had they arrived than they discovered their mistake. Forty of them, including the Lord of the Isles, were at once thrown into prison; and the most formidable of them were tried and executed. The majority, however, including Alexander, were allowed to go free after a short imprisonment; and for a brief period there was peace. Two years later (1429),   1429
however, Alexander again took up arms and with

a strong force attacked and burnt Inverness, the scene of his late humiliation. His triumph was short-lived. James, hastily collecting an army, came up with him in a marsh in the district of Lochaber, and inflicted on him a total defeat. Alexander's fortunes were now desperate; and in a strange fashion he gave in his submission to James. On the Feast of St Augustine, he appeared in his shirt and drawers before the high altar of Holyrood Church, and presented his sword to the king in presence of the assembled court. After an imprisonment in Tantallon Castle, Alexander was suffered to go at large. In 1431 his cousin-german, Donald Balloch, inflicted a severe defeat at Inverlochy on the king's representatives, the earls of Mar and Caithness; but in this rising Alexander had no part, and Balloch had to flee to Ireland, whence he reappeared in the succeeding reign to take his part in a more formidable rebellion.

By his wars and executions James had sought at once to strengthen the crown and to give peace to his kingdom. The first of these ends he tried to accomplish by still more effectual means. On the execution of the Earl of Lennox in 1425, James took possession of his estates and earldom, and retained them to the close of his life. In the case of three other earldoms he proceeded in the same uncompromising fashion. On the groundless pretext that it was a male fee, he deprived Malise Graham of the earldom of Strathearn[1] (1427); and sent him as a hostage to England, where he remained for twenty-four years. George, Earl of March, was the next to find himself at James's discretion. He was the son of the renegade March who had given so much trouble in the reign of Robert III; but he had himself been in all respects a loyal subject. It was now maintained, however, that Albany had gone beyond his powers in restoring his father to his estates,

---

[1] To Graham was nominally granted the inferior Earldom of Menteith, but even its lands remained in the hands of James. *Exchequer Rolls*, iv. p. 117.

and on this ground he was deprived of the earldom and imprisoned in the castle of Edinburgh. By way of compensation, the earldom of Buchan, a miserably inadequate substitute, was given to the deprived noble—the earldom of March being forfeited to the crown. The death in 1435 of Alexander, Earl of Mar, the natural son of the Wolf of Badenoch and the hero of Harlaw, brought another opportunity not to be lost. The rightful heir of the earldom was Robert Lord Erskine; but James put his claim aside and appropriated the earldom and estates to the crown.

In the foreign relations of James there is only one event of importance—the unhappy marriage of his daughter Margaret to the Dauphin of France, afterwards Louis XI. The circumstances under which the alliance was formed gave special satisfaction to the Scots. The French were being still hard pressed by the English; and they had had recent experience of the value of the Scottish alliance. Accordingly, in 1428, an embassy arrived from France bearing the offer of the Dauphin's hand in marriage. As coming 1428 spontaneously from such a country as France the offer in itself was gratifying; and the ambassadors who brought it—the archbishop-duke of Reims, John Stewart of Darnley "Constable of the Scots in France," and the famous Alain Chartier,—gave additional grace to the offer. James, who bore no love to the English, gladly responded to these overtures, and in 1436 Margaret was sent to France and united to a husband whose brutal ill-usage sent her to an 1436 early grave.

These cordial relations between Scotland and France naturally excited the apprehensions of the English government. In the treaty regarding James's ransom a truce of seven years had been arranged between the two countries; but the year after the French embassy, the English thought it prudent that the treaty should be confirmed. Accordingly, at a meeting (1429) at Dunbar, between James and Cardinal Beaufort, the

truce was renewed till 1431—the original date of its expiry.
As neither country was in a position to declare war against the
other, the truce was again extended till 1433. But the
approaching French marriage rendered it more and more
difficult for the two nations to remain on friendly terms. In
1433 Lord Scrope came to Scotland with a proposal to restore
Roxburgh and Berwick on condition of a perpetual peace.
Bound as they were to France, the Scots were not in a position
to accept the offer, and thenceforward, during the brief space
that still remained to James, the two countries considered
themselves free to indulge in mutual hostilities. In 1435 an
English expedition under Sir Robert Ogle was met at Piperden
by William, Earl of March, and defeated with severe loss—Ogle
himself being among those taken. Another proceeding of the
English awoke in James all the wrath of which he was capable.
On the voyage of his daughter to France in 1436 an English
fleet attempted to repeat the exploit which had been so successful in his own case, and the vessel in which Margaret sailed
escaped only by a lucky accident. For the first and last time
(1436) James now led an army to the English border and laid
siege to the castle of Roxburgh. Though he had a great host
behind him, equipped with all the weapons his kingdom could
supply, no success attended his effort, and after fifteen days
he disbanded his force with as little glory as Albany in the
"Foul Raid."

James had now reigned for twelve years, and had governed
the country with an energy and ability of which it had had no
experience since the days of the great King Robert. Yet with
no class of his subjects does he appear to have been really
popular. The tax of twelve pennies in the pound with which
he had begun his reign had given deep offence to the country.
This tax had been exacted only for two years, but in 1431
a tax of two pennies had been imposed in connection with
the marriage of his daughter. Whatever benefits were derived
from James's firm government, therefore, were more than

counterbalanced by impositions which the Scottish Commons regarded as an unlawful grievance to which they had never been subjected in the days of the Dukes of Albany. As for the nobles James had dealt so arbitrarily with them as a class that none of them could feel secure in the possession of their titles and estates. Another bitter complaint they had against James was the detention of their relatives in England as hostages for payment of his ransom. To one great noble, however, is attributed the origin of the conspiracy which ended in James's destruction. This was the Earl of Athole, grandson of Robert II by his second marriage. In the opinion of many the children of Robert II by his first wife, Elizabeth Mure, were illegitimate, and in that case Athole was the rightful king of Scotland. James had done his best to conciliate Athole, and had made him great Justiciary of Scotland and Earl Palatine of Strathearn for life. Athole himself was near his seventieth year; but he found willing and capable agents in his grandson, Sir Robert Stewart, and above all in that Sir Robert Graham, whom James had sent to prison in the first year of his reign. At Perth on the 20th or 21st of February, 1437, the conspirators found their opportunity.

To receive a papal legate who had been sent **1437** to Scotland a great council had been summoned in that town, over which James was to preside in person. As Perth Castle was in disrepair, he had taken up his abode in the Blackfriars Convent immediately outside the town-wall. Athole's grandson was the king's private chamberlain, and was therefore in a position to make the way clear for the work that was in hand. Just as James was retiring for the night the murderers—Sir Robert Graham and seven others—burst into the chamber when he was in the act of undressing. On hearing the sound of armed men he had sought refuge in a closet; but he was immediately discovered and slain on the spot—the queen herself receiving a wound in the confusion[1]. Within a month

[1] The details of the death of James usually given are taken from the

the Earl of Athole, Sir Robert Graham, and their chief
associates were taken, and put to death with a refinement of
cruelty which excited horror even in that age

During his reign of thirteen years James was as energetic
in making laws as in enforcing them.   His reign, indeed, is of
special interest in the constitutional development of Scotland.
During his imprisonment in England he had acquired notions
regarding the powers and functions of Parliament which he
endeavoured with partial success to apply to his own kingdom.
He reigned thirteen years and he held in all thirteen Parliaments.   The most notable of these was that which met at Perth
in 1428.   To relieve the smaller barons from attendance it was
enacted that they should send two "wise men" from each shire[1]
to represent them.   By a further enactment these representatives
were to choose "a Common Speaker of the Parliament"   In
neither case, however, did these innovations take effect.   In
other reforms James was more successful.   He founded a
system of Statute Law, he introduced the court known as The
Session, and he set the example of promulgating the laws in
the Scottish tongue.   The details of James's social legislation
cover the whole life of his people   For the defence of the
country the practice of archery was pressed on his subjects with
special emphasis.   The encouragement of hostelries, the sowing
of peas and beans, the preservation of wood, the selling of
horses, the fulfilment of contracts, the destruction of wolves,
provision for lepers, the sale of salmon, the disposition of

so-called "Contemporary Account of the murder of James I," which
is printed by Pinkerton (Vol 1 p 462).   A more accurate text of the
Account will be found in a volume edited by Joseph Stevenson for the
Maitland Club (1837)   But neither the style nor the substance of this
document is such as to inspire confidence; and I have preferred to keep
mainly to the concise narrative of Bower.

The heart of James was carried to the East, and was brought home
from Rhodes by a Knight of St John.   *Exchequer Rolls*, Vol. v. pp XLIV.
156, 179

[1] Kinross and Clackmannan were to send one representative each

wrecks—such are among the subjects on which the Parliaments of James industriously passed laws, which an inadequate executive could but feebly enforce.

In religion and the Church, James took as strenuous an interest as in politics. Against heresy he displayed special zeal. The Parliament of 1425 passed a fresh law against heretics which bore fruit (1433) in the burning of Paul Craw, who had come all the way from Bohemia to teach his doctrines in Scotland. Nor did James spare the Church itself in its own backslidings. A letter he addressed to the Abbots and Priors of the Benedictine and Augustine monasteries in Scotland is a formidable indictment against these institutions. One magnificent proof he gave of his genuine zeal for the Church. Though he is said to have denounced David I as "a sore saint to the Crown," he himself founded (1429) the great Carthusian Convent at Perth—the only establishment of that order that ever existed in Scotland.

In his last agonies, Sir Robert Graham, the chief of James's assassins, is reported to have made a singular statement. Posterity, he said, would justify his act as the destruction of a cruel tyrant. So far was his prediction from the truth that James I came to take his place after David I and Robert I in the roll of Scottish sovereigns. Much of his good repute, indeed, he has owed to two extrinsic circumstances—his violent death and the story of his early love as told in the King's Quhair. Of recent years, however, his laurels have in some degree been tarnished. As a poet he now stands in a somewhat dubious light. Every flower is being successively plucked from his poetic garland. Christ's Kirk on the Green, Peebles to the Play—poems once confidently assigned to him—are now definitively dissociated from his name; and it has even been maintained, though probably on insufficient grounds, that the King's Quhair itself, the crown of his poetic glory, must be assigned to another hand than his[1]. As a king, also, he must

[1] See "The Authorship of the King's Quhair, a New Criticism," by

now be regarded with somewhat qualified admiration. That he was rapacious, that he was violent to imprudence, that he aimed as much at the greatness of the Crown as at the good of his people—all this his subjects appear to have believed, and in the record of his acts there is much that goes to prove that they were not mistaken in their judgment[1].

J. T. T. Brown (Maclehose and Sons, 1896) M Jusserand has replied to Mr Brown's arguments in the *Révue Historique* for 1897 (May—June).

[1] Æneas Sylvius Piccolomini (Pope Pius II.) has left an interesting account of a visit to Scotland which he made during the reign of James I This account will be found in *Early Travellers in Scotland* (David Douglas, Edinburgh, 1891).

Information regarding other visits of foreigners to Scotland during James I's reign is given in M. Jusserand's *The Romance of a King's Life* (Fisher Unwin, 1896).

CHAPTER V.

JAMES II, 1437—1460.

English King.	French King.
Henry VI ...... 1422—1461	Charles VII ...... 1422—1461

THE period covered by the twenty-three years of James II's reign was a memorable one for Christendom at large. During this period England saw the close of the Hundred Years' War with France, and found herself deprived of all her possessions in that country with the exception of Calais. During these years, also, began her Wars of the Roses, which so effectually crippled her in her relations with the Scottish kingdom. For France the same period was of the first importance in the consolidation of territory and in the growth of the national spirit. By the expulsion of the English and the annexation of Aquitaine northern as well as southern Gaul were at length united, and a vast stride was taken towards the compacted kingdom of Francis I. In Florence began the ascendency of the Medici, which forms the most interesting chapter in the political history of mediæval Italy. But for Christendom at large the most momentous event was one which had long been dreaded by the pious souls and politic heads of the countries of the west—the capture of Constantinople by the Turks in 1453.

During the reign of James II Scotland passed through an ordeal such as she had not known since the days of William the Lyon and Malcolm IV. For nearly six years the ambition and resources of two great subjects threatened the ruin of the existing dynasty and the disintegration of the kingdom. On a reduced scale the six years' struggle between the Stewart and the Douglas is the Scottish parallel to the wars of Lancaster and York. That the struggle was not further prolonged and that it ended as it did, was indubitably owing to the vigour and enterprise of James himself[1].

After the murder of the late king Perth was hardly a safe place for his son and heir; and the queen seems to have made haste to Edinburgh, where she took up her abode in the castle[2]. It soon appeared that the great barons had at least no immediate intention of profiting by the new situation. On the 25th of March the Estates met in Edinburgh, and proceeded to adjust the affairs of the kingdom. Their first act was the coronation of the king, now in his seventh year—the ceremony being performed in Holyrood Church, as Scone for the present was somewhat dangerous ground. One of the enactments of this Parliament proved that the crown had real well-wishers, able to give effect to their desires. Till the king reached the age of twenty-one, it was declared, there should be no alienation of the royal lands or property without the consent of the Three Estates. Two other matters of importance appear to have completed the business of the first Parliament of this reign[3]: Archibald, fifth Earl of Douglas, was made king's

---

[1] In the following account of James II's reign I have kept closely to the authorities cited at the end of this volume. Hector Boece's narrative of this reign, which is virtually translated by Pitscottie, and is reproduced by Buchanan, Leslie, and Drummond of Hawthornden, cannot be accepted as an authority. John Major, also, though he was born only twenty years after James's death, is very ill-informed regarding the events of this reign. Scanty as the authentic chronicles are, however, they enable us to relate James II's reign in greater detail than those of the first three Stewarts.

[2] The Palace as distinct from the Abbey of Holyrood appears to belong to the reign of James II. *Exchequer Rolls*, vol. v. p. lxxv.

[3] The records of this Parliament are mutilated.

lieutenant, and ambassadors were despatched to England, who subsequently arranged a truce of nine years, dating from the 1st of July, 1438.   1438

So scanty are the authentic records of the next few years that we catch only a glimpse of one or two outstanding events. What is remarkable is that the men who appear to have managed the kingdom did not belong to the great nobility of the land. Of the action of the king's lieutenant, Douglas, we hear nothing; but the country is distracted by the rivalries of two minor barons for the possession of the young king One of these was Sir Alexander Livingstone, of whom it is recorded that he took part in the negotiations for the liberation of James I, and that he was one of those who sat in judgment on the Regent Murdoch. The other, Sir William Crichton, had been a trusted servant of James I, who had made him Master of the Royal Household, Sheriff of Edinburgh, and Keeper of its Castle At the outset the advantage lay with Crichton, since as keeper of Edinburgh Castle he received the king and his mother on their flight thither from Perth Yet the next ascertained fact is that Livingstone is the predominating person in the country. By the 13th of March, 1439, he had the king in his hands at   1439 Stirling Castle[1], and was sufficiently powerful to dictate terms to Crichton. A compromise between the two rivals enabled them for a time to follow common counsels, and Crichton was made Chancellor of the kingdom Douglas, the lieutenant, had troubled himself so little with the responsibilities of his office that his death in June 1439 left things as they were, and for the time no successor in the lieutenancy was appointed His death, however, may have prompted a singular step on the part of the queen-mother; for she immediately married Sir James Stewart, younger son of Sir John Stewart of Invermeath, and

---

[1] Boece's story of the Queen's carrying off her son in a chest to Stirling is quite in his usual manner. In many of his details, moreover, he is demonstrably inaccurate

known as "the Black Knight of Lorn." If her object in this union was to find a protector for herself and her son she speedily found her mistake.   On the 3rd of August, Livingstone, his son, and his brother, broke into her chamber in Stirling Castle, beat off her domestics, seized her person, and placed her in durance in another part of the Castle.   In completion of this act her husband and his brother were thrown into the dungeons and placed in fetters   The proceedings that followed prove to what extent Livingstone was master of the situation.   On the 4th of September, a General Council met at Stirling, and formally gave its sanction to the following arrangements.   Livingstone was to have the custody of the king till he attained his majority; and at no future time were he and his associates to be called in question for their recent doings.   On her part the queen was to have the use of Stirling Castle with an allowance of 4000 marks, and she was permitted to see her son in the presence of proper persons.

How far the Chancellor Crichton was responsible for these proceedings at Stirling it is impossible to say, but in an

1440

audacious deed of the following year (1440) he acted in full understanding with Livingstone. The late Earl of Douglas had been succeeded by his son William, a boy of sixteen.   In 1440 the new earl was still only in his eighteenth year; but he had already given evidence of a temper which threatened to mar the arrangements of the two confederates.   Douglas, it would appear, was on friendly terms with the young king, who is said to have greatly admired his bold and haughty ways.   However this may be, on the 24th of November Livingstone and Crichton found the opportunity of seizing, in Edinburgh Castle, not only the young earl himself, but his only brother and their chief adviser, the aged Malcolm Fleming of Cumbernauld, brother-in-law of the Regent Murdoch.   After the form of a trial, of which we know nothing, Douglas was summarily beheaded on the Castle Hill— his brother and Cumbernauld sharing the same fate three or four days later[1]. As the earl had suffered death on a charge of treason, the forfeiture of his estates should have followed by course of law[2]. But no such forfeiture took place, and we can only conjecture why the law was not carried out in its full rigour. The formidable resources of the Douglas kin may have deterred the Chancellor and his ally from proceeding to extremities; but another reason is more probably the true one. The successor to the murdered Douglas was his great-uncle, James, Earl of Avondale, whose previous record and whose subsequent conduct raise the strongest suspicion that he had known something of the purposes of Livingstone and Crichton. During the three years that he held the earldom, James the Gross, as he was called on account of his obesity, gave not the slightest trouble to the two men who had slain his kinsmen—a course of conduct singularly alien at once to the spirit of the time and the tradition of the Douglas blood.

For the next three years Livingstone and Crichton appear to have worked in concert, and they further attached Douglas to their interests by making his second son Earl of Moray. One event only, however, is recorded of this time of reconciliation. In 1441 ambassadors came   1441 to Scotland from John, Duke of Brittany, with an offer which was readily accepted. This was a proposal of marriage between the duke's eldest son and Isabel or Elizabeth, the second daughter of James I. A Scottish embassy despatched to

---

[1] This murder was known as the " Black Dinner," and is commemorated in the following stanza :—

> Edinburgh Castle, towne and toure,
> God grant thou sink for sinne!
> And that even for the black dinoir
> Erl Douglas gat therein.

[2] The Duchy of Touraine acquired by the fourth Earl of Douglas died with this William; Galloway and Bothwell passed to his sister the " Fair Maid of Galloway"; and Annandale lapsed to the Crown.

France having concluded the necessary arrangements, the

1442 marriage took place in Brittany on the 30th of October, 1442.

The death in 1443 of James the Gross, Earl of Douglas, gave a new turn to the affairs of the country. His son William, who succeeded him, proved a very different person from his politic and corpulent father. During the nine years he held the earldom the power of his family became for the first time a serious menace to the unity of the kingdom. In the year of his succession he formed a coalition with Livingstone with the express purpose of crushing the Chancellor Crichton. Having procured his appointment as lieutenant, he at once proceeded

1443 with fire and sword against Crichton and all who were attached to his interests. In August of 1443 he demolished Barnton House, near Edinburgh, the possession of Sir George Crichton, admiral of Scotland and a kinsman of the Chancellor; and in November a General Council held at Stirling "put to the horn[1]" the whole Crichton kin, and removed the head of the family from the office of Chancellor. But the ex-Chancellor was still master of Edinburgh Castle, and from this stronghold was able to retaliate on

1445 the Douglases by harrying the lands of their friends. At length, in 1445, after a siege of nine weeks, Crichton was forced to capitulate, but on terms which prove that his enemies recognized his importance in the country. All his past offences were remitted, and he himself was again received into the favour of the king.

During his struggle with Crichton Douglas had both added to his domains and increased his influence in the country. On the execution of William, the sixth Earl of Douglas, the lordship of Galloway had passed from the possessions of his family, but he found a simple means of recovering it The lordship was now in the hands of his cousin Margaret, well-known in her time as the Fair Maid of Galloway; and having

---

[1] Outlawed.

obtained the necessary dispensation, he brought such effective means to bear upon that lady that the cousins were married and their lands reunited. By another arrangement he was able to make, Douglas still further increased his predominance in the country: he procured for his brother Hugh the Earldom of Ormond in connection with the lands of Ardmanach in Ross. Thus powerful in his own resources, he entered into an alliance by which his successor was to profit more than himself. To the north of the Forth the most formidable potentate at this time was David, third Earl of Crawford. In the counties of Perth, Angus, and Kincardine, this noble exercised an influence which made him the terror of his neighbours, and of which we shall presently see notable proof. With Crawford Douglas now entered into relations which could have only one of two objects—the weakening of the crown or the overthrow of the House of Stewart.

It is now that we meet with a name of happy omen in Scottish history—that of James Kennedy, a nephew of James I and at this time Bishop of St Andrews. In the growing ascendency of the Douglases Kennedy saw the most serious danger to the country, and as the best means of checking it he made common cause with the ex-Chancellor, Crichton. The immediate result of this alliance was not encouraging. In 1445 the Earl of Crawford, Sir James 1445 Livingstone (the rival of Crichton), and the whole Ogilvy[1] kin, broke into Kennedy's diocese, carried destruction far and wide, and retreated with abundant booty. The bishop had only spiritual weapons with which to retaliate, but he used them with special vigour, and, as the world was afterwards to see, with striking effect. Continually for the space of a year he excommunicated the perpetrators of the late outrage "with

---

[1] At this time Alexander Ogilvy of Innerquharady was a member of the king's Council. By an indenture made at Edinburgh (July 7, 1445), between the king's Council and Walter Ogilvy of Beufurdre, the latter became bound to defend the king in all his actions and quarrels.

mitre and staff, book and candle," and laid under interdict every place where they were harboured. Exactly one year had elapsed from the day of the harrying of the bishop's territory, when the judgment of heaven overtook the chief offender. Late on a Sunday night in January, at the gates of the town of Arbroath, a bloody encounter took place between the Earl of Huntly and the Ogilvies on the one hand, and the Lyndsays and their friends on the other. Crawford and his son, afterwards known as Earl Beardie or the Tiger Earl, remained masters of the field; but Crawford himself received a mortal wound, of which he died in the course of eight days. In the coincidence of his death and his sacrilege his retainers saw the manifest hand of God, and they left him unburied till the bishop was induced to send proper persons with full powers to perform the last offices to the unhappy earl.

In the year 1448 the Douglases did signal services to their country against the common enemy, England.

1448   The nine years' truce concluded at the beginning of James's reign had now expired, and the men on either side of the Border appear to have been alike eager to make up for their long inactivity. The game began with the burning of Dunbar in May by Sir Robert Ogle and young Percy, afterwards third Earl of Northumberland. In the following month the Earl of Salisbury set fire to Dumfries. The turn of the Scots came next. On the 3rd of June the Earls of Douglas, Angus, Ormond, and Orkney (three of them Douglases), gave Alnwick to the flames, and carried destruction far and wide. A month later (July 18th) they repeated their work—on this occasion burning the town of Warkworth. It was in October of the same year, however, that the Scots achieved their most notable success in this petty warfare, and once more it was a Douglas who was the champion of his country. To chastise the Scots for their late proceedings young Percy was despatched across the Border to carry fire and sword into Dumfriesshire. But he never reached his destination. With a force of 5000 men Hugh, Earl of Ormond, brother of the Douglas, met him near Gretna, on the banks of the Sark. The victory of the Scots was complete—Percy and other two leaders being taken, and many of their followers drowned in the river.

To the great resources of the Douglases was now added the prestige of their deeds against England ; but the measure of their greatness was nearly full. The king was now in his eighteenth year, and must henceforth be a factor in the state. It is with his marriage in 1449 that he first comes before us as a personal agent in the management of his kingdom. In 1448 an embassy had been sent from Scotland to seek a suitable match among the princesses of France. In France, however, no eligible person was to be found, and the ambassadors were sent on to Philip the Good, of Burgundy, who recommended to them his niece, Mary, daughter of Arnold, Duke of Gueldres. The alliance commended itself to the Scots, and in 1449 the lady landed at Leith and the mar- 1449
riage was celebrated on the 3rd of July. Of Mary of Gueldres we know little that is definite ; but she appears to have been a woman of high spirit and capable of playing a part in the affairs of the country.

A step which James now took proves that he had both the power and the will to carry out the policy on which he had set his mind. Within three months after his marriage, Sir Alexander Livingstone, his sons James and Alexander, and other adherents of their house, were summarily seized and laid in the Castle of Blackness. Nor were they long left in doubt as to their fate. In James's first Parliament, held in Edinburgh on the 19th January, 1450, 1450
Sir Alexander Livingstone was forfeited and his two sons found guilty of high treason—their execution following on the third day of the sitting of the Estates. The ruin of the Livingstones was complete ; but while the power of the Douglases was unbroken, James never could be master in his

own kingdom.   Meanwhile, the fall of his old allies the Livingstones seemed to have brought additional strength to the great earl, as he was among those who had their share in the forfeited estates of that family.   It could hardly bode good to him, however, that his old adversary Crichton now stood high in the king's favour, and had lately been restored to the office of Chancellor.

In the year 1450 began the great struggle between the House of Douglas and the House of Stewart for the first place in the country.   At the accession of Robert II we have seen that William, the first Earl of Douglas, made a claim to the crown which was compromised by his son's marriage to the king's daughter, Isabella.   Though in the authentic records of the contest that now ensued there is no hint of a dynastic claim on the part of the Douglases, such a claim was familiar to the mind of the country[1].   In point of resources and popular esteem the advantage lay rather with the Douglas than the Stewart.   In the defence of their country the successive Earls of Douglas had a far more brilliant record than the kings of the house of Stewart.   The deeds of their famous ancestor, the Good Sir James, had been emulated at Otterbourne, at Homildon Hill, and on the banks of the Sark[2].   The undoubted popularity derived from these services was supported by possessions far more extensive than those of any other family in Scotland.   As lords of Galloway and Annandale they were the virtual masters of the South of Scotland ; and these districts, moreover, were from their proximity to England precisely the most warlike in the whole country.   When to these resources of the earl himself we add those of his

---

[1] We receive this impression from Bower.—*Scotichronicon*, Vol. II. p. 382.   See above, p. 186.

[2] The warlike spirit of the Douglases is commemorated in the well-known couplet :—

> So many, so good, as of the Douglases have been,
> Of one sirname in Scotland never yet were seen.

brothers, the Earls of Moray and Ormond, we see with what advantage he entered on the contest with the crown. Fortunately for the integrity of the kingdom James II was found to possess the very qualities needed in the crisis that awaited him. According to John Major, who was born twenty years after his death, James was peculiarly a soldier's king. Without the graces and accomplishments which his father had acquired in England, he possessed similar vigour of mind and body[1]. In military expeditions he was careless of his personal comfort and mingled freely with his men, who would offer him their own food and drink in the easy fashion of the camp. As showing his unsuspicious temper, it is noted that he asked no one to eat or drink before he partook himself.

The immediate occasion of the struggle was the temporary absence of Douglas from Scotland[2]. The year 1450 was a jubilee in the Church, and about the month of November the earl set out for Rome with a train so numerous and magnificent that it ensured him a princely reception both at Rome and afterwards in England. During his absence disturbances occurred in his domains which induced the king to put forth his authority to check them. With the advice of Turnbull, bishop of Glasgow, and the two Crichtons, Sir William and Sir George, he entered the Douglas territory, laid siege to various strongholds, slew many freeholders, and received the rest to mercy on their taking the oath of fealty. In the beginning of April, 1451, Douglas returned; but   1451
James still continued his efforts against him, and demolished Douglas Crag, a small fortress of the earl's in Ettrick Forest. In the course of the year, however, a temporary reconciliation took place between the king and his great subject. On the 15th of April Douglas was appointed one of the commissioners

[1] From a red birth-mark on his cheek, James was known as "the king with the fire-mark in his face."

[2] As we learn from a Charter, dated Edinburgh, Nov. 15, 1449, James was on good terms with Douglas till the close of that year.

to treat with England regarding the late hostilities on the borders, though he seems merely to have sent his seal with the other Scottish representatives On May 12, also, a safe-conduct, good for a year, was sent from England for the benefit of himself and his brothers. Apparently Douglas himself remained at home, but his brother James proceeded to the English court and made so long a stay that he raised the suspicions of the friends of the House of Stewart Other proceedings of the same year gave further proof of the good understanding between the earl and the king. In a Parliament which met in Edinburgh on the 25th of June, Douglas "put himself, body, lands, and goods in the king's grace"; and at the express wish of the queen and the three Estates received back all the lordships which had lately been taken from him. Four months later a Parliament held at Stirling not only confirmed this transaction, but made the further grant of the earldom of Wigton and the lordship of Stewarton, which had not been included in the charters of June.

The reconciliation was as shortlived as it was hollow. Within his own dominions Douglas carried it with so high a hand as to set the royal authority at defiance[1]. What was still more unpardonable in a subject, Douglas now entered into a bond with the Earls of Crawford and Ross[2], which must sooner or later have endangered the peace of the kingdom With the view, perhaps, of effecting a mutual understanding, James, in February 1452, sent a special invitation to Douglas to visit him at Stirling. As showing the relations between them it is noteworthy that it was deemed necessary that the king should provide the earl with a safe-conduct. On the 21st of February

1452

---

[1] It is to this period that Pitscottie—the sole authority—assigns the story of the execution of McLellan, Tutor of Bomby, by Douglas, in defiance of the request of James through McLellan's kinsman, Sir Patrick Gray.

[2] This is probably John, Lord of the Isles and Earl of Ross, who succeeded his father Alexander in May, 1449.

Douglas appeared at Stirling, and was received by the king with apparent cordiality. The following day they dined and supped together in the castle; and at the close of supper James at length approached the earl on the subject of his league with Ross and Crawford. When urged by James to break the bond, Douglas replied that he neither might nor would break it. "If you will not," exclaimed the king in an access of passion, "this will", and struck his dagger into his neck and body. The courtiers who stood by finished the work, and the Douglas lay dead with twenty-six wounds.

The wild deed of James could only discredit him at home and abroad. To France, the country with which he was specially anxious to stand well, he thought it necessary to send a message to put the best face he could on his crime. In Scotland the year of Douglas's murder was distinguished by a series of events which showed the unsettlement of the country. The Douglases themselves soon gave proof of their continued contempt for the royal authority, and their indignation at the murder of their chief. The murdered earl was succeeded by his younger brother James, who was to prove as formidable an enemy of the crown as any of his race. His first public act after his accession showed the country what might be expected of him. Accompanied by his brother, the Earl of Ormond, and James Lord Hamilton, he rode into Stirling (March 27) at the head of a force of 600 men and went through all the formalities of feudal defiance. With the blast of twenty-four horns they signified the withdrawal of their allegiance; tied to a horse's tail, the safe-conduct which James had given to Douglas was dragged in contempt through the street; and finally the town itself was spoiled and given to the flames. The friends of the Douglases, also, were not idle. In the north the Tiger Earl of Crawford gave such trouble that James sought to join forces with his lieutenant, the Earl of Huntly[1],

[1] Alexander Seton, Lord Gordon, married Elizabeth Crichton, daughter of the Chancellor. He was created first Earl of Huntly between 3rd October,

in putting him down. In his own strength, however, Huntly
was able to inflict a severe check on Crawford. On a moor
near Brechin, Huntly with a greatly superior force encountered
him (May 18), drove him from the field, and marched through
Angus at the head of three or four thousand men[1].

To deal with recent events a Parliament was summoned to
meet in Edinburgh on the 12th of June. On the 2nd of that
month Douglas had sent his mother and the widow of the late
earl with an offer of personal homage to Henry VI; and now
he took the opportunity of formally renouncing his allegiance
to the King of Scots. Under cover of night a letter full of
defiance and abuse, and bearing the seals of Douglas, Ormond,
and Hamilton, was affixed to the door of the hall where the
Estates met. The Parliament, however, proceeded with its
deliberations, and in its session of fifteen days took decided
measures for the peace of the country The slaughter of
Douglas was justified on the ground that he had renounced his
allegiance and was a proved traitor; the Earl of Crawford was
attainted; while, as a reward for their loyalty, Sir James Crichton, the Chancellor's eldest son, was made Earl of Moray; Sir
George Crichton, the Admiral, Earl of Caithness; and Lord
Hay, Earl of Erroll. Most important of all its resolutions,
however, was the summons for the immediate muster of an
army on Pentland Muir, in the neighbourhood of Edinburgh.

An army to the number of 30,000 men duly met on Pentland Muir, and with the king at its head marched into the
domains of the Douglas. According to the chronicler, who
records the expedition, its performances did little credit to its
leader. Marching by way of Peebles, Selkirk, and Dumfries,
it did as much harm to friends as foes, destroying grain and

1444 and July 3rd, 1445. *The Records of Aboyne,* p. 383. (New Spalding
Club.)

[1] About this time, also, John, Earl of Ross, was giving trouble in the
north; but apparently his doings had no connection with the murder of
Douglas. But this must remain uncertain.

grass wherever it passed. Yet in its main object the expedition
was signally successful. On the 28th of August Douglas signed
an "appointment" in conjunction with Hamilton, in which he
made his unconditional submission to the king   In this document he leaves it with James and his queen to restore to him
the earldom of Wigton and the lordship of Stewarton ; under-
takes to seek no revenge on any concerned in his brother's
death and to form no alliance prejudicial to his sovereign ; and
promises to do his utmost in discharge of his office as Warden
of the Marches[1].

If the reconciliation was shortlived, it had at first the
appearance of cordiality.   James at least seemed to show that
he had laid aside all suspicions and fears of his formidable
subject   With his express consent Douglas obtained a dispensation (February 26, 1453) to marry his brother's
widow, the Fair Maid of Galloway, thus strength-   1453
ening his titles to his lands in that province   Later in the
same year James gave another apparent proof of his confidence
in the earl's good faith.   On the 18th of April he appointed
him a commissioner to England to treat regarding a truce.   It
would seem, however, that Douglas did not return the confidence of his master. While in England he dealt a stroke which
in view of future contingencies was wholly in his own interest
and against that of James.   On his special petition Malise
Graham, Earl of Strathearn, who for twenty-five years had been
a hostage for the ransom of James I, was permitted to return
to Scotland.   The presence of Graham in the country could
be productive only of mischief   Against the House of Stewart

---

[1] In the Laing Collection of Charters about to be published under the
editorship of the Rev. Mr Anderson of the Register House there is an
interesting document connected with this expedition of James against
Douglas.   It is an instrument bearing that in the tent of the Chancellor
Crichton at Corhead on 18th July, 1452, his lands were regranted to
Alexander Cunningham of Kilmaurs on his resigning them into the hands
of James   I have to thank Mr Anderson for calling my attention to this
document

he had every reason to feel all the hatred of which he was
capable[1].   James I had deprived him of his earldom and condemned him to exile during the best part of his life.   In the
eyes of some, moreover, Graham as a representative of the
second family of Robert II had a better right to the throne
than the reigning house.   In effecting his return to Scotland,
therefore, Douglas must have known that he was strengthening
his own hands in the event of a renewed contest with the crown
In the same month (July) in which Graham was liberated,
Douglas was in all probability the cause of serious trouble on
the west coast.   In May he had paid a visit to the young Lord
of the Isles in Knapdale, which in the opinion of the country
boded no good.   Within a month men were left in little doubt
as to the meaning of the conference.   Donald Balloch (of
whom we have already heard), cousin-german of the Lord of the
Isles[2], with a fleet of a hundred galleys, fell upon Inverkip in
Renfrewshire, harried the island of Arran, demolished the castle
of Brodick, and exacted heavy tribute from the inhabitants.

James could hardly have been ignorant of these doings of
Douglas, yet two years elapsed before the sword was again
drawn between them.   Of the immediate occasion of the contest we have no authentic record.   In the relations of the two
parties, however, we have the adequate explanation of everything that now followed.   To the king it must have become
more and more evident that Scotland could not contain himself
and the Douglases   So strongly was this borne in upon him
that according to Major he had at one time serious thoughts of
withdrawing from the country.   Douglas, on his side, had
many reasons for doubting the good faith of the king, and for
seeking revenge against his house   James had slain his eldest
brother, and deprived another of the Earldom of Moray ; and
the queen now held his own lands of Wigton and Stewarton.
In view of these past relations Douglas must have known that
James only waited the opportunity of crushing himself and his

_____
[1] See above, p. 214.   [2] See above, p. 214.

family once and for all. To all these provocations to rebellion against his sovereign was added the encouragement he received from the Yorkist faction in England, with whom he had long been in communication. At the period at which we have arrived—the spring of 1455—the York-   1455 ists had lost their temporary supremacy, and were about to break into the revolt which ended in their triumph at St Albans, the first battle of the Wars of the Roses (May 22nd). Since their last trial of strength, it may be added, Douglas and James had both lost powerful supporters—the Tiger Earl of Crawford having died in 1453, the Chancellor Crichton and his brother the admiral in 1454. It remained, therefore, to be tried on which side the greater prudence and resources now actually lay.

In the beginning of March James opened the campaign with a vigour that swept all before it. Having demolished the castle of Inveravon, he hastened to Glasgow, and gathering a force of Westland men and Highlanders, he carried fire and sword into Douglasdale, Avondale, and the lands of Lord Hamilton. Returning to Edinburgh, he collected another army with which he marched into Ettrick Forest, and wrought similar destruction. Douglas's castle of Abercorn was the next object of his attack; but so strong was the place that the month of April was consumed before it surrendered. The energetic action of James appears to have struck his enemies with dismay. Douglas himself with four or five companions made haste to cross the Border. His kinsman, Lord Hamilton, did what he could to procure assistance in England, but at this moment the Yorkists had their own battles to fight, and had no strength to spare. Despairing of his cause, Hamilton took a step of which we shall afterwards see the notable result. In the guise of a suppliant he appeared before James at Aber- corn[1], and though for the time he was committed to Roslin

---

[1] The story told by Boece of the meeting of the armies of Douglas and the king on the banks of the Carron has no support in any contemporary authority.

Castle, he was assured of safety and favour. The adherents of Douglas, however, were not yet crushed. In Ewisdale his three brothers, the Earls of Ormond and Moray, and Douglas of Balveny, still held together and made destructive inroads into the neighbouring country. But their career was speedily checked. On the 18th of May the king's troops came up with them at Arkinholm, now partly covered by the town of Langholm, and gained a decisive advantage. The Earl of Moray fell on the field; Ormond being taken suffered the death of a traitor; and Balveny sought refuge in England. The victory of Arkinholm was followed by the destruction of the castles of Strathavon, Douglas, and others—the fortress of Threave, the strongest in Galloway, alone continuing to hold out against the king[1]. Built by Archibald the Grim on an island in the Dee, Threave defied for some months all the forces brought against it; but with its fall the triumph of James was complete. Even while the siege was proceeding the law had taken its course against the doomed family. On the 10th of June a Parliament held in Edinburgh attainted the great earl himself, and two days later a similar decree was pronounced against his mother, his brother Archibald the "pretended Earl of Moray," and Douglas of Balveny. Another Parliament convened in August gave the final blow to the House of Douglas. Their estates were either attached to the crown or bestowed on such nobles as had aided in their overthrow; and it was stringently forbidden to harbour any of their name. In view of the ill use to which the Douglases had put their powers, the office of March Warden was declared to be no longer hereditary and its privileges were largely curtailed.

The great achievement of James II was the suppression of the House of Douglas: of the five years that remained to him there are few events of importance to relate. We know enough, however, to conclude that he reigned with vigour and prudence.

---

[1] Douglas made a nominal surrender of Threave to Henry VI for which he received an annuity of £500.

As will afterwards be seen, the records of his Parliament show that he had all the interest of his father in the social well-being of his people. From casual entries in the Exchequer Rolls we also learn that he was indefatigable in visiting the various parts of his kingdom. He made it his special aim to conciliate his great nobles, and during the remainder of his reign he appears to have had no further trouble from any of them. By tact and timely concession he even succeeded in attaching to his interests that young Lord of the Isles who had conspired with Douglas in Knapdale.

It was in his relations with England that James found most trouble during the last five years of his reign. Of his treatment by that country throughout his struggle with the Douglases he had good grounds for complaint. All through that struggle Douglas had received encouragement from England, and now after his overthrow he was entertained at the English court, and was nominally in receipt of an annuity of £500. Besides these grounds of complaint there were other reasons that now induced James to begin open hostilities. Roxburgh Castle and Berwick were still in English hands, and he owed it to his country to recover them. The time, moreover, was opportune. During the spring and summer of 1455 England was distracted by the quarrel of York and Lan- 1455 caster; and in similar circumstances the predecessors of James had often found their opportunity. Shortly after the battle of St Albans (May 22), indeed, and before the final overthrow of the Douglases, he had made an unsuccessful attempt to possess himself of Berwick. It had been told him that the town was so carelessly guarded that it might be surprised by a sudden attack. On his army approaching the walls, however, the enemy was found to be fully prepared for its reception. An Englishman, then in Scotland under a safe-conduct, had broken his pledge, and carried to his countrymen the news of James's intention.

Baffled in this enterprise, James did not abandon his hostile purpose; and an insulting letter from England (July 26) must have whetted his desire for revenge[1]. To gratify his desire he left no stone unturned. In November he sent ambassadors to Charles VII with proposals for a simultaneous attack on Calais and Berwick; but the suggestion did not fall in with the interests of France. The following year (1456) **1456** James on his own account took active steps against his enemy. After some fruitless attempts at negotiation, he led an army to the Border with the intention of entering Northumberland. On the banks of the Cale, the eastmost tributary of the Teviot, he was met by ambassadors from England who by a "fraudulent promise" persuaded him to retrace his steps. Discovering that he had been cheated, James within twenty days returned with a greater force than before, and for six days and nights harried the north of Northumberland. An army sent against him under the Duke of York and the Earl of Salisbury effected nothing through the dissensions of its leaders.

In fresh communications with Charles VII James still urged him to make common cause against England; but Charles would neither join in open war nor supply the Scottish **1457** king with arms or money. In 1457 the temporary restoration of Henry VI disposed James to other counsels. It was with the Yorkists who had made a tool of Douglas that he had a special quarrel: with the Lancastrians he had on the whole been in friendly relations from the beginning. Accordingly, on the 6th of July a truce was concluded between the two countries which was to last till July 6, 1459, by land, and till July 28, 1459, by sea. If we may believe one authority[2], the truce was broken by England in

[1] In a Charter, dated Peebles, July 12, 1456, James mentions that he has granted remission to all his lieges and subjects who had lately been with his army at the Water of *Calne.*

[2] MS. of John Law in the Library of the University of Edinburgh. See Tytler, *Hist. of Scotland,* IV. 145 (Edit. 2nd).

October of 1458. At that time the Yorkists were again in the ascendant, and in the interests of the Douglases a strong force was sent into Annandale. At Lochmaben, however, it was encountered by the Scots and utterly routed—600 of the English being slain and 1500 captured. Another revolution in England at length engaged James in the enterprise which was to be his last. On the 10th of July, 1460, the victory of the Yorkists at Northampton placed Henry VI in their hands and gave them the predominance in the country. As it was with Henry alone that James had been in friendly relations, he now considered himself free to take what steps he pleased against the victorious faction in England. At this moment, James was specially prepared for hostilities on a large scale, and he decided to seize the opportunity of recovering the long lost castle of Roxburgh. Towards the end of July he led southwards a great army, equipped with all the warlike implements of the age, and prepared to lay siege to that stronghold. As the accounts of the kingdom show, James had taken special interest in the cannon known as bombards, which had begun to play an important part in warlike operations, and on this expedition he had several of these with him. On Sunday, the 3rd of August[1], while watching one of these cannons in company with the Earl of Angus, the piece exploded—one splinter wounding the earl, and another all but instantaneously killing the king. In the grounds of Floors Castle, the spot is still shown where he is said to have fallen.

At his death James was only in his 30th year, yet he had proved himself one of the most vigorous and capable of Scottish kings. His slaughter of the Douglas, like the similar deed of Bruce, is the one act recorded of him that betrayed folly and passion. In his subsequent career, as in that of Bruce, it is precisely the combination of caution and enterprise that enabled him to cope with difficulties that would have

1460

---

[1] According to some authorities, the third Sunday of August.

overwhelmed a weaker king. It is when we compare his conduct with that of his son in similar circumstances that we realize his superiority as a ruler of men. Compared even with his more distinguished father, he appears to have had the advantage of uniting equal vigour with a higher tact and a more conciliatory temper. In his struggle with the Douglases he had a more difficult task than any that fell to James I, and at the close of his reign he left all classes of his people happier and more contented than he had found them.

The mere record of the chief events of James's reign may easily mislead us as to the real state of the country. The insubordination of such vassals as the Earls of Douglas, Crawford, and Ross, seriously interfered with the administration of the law, and their retainers were a frequent terror to peace-loving subjects. When we compare Scotland at its worst, however, with contemporary England and France, it does not seem that the country as a whole was more unhappy than its neighbours. In England and France law was not more successfully enforced; the barons and their vassals gave as much trouble to their kings; and the disbanded soldiers of the Hundred Years' War (in France known by the significant name of *Écorcheurs*) inflicted miseries on the people beyond anything that is recorded of the Wolf of Badenoch or the Tiger Earl. But we have conclusive proof that the subjects of James II had both the will and the opportunity to cultivate the arts of peace and even to attain to a degree of luxury that seemed to call for repression rather than encouragement. Alike from the Exchequer Rolls and from Parliamentary legislation we derive the picture of a society energetic, intelligent, and eager to keep its place in the community of nations.

It is to the years when James himself actually reigned that the most important legislative enactments belong. Most notable of all his Acts in its practical bearings was the appropriation of lands to the crown by the Parliament of August, 1455. On the ground that the poverty of the crown implied the poverty of the people, this Parliament sought with all its might to guard against such an evil in the future. James I had laid his hands freely on the estates of his barons, but in this he was far outdone by his son, whose appropriations, however, were at the expense of proved traitors to their country. After declaring that the whole customs which had been in the hands of James I at his death belonged of right to his successor, the Act in question proceeds to enumerate the various lands that were thenceforth to be inalienably annexed to the crown. The list is a long one, but in view of subsequent events it is of special interest and importance. The lands appropriated are as follow: Ettrick Forest, the lordship of Galloway, the castle of Edinburgh with the lands of Balincrief and Gosford, the castle of Stirling with the neighbouring crown lands, the castle of Dunbarton with the lands of Cardross and Rosneath; the earldom of Fife with Falkland Palace; the earldom of Strathearn; the lordship of Brechin; the castles and lordships of Inverness and Urquhart, and Red Castle with the lordships in Ross that pertained to it[1].

Next in interest and importance to this Act is one that was passed in the Parliament of January, 1450, though, in this case as in the other, legislation proved of little avail to cure the evil at which it was aimed. "For the safety and favour of the poor people who labour the ground" it was enacted that their leases should hold good though the lands leased should change owners. Long after the passing of this Act, as Major complains, precarious leases in Scotland were at once a grievance to the small farmers and a serious drawback to the prosperity of the country.

The administration of justice had often engaged the attention of previous kings; but to the reign of James II belongs an Act which gave a precision to legal machinery that had hitherto been unknown in Scotland. In the Parliament of

---

[1] Certain minor domains have been omitted. For the correct text of the Act see *Exchequer Rolls*, vol. VI. p. cxlvii.

March, 1458, it was enacted that a Court or Committee, consisting of nine persons representing the clergy, nobles, and burghs, should meet twice in the year for the administration of justice in Edinburgh, Perth, and Aberdeen   Of the efficiency of this Court and of its subsequent developments there will be occasion to speak in connection with James's immediate successors

The miscellaneous social legislation of James's reign gives us an interesting glimpse into the life of the time.   The sumptuary laws, especially, may convince us that in spite of English raids, the feuds of nobles, and the miscarriage of justice, all classes of the people had both the leisure and the disposition to attend to the decoration of life.   The whole realm, in each estate—so runs an Act of March 1458—is greatly impoverished through sumptuous clothing both of men and women, and in special within burghs and commons to landward.   To cure this formidable evil the following restrictions among others are imposed on the king's lieges : in burghs only persons in dignity (such as aldermen and bailies) and their wives are to wear clothes of silk and costly scarlet and the fur of martens, women are to wear short kerchiefs with little hoods as is the custom in Flanders, England, and other countries ; women are not to wear tails "of unbecoming magnitude" except on holidays , on working-days labourers are to restrict themselves to clothes of gray and white, on holidays to light blue or green or red ; women going to kirk or market must muffle their faces under pain of the escheat of their kerchiefs.

From the following miscellaneous enactments we may infer what were the main national interests in the reign of James II. On pain of having their ears nailed to a tree, all sorners, masterful beggars with horses and hounds, pretended fools, bards, and other such runners-about, are commanded to desist from their practices , under pain of treason no poisons of any kind are to be imported into the country , a system of beacon fires from the east Border to Stirling is to be arranged so as to give effective warning of any invasion from England; freeholders, spiritual and temporal, are to plant woods, hedges, and broom in all convenient places; wild fowl "fit for the sustenance of man" are to be carefully preserved; six pennies are to be paid for every fox's head, he that slays a wolf is to have a penny from every householder in the parish; every tree from which the young of birds of prey are allowed to escape is to be forfeited to the king with the alternative of a fine of five shillings[1].

The foundation of Glasgow University by Bishop Turnbull in 1451 is a further proof that the country was not wholly preoccupied with its own miseries. At the same time, it would appear that the new university did not meet a real demand in the country. For more than a century after its foundation its students were so few and its endowments so scanty that it was permanently on the verge of extinction. But between the sees of St Andrews and Glasgow there was a traditional rivalry, and now that St Andrews had a university, it was incumbent on Glasgow to possess one also. In spite of the advantages now offered them at home, however, Scottish students still flocked to the continental universities, and specially to Paris, whence they returned with a prestige of learning and experience which they could not have acquired in their own country.

---

[1] We have an interesting description of Scotland at this period by the English Chronicler, John Hardyng, who visited the country shortly after the death of James II His description was written to serve as an itinerary to Edward IV in view of an invasion of Scotland. As Hardyng spent about three years and a half in the country he speaks with real knowledge of what he writes. From his description we learn that wherever the soil permitted, the Scots had assiduously and successfully applied themselves to its cultivation. See my *Early Travellers in Scotland*, p. 16.

CHAPTER VI.

JAMES III, 1460—1488.

English Kings.		French Kings.	
Henry VI	... 1422—1461	Louis XI	... 1461—1483
Edward IV	... 1461—1483	Charles VIII	... 1483—1498
Edward V	... 1483		
Richard III	... 1483—1485		
Henry VII	... 1485—1509		

At the close of the reign of James II Scotland enjoyed a happiness and prosperity which she had not known since the last days of Robert Bruce; and if a king of equal capacity had succeeded him the next quarter of a century might have presented a very different page in Scottish history. Carried out with equal ability, the policy of James I and James II would have left the country where France and England found themselves at the close of the 15th century—with a despotic monarch, a powerless nobility, and a consolidated kingdom. When the kingdom passed from the hands of James III in 1488, the nobility had reached the height of their power and audacity, and the crown was as impotent as it had been during the reigns of Robert II and Robert III. Yet in a policy which aimed at checking his barons and fostering the commons, James had advantages beyond those of his two predecessors. By the wholesale confiscation of lands during the two preceding reigns the crown had now attained a predominance against which no single subject could hope to contend

with success. The overthrow of the great house of Douglas
was a lesson which only the singular weakness and folly of the
king could make men forget. The condition of England
during the whole of James's reign would have brought another
advantage to a ruler of ability: during his reign of twenty-
eight years James had no fewer than five contemporaries in
England; and the position of each of them rendered it for the
most part more prudent to cultivate the friendship of Scotland
than to attempt to subdue her. The opening years of James's
reign afford convincing proof of the advantages with which it
began. During the first five years of his minority the country
was mainly administered by Kennedy, bishop of St Andrews,
and his administration was distinguished by notable successes
both at home and abroad. It was with the actual reign of
James himself that the troubles and disasters of his reign
began; and his tragic end was but the natural result of a
feeble and exasperating rule which alienated all classes of his
subjects by its manifest disregard for the true interests of the
country. Materials are lacking for a detailed narrative of
James's conduct, but the merest outline of events leaves us in
little doubt of its character and tendency. The number and
variety of the troubles that overtook him must have been due
to his own incompetence rather than to mere ill-fortune.

On the death of James II those responsible for the government of the country acted with unanimity and decision. As
had often been proved in the past, it was of the highest importance for the public peace that there should be as brief an
interval as possible between the death of one king and the
coronation of his successor. James II fell on Sunday the 3rd of
August; his widow and his heir, now at the close of his ninth
year[1], were in Kelso on the 8th; and on Sunday the 10th the
coronation took place in the Abbey in presence of the bishops

---

[1] This appears to have been his true age. Cf. *Accounts of the Lord
Treasurer of Scotland*, edited by Dr Dickson, p. xxxvii, note.

and chief nobility of the country. Under their new king the Scottish leaders carried out with vigour the enterprise in which his father had been engaged at the time of his death. Roxburgh Castle was captured and destroyed, so that of Scottish territory Berwick alone remained in the hands of the English. As the condition of England now presented the most tempting opportunity, they pursued their success still further. Crossing the Tweed, they captured and dismantled the castle of Wark, at the same time ravaging the neighbouring country[1].

In these achievements the leaders of the Scots appear to have been engaged till near the close of 1460, and as yet there had been no opportunity for holding an assembly of the Estates. Events both at home and abroad, however, made it urgent that they should meet at the earliest date possible. In the outlying parts of the country the usual advantage was being taken of the embarrassments of a new reign. Either at the close of this year or at the beginning of the next, "the first slaughter" under the new king took place. John Keir of Lorn, a nephew of the redoubtable Donald Balloch, imprisoned his brother in the island of Kerrera with the intention of seizing his heritage. The cousin of both brothers, however, was Colin, Earl of Argyle, who fell upon the offending John, burnt his ships, and slew nearly a hundred of his followers[2].

At length, on February 22, 1461, the first Parliament of James III assembled in the castle of Edinburgh, now its usual place of meeting. Unfortunately the record of its doings has not been preserved, and of contemporary notices we have only the scanty details of the *Auchinleck Chronicle.* In the difficulty of the matters with which it had to deal we have perhaps a partial explanation of the delay in calling it together. Three pressing questions had to be settled if its work was to be done thoroughly—the choice of a regent, the appointment of a guardian for the king, and

1461

---

[1] *Auchinleck Chronicle.*
[2] *Ibid.*

the future policy with regard to England. On all three questions there were serious differences among the chief persons in the country, and during the sitting of the Estates there was imminent danger of bloodshed. At the head of one party was the queen-mother, Mary of Gueldres, at the head of the other Kennedy, bishop of St Andrews, and George Douglas, fourth earl of Angus[1]. Apparently the queen-mother had the stronger following, for at the close of the session the chief power in the country was left in her hands. No regent appears to have been appointed; but the king was committed to her charge, and she was able to place the castles of Dunbar, Edinburgh, Stirling, and Blackness, in the keeping of friends of her own. The Privy Seal she gave to James Lindsay, Provost of Lincluden, a person specially obnoxious to the opponents of the queen[2].

During the next few years the history of Scotland is mainly the history of its relations to the two factions which were now contending for the mastery of England. The policy of James II had been to give his support to the Lancastrians, and it was partly in their interest that he had engaged in the enterprise in which he met his end. This policy the party of Kennedy[3] and Angus were prepared to further to the best of

---

[1] New light has been thrown on the first three years of James III's reign by a despatch of Bishop Kennedy to Louis XI, discovered in the Bibliothèque National, Paris, and published by the Société de l'Histoire de France in the *Anchiennes Croniques d'Engleterre*, par Jehan de Wavrin, Tome III p. 164 et seq. The despatch was written between March 6 and April 20, 1464. What the despatch proves is that Kennedy strenuously supported Henry VI, while Mary of Gueldres then favoured the Yorkists, and that there was imminent danger of civil war between their respective adherents. Buchanan had affirmed that this division had existed, but Pinkerton treated his statement as "fables," and subsequent historians have followed Pinkerton. On certain other points in his account of James III Buchanan also proves to be right, though on these very points he has been severely taxed by Pinkerton and Tytler.

[2] *Auchinleck Chronicle.*

[3] Kennedy's Despatch

their power, and for a time it had also the support of the queen-mother. The occasion soon came when the Lancastrians needed all the help the Scots could give. In January 1461, before the meeting of the Estates, Margaret of Anjou with her son Edward appeared in Scotland with the object of obtaining men and supplies. She was hospitably received by both parties in the state. At Lincluden Abbey, near Dumfries, she was entertained by Mary of Gueldres, and during a stay of ten or twelve days it is recorded that three bolls of salt and three pipes of white wine of Poitou were consumed by the company[1]. To secure the support of Mary of Gueldres for the House of Lancaster Kennedy proposed a marriage between Prince Edward and James's sister, the Lady Mary[2], but the proposals did not bear fruit, and meanwhile Margaret was called to England, where further misfortunes awaited her. She was no sooner gone than the Yorkists took steps to detach the Scots from her interests. As soon as the Earl of Warwick, the mainstay of that party, had heard of her visit to Lincluden, he communicated with Philip, Duke of Burgundy, the uncle of Mary of Gueldres. Friendly as he was to the House of York, Philip at once despatched to the Scottish court Louis of Bruges, Lord of la Gruythuyse. So successful was the mission of this personage that thenceforward the Scottish queen ceased to favour the House of Lancaster and placed herself in opposition to Kennedy and the lords who sought to maintain the policy of James II[3].

But the course of events in England gave the advantage to the party of Kennedy. In the spring of 1461 a

1461

succession of battles decided for a time the fate of England. On March 27 the Lancastrians were routed at Ferrybridge, and two days later at Towton. For the moment the fortunes of Henry VI were desperate, and with his consort

[1] *Exchequer Rolls*, vol. VII. pp. xxxv. 8.
[2] Kennedy's Despatch.
[3] De Wavrin, II. 302; Buchanan.

and a company of his friends he sought an asylum in Scotland[1]. To ensure a favourable reception he bestowed a gift on the Scots which would confirm the ascendency of Kennedy and Angus. On the 25th of April[2] Berwick, once the key of Scotland and its most flourishing city, was placed in their hands as a proof of his gratitude and a pledge of his future good faith. With the exception of a few brief intervals Berwick had been in the hands of the English since its capture by Edward I, and its recovery was a national triumph. The Scots were not slow to prove their gratitude for this great acquisition. For more than a year the English royal family were entertained, first in Linlithgow Palace and subsequently in the Dominican Convent in Edinburgh. To aid Henry's cause in England also, they crossed the Border with a large army and laid siege to Carlisle in the month of June. But the enterprise proved unsuccessful. Attacked by Lord Montagu, brother of the Earl of Warwick, they were compelled to raise the siege, and to retire to their own country with a loss of 6000 men[3].

In the divided state of England it was of high importance to Edward IV, who had been crowned on June 28, that at least the whole nation of the Scots should not combine against him; and in the condition of their own country he found the opportunity of holding them in check. The queen-mother, we have seen, though circumstances had gone against her, was using what influence she possessed on the side of York. But there was another personage in Scotland who might serve Edward's purpose more effectively than Mary of Gueldres. This was that John, Earl of Ross and Lord of the Isles, who had been won over by James II and whom that king had left a law-abiding subject. In the opportunity of the nation's divided counsels, however, he was showing signs of restlessness which portended coming mischief. In this potentate, therefore,

---

[1] *Paston Letters*, II. 46 (ed. Gairdner).

[2] Ramsay, *Lancaster and York*, II. 274.

[3] *Paston Letters*, II. 13.

Edward IV found a tool whom he could use effectively against Kennedy and his party[1]. He had at hand, also, one who by his past history was well-fitted to approach Ross successfully—that exiled Earl of Douglas who had been crushed by the energy of James II Accordingly, in June of 1461 Douglas and his brother of Balveny were despatched to Scotland to open negotiations with Ross As the sequel was to show, their mission was attended with complete success. On the 19th of October Edward IV promised protection to every Scot who would assist Douglas in his attempt to conquer the country. In the beginning of the following year (February 13) a treaty was signed at Westminster which was to settle the fate of Scotland[2]. By this arrangement Ross and his kinsman, Donald Balloch, who in the two preceding reigns had proved himself such an unruly subject, were to subdue the country beyond the Forth and divide it between them, while Douglas on the conquest of the south was to be reinstated in all his possessions In return for his support in the achievement of these ends Edward was to be recognized as Lord Paramount of Scotland, and pending the accomplishment of their schemes he was to pay liberal pensions to his three prospective vassals. In what notable results these negotiations were to issue we shall presently see.

1461

1462

While he was thus laying a train with the Lord of the Isles, Edward had not been neglecting his other ally in Scotland, Mary of Gueldres. The prevailing party in the country was that which favoured Lancaster ; but the departure (April 2, 1462) of the indefatigable Margaret of Anjou left the Scottish queen at greater liberty to work out her schemes. In the very month that Margaret sailed for France Mary and her son met the Earl of Warwick at

1462

---

[1] While the young lords of Scotland favoured York, the old lords favoured Lancaster. *Paston Letters*, II. 111

[2] Rymer, *Fœdera*, XI. 484.

Dumfries, where a proposal was made to her which she was not the person to reject. In the interest of the two kingdoms it was suggested by Warwick that a marriage should be arranged between her and the English king[1]. Though nothing came of this proposal, the Scottish queen persevered in her approaches to the Yorkists. In June she met the Earl of Warwick at Carlisle with the result that Douglas was commanded to abstain from further forays into Scotland, and was sent to the Abbey of St Albans "a sorrowful and a sore rebuked man[2]." To give effect to these negotiations with Warwick, Mary of Gueldres desired a Parliament to meet at Stirling ; but through the influence of Kennedy it was prevented from assembling[3]. So effective, however, were the measures she had taken that by the autumn ambassadors were coming and going between the Scottish government and the English king Nevertheless, Henry VI was still an honoured guest in Scotland, and the events of the following year were to prove that the strongest party in the kingdom was still Lancastrian in its sympathies.

Meanwhile Edward's intrigues with John of the Isles had effected a crisis in the Highlands. In October of 1461 John had assumed the kingly style, and had despatched ambassadors to England on his own account. The result of the embassy, we have seen, was the treaty of February 1462, in which Edward assigned to Ross and Donald Balloch all the country to the north of the Forth. At once, it appears, John took upon him the functions as well as the style of a monarch. To the inhabitants of the sheriffdoms and burghs of Inverness and Nairn he issued injunctions commanding them to yield obedience to his son Angus, whom he had appointed his lieutenant. The crown rents and customs were to be paid to himself, and penalties were threatened against the refractory. In true kingly fashion, also, he granted respites and remissions

[1] Kennedy's Despatch; William of Worcester.
[2] *Paston Letters*, II. 110, 111.
[3] Kennedy's Despatch.

at pleasure within the bounds of the above-named districts. When the news of these doings reached the authorities, John was duly summoned to appear at the next meeting of the Estates ; but he knew his own strength and the difficulties of the government, and contumaciously refused to recognize any power higher than his own.   He was one day to learn that he had only postponed the reckoning that awaited him[1].

The events of 1463 proved that the Scottish party favourable to the Lancastrians was still in the ascendant.   In September of the preceding year

1463

Margaret of Anjou, with a force of some 800 men, led by a famous French captain, Pierre de Brézé, had landed on the coast of Northumberland in the hope of a rising in her favour. Her only success, however, was the capture of the castles of Alnwick, Bamborough, and Dunstanborough—the last two of which were recovered by Edward before the close of the year. In the beginning of 1463 the Scots took up Margaret's battles, though with results so little encouraging that they were eventually led to consider the prudence of a change in their policy Through their aid, indeed, Margaret recovered two castles in Northumberland ; but they must have seen that her cause was desperate   In England it was clear that she had little support, and no foreign aid was likely to turn the scale in her favour. Moreover, they had their own troubles at home which required all the vigilance of those in authority.   John of the Isles was bidding defiance to the government; the exiled Douglas, all through the spring and summer, was again at his old work of harrying the West Marches; and a threatened invasion by Edward himself so alarmed the nation that Bishop Kennedy, in order to put spirit into his countrymen, was preparing to head an army in company with the young king[2]   The defeat of

---

[1] *Auchinleck Chronicle*; *Acts of the Parliament of Scotland*, II. 109 Boece has a characteristic story regarding this rebellion of Ross, which was repeated by the historians who succeeded him.

[2] Kennedy's Despatch.   According to the Auchinleck Chronicle the

Douglas, however, and the capture and death of his brother of
Balveny relieved the Scots from what had been a pressing
danger.   Two events of the year must also have disposed the
Scots to come to terms with the Yorkists   The Earl of Angus,
who had been an ardent supporter of the Lancastrians, and
whom Margaret had bound to her by the promise of an
English dukedom, died in the spring of 1463; and in the
autumn a truce was concluded between Edward IV and
Louis XI—the first that had been made between France and
England for fourteen years[1]. In these circumstances the
course of the Scots was clear; and at the instance of Kennedy
himself they entered into negotiations with Edward IV.   In
December certain envoys from Scotland met him at York with
the result that a truce was arranged which was to last till the
31st of October, 1464[2]

The close of the year 1463 saw Bishop Kennedy the chief
person in the country   The Earl of Angus had died in the
spring, and on the 1st of December[3] his death was followed
by that of the queen-mother   She was not more than thirty
years old, and had she lived a few years longer the reign of her
son might have had a different course and a different ending.

following arrangement was made with regard to the king and his mother—
"the king suld cum be him self and his, and the quene be hir self and
hirris, bot the king suld ay remane with the quene, bot scho suld nocht
intromit with his profettis, bot allonerlie with his person." Apparently
this settlement was made between March 1, 1461, and July 1462 (*Exchequer
Rolls*, vol VII pp. xlvi, xlvii).   The king could not have been long in his
mother's charge, however   From a document recently published we learn
that against the Estates Lord Hailes had carried him off from Kennedy in the
interest of the queen. (Philippe de Cran to Louis XI, July 15, 1463,
De Wavrin, III 163.)   Buchanan mentions this fact; but Pinkerton derides
the statement as one of his "fables"   Lord Hailes, it should be said, was
one of the reputed paramours of Mary of Gueldres.

[1] From Kennedy's Despatch we learn that this truce greatly disturbed
the Scots lords who had favoured Lancaster.

[2] Kennedy's Despatch; Rymer, *Foedera*, XI. 509, 510

[3] This appears to be the real date   *Exchequer Rolls*, vol liv p. VII

After the death of her husband her conduct had not been discreet[1], but her energetic character had led her to play a considerable part in public affairs, and it was she who had headed the party known as "the young lords," which was opposed to that of "the old lords" who followed Angus and Kennedy. By the magnificent Trinity College Church and Hospital[2], erected by her in fulfilment of the desire of her husband, her name was long preserved in Edinburgh.

For about a year and a half Kennedy managed the kingdom, and according to the unanimous testimony of Scottish historians he discharged his trust with equal prudence and good fortune. The best testimony to the wisdom of his rule is that no sensational events are recorded of it. With Edward IV the good relations which had prompted the truce of December 1463 remained undisturbed. Only for a moment in the beginning of the following year was there danger of a breach. The Duke of Albany, next brother of the king, was seized by an English ship while on his way home from a visit to his uncle in Gueldres. On the representation of Kennedy, however, he was at once released, and on the 3rd of June the truce between the two countries was prolonged for fourteen years. So far as Scotland was concerned, the interests of the House of Lancaster no longer conflicted with those of the House of York. In March, 1464, Henry VI had been removed from Scotland by his supporters, who at the subsequent battles of Hedgely Moor and Hexham were so completely broken that Edward IV at length found himself the real master of the country.

In July, 1465[3], died Bishop Kennedy, who with Cardinal Beaton and Archbishop Hamilton completes the list of the

[1] William of Worcester gives this impression as well as the Scottish historians. Annals, *sub anno* 1462.

[2] It stood on the present site of the North British Railway Station.

[3] This is probably the correct date. See *Accounts of the Lord High Treasurer*, I. p. xl, note; *Exchequer Rolls*, VII. p. lvi, note.

great Catholic churchmen of Scotland. By his character and
public deeds, however, he left a very different
memory from that of Beaton or Hamilton.   1465
"Among our fellow-countrymen," says John Major, "I have
found none who has done more signal public service than this
prelate", and the Protestant Buchanan bears similar testimony.
Of Kennedy's public acts three are commemorated by all the
historians—the foundation of St Salvator's College at St
Andrews, the building of a great vessel known as the Bishop's
Barge, and the erection of a magnificent tomb to his own
memory. All three achievements alike filled his contemporaries with wonder. "Through the whole land," says
Bishop Leslie, "the common speaking was that these three
were all of one and the same price, all alike sumptuous."

The loss of Kennedy was not long in being felt. At
Stirling on February 10, 1466, three persons
entered into relations with each other which were   1466
fatal to good order and just government. The three persons,
all men of standing and influence, were Robert Lord Fleming,
Gilbert Lord Kennedy, and Sir Alexander Boyd. Fleming
was a son of that Malcolm Fleming who had suffered death
with the sixth earl of Douglas in 1440, and had been Steward
of the Household of James II; Kennedy was a brother of the
late bishop, and possessed great influence in the west of
Scotland; and Boyd was brother of Robert Lord Boyd of
Kilmarnock, and held the offices of king's instructor in military
exercises and Governor of Edinburgh Castle. In a bond drawn
up between them they pledged themselves to stand by each
other in all quarrels and against all persons. The very qualifi-
cations they made to their bond showed the measure of their
power. In the case of all three there were previous pledges to
other leading persons in the country, and in favour of these
there was to be an exception in the present understanding.
The two important clauses in the document exhibit the spirit
and aims of its authors. Fleming on his part was to leave the

king in the hands of Kennedy and Boyd, while they pledged themselves to put in Kennedy's way any "large thing" that should fall to the crown[1].

A few months later the three confederates found an opportunity of carrying out their schemes In June there was an audit of the royal revenues at Linlithgow, at which the king was present with his chief officers of state. Towards the close of the audit, on the 9th of July, they effected their purpose by one stroke. On the pretext of a hunting-party the king was decoyed from the Palace by Boyd and Fleming and carried off to Edinburgh Castle. For reasons unknown Kennedy offered a show of resistance, and was actually for a time imprisoned in the Castle of Stirling[2]. But the sequel showed that the plot was both deep and wide. On October 9 a Parliament met in Edinburgh Castle, and its doings proved that the Boyds were masters of the situation. On the fifth day of its sitting a curious scene took place which must have been carefully rehearsed beforehand. In presence of the assembled Estates Lord Boyd knelt before the king and besought him to say if his removal from Linlithgow had been carried out against his will. The reply was that everything had been done by the royal consent, and in further proof of Boyd's loyalty he was appointed guardian of the king and his two brothers, and keeper of the royal fortresses[3]. Nor did the honours that fell to the Boyds cease here. The act of attainder which was soon to overtake them shows the extent of territory they contrived to acquire; but the pride of their house reached its limit in the fortunes of Thomas Boyd, eldest son of Lord Boyd. The rapid rise of the family is sufficient proof of their audacity and talent; but in the case of Thomas Boyd we have distinct testimony to the brilliant qualities that led to his ascendency.

[1] This bond is printed in the Notes and Illustrations to vol. v. of Tytler's *Hist. of Scotland*
[2] Buchanan; *Exchequer Rolls*, VII. pp lix, 443, 458.
[3] *Acts of Parl. of Scot.*, II. 85.

In the words of an English contemporary who speaks from personal acquaintance with him, he was "the most courteous, gentlest, wisest, kindest, most companionable, freest, largest, most bounteous knight"... .."the lightest, deliverest, best spoken, fairest archer, devoutest, most perfect, and truest to his lady of all the knights that ever I was acquainted with[1]." Supported by these gifts and graces, the influence of his family did the rest; and in the beginning of 1467 he received the title of Earl of Arran and was married to the Lady Mary, eldest sister of the king. By the grants of land which followed Arran became the first subject in the country; and but for an ill-advised step might have maintained the position which his capacity and his influence seemed to assure him[2].

1467

The ruin of the Boyds is connected with one of the fortunate strokes of policy in Scottish history. James III was now approaching a marriageable age; and it became incumbent on his councillors to find him a suitable consort. At this time, as it happened, exigencies of state pointed to Denmark as the country with which it was advisable to form some close alliance. The "annual" due for the Western Islands had gone on accumulating since the days of James I; and Denmark had on more than one occasion given out threats of insisting on its payment. In 1457 Christian I, king of Denmark, Norway, and Sweden, had appealed to Charles VII of France to use his influence with the defaulting Scots; and in 1460 Charles had suggested that the two countries should make up their quarrel by a marriage between the heir to the Scottish crown and the daughter of Christian. The suggestion was welcomed by both countries; but the death of James II had put a stop to further negotiations. In the Parliament of 1466, however, the question was again raised, and the marriage of the king was discussed in connection with the Norway annual. No

---

[1] *Paston Letters*, III. 47.
[2] *Reg. Mag. Sig.* VII. Nos. 115, 116, 117, 118.

immediate result followed the discussion; but a series of communications from Christian gave the Scots to understand that they must take decided steps to heal the quarrel A certain bishop Tulloch had been seized and imprisoned by the Earl of Orkney, who by other refractory actions had defied his liege lord the king of Norway. It was accordingly in tones of menace that Christian demanded the correction of the noble, and the immediate payment of the Norway debt. Under this pressure the Scots at length took up the matter in earnest In a Parliament held at Stirling in January 1468 it was resolved to send an embassy to Denmark to negotiate a marriage treaty. To defray the expenses of the embassy the barons, clergy, and burghs were to contribute £1000 each; and chief among the envoys was to be the king's brother-in-law, the Earl of Arran The embassy was as successful as could have been desired; and a treaty of marriage between the King of Scots and Margaret, daughter of Christian, was signed on September 8, 1468 As things afterwards went, the Scots found that they had made an excellent bargain For her jointure Margaret was to receive Doune Castle and the Palace of Linlithgow, and in the event of her surviving her husband one-third of the royal revenues. Christian on his part was to give as his daughter's dowry 60,000 florins, of which 10,000 were to be paid before she left Copenhagen, the Orkney Islands to be given in pledge for the rest; while he was to give a full discharge for the Norway annual and all arrears To report these arrangements and to receive further instructions Arran came to Scotland before the close of the year, and in an evil day for himself returned to Norway in the spring of 1469. When the time came for the princess to leave her home, however, Christian found himself in straits Of the 10,000 florins he had undertaken to pay on her departure he could muster only 2000, and as a pledge for the remainder he was forced to give up the Shetland Islands, which,

1468

1468

1469

unredeemed like the Orkneys, have remained a Scottish possession from that day to this[1].   At length, in July, Margaret arrived in Leith, and in the same month the marriage was celebrated with unusual magnificence in the Palace of Holyrood—the king being in his eighteenth year and his bride in her twelfth. Margaret was to play no such part in the country as Mary of Gueldres, but on the other hand her prudence and virtuous living were to endear her to every class of her subjects.

In the crowning act of his embassy the brilliant Arran had no part.   In their sudden rise to such power and place the Boyds had made many enemies; and in the long absence of Arran these had found their opportunity.   By the time he had arrived at Leith with the royal bride the ruin of his house was decreed   From the fate that awaited him, however, he was saved by the devotion of his wife, the Lady Mary   Secretly joining him on board his ship, she warned him of his changed fortunes, and in one of the Danish vessels sailed with him to Copenhagen to the indignation and disgust of her brother the king Two victims still remained—Lord Boyd, the Chamberlain, and his brother, Alexander, James's military tutor; and they were not kept long in suspense.   In November a Parliament, held in Edinburgh, found them guilty of treason in seizing the king at Linlithgow, and of retaining him and his brothers in their power to the detriment of the state.   Forfeiture and sentence of death followed—the elder Boyd avoiding his fate by flight to England, where shortly afterwards he died at Alnwick[2].   The fall of the Boyds removed three dangerous subjects, but it also brought a direct increase of strength to the crown in the confiscation of the chief part of their great domains, which were attached inalienably to the inheritance of the king's eldest son.   To what extent James himself was responsible for the ruin of his former favourites it is impossible to say.

[1] *Torfaei Orcades*, pp. 187, 189.   It may here be stated that in February, 1472, Orkney and Shetland were annexed to the crown.

[2] *Acts of the Parl. of Scot.* II. 186, Buchanan.

In a subsequent proceeding, however, we seem to discover the direct expression of his own feeling. Arran and his wife, we have seen, had made their way to Denmark; but on the representation of the King of Scots he was forced to leave that country and to find a home elsewhere. The fortunes of her husband being thus desperate, Mary was induced by the appeals of her royal brother to return to Scotland and to enter into an alliance on which he appears to have set his heart. In the course of a few years[1] she was married to that Lord Hamilton, who in the reign of James II had deserted the cause of the Douglases when their cause had become hopeless, and had thus laid the foundation of the greatness of his house. In the union which he thus eagerly pressed James little dreamt what trouble he was preparing for one of his descendants. From this second marriage of his sister sprang that claim of the Hamiltons to the crown which was to be a permanent source of disturbance to Scotland throughout the reign of Mary Stewart.

It is not till 1472 that we again meet with an event of national importance. On August 17th of that year St Andrews was erected into an archiepiscopal and metropolitan see, with jurisdiction over the whole of Scotland together with Orkney and the Isles. There were excellent reasons why this honour should have been gratifying to the Scottish people. The archbishops of York had never abandoned their claim to supremacy over the Scottish church, and the creation of a metropolitan definitively foreclosed this claim. Even had the Scottish clergy been willing to recognise an English superior the relations of the two countries since the days of Edward I had made it imperative that some other arrangement should be effected in the interests of their church. It would seem, however,

1472

---

[1] Some difficulty exists as to whether the Lady Mary was a widow or a divorced wife when she married Hamilton. The question is discussed by Mr Burnett in the 8th vol. of *Exchequer Rolls*, pp. xlix, et seq.

that the pope's boon was regarded as a doubtful blessing at once by the king, his nobles, and the leading clergy. According to all the historians[1] the reign of James III was marked by a rapid declension both in the morals of the clergy and the government of the church. By the sale of benefices and the appointment of unfit persons to important offices the king and his courtiers gave abundant proof that the good of religion was not very near their heart. In the strange proceedings connected with the new see, therefore, James and his advisers can hardly be credited with a special desire for the spiritual well-being of the national church. The proceedings carry us to the year 1478; but any interest or importance they possess will appear only from a connected narrative.

On the death of Kennedy, bishop of St Andrews, he was succeeded (Nov. 4, 1465) by Patrick Graham, his uterine brother, and a kinsman of the king. From the first Graham had many and powerful enemies, and he consequently betook himself to Rome, where he seems to have made his residence. Without due consultation with the Scottish king and clergy, as was at least alleged against him, he put his case so strongly before the papal court that he had himself made metropolitan of Scotland—the office of nuncio being subsequently conferred on him for the space of three years. When news of Graham's doings reached Scotland, the king, clergy, and courtiers, were alike indignant. So eager, indeed, were the clergy in their opposition that they made a gift of 12,000 marks to the king to quicken his zeal in their cause. As it happened, there was then at the court a person who by his talents, his ambition, and his good graces with the king, was precisely fitted to serve their ends. This was William Scheves, who at the present moment was fulfilling the various functions of king's physician, astrologer, and officer of the wardrobe. Accordingly, on

[1] The Catholic historians Ferrerius and Bishop Leslie as well as the Protestant Buchanan.

Graham's return to Scotland towards the close of 1473, a
phalanx of adversaries, led by Scheves, sought by all the means
in their power to work his ruin. Their triumph was complete.
A papal bull (Jan. 9, 1478), obtained at their instance, declared
him guilty of various crimes against the church, deposed him
from his office, and condemned him to spend the remainder of
his life in religious seclusion. From the materials that have
been preserved it is impossible to speak with certainty of the
real character of these proceedings against the unfortunate
archbishop. As far as James and his courtiers were concerned,
it was their interest, as it had been their policy, to wink at
abuses in the church ; and their opposition to Graham cannot
be regarded as any proof that his conduct deserved reprehen-
sion. As for his principal adversary, Scheves, from the little
we know of him, he appears as something of an adventurer ;
and it raises suspicion of his righteous zeal that he stepped
into the place of his victim[1]. In explanation of the conduct of
the clergy it is affirmed that they objected to one of their own
number being placed over them[2]; yet after the deposition of
Graham we hear of no further complaints against a metropolitan
on this ground. The real character and aims of Graham
himself are equally obscure. The charges adduced against
him in the bull of condemnation raise suspicion alike by the
terms in which they are couched, and by the testimony on
which they are based. In view of all the circumstances, as
they are known to us, there is no improbability in the statement
of Buchanan that Graham was an honest reformer, and the
victim of a rapacious court and a purblind clergy[3].

[1] Scheves had been made Archdeacon of St Andrews, and afterwards
co-adjutor of Graham on the ground of the latter's mental incapacity.

[2] Another reason for their opposition to Graham was that he had come
to Scotland with a commission to raise a tithe of their benefices for a war
against the Turks.

[3] All the authorities regarding the dispute will be found in Robertson's
Concilia Scotiae, pp. cix, et seq.

For several years after the truce of 1464 there was no
serious misunderstanding between Scotland and
England. In 1471, however, there were dis-   1471
turbances on the Borders which demanded the consideration
of both governments. At this date there were special reasons
why Edward IV should wish to be on good terms with the
Scots On the field of Tewkesbury (May 4) he had crushed
the last effort of the Lancastrians, and he was now meditating
a war with France But, as his predecessors had so often
found, to invade France with the possibility of a Scottish war,
was seriously to increase the risks of the enterprise. Accordingly, in August 1471, Edward granted safe-conducts to
commissioners from Scotland to meet representatives of his
own with the object of discussing the late troubles and of
confirming the existing truce At Alnwick in September
and at Newcastle in April of the following year, the way
was prepared for a friendly understanding. In
the beginning of 1473 Edward's desire was still   1473
further quickened for a definitive arrangement with the Scots.
His brother-in-law, Charles the Bold, besought his assistance
in his quarrel with his liege lord, Louis XI of France. The
reply of Edward was that he would willingly give the help
Charles needed, if he could be sure of the Scots. But since
the union of Mary of Gueldres and James II, Burgundy and
Scotland had been in the closest relations, and at the instance
of Duke Charles, the King of Scots agreed to a renewal of the
truce with England (March 25, 1473).

This arrangement could not have been long made before
an appeal came to James which threatened to commit him to
a very different policy. An envoy from Louis XI, one of the
distinguished Scots in France, William de Mennypenny,
seigneur de Concressault[1], brought him a singular offer and
request. On condition of his conquering it, he was offered the

---

[1] Some interesting facts regarding this Mennypenny will be found in
De Wavrin, III. 186, note.

duchy of Britanny, the acquisition of which we know to have been a grand object of Louis's own desire. It would even seem that James had serious thoughts of engaging in the enterprise. But his councillors were wiser than himself. In a Parliament which met at Edinburgh in July he was told that it was impolitic for him to pass out of the realm at that time, and that if he were bent on crossing the sea the only honourable mission he could undertake would be to act as mediator between France and Burgundy[1]

In September of 1473 the articles adopted at Newcastle in the previous March were formally ratified at Alnwick by commissioners from England and Scotland. Yet the relations of the two countries still remained unsatisfactory. In the beginning of the following year it seemed as if the truce had been thrown to the winds. On the 12th of March the great ship built by Bishop Kennedy was wrecked on the coast near Bamborough, and many of those on board were drowned. Among those who escaped was the Abbot of St Colme; but though it was a time of truce those into whose hands he fell would let him go only on the payment of 80 pounds sterling. In the following month a more serious breach of amity seemed imminent. The Duke of Gloucester, brother of Edward IV, was then acting as Warden of the Marches, and the report reached the Scots that he was preparing to invade their country. To meet the enemy their fighting men were ordered to assemble at Lauder; but Gloucester never came, and no actual fighting appears to have taken place. It was evident, however, that if peace was to be preserved, some closer bond must be found to unite the two nations[2]

Fortunately the means were at hand for effecting a permanent understanding. On March 17, 1473[3], a son, afterwards

---

[1] *Duclos*, II. 73, 75.

[2] Ferrerius; *Accounts of the Lord High Treasurer*, I. pp. lv, 49

[3] This is apparently the correct date. See *Accounts of Lord High Treasurer*, I. p. xlv, note.

James IV, had been born to the King of Scots; and it was now proposed that a marriage should be arranged between the infant prince and Cecilia, youngest daughter of Edward IV. Accordingly, a Parliament held in Edinburgh (May 9, 1474) ordained that an embassy should pass to England with the double object of seeking redress for the affair of the Bishop's Barge and of furthering the proposed royal match. As Edward was on the point of carrying out his intended invasion of France, he readily responded to the overtures of the Scots. In October, his ambassadors, charged with the settlement of the union, arrived in Edinburgh; and on the 18th of that month the espousals were contracted in the Low Church of the Greyfriars. The terms of the treaty [October 26] attest that Edward at least was eager for a lasting peace. The marriage was to take place as soon as the Scottish prince reached his majority; for her dowry the princess was to bring 20,000 marks, English money, the payment of which in seventeen instalments was to begin the following February; should the marriage not take place, the money was to be repaid if it exceeded 2,500 marks; in the event of the death of either party, the heir of the King of Scots was to marry another daughter of the King of England; and the truce concluded at Newcastle in 1465 was again confirmed. To leave no grievance on the side of the Scots an indemnity of 500 marks was paid for the breach of truce connected with the Bishop's Barge[1]. Never, it may be said, did an English king concede so much to a King of Scots; but Edward was playing his own game, and time was to show that it was only the circumstances of the moment that constrained him to such an excess of generosity.

The new treaty with England was soon to bring a further substantial benefit to the Scottish crown. That John of the Isles who in 1463 had set the government at defiance was at length to be brought to account. During the twelve years

1474

---

[1] Rymer, *Fœdera*, XI. 820, 825, 836, 850; *Rotuli Scotiae*, II. 446.

that had elapsed since his secret treaty with Edward IV, he had not ceased to bear himself like an independent potentate—his feuds with the Earl of Huntly being an especial source of disturbance. At the meetings of the Estates he never condescended to appear; but on every occasion of their assembly he was careful to send a deputy. In the new relations with England, however, the government found itself in a position to deal more effectively with this restless subject. It is possible, indeed, that the extent of his treason with England may now have been learned for the first time. However this may be, he was now to be taught that unsupported by England he was no match for the King of Scots. On the 16th of October, 1475, he was cited in his castle of Dingwall to appear before the Parliament that was to meet in Edinburgh in the following December. The Parliament met, but John did not appear, and a commission was granted to Colin, Earl of Argyle, to fall upon him with fire and sword[1]. Attacked simultaneously by the Earls of Argyle, Crawford, Athole, and Huntly, his power was speedily broken, and he was induced (July 15, 1476)[2] to place himself at the mercy of the crown. Considering his whole conduct during the present and the preceding reigns, he had no reason to complain of his treatment. On the express intercession of the queen, he was allowed to retain all his possessions with the exception of Knapdale, Kintyre, the castles of Inverness and Nairn, and the Earldom of Ross; and thenceforward he was to sit in Parliament as Lord of the Isles, a title which now for the first time received legal recognition. A formidable subject had thus been crushed, and by the permanent annexation of the Earldom of Ross the crown received a further addition to its now vast domains[3]

1475

1476

---

[1] *Fourth Report of Historical MSS. Commission*, p 487.

[2] In a document dated Edinburgh, July 15, 1476 John gave in his formal submission on the terms offered him by the government

[3] *Accounts of Lord High Treasurer*, I. p 48; *Acts of Parl. of Scot.* II. 109, III, 113.

Till the date we have now reached the reign of James III had been attended by a good fortune which promised to give it a place apart in the annals of the country   The acquisition of Berwick, Roxburgh, Orkney, Shetland, and the advantageous marriage-treaty with England, made up a series of events which few other reigns could boast   From this point onwards, however, the reign of James III was to have a very different fortune. Hitherto, the advisers of James, in whose choice he had little part, had been responsible for the guidance of the country; but James had now passed his twenty-fifth year, and henceforward it is himself who chooses his own councillors and gives its character to the national policy.

It is in the year 1479 that we first hear of those troubles in James's government which were to beset him to the end.   As in the closing struggle of his life,   **1479** so at the beginning, it was those nearest him in blood against whom he found himself in open strife   It is now his two brothers, Alexander, Duke of Albany, and John, Earl of Mar, younger by three and six years respectively than himself, who are his foremost enemies.   From the meagre and contradictory accounts that have come down to us it is impossible to trace in detail the growth of this antagonism   In the character of the three brothers, however, we find a satisfactory explanation of the misunderstandings that arose between them.   By his love of seclusion, his distaste for all the activities and accomplishments of a feudal king and knight, James alienated the sympathies of every class of his subjects.   To the commons a ruler of this type was as repugnant as to the nobility.   It was in the choice of his immediate followers and advisers, however, that James most sorely tried the loyalty of his people.   On a tragic occasion the chief among these persons will afterwards come before us.   Most notable of them was Thomas Cochrane, by profession an architect, whose ascendency over James was the main cause of the disasters of his reign.   William Roger, a musician ; James Hommyle, the king's tailor, William

Torphichen, and two others, Preston and Leonard, are also named among James's closest intimates That certain of these men possessed high talents and accomplishments there is some evidence to prove. Of Roger especially it is recorded that in the succeeding century it was the boast of many musicians that they had been trained in his school[1]. But in the amusements of a dilettante James put aside the business of the country, and suffered himself to be guided in public affairs by these professors of the fine arts. In James's two brothers the people saw a different type of character and one which they could understand and admire as befitting men born to rule over them. Both, it would appear, possessed all the gifts and graces of accomplished knights The premature end of the youngest brother, the Earl of Mar, leaves us in doubt as to his real character and aims; but the devious career of Albany gives us the measure of his talents and his ambitions So preeminent was he in all knightly accomplishments that in France he was afterwards known as "the father of chivalry[2]." On the other hand, he had little of the prudence and constancy of a statesman or a great captain ; and the part which he played has given him a place among the equivocal figures in the history of his country.

Such being the character of the brothers, it could be only a question of time when their interests and their aims would provoke them into mutual hostility. Of the two causes that are said to have occasioned their quarrel, both are in keeping with all that we know of James. By the intrigues of his favourites, we are told, he was led to suspect Mar and Albany of intentions against his person and his throne The other cause was as characteristic of the age as it was of James himself One Dr Andrews, an astrologer, whom he entertained at his court, had made a prediction which confirmed his suspicion

[1] Ferrerius, 391.

[2] Leslie. In giving Albany this title, Leslie may have confounded him with Bernard Stewart, Lord Aubigny, of whom we shall afterwards hear.

regarding his brothers. The action which James now took must have been both sudden and unexpected : Mar and Albany were seized before they could offer resistance—the one being imprisoned in Craigmillar Castle, the other in the Castle of Edinburgh. By an unfortunate coincidence Mar died during his confinement, and the natural suspicion arose that he had met with foul play. Beyond the course of events we have no evidence of James's guilt, but that men deemed him capable of the crime may be regarded as a proof that he was not well thought of among his subjects. To the end the death of Mar remained a stigma on his name; and at a later day it was alleged as a pretext for his deposition that his own son was not safe in his hands. The Duke of Albany was more fortunate than his brother. Having broken from his prison by slaying his gaolers, he escaped to a ship which was ready for him at Leith, and made his way to France after a brief stay in his castle of Dunbar. In the suppression of his two brothers, James had only in one case to resort to actual fighting. Before his flight Albany had garrisoned Dunbar Castle, and left commands that it should be defended in his name. After a siege of some months, however, it was captured for the king by the chancellor, Lord Avondale; and no other place appears to have made a stand for the exiled duke[1].

James had for the time effectually rid himself of Albany; but he was encompassed with difficulties with which his tastes and his aptitudes little fitted him to cope. In his own kingdom he had to face a disaffected nobility, whom he had gradually driven to desperation, and whose action was soon to show that they were ready for the most desperate measures. England, also, was no longer in the mood that prompted the

---

[1] Buchanan Ferrerius; Leslie: *Exchequer Rolls*, XVIII. pp. lxx.—567; Chronicle at end of Wyntoun (Pinkerton, I. 503). Between the conflicting authorities it is impossible to fix with certainty the exact sequence of these events.

marriage-treaty of 1474. At that period Edward was on the
point of a war with France ; and it was his policy to do all in
his power to conciliate the Scots. In the following year, however,
he had come to an understanding with Louis XI in the treaty of
Pecquigny ; and he was not long in showing that his bargain
with the Scots had been wrung from him only by his temporary
needs. Henceforward, till his death in 1483, he lost no opportunity of seizing every advantage against the Scots. It was not
till 1477, however, that he gave distinct intimation of his unfriendly intentions. Encouraged
by the advantageous alliance he had made for his eldest son,
James proposed two other marriages with the object of
strengthening the friendly relations of the two countries. The
one proposal was for a marriage between the Duke of Albany
and Margaret, the widow of Charles the Bold ; the other, for
the marriage of Edward's brother, the Duke of Clarence, and
James's sister, the Lady Margaret. As it happened, neither
match was at the moment acceptable to Edward , and his
answer to the Scots was a civil rebuff   Still more significant
of his purposes was his neglect to pay the instalment of the
Princess Cecilia's dowry, which became due in February, 1477.
As the sequel was to show, James had good reason to avoid an
open rupture with England, and he did what he could to avoid
it. In 1478 he made a proposal of marriage
between his sister, the Lady Margaret, and Earl
Rivers, the favourite of the English king , and on this occasion
the proposal was accepted. In October, 1479,
she was to have proceeded to England for the
celebration of the union, but for a sufficient reason she did not
leave her own country. Four months before she was to have
gone, Edward was conferring with the herald of John, Lord of
the Isles, and concocting schemes which could not be in the
interest of the King of Scots   Yet no open breach immediately
followed ; and later in the year Edward even granted a safe-
conduct to the Scottish king, pressing him to pass through his

dominion on his projected pilgrimage to the shrine of St John at Amiens[1].

It was apparently at the pressing instance of Louis XI that James was led into open hostility against England. Alarmed at the friendly intercourse between Edward and Maximilian of Austria, Louis had recourse to the time-honoured policy of his predecessors, and sought to give Edward occupation in a Scottish war. With this object he despatched (1479) envoys to the court of James, the chief   **1479** of whom appears to have been a person after James's heart— Robert Ireland, a Scot naturalized in France, a doctor of the Sorbonne, and one of the learned men of the time. Ireland's mission was twofold—to reconcile James to his brother Albany and to persuade him to send an army across the Border; but in neither object was he successful. However, Louis did not despair of gaining the Scots to his purpose; and another embassy the following year, also with Ireland at its head, returned triumphant[2]. In the spring of 1480 the Scots began the old work on the Border   **1480** —burning villages and carrying off provisions[3]. With a strong force Archibald, sixth Earl of Angus, known to Scottish history as Bell-the-Cat, even made his way to Bamborough, which he gave to the flames, and returned with the old Scotch boast that he had lain three days and nights on English ground[4].

Alike from his circumstances and his natural temper, James was still desirous of peace ; and to secure this end he despatched a herald and pursuivant to the English court. If Edward would abstain from aiding Maximilian against France, the Scots, he was to be told, would willingly renew the truce. But at this moment the idea of truce was as far

---

[1] *Fœdera*, vol. XII.; *Acts of Parl. of Scotland*; Ramsay, *Lancaster and York*, II. 434 et seq.

[2] Ferrerius.

[3] Rymer, XII. 117.

[4] Chronicle at end of Wyntoun.

as possible from Edward's mind, and he had already taken measures to chastise the Scots for their doings of the preceding year. About the middle of April, 1481, he sent a fleet under Lord Howard to do as much mischief as it could on the shores of the Firth of Forth. At various points Howard was met and repulsed by the Scots; but he succeeded in burning Blackness and in carrying off eight large vessels besides injuring many others[1]. Having thus had his revenge, Edward at length dismissed the two Scottish envoys, and in a manner that was studiously insulting[2]. But before the return of their envoys the Scots had been preparing for either emergency. In a Parliament which met in Edinburgh on the 11th of April, they had issued a summons for the assembly of an army and imposed a tax for the victualling and defence of Berwick, which they knew to be the grand object of all Edward's designs. According to a contemporary chronicle the past winter had been one of unexampled severity : from New Year's eve there had been continuous frost and snow. It was at the close of this time of hardship that the summons now came for the Scots to meet for the defence of their country. In answer to the summons a great army came together from every corner of the country ; and among the rest the versatile Lord of the Isles, doubtless prepared to wait on the fortunes of either king. At the head of this formidable force James was about to cross the Border when his march was suddenly stayed. A message from a papal envoy then in England threatened him with an interdict if he proceeded with his present enterprise—the reason alleged being that the time had come for all Christian princes to turn their arms against the Turk. On the understanding that the English should also abstain from hostilities James led back his host without striking a blow. He had hardly turned his back,

_1481_

---

[1] Ferrerius, 394.
[2] Leslie, Ferrerius, Buchanan, *Acts of Parl. of Scot.* II. 138.

however, when to the indignation of the Scots the English attacked them both by sea and land[1].

The nation was now in the full tide of a war with England, and was, moreover, in the midst of manifold evils besides. In the contemporary chronicle mentioned above we have the following picture of the state of Scotland in the year 1482. "Thar was ane gret hungyr and deid in Scotland, for the boll [six bushels] of meill was for four punds; for thair was blak cunye [debased coinage] in the realm, strikkin and ordinyt be King James the Thred, halfpennys, and three-penny pennies, innumerabil, of coppir. And thai yeid [went] two yer, and mair. And also was gret wer betwix Scotland and Ingland, and gret distructionn throw the weris was of corne and catell. And thai twa thyngs causyt bayth hungar and derth, and mony pur folk deit of hungar[2]."

From the number and importance of its events the year 1482 is, in truth, one of the memorable years in Scottish history. In the crowd of troubles that 1482 beset the country the danger from England was most alarming; and energetic steps were taken to meet it. At an assembly of the Estates in Edinburgh (March 13) the one absorbing business was the preparation for the threatened English invasion. The spirit in which they met is expressed in a phrase in which the English king is styled "the revare [robber] Edward, calland himself king of England." For the defence of the kingdom it was enacted that all the fighting men should be ready to appear on a warning of eight days, that Berwick and a number of castles on the Borders should be more strongly garrisoned, that in the event of Edward leading his army in person James should do likewise, and that an embassy should be sent to France to demand aid. As the exiled Douglas was making himself specially active against his country, a price was set upon his head, and upon those of his followers[3].

[1] Ferrerius, Leslie.   [2] Pinkerton, II. 503.
[3] *Acts of Parl. of Scot.* II. 137—140.

All that the Scots could do in defence of their country was certainly needed; for Edward was about to receive an ally who was peculiarly fitted to assist him in his designs—the Scottish king's own brother, the exiled Duke of Albany. On his flight to France Albany had been handsomely received by Louis XI, who taking pity on his destitute condition had given him in marriage Anne de la Tour, daughter of the Count of Boulogne and Auvergne. Louis's attempts to reconcile him to James, however, were not successful; and a process of forfeiture was still hanging over him in the Scottish Estates. Having no further hopes from the King of France, therefore, he crossed to England towards the end of April 1482[1]. To Edward there could not have come a more welcome guest; and during a quiet retreat together at Fotheringay Castle they came to an understanding as to the future of Scotland. On the 10th and 11th of June two treaties containing the following clauses were arranged between Edward king of England and "Alexander king of Scotland," as Albany chose to describe himself. With the assistance of Edward Albany was to make himself master of Scotland on these conditions: within six months after the conquest he was to do homage for his kingdom; he was to break off all alliances with France; and within fourteen days after entering Edinburgh he was to surrender the town and castle of Berwick. Within a year, also, Albany was to be united to the Lady Cecilia, who had been destined for his nephew—though on the condition that "he could make himself clear of all other women according to the laws of the Christian Church[2]." Nor was this treaty to remain long a dead letter. Before the end of June an army under the command of the Duke of Gloucester, accompanied by Albany, began its march towards the Scottish border[3]

About the same date as the English left York, the King of Scots led a force from Edinburgh, and encamped in the town

---

[1] Ramsay, *York and Lancaster*, II. 443.
[2] Rymer, XII. 156   [3] Ramsay, II. 444.

of Lauder. With a fatuity which it is difficult to understand, he took in his train the whole band of court minions whom every class of his subjects was unanimous in regarding as the cause of all the evils in the country. He was soon to learn that he had presumed too far on the forbearance of the nation. He had been encamped some days at Lauder when in the early morning a force considerably stronger than his own made its way to the town. It was led by the Earls of Angus, Huntly, Lennox, and Buchan, the Lords Gray and Lyle, and other leading men in the country. At a meeting held in the town church, the lords at once took counsel as to their future proceedings, and despatched certain of their number to report their decisions to the king. On two conditions only, he was told, would they consent to follow him against the English enemy. He must recall the debased coinage then in circulation without loss to existing interests, and he must unconditionally surrender his favourites to their discretion. In high indignation James peremptorily refused both demands. Considering all the circumstances the Lords had confidently reckoned on James's compliance, but they had gone too far not to go further. Breaking into the royal quarters, they seized the wretched favourites—Cochrane, Roger, Torphichen, Preston, Leonard, and others unnamed, and hanged them without ceremony[1]. As things now were, combined action against the invader was impossible, and James was conducted to the castle of Edinburgh, where he was placed under the charge of his uncle, the Earl of Athole[2].

[1] The early historians assert that James Hommyle, the king's tailor, was among the victims at Lauder; but this has been shown not to be the case. *Exchequer Rolls*, IX p xlv

[2] Ferrerius, pp. 394 et seq.—In this account of the affair at Lauder Bridge I have followed Ferrerius, and for these reasons· that his narrative is most intelligible, that he had his information from contemporaries, and that his aim as a historian seems to have been to tell the simple truth. The story usually given is that of Pitscottie, which bears on the face of it the characters of romance.

Meanwhile, the enemy led by Gloucester and Albany had not been idle. After a brief siege the town of Berwick was taken, though the castle still held out; and as far west as Jedburgh the country was laid waste. As the enemy still continued to advance, the Scottish nobles who now directed affairs were convinced that resistance was hopeless and made overtures for a peaceful understanding. Accordingly, on the second of August a treaty was struck at Edinburgh between Albany on the one part, and on the other, the Archbishop of St Andrews (Scheves), the Bishop of Dunkeld, the Earl of Argyle, and the Chancellor, Lord Avondale. Certain expressions in the treaty show that the Scots were fully aware of the extent of Albany's treason; and, considering his late arrangement with Edward, it is noteworthy that Albany agreed to sign it. Yet he had little reason to complain of its terms. On condition of owning allegiance to his brother, he was to be secured from all prosecution for past offences, and he was to be restored to all the estates and offices which he had held at the time of his flight from the country[1]. What is singular is, that no arrangement was made which brought any special gain to England. On the 4th of August, indeed, the magistrates of Edinburgh undertook an engagement; but it was hardly an adequate return for the English king's outlay in connection with the invasion of Scotland. Should Edward desire to break off the match between his daughter Cecilia and the Scottish prince, they undertook to repay all the instalments of her dowry which he had already advanced[2]. But before the English left Scotland, they were to achieve what had been Edward's real object in sending his army into the country. On his return march, Gloucester made himself master (Aug. 24) of the castle as well as the town of Berwick, which after twenty-one years thus finally passed from the hands of the Scots[3].

[1] Rymer, XII. 160.
[2] *Ib.* XII. 161.   [3] Ramsay, II. 446.

The country was now in a singular position. The king was in ward in the castle of Edinburgh; and the administration of affairs was mainly in the hands of Albany, Argyle, Avondale, the Archbishop of St Andrews, and the Bishop of Dunkeld. Fortunately, the King of England was not in a position to pursue his late advantage, otherwise the divisions in Scotland must have presented the best of opportunities. Towards the end of August, Margaret the king's sister was to have proceeded to England to celebrate her marriage with Earl Rivers; but for a personal reason she could not leave her own country. In October the projected union between the Lady Cecilia and the Scottish prince was likewise broken off; and the city of Edinburgh repaid the English king the instalments of his daughter's dowry[1]. Till Edward's death the following year these were the only public relations between the two countries. Secretly, however, Edward never ceased to interfere in the affairs of the country and to turn them to his own account.

It was not long before fresh quarrels in Scotland led to another crisis. The understanding between Albany and his confederates did not last beyond the autumn. After a visit which they made in company to the queen at Stirling, a difference arose among them as to their treatment of the king. From motives which we can only conjecture Albany resolved to rescue his brother from Edinburgh Castle; and with the aid of the provost and citizens of the town he succeeded in effecting his end. For a brief space the country now saw the two brothers in the happiest relations, and it was told that they even shared the same bed[2]. A Parliament which met in

---

[1] Rymer, XII. 164—167. In return for their service in rescuing the king, the citizens of Edinburgh received what they called their "Golden Charter"—investing their chief magistrate with a right of sheriffdom within burgh.—Drummond, *Hist. of the Five Jameses*, p. 102; *Reg. Mag. Sig.* X. 79, 80.

[2] Ferrerius, Leslie.

Edinburgh on the 11th of December proved by its enactments
that Albany was for the time the most powerful person in the
country. In addition to his former estates and honours, he
now received the Earldom of Mar and Garioch, and was
appointed Lieutenant-General of the Realm[1]. Had James been
a mere weakling he would have acquiesced in the ascendency
of his brother, as Robert II and Robert III had given place to
the Albany of their day. But though James had little aptitude
for affairs, his history proves that he was both stubborn and
self-willed, and not without the skill to compass his own
ends. Before long it was seen that the country could not
hold the two brothers without civil war James steadily set
himself to undermine Albany's influence, and with such success
that Albany was once more driven to renew his secret negotiations with England. Through three representatives at the English
Court, the Earl of Angus, Andrew Lord Gray, and Sir James

1483

Liddell, he entered into a treaty with Edward
(Feb. 11, 1483) similar to that of Fotheringay in
the preceding year[2]. With the assistance of Edward he was to
do his utmost to make himself King of Scots, and on attaining
this object he was to acknowledge Edward as his superior and
to break off all connection with France. Before many weeks
his secret treaty was perfectly well known to James, whose
position, however, did not allow him to proceed to an open
quarrel On the 19th of March an indenture between the two
brothers was signed by Albany at his castle of Dunbar, which
throws a curious light on their relations to each other   From
this document it appears that there was a rumour abroad that
in the king's presence an attempt had been made to poison
Albany, and that Albany had even arrested certain persons
whom James had charged to cut him off. According to the
arrangement in the indenture, Albany was not to come within
six miles of the king's presence ; he was to demit the office of

[1] *Acts of Parl. of Scot.* II. 142
[2] Rymer, XII. 173, 176.

Lieutenant-General, and he was to cease communication with all those who had been his confederates in the treason with England[1]. But the strife of the brothers was beyond healing by any arrangement on paper. Within his castle of Dunbar Albany still continued his intercourse with his old confederates, and still carried on his dealings with England. But James, it would appear, was proving too strong for him, and before the death of Edward IV (April 9) Albany was forced to cross the Border, though not before strengthening his castle with an English garrison. The death of Edward IV, whose interest had been so closely bound up with his own, was fatal to Albany's ambition; and in a Parliament which met on the 27th of June James was at length able to effect his ruin by sentence of attainder.

James had still five years to reign, and the course of late events seemed to promise a happier future both for himself and the country. He was now rid of Albany, who had been the chief cause of disturbance at home. The death of Edward IV, also, had removed an enemy who of late had lost no opportunity of doing him injury; and the two successors of Edward, Richard III and Henry VII, were so fully occupied with their own affairs that they were disposed rather to make a friend of the King of Scots than an enemy. That James failed to profit by these favourable circumstances, and for the third and even a fourth time brought about a crisis in his kingdom, is conclusive proof that he was pre-eminently devoid of the qualities of a prudent ruler.

For a time everything seems to have gone well, and James's public acts show that he was now really master in his kingdom. In the Parliament which met in February, 1484, **1484** he dealt an effectual blow at the supporters of Albany by passing the doom of forfeiture on Lord Crichton

---

[1] This Indenture is printed in a supplement to the Acts of Parliament at the beginning of Index volume, p. 31. Cf. also *Exchequer Rolls*, ix. p. xlix

and about thirty others of more or less note[1]   In the course
of the spring, also, he began the siege of the castle of Dunbar,
into which Albany had introduced an English garrison[2].   It
was not till two years later that the castle fell into his hands;
but in the month of July a stroke of good fortune rid him of
two enemies at once.   On St Magdalene's Day (July 22)
Albany and the exiled Douglas made their way to Lochmaben
at the head of a chosen band of 500 horsemen.   Lochmaben
was the centre of a district where both nobles might expect to
find many friends, and they had chosen the occasion of the
town fair for their enterprise.   But though they were joined by
many supporters, and fought with desperate courage, the result
was disastrous to Douglas and Albany—the former being made
prisoner, and the latter escaping only by the speed of his
horse[3].   If ever subject deserved the death of a traitor, it
was this last of the Black Douglases; but whether from policy
or commiseration his life was spared, and he was confined for
the rest of his days in the Abbey of Lindores[4].   It was the
last time, also, that we hear of Albany in connection with
Scotland.   Despairing of further support from England, he
withdrew to France, where a year later he was killed by the
splinter of a lance while looking on at a tournament[5].   At a
later period of Scottish history, his only son by his second
wife, Anne de la Tour, was to play a part more important
than his own.

Thus fortunate at home, James's relations with England
under Richard III were likewise all that could be desired.   On
July 21, 1484, he acknowledged a communication he had
received from Richard III, in which proposals were made for a

---

[1] *Acts of Parl of Scot* II 147 et seq.

[2] *Exchequer Rolls*, IX. 432, 433.

[3] Buchanan.

[4] Regarding the last days and death of Douglas, see *Exchequer Rolls*,
vol. x.   Preface to Appendix, No. 1.

[5] See Le Laboureur, *Les Tombeaux des personnes illustres*, pp 113, 114.

permanent peace by some fitting marriage between the royal houses[1]. As both kings were in earnest, the negotiations were not protracted; and at Nottingham on the 21st of September two treaties were concluded between them. By the first a truce of three years was arranged—a special agreement, however, being made in the case of Dunbar. At the close of six months, it was stipulated, the Scots might do what they could to recover it on condition of observing the truce elsewhere. By the second treaty there was a provisional betrothal between the heir to the Scottish crown and the niece of Richard, the Lady Anne, daughter of the Duke of Suffolk. Not till the 8th of September, however, were the terms preliminary to the marriage to be finally arranged[2].

The death of Richard III at Bosworth Field (Aug. 22, 1485) did not interrupt these friendly relations. The projected marriage, indeed, never took place; but the truce remained, and during the first years of Henry VII, James contrived to recover the castle of Dunbar. With Henry James showed an eagerness to be on friendly terms that confirms a charge which his subjects brought against him of undue leanings towards England. On the 27th of November, 1487, an indenture was signed by the Carlisle Herald 1487 for England and the Snowdon Herald for Scotland, which though it came to nothing, deserves a passing mention as showing the inclinations of James immediately before his final disaster overtook him. In this document it is proposed that for the permanent harmony of the two kingdoms three marriages should be arranged at as early a date as possible—between James himself and the widow of Edward IV[3], between his son

---

[1] *Letters of Richard III*, I. 63, 64.

[2] Rymer, XII. 232—247.

[3] Queen Margaret had died at Stirling in 1486, probably on July 29 (*Accounts of Lord Treasurer*, I. p. lxiv, note). Like most of his race, James III, in his marriage relations, did not show a good example to his subjects. One of his mistresses, known as the *Daisy*, was specially notorious.

the Marquis of Ormond and the third daughter of Edward IV,
and lastly between Prince James and another daughter of the
same king. For the settlement of terms representatives of both
kingdoms were to meet at Edinburgh on the 24th of January,
1488; and an interview between the two kings was to take
place in the July following[1]. In no circumstances would these
singular proposals have been likely to take effect; but the
weakness and folly of James were about to raise the final issue
between him and his people.

From the confused accounts that have been preserved it is
impossible to speak with precision of the events that now
followed. Everything, however, points to the fact that only
sheer misgovernment on the part of James could have led up
to them. At the date at which we have arrived, his chief
confidant was one Sir John Ramsay, afterwards Lord Bothwell,
who had been spared at Lauder on account of his youth
and at James's own special intercession. As his subsequent
career was to show[2], Ramsay was a person fit for desperate
undertakings; and his insolent ascendency made him hateful
alike to the nobility and the commons[3]. Yet Ramsay was
only one of many familiars who excluded the king's natural
counsellors, and led him into courses which were distasteful
to every class of his subjects. Chief among the complaints
against these persons was their abetting the king "in the
inbringing of Englishmen to the perpetual subjection of
the realm[4]." On the other hand, there was a numerous body
of the greater and lesser barons who had good reasons both to
hate and to fear their king. In the extensive forfeitures of
those who had supported Albany they saw what would be their
own fate whenever James had the power to inflict it. It was
in self-defence, therefore, as well as from the desire to remedy

---

[1] *Rotuli Scotiae,* II. 480; Rymer, xii. 328.
[2] He afterwards became a spy of Henry VII.
[3] Ferrerius, 398—399.
[4] *Acts of Parliament of Scotland,* II. 216.

undoubted abuses that they now entered on what was to prove a revolution.

The first half of the year 1488 saw the beginning and end of the struggle. In a Parliament which met on the 29th of January an Act was passed which at 1488 least must have quickened the action of the insurgent barons. Some years previously James had annexed the revenues of Coldingham Priory to the Chapel Royal in Stirling Castle, which was of his own foundation. But these revenues were regarded by the Humes as their patrimonial right, and that family having formed an alliance with the Hepburns steadily opposed this exertion of James's authority. In the Parliament of January, however, it was decreed that action should be taken against all such as opposed the transference of the revenues. Thus, the Humes and the Hepburns, and their numerous and powerful allies, were in the mood for any enterprise that might promise the recovery of their rights. Within the next three months a conspiracy was formed before which a bolder spirit than that of James might have quailed. In its ranks were the Earls of Angus and of Argyle, the Lords Gray, Hume, Hailes, Drummond, and Lyle[1]; and so powerful and numerous was their following that James found it necessary to take refuge in the north, where many nobles were still faithful to him. Meanwhile the insurgent barons made the most of his flight. They seized the castle of Dunbar, which at that moment was specially well furnished with all the means of war; and at Leith they were fortunate enough to possess themselves of much of James's own baggage. In view of a protracted civil war, also, they made overtures to Henry VII, who in May granted a safe-conduct to the bishops of Glasgow and Dunkeld, the Earl of Argyle, Lord Hailes, Lord Lyle, the Master of Darnley, and the Master of Hume[2], all of whom were in the number of James's enemies. But another stroke of the rebel lords was still more significant and menacing. The Duke of

---

[1] Ferrerius.   [2] Rymer, XII. 340.

Rothesay, the heir-apparent, had been placed for safety in Stirling Castle under the charge of James Schaw of Sauchie; but by threats or promises Schaw was seduced to surrender the prince into the hands of his father's enemies. The prince was only in his fifteenth year; but his very presence was a source of strength to the insurgents, for they could now give assurance to the nation that the son would in due course take the place of his father.

In the north country James had found a ready response to his call for support; and with the help of the Earls of Huntly, Errol, Crawford, Athole, Rothes, Sutherland, Caithness, the Earl Marischal, and many of the minor barons, he succeeded in collecting a considerable force[1]. By the beginning of May he was able to take the field; and the two armies met at Blackness on the south shore of the Firth of Forth. After an indecisive skirmish proposals were made by both sides for an interchange of their respective objects and desires. In the negotiations the king was represented by the Bishop of Aberdeen, chancellor of the realm, the Earls of Huntly and Errol, the Earl Marischal, Lord Glamis, and Alexander Lyndsay; and the lords by the Bishop of Glasgow, the Earls of Angus and Argyle, Lord Hailes and Lord Lyle. The result of the conference had the appearance of a compromise, but in reality the two parties were left precisely where they had been. James was to retain the royal authority and estate, and to pledge himself to take as his counsellors those to whom that office naturally belonged. On the other hand, the prince was left in the hands of the insurgents—a condition that nullified the whole arrangement[2]. Such as it was, however, the treaty stayed further hostilities for the space of a few months. For the short time that still remained to

---

[1] Ferrerius.

[2] The "Pacification of Blackness" is printed in Pinkerton, Vol. I. pp. 505–6; and is contained in an Act of the Scottish Parliament of Oct. 17, 1488.

him James took up his abode in the castle of Edinburgh; and with the object of strengthening himself against further contingencies, he bestowed honours on such as might one day be of service to him. The Earl of Crawford he made Duke of Montrose, and Lord Kilmaurs, Earl of Glencairn. But what was most significant, he conferred on his second son the title of Duke of Ross, thus signifying in what light he regarded the conduct of the heir-apparent. But the rebel lords had never laid down their arms; and in the beginning of June James was again forced to take the field. On St Barnabas's Day, the 11th of June, the two armies met at Sauchieburn, almost on the field of Bannockburn. Among James's weaknesses superstition was not the least prominent; and it was doubtless by way of happy omen that in this his last enterprise he armed himself with a sword that had belonged to the great King Robert. From the conflicting accounts of the battle that ensued it is impossible to speak with confidence of the various events of the day. Before the fighting was over James had sought safety in flight, and left his sword on the field[1]. In the existing state of the country it would have been difficult for the unfortunate king to distinguish his friends and his foes. He had not ridden far, therefore, before he leapt from his horse, and took refuge in a neighbouring mill, with the intention of lying concealed till dusk. But the victory of the insurgents would have been but half-gained if the king had escaped; and the pursuit was eager. The discovery of the king's horse was a sure token that his master could not be far off; and before nightfall the unhappy king was found in his hiding-place, and slain in cold blood[2].

[1] It was picked up on the field of battle.—*Exchequer Rolls*, Vol. x. p. xxxix.

[2] Pitscottie's lively account of James's death is the one usually followed; but like most of his narratives of the kind it does not inspire confidence. Leslie merely says that James was slain; Buchanan and Ferrerius are more precise, and in the main tell the same story. For reasons already stated I have followed Ferrerius.

A comparison has been made between James III and his contemporary Louis XI[1]; and in many points the resemblance is interesting. It was the peculiarity of both that they gave their confidence to men of low birth; and both in consequence had to reckon with the determined hostility of their nobles. Both were equally superstitious and equally interested in astrology, whose professors they held in special honour. In their avarice, their suspicious temper, their love of seclusion, we find other traits they had in common; and such was the impression of their character that justly or unjustly their subjects believed them capable of the blackest of crimes: as Louis was accused of murdering his brother the Duke of Berri, so was James accused of the death of the Earl of Mar. But, while they had so many characteristics in common, the course and the result of their respective reigns are sufficient proof that they belonged to different types of men. From all we know of James we are led to believe that he was essentially a dilettante and incapable of conceiving a national policy, or, at least, of consistently carrying it out. Of the political craft and the undeviating purpose of Louis he possessed little, and the tragic end of his reign was not the result of chance combinations but the natural issue of his own incapacity.

Troubled as was the reign of James III, it escaped the calamity of protracted war; and it saw no serious breach in the national life. The Estates met year by year with the utmost regularity—Edinburgh being now their usual place of assembly. From the mere narrative of the events of the reign some notion may be gained of the part which they now played in the government of the country. The one salient fact is that they were the mere instruments of the faction that chanced to be in the ascendant. In the Parliament that met in October, 1466, the Boyds dictated their own pardon for their seizure of the king, and otherwise disposed its proceedings in their own

[1] Pinkerton, I. 274.

private interests. By November, 1469, however, they had fallen before a new combination of the nobles, and the Parliament of that date effected their ruin at one stroke. Similarly, during the brief period of Albany's supremacy, the Parliament of November, 1482, merely registered his wishes, appointing him lieutenant-general of the realm, and strengthening his hands in the ways that seemed best to himself.

In no previous reign was seen more clearly the true character of the "Lords of the Articles." Chosen at the close of the session, they were the virtual masters of the country so long as their party held together, and whether they were the nominees of the king or of a faction their existence was equally unfavourable to the growth of a constitutional Parliament. The number of those who had a right to be representatives was about 190; but the average attendance was only about 60[1]. In an assembly like the Scottish Parliament the representatives of the burghs could have but little influence, and, as things now were, there was no prospect of their influence increasing. Neither the king nor the clergy made common cause with them; and in themselves they were not sufficiently powerful to compel a reciprocation of favours such as ensured the growth of the Commons of England. In a separate chamber and with a larger representation they would have attracted the smaller barons whose interests as a class were identical with their own; and together they would have formed a body which would have held its own with the other powers in the state. In 1560 such a combination actually took place, with the momentous result that in spite of the higher clergy and many of the nobles they gave the country a new religion.

Of James's Parliaments that of November, 1469, is perhaps the most important. Its forfeiture of the Boyds made an

---

[1] In the Parliament that met on June 1, 1478, there were present 16 ecclesiastics, 23 barons, and 14 commissioners of burghs. These numbers may be taken as representing the relative proportions of the three constituent parts of the Estates.

epoch in his reign by giving him the opportunity of showing
that he could act as his own master. But it also passed other
Acts that call for mention. In the reign of James II we
have seen that an Act was passed in favour of small tenants
in regard to their leases One of equal importance now
declared that the tenant should not be held responsible for his
landlord's debts. Another of the Acts of this Parliament is a
significant comment on the condition of society that rendered
it necessary By reason of the frequency of murder and homi-
cide it was enacted that man-slayers should not in future have
the benefit of sanctuary. Two Acts of the same Parliament
have been supposed to point to a deliberate purpose on the
part of James and his advisers to increase the powers of the
Crown. On the pretext that the annual elections were attended
by reprehensible disturbances, the right of choosing their
magistrates was taken from the citizens of the burghs, and
vested in the retiring town council By this arrangement the
Court could easily secure the election of persons favourable to
its interests both in the burgh itself and in the Parliament to
which the magistrates were sent as representatives In the
other Act certain words are used regarding the Parliament
which might imply a set purpose to restrict the government of
the country to the hands of a junto. "It is seen expedient,"
this Act runs, "that the courts of Parliament, Justice Ayre,
Chamberlain Ayre, or such like courts, that have continuation,
need not be continued from day to day, but that they be of
such strength and force as [if] they had been continued from
day to day unto the time that they be dissolved, the Parliament
by the king, the Justice Ayre by the Justice, the Chamberlain
Ayre by the Chamberlain, and other such courts."

From other Parliaments of James we have legislation that
gives us a glimpse into the social conditions of the time. As
in previous reigns, sumptuary laws are passed as a means of
checking "the great poverty of the realm." In 1471 it was
ordained that none except knights, minstrels, or heralds, should

wear silk in gown, doublet, or cloak. The importation of English cloth was held to be another cause of the impoverishment of the country. In exchange for salmon, cod, and other fish, the Scots were in the habit of taking cloth from English traders; whereas, says an Act of 1473, they might have good money in silver and gold, of which the country was in such need. On pain of forfeiting their cloth and of further punishment, therefore, such traders, both Scots and English, were forbidden to continue their barter. The careless or dishonest workman was also the object of legislation. Thus in 1478 a stringent Act was passed against incompetent or drunken smiths. If they injured a horse in the process of shoeing, they were to supply another horse to its master till his own was recovered: should the horse be permanently maimed, one of equal value must be given in compensation. Ferrymen appear to have been an especially knavish class; and in 1485 they were threatened with pains and penalties for taking double and triple fare of the king's lieges.

But the most absorbing subject of legislation throughout the reign of James III was the state of the coinage. In the latter years of James I there had been a serious debasement of the currency, and the evil reached its height in the reign of James III. To the evils of this debasement were added the complications arising from the circulation of French, Flemish, and English coins; and the fixing of the relative value of Scottish and foreign money exercised the ingenuity of successive Parliaments In the reign of James I the relative value of English and Scottish money was estimated at two to one; under James III at three to one. During the ascendency of the court favourite, Cochrane, the state of the coinage became the crying grievance of the country. The issue of two coins, respectively valued at a halfpenny and a penny, was in fact among the most potent of the causes which led to the tragedy at Lauder

The continuity of Parliaments, such as they were, proves

that the public business of the country was never interrupted by James's personal troubles. What is further interesting is that there was now a cultivated opinion in Scotland which called forth a vigorous vernacular literature. From Dunbar's "Lament for the Makars" we learn that throughout the latter half of the 15th century there was a crowd of poets of various degrees of merit, whose very existence proves that they could count on a following of interested listeners. In two poets who flourished during the reign of James III we find the vivid expression of the feelings and interests of different sections of the community. It was in the households of the nobles, according to Major, that Blind Harry found his audiences. In the hatred of all things English which gives its character to his "Wallace," Blind Harry expressed a real feeling of his age, though in the landward districts it existed more strongly than in the towns. We have seen that the insurgent nobles made it a ground of accusation against James that he showed dangerous leanings towards Englishmen ; and both in Acts of Parliament and in other documents there is proof of a constant apprehension of English influence in the country[1].

Robert Henryson, "Chaucer's aptest and brightest scholar," belongs to a very different order of spirits, and was the spokesman of another class of his countrymen. It would have made us think better of James III, if, in his patronage of the fine arts, he had discovered and appreciated the rarest genius among his subjects. As the product of his country and his age, what interests us in Henryson is the general tone of his work and the general standard of expression which he maintained in it. In the poems where he speaks with the deepest feeling we have the natural reflection of a time when thoughtful observers could not but look with anxiety on the future of their country. It is on the triumph of wickedness, the uncertainty of life, the happiness of death, that he strikes his

---

[1] See Dr Dickson's remarks on this subject. *Accounts of the Lord High Treasurer*, Vol. I. p. lxvi. and note.

deepest note and most directly suggests that he is giving utterance to the higher consciousness of his time. But if he represents the age by this seriousness of tone, the quality of his style speaks as clearly for the existence of a cultivated opinion. Though he is not to be compared with Chaucer for variety and abundance, he is his superior in economy of language and pregnancy of reflection; and this is but to say that he belongs to a higher stage of national development. That a poet like Henryson appeared in Scotland in the latter half of the 15th century is convincing proof that the country was in living contact with the advancing thought of Europe, which had led to the Revival of Letters and was soon to issue further in the breaking-up of Christendom.

CHAPTER VII.

JAMES IV. (1488—1513).

English Kings.		French Kings.	
Henry VII	... 1485—1509	Charles VIII	... 1483—1498
Henry VIII	... 1509—1547	Louis XII	... 1498—1515

Popes: Innocent VIII, Alexander VI, Julius II.

THE period covered by the reign of James IV was one of the most important in the history of Western Europe since the introduction of Christianity. During these years began what is distinctively known as Modern Europe in contradistinction to the Middle Age which preceded it. In spirit and aim and scale of action the difference between the two epochs is so great that it marks two distinctive phases of the human spirit. In the sphere of thought the development is distinguished by the decay of that scholastic theology which had dominated men's minds since the 11th century, and by the spread of the ideas and aspirations which had their origin in the direct study of Greek and Roman antiquity. This revelation of a larger world by contact with Greece and Rome was reinforced by events and circumstances that gave an impulse to human life such as it had not experienced since it had received the gift of a new religion. The invention of printing (introduced into Scotland during the reign of James IV) made Europe an intellectual commonwealth in a degree which had not been realized even in the days of the greatest of the schoolmen; and the discovery of America and of the route to India by the Cape of Good Hope was of the nature of an analogue to the widened scope of spiritual and intellectual aspirations. By many of his qualities James IV was peculiarly fitted to rule men in such a time of transition. Curious, restless, and enterprising, he gave ready welcome to all forms of novelty, and was eager even to rashness in giving effect to what he considered an improvement on the ways of his predecessors. By the peculiarity of his position as a ruler, also, James was still further fitted to play his part in the new order which had begun for Europe at large. At the close of the 15th century the three chief powers in Christendom, Spain, France, and England, were at once consolidated in territory, and swayed by rulers whose powers enabled them to choose their own ends and to direct the national resources at will. In the circumstances of his predecessors, who were either effaced or held in check by their nobility, James could have played no part in the new condition of the leading powers of Europe; but from the time he reached manhood he became as imperious and absolute a master of his subjects as any of his contemporary sovereigns. In the case of the two most important actions of his reign we shall see that it was in the teeth of all that nobles and commons could urge that he carried out a policy which gratified his own whims at such terrible cost to his people. Thus master of his own kingdom, he was able in spite of its comparative insignificance, to make it a real force in the rivalries of the greater European powers.

Prince James and his supporters could have no doubt as to their decisive victory at Sauchieburn; but they did not immediately learn the fate of his unfortunate father. Having proclaimed his son king, however, the insurgent lords at once marched to the capture of Edinburgh, which had been left in the possession of the late king's friends. The castle offered no resistance; and steps were immediately taken to regulate the affairs of the country. As the new king was but in his 16th year, he could be only the passive instrument of the arrangements that were now made. In these arrangements personal ambition was doubtless gratified; but the conduct of James's advisers contrasts favourably with that of the Boyds and Crichtons and Livingstons in similar circumstances. The great offices of state were thus assigned: the Earl of Argyle was made Chancellor; Patrick Hepburn, Lord Hailes, Master of the Household; Robert, Lord Lyle, Justiciar, and Alexander, Master of Home, Great Chamberlain—the Earl of Angus being charged with the guardianship of the king[1].

The government being thus arranged, vigorous action was at once taken to set the country in order. On June 17th what remained of the great treasure accumulated by James III was seized in Edinburgh Castle; and in the last week of the same month the new king was crowned at Scone. There were still some supporters of the late king who refused to give in their submission, and stern measures were now adopted to prevent them from becoming dangerous. On the ground that they had been made against the common good of the realm, all grants of lands and offices by the late king since the 2nd of February, 1488, were declared to be null and void; and at the same time summons of treason was issued against all persons who still held out against the new government. To ensure the good will of England, an embassy was despatched to Henry VII, with whom the truce of 1486 was renewed on the 26th of July[2].

The first Parliament of James IV met on September 4, 1488; and the number of its representatives

1488

(many of whom had been among the supporters of the late king) showed the interest that was taken in its proceedings. The first business was to dispose of those who had been summoned to appear on a charge of treason—chief

---

[1] *Accounts of Lord High Treasurer*, p. lxix.
[2] *Acts of Parl. of Scot.; Accounts of Lord High Treasurer*, p. lxx. et seq.; Rymer, XII. 346.

among whom were the Earl of Buchan; Ramsay, Lord Both-well, the favourite of James III; and Ross of Montgrenane, who had lately been king's advocate. Buchan, having sub-mitted to the king's mercy, received a full pardon, but the others were attainted, and their honours and estates divided among the new councillors—the Humes and Hepburns re-ceiving the best part of the spoils. Other legislation of the same Parliament proved that the country was still unsettled. To secure the public peace different districts were placed under the special charge of powerful barons—two of whom, we shall see, proved faithless to their trust. As a further means of strengthening the government it was enacted that the heirs of such as had fallen at Sauchieburn should succeed to their estates if their predecessors had died in the king's peace. But the most important matter dealt with was the late revolution which had issued in the battle of Sauchieburn and the death of James III The advisers of the young king appear to have been fully aware of the opprobrium that might attach to their action both at home and abroad. In a formal document, therefore, they sought to justify their proceedings in the eyes of Christian Europe. The late catastrophe, they affirmed, was solely due to the evil doings of James III and his councillors, and as for themselves they were "in-nocent, white, and free" of all the mischiefs that had occurred Signed and sealed by the king and members of the Estates, this document was distributed to the courts of England, France, Burgundy, and Austria, and it was doubt-less on the strength of its assertions that Pope Innocent VIII was induced to grant absolution to all who had a part in the late rebellion[1].

The events of the following year justified all the precautions that had thus been taken Among those who had been charged with the preservation of peace   1489
were Lord Lyle, the Justiciary, and the Earl of Lennox,

---

[1] *Acts of the Parliaments of Scotland*, II. 201—205.

Governor of Dunbarton Castle. In the late reign both Lennox and Lyle had been on the side of the insurgents; but apparently they had been dissatisfied with the distribution of favours, for in the month of April they openly revolted against the government. Having garrisoned the castles of Dunbarton, Crookston near Paisley, and Duchal in the parish of Kilmalcolm, they refused to open the gates on the summons of the king. At the same period, a rising in the North gave a more formidable turn to their revolt. In Aberdeenshire Lord Forbes drew together a body of men, and with the bloody shirt of James III as a standard bade defiance to the government of his son The king and his advisers, however, acted with energy and decision. In a Parliament which met in Edinburgh on June 26th, decree of forfeiture was passed against Lennox and Lyle, and arrangements were made for a simultaneous attack on the three garrisoned castles. Before the end of July both Duchal and Crookston had surrendered, though Dunbarton still held out. But a movement of Lennox was the means of bringing the revolt to an end. With the view of gaining new allies he marched northwards with some 2,000 men in the beginning of October; and on the 11th of that month, in the darkness of night, he was surprised and defeated at a ford of the Forth in the parish of Aberfoyle. The recovery of Dunbarton followed in the beginning of December, and the close of the year saw the country once more at peace[1].

To the year of this revolt two other events appear to belong which brought greater glory to the nation
1489　　The hero of both was Sir Andrew Wood of Largo, one of the notable figures in Scottish history. In Wood were conjoined in curious fashion the various parts of feudal baron, merchant, naval commander, and pirate He had distinguished himself by his fidelity to James III; and it was only after being assured of that king's death that he gave in his

[1] *Accounts of Lord High Treasurer*, pp. lxxxviii. et seq.

allegiance to his successor. As the creation of a navy came
to be the special object of James IV, Wood found a high place
in his favour at once by his knowledge of naval affairs and his
boldness and skill as a commander. Of these qualities he
now gave brilliant proof in the second year of James's reign.
Though Scotland and England were now at peace, piratical
encounters between the vessels of the two countries were of
constant occurrence, and at this time a fleet of five English
ships were doing wide mischief to Scottish craft in the Firth of
Forth. At the request of the king and council, therefore,
Sir Andrew Wood, with his two ships the *Yellow Carvel* and
The Flower, undertook to give an account of the enemy. The
engagement took place off the castle of Dunbar, and resulted
in the complete triumph of Wood, who bore his five prizes and
their crews into the harbour of Leith   Later in the year Wood
was the hero of a more desperate encounter   To revenge the
late defeat one Stephen Bull was sent by Henry VII to try his
strength against the redoubtable Scot. Accordingly, with
three stout vessels Bull entered the Firth of Forth with the
purpose of intercepting Wood on his way home from Flanders.
At length, early in a summer morning, the two vessels of
Wood hove in sight, and no time was lost in coming to action
The fight began off St Abb's head; and through the whole
summer day it raged in sight of the inhabitants who lined the
shore. Night parted the combatants; but the next day the
struggle was renewed with such obstinacy that the ships of
both parties drifted with the ebb tide to the mouth of the Tay.
Fortune at last declared for Wood, and with the English
captain and all his three vessels as his captives he sailed into
the port of Dundee[1].

With the exception of one sensational event the year 1490
was one of repose for the country. In a Parliament which

---

[1] Pitscottie is our only authority for these exploits; but they can hardly
be pure invention, as Pitscottie tells us that he was personally acquainted
with Sir Andrew Wood, son of the above-named hero

met in the Tolbooth on February 3rd, fresh measures were
passed for the healing of the late divisions.   The
1490 forfeitures of Lennox and Lyle were rescinded,
and a Secret Council of six was appointed to advise with the
king and to be responsible to the Estates for the advice which
they gave.   As a grievous source of the troubles of the late
reign the coinage received its special attention.   To prevent
such tampering with the coin as had been practised by
Cochrane it was enacted that "a trew substantious man"
should be appointed specially to superintend the mint; and
that the value of the groat should be fourteen pennies, ten of
which were to weigh an ounce[1].   To the autumn of this
year belongs one of those hideous incidents which from time
to time occurred in the history of the Highlands.   Between
the Drummonds and the Murrays, two great families of Perthshire, there was a feud of ancient standing, and at this time
an occasion arose which brought them into direct conflict.
George Murray, abbot of Inchaffray, sought to levy from the
parish of Monzievaird in the lands of the Drummonds a larger
amount of teind than they held to be just.   In the act of
levying the teind the Murrays were attacked by a body of the
Drummonds, and shut up to the number of six or eight score
in the church of Monzievaird   Content with this triumph, the
Drummonds were marching off, when a shot from the church
slew one of their number.   In their rage the Drummonds took
a terrible revenge   Setting fire to the church, they burnt it to
the ground, only one of the Murrays escaping destruction.
The crime was speedily punished, for in October the chief
offenders were brought to trial and executed at Stirling[2].

Of the next two years no event of importance is recorded.
From the record of a Parliament that met in
1492   February, 1492, we gather, indeed, that Sauchie-

[1] *Acts of Parliament of Scotland.*
[2] With the account given in the Scottish historians, compare *Accounts
of Lord High Treasurer*, CII ; and *Exchequer Rolls*, X. p. l.

burn was not yet forgotten; since to check "the heavy murmur and voice" of the people a reward of a hundred merks of land was offered to any one who would discover the persons who had slain the late king. But in spite of some unpopularity the government had no enemies sufficiently formidable to raise their hands against them; and thenceforward James and his advisers were at full liberty to give their attention to other matters than those of home policy.

The year 1493 is a memorable one in Scottish history, for in that year the Lordship of the Isles, which had existed since 1346[1], and played so great a part in the affairs of the country, came at length to an end. We have seen that in 1476 John, Lord of the Isles, gave in his submission to James III, and was stripped of the earldom of Ross, as well as of the lands of Knapdale and Kintyre; but since that date there had been wild doings in the West Highlands and the Isles. The submission of John gave deep and wide dissatisfaction to many of the sub-chiefs, who soon found a leader more after their own heart. This was a natural son of John, Angus by name, who by his marriage with a daughter of the Earl of Argyle had further strengthened the ascendency which his energetic character had already secured to him For fully ten years (1480—1490) Angus was virtual Lord of the Isles. Shortly after 1480 he broke into Ross with the intention of recovering that earldom, and was driven back only by the combined forces of the Earls of Crawford, Huntly, Argyle, and Athole. Expelled from the mainland, he made himself master of the Isles by a decisive naval victory over his father near Tobermory. When next we hear of him he is again at work on the mainland. By some stratagem his son, Donald Dhu, who was in his day to prove worthy of his father, was carried off from Isla by the Earl of Athole and placed in the keeping of Argyle. Angus's revenge was swift and terrible.

[1] This is the date given by Gregory; but cf. *The Clan Donald*, I. 131.

1493

Bursting into the territory of Athole, he ravaged it with fire and sword, and bore off the Earl and Countess from the chapel of St Bride, where they had vainly deemed themselves safe.   The assassination of the terrible Angus (1490) by an Irish harper in Inverness promised a more peaceful future, since the aged John now recovered his authority in the Islands. In an evil day for his race, however, John committed the charge of his dominion to his nephew, Alexander of Lochalsh, who proved to be as restless a spirit as Angus himself. Apparently with the consent of his uncle, Lochalsh revived the claims on the Earldom of Ross, and set himself to recover it with the strong hand.   His attempt wrought the ruin of his house.   Defeated and wounded in an invasion of the disputed territory (1491), he was not again heard of for some time.   But the doings of recent years must have proved to the government that only one course was open if the dominion of the Isles was to become a law-abiding portion of the kingdom   A Parliament that met in May 1493 took the decisive step, and passed a final sentence of forfeiture on the Lord of the Isles.   The time-stricken John, the last representative of his title, was in no position to offer resistance to this decree, and in August the king visited his head-quarters and received the submission of several of his chief vassals.   In January of the following year John himself appeared before the king and made formal surrender of his lordship.   Thus the triumph of the King of Scots over his formidable subject seemed at length complete, but as the sequel will show, many years were yet to pass and James was still to have an infinity of trouble, before the royal writs should run in the dominion of the Lords of the Isles[1].

John Knox is our authority for an incident of the year 1494, to which the subsequent history of Scotland was to give a special significance.   Since

1494

[1] Gregory, *History of the Western Highlands and Islands of Scotland*, p. 51 et seq.; *Accounts of Lord High Treasurer*, p. cxiii. et seq.; *Exchequer Rolls*, vol. x. p. lvi. et seq.

the burning of Paul Craw in the reign of James I we have heard nothing of those heretical opinions which had alarmed the Church in the opening of the 15th century. From this story told by Knox, however, we gather that these opinions were still sufficiently widespread to raise anxiety among good churchmen. In the year of which we are speaking Robert Blackadder, archbishop of Glasgow, cited no fewer than thirty persons on a charge of heresy from Cunningham and Kyle, in the county of Ayr. On thirty-four points these "Lollards of Kyle" were accused of diverging from the teaching of the Church; and, as recorded by Knox, some of their tenets were certainly startling. Every faithful man is a priest; the pope is not the successor of Peter; the pope deceives the people by his bulls and indulgences and pardons: such were a few of the heresies laid to their account. Fortunately for the thirty heretics, the young king in whose presence they were examined was not of the stuff of which inquisitors are made, and he good-naturedly contrived to end the trial in a jest. Yet, if James had known, the zealous archbishop was justified to the full in his alarm at what this wild teaching might one day involve. To these Lollards of Kyle John Knox looked back as to his spiritual ancestors; and it was in Ayrshire that George Wishart and himself were one day to find the quickest response to that teaching which was to issue in the ruin of the ancient Church[1].

During the next three years (1495–1497) the relations with England were the main concern of James and his advisers. Since the beginning of the reign there had been various attempts to establish a friendly understanding between the two countries. In June 1488 an embassy had been despatched to the English court to explain and justify the overthrow of James III; and in October of the same year a truce of three years was concluded at Coldstream[2]. In 1489 the victories of

---

[1] Knox, *Works*, I. 6 (Edit. Laing).
[2] *Rot. Scot.* II. 488.

Sir Andrew Wood must have been a source of exasperation to
the English king; and to the year 1491 belong certain events
which prove that Henry did not scruple to work in underhand
fashion against the country with which he was nominally at
peace.   On the 16th and 17th April of that year he entered
into a secret arrangement with certain Scots, which probably
sounds more formidable than in reality it was.   The traitorous
Scots were Ramsay, the favourite of James III (who had been
permitted to return to his own country), Sir Thomas Tod
of Sereschaw, and James, Earl of Buchan: and the undertaking to which they pledged themselves was to deliver to the
King of England the persons of the King of Scots and his
brother, the Duke of Ross[1].   As Ramsay continued to reside
at the Scottish court, James was probably ignorant of this plot:
of the treachery of another subject in the same year, however,
he was fully informed.   Archibald, Earl of Angus, the head of
the House of Douglas, and the first subject in the country,
probably in November of this very year[2], likewise entered into
a secret engagement with Henry VII.   Together with his son
he bound himself to do his utmost to prevent James from
making war on England.   Should war actually supervene,
however, he bound himself to surrender his own castle of
Hermitage to Henry on condition of receiving an equivalent in
England.   The treason of Angus appears to have been discovered; for on the 29th of December he was deprived of his
domain of Liddesdale with its castle of Hermitage, receiving in
return the less dangerous ground of the lordship of Kilmarnock.
Yet in spite of these untoward circumstances peaceful communications still went on between the two countries.   In the
very month (Dec. 21) in which the treason of Angus was

[1] Rymer, XII. 440.
[2] Gairdner, *Letters and Papers of Richard III and Henry VII*, i. 385.
The date affixed to this document is in a modern hand, so that Angus's
treason may have been earlier. Cf. *Accounts of Lord High Treasurer*,
p. cvi.

discovered a further truce of five years was concluded at Coldstream[1], though in terms so vague that in the following year both kings appointed commissioners to guard against its infringement. In 1493 Henry gave further proof of his desire to be on good terms with his neighbours, for in May of that year he proposed a marriage between the King of Scots and Catherine, the granddaughter of Henry's uncle, Edmund, duke of Somerset. Nothing, indeed, came of the proposal, but the truce was continued till the last day of April 1501; and James received an indemnity of a thousand marks for damages in breach of the existing treaty[2].

These uncertain relations with England had been rendered still more precarious by the old ties with France. Following the usual precedent, James's Council had decided to send an embassy to the French court to renew the old alliance between the two peoples. Owing, however, to the troubles at the outset of the reign the embassy was not sent; and, meantime, an attempt was made from a new quarter to divert the Scots from friendly overtures to France. In July of 1489 they were honoured by an embassy from personages no less than the Catholic kings, Ferdinand of Aragon and Isabella of Castille. In the schemes of Ferdinand, the arch-plotter of Europe, it was the prime object to array all the other powers against France; and it was in furtherance of this aim that his representatives found their way to Scotland. Here the same inducement which had been successful in England was held out to the Scots. As Henry VII had been won over by a proposal of marriage between his son Arthur and Katharine, the daughter of Ferdinand and Isabella, so the hand of another princess was offered to the King of Scots. In point of fact, however, no other legitimate princess existed; and as the Scots prepared to send an embassy to Spain, Ferdinand's ambassador La Puebla was directed to undeceive them[3]. Of these astute

---

[1] Rymer, XIII. 465.   [2] Rymer, XII. 529.
[3] Bergenroth, *Calendar of Spanish Papers*, Vol. I no. 41.

dealings nothing came, and the old friendship for France once more prevailed. In 1491 Patrick, Lord Bothwell, and the Bishop of Glasgow were despatched to the French Court for the purpose of renewing the traditional alliance. Beset as he was by the wiles of Ferdinand, Charles VIII could not afford to reject the offer of the Scots, and the result of Bothwell's embassy was not only the renewal of past treaties, but a secret arrangement binding the Scottish king to attack Henry of England should he ever make war on France[1].

It was in the year 1495, as has already been stated, that the relations with England became the first interest of the Scottish government. For the policy now adopted it was undoubtedly James himself who was mainly responsible. He was in his twenty-second year, and such as he was then he remained to the end; for like others of the Stewart race he early reached all the maturity of which he was capable. From the glowing portrait of him drawn by the Spanish envoy Pedro d'Ayala large deduction must certainly be made; yet after every abatement it is clear that James possessed many qualities that endear kings to their subjects. His personal appearance was prepossessing. Of middle stature, he was strongly yet elegantly formed and he was an adept in all manly exercises. His face also was handsome, and it is noted that he never cut his hair or his beard—a fashion, we are told, that "became him very well." Of his character as of his external appearance we have fuller details than of any of his predecessors. His temperament was in excessive degree mercurial, the highest spirits varying in him with the extremest depression. From the accident of his history the morbid element of his character was associated with the violent death of his father[2]. His remorse for his share in

---

[1] *Inventaire Chronol des Documents relatifs à l'Histoire d'Écosse*, p. 53 (Abbotsford Club.)

[2] In his later years James's morbid tendency must have been aggravated

his father's end displayed itself in ways which revealed the romantic gloom of his temper. By way of penance he constantly wore about his waist a chain of iron to which he added a few links every year, and in the midst of his pleasures the cloud would suddenly descend upon him, and he would bury himself in some house of religion, or work off his depression by a solitary ride to some distant shrine such as that of St Duthac at Tain, or St Ninian in Wigton. His religion had little connection with morals, for in sheer sensuality he held his own with any of his stock, and his example made his court the rival of that of any southern prince in open and promiscuous debauchery. In the higher qualities of a king he was seriously lacking. He was clever and intelligent[1], and possessed the courage and high spirit that were so necessary to a King of Scots in holding his own against a truculent nobility; but the critical actions of his life gave disastrous proof of his signal deficiency in sagacity and self-control, and in real sense of the responsibility that he owed to his people. Writing to Henry VII, the traitor Ramsay speaks of James's "young adventurousness" and his "simple wilfulness[2]", and the two phrases give us a deeper insight into James's character than all the vague eulogy of the Spanish ambassador.

Since the spring of 1492 Henry VII had been kept in uneasiness by the proceedings of the brilliant adventurer, Perkin Warbeck, who had given himself out as Richard, Duke

---

by the fact that only one of his six legitimate children survived infancy. A pilgrimage to Rome was one of the cherished projects of James in his later years.

[1] Ayala makes James an accomplished linguist and a "good historian." Buchanan, on the other hand, says that James was "vitio temporis ab literis incultus," which, considering the circumstances of his upbringing, is probably nearer the truth. James's interest in alchemy is specially noted.

[2] Ramsay's letter is given in Pinkerton, I. 438—9.

of York, the elder of the two princes supposed to have been murdered in the Tower. From the beginning of his career Warbeck had been in communication with the Scottish government[1]; but in the year 1495 James had come to the determination to take active measures in his support. In June four ambassadors bore from him certain significant proposals to Maximilian, king of the Romans, then holding his court at Worms. Maximilian was a zealous patron of Warbeck, and James undertook to give his support to the pretender if Maximilian would make a league with the Scots against England. In the event of a successful war the Scots should be rewarded with their lost town of Berwick[2]. The news of James's intentions must have reached Henry and caused him some alarm, for he now prepared to make a serious effort to secure the goodwill of the Scots. On June 21 he appointed commissioners to convey to James the offer of his daughter Margaret's hand in marriage[3]. Henry's ally, Ferdinand, also, took an opportunity presented to him of trying to detach the King of Scots from his alliance with France. Robert, archbishop of Glasgow, had been sent to Spain with the object of cementing friendship with Ferdinand, and probably of furthering the proposed marriage between his master and a Spanish princess[4]. On Ferdinand's part the proposed alliance was only a lure to gain his own ends; but, as was soon to be proved, neither the prospect of an alliance with England or Spain availed to divert James from the policy on which he had set his heart.

In the course of the autumn Warbeck must have received an express invitation to come to Scotland; for

1495

on the 20th of November he appeared before the Court at Stirling with a considerable retinue. James lost

---

[1] *Accounts of Lord High Treasurer*, p. cxxv.

[2] Rawdon Brown, *Calendar of Venetian State Papers*, Nos. 643, 645, 647, 633.

[3] Rymer, XII. 572.   [4] Bergenroth, vol. I. no. 103.

no time in showing that he was in all earnest in taking up
Warbeck's cause.   He gave him a pension of £1200 a year,
introduced him to the leading nobility; and, as a proof to all
the world that he was assured of the justice of Warbeck's
claims, married him to his cousin, Lady Catherine Gordon,
daughter of the Earl of Huntly, in January, 1496.   The month
following Warbeck's arrival representations were made to James
both by Ferdinand and the pope; but he had gone too far to
retreat, and with all his faults as a king, James had a keen
sense of personal honour.

It was not till the autumn of 1496, however, that James
took direct measures to make good the cause of
Warbeck.   The obstacles in the way were such   1496
as might have turned from his purpose a less resolute ruler
than James.   It was against the will of his subjects that he
took up Warbeck's cause at all; the tax imposed to meet
the expenses of the army that was to invade England proved
to be inadequate; and he had to eke it out by coining his own
" chains, plate and cupboard[1] ".   In June or July the Spanish
agent Pedro de Ayala, of whom we shall presently hear more,
came at Ferdinand's desire to try once again to win over James
to the league against France[2].   On September 22nd, also, on
the very eve of his invasion, Henry VII sought to divert
him from his purpose by renewing the offer of his daughter's
hand[3].   As was to be fatally shown at a later day, however,
obstacles only urged James along the course on which he had
resolved.

By the 12th of September James's preparations were complete, and on the 19th he was at Ellem Kirk, ten miles from
the Border, at the head of his army.   With Warbeck he had
come to a definite agreement before crossing the Border.
Warbeck was to restore Berwick to the Scots and to pay

---

[1] Pinkerton, II. 440.
[2] Bergenroth, I. no. 107.
[3] Rymer, XII. 635.

50,000 marks in two years[1]. To prepare the way for the
invasion a proclamation was now issued in the name of the
Duke of York offering protection to all Englishmen who were
willing to fight in his quarrel. On the 20th the Scots appear
to have entered England; but the campaign was short and
inglorious. As James told the French ambassador, Concressault, they had many scores to settle; for, though it was
nominally a time of truce, the English both by sea and land had
of late done much mischief to Scottish property. In the
present opportunity, therefore, his army lost no time in re-
taliating with interest, and plundered and ravaged at will. It
soon became evident, however, that the main object of the
expedition was hopeless. To the proclamation that was made
there was no response whatever; and, as James had been led
to expect a rising in Warbeck's favour, friction at once rose
between them. Warbeck, it is said, objected to the method of
conducting the enterprise, and James replied with a bitter
sarcasm at his concern for a people who showed such little
interest in himself. After two days on English ground Perkin
returned to Scotland, leaving James engaged in besieging the
House of Heiton. A few days later James himself recrossed
the Tweed, arriving in Edinburgh by the 8th of October[2].

After this flagrant act of hostility on the part of the King
of Scots there was no alternative but war. The King of England,
indeed, had a double reason for being provoked at James's
invasion. To raise a force to chastise the Scots he was compelled to have recourse to a loan and a subsidy which roused a
revolt in Cornwall, and instead of sending his army against the
Scots he had to employ it against his own subjects. For the
rest of the year, therefore, Henry was not in a position to hold
a reckoning with his enemy; and with the be-
ginning of 1497 the Scots were again across the
Border. By the express command of James, Lord Hume, the

1497

---

[1] Ramsay to Henry VII (Pinkerton, II. 438).
[2] *Accounts of Lord High Treasurer*, p. cxlii.

Warden of the East Marches, broke into Northumberland on February 12th, and in view of an English invasion many of the Border castles were reinforced with men and ordnance. Though he appointed Lord Dacre lieutenant of the North, however, Henry took no immediate steps to invade Scotland on a large scale; and the first half of the year was occupied in petty raids on the part of both countries.

As long as Warbeck remained in Scotland there could be no peaceful arrangement between the two kings. Yet, in point of fact, it was no longer in Warbeck's interest that James maintained his hostile attitude. Since the day when they had their misunderstanding, a coldness appears to have sprung up between them; and during the nine or ten months during which Warbeck remained in Scotland we hear nothing of mutual good offices. It was, in truth, only a regard to his personal honour that seems to have bound James to his equivocal guest; for on grounds of policy there were several reasons which might have led James to part with him. Both the nobility and the commons had looked askance on Perkin from the first; the French king, it is said, offered 100,000 crowns for his surrender[1]; and Henry made liberal promises to have him placed in his hands[2]. It was in honourable fashion, however, that James at length saw the unfortunate adventurer safely out of his kingdom. In the second week of July Perkin sailed from Ayr in a ship named the "Cuckoo," commanded by Robert Barton and equipped in a manner befitting the rank to which he aspired[3].

The departure of Warbeck made no immediate change in James's intentions towards England. In the beginning of the

---

[1] Ramsay to Henry VII (Pinkerton, II. 439).

[2] Gairdner, *Letters and Papers, &c.* I. 104.

[3] Perkin's wife accompanied him. In Ayr he left his brown horse in pledge.—*Accounts of Lord High Treasurer*, p cliii. To the sojourn of Warbeck and his followers is assigned the appearance of the *grand-gore* (*morbus gallicus*) in Scotland.

year he had formed the plan of a raid on a larger scale than that of the previous autumn ; and now that Warbeck was gone the preparations went on apace To meet the costs a spear-tax was again levied, and so eager was James to equip an adequate force that he coined "the great chain[1]" and other ornaments, raising at the same time considerable sums from various persons in the country. On the 20th of July he met his assembled army at Melrose, and on the 29th he encamped at Upsettlington, on the north bank of the Tweed, opposite the castle of Norham Despatching his light horsemen to harry the surrounding country, he laid siege to Norham with his main body. In view of the impending invasion of the Scots, however, the castle had been strongly garrisoned by Fox, bishop of Durham, in whose diocese it lay , and for several days James assaulted it in vain. While thus engaged, news came to him that the Earl of Surrey was within two days' march at the head of 20,000 men ; and as this was a force superior to his own he at once retired within his own kingdom It was now the turn of Surrey to redress the balance of mischief. Crossing the Tweed, he levelled the castle of Coldstream, and after similar handling of other strong places, prepared to besiege the important castle of Ayton In this attempt, however, he was checked by the approach of a Scottish force , and in a meeting at Dunbar between James and the English governor of Berwick an arrangement was made which led to Surrey's withdrawal from Scottish ground[2].

Now that James was no longer abetting Warbeck, the English king only desired to be at peace with his neighbour,

---

[1] "The 'great chain' consisted of seven score and six links, weighed about thirteen pounds and a half, and was therefore worth upwards of £1500.—*Accounts of Lord High Treasurer*, Editor's note, p. cliv.

[2] According to Hall (p. 481, Ed. 1809), Surrey actually took the castle of Ayton, but this is not borne out by the dates of the movements of the Scots and English. Cf. *Accounts of Lord High Treasurer*, p. clvii, and *Exchequer Rolls*, XI. lxiii. Hall also records that James challenged Surrey to personal combat, which Surrey for good reasons declined.

and in this policy he had the strong support of his ally, Ferdinand. As it happened, also, the English ambassador of Ferdinand, Pedro de Ayala, stood high in the good graces of the Scottish king, who appears to have had implicit faith in the excellence of his intentions towards himself. We have seen that in June or July of 1496 Ayala had come to Scotland on the fruitless errand of trying to persuade James to give up the cause of Warbeck, and he was now in Scotland once more on a mission of peace. On this occasion his success was complete. Mainly through his endeavours a truce of seven years was concluded at Ayton on the 30th of September[1].

But the hostilities of the last three years had borne their fruit; and on both sides of the Border there was every disposition to pick a fresh quarrel. The   1498
year after the arrangement at Ayton a trifling incident as nearly as possible renewed the war. A small band of Scots having crossed the Tweed at Norham on some peaceful errand, they were attacked by the garrison of the castle and several of their number slain. In bitter indignation James protested against this breach of the truce; and it was only the prudent conduct of Henry that averted a renewal of strife. A terrible pestilence that raged in Scotland during the years 1499 and 1500 may also have helped to cool the temper of James, and Henry's conciliatory overtures at length led up to the most important arrangement that had ever been made between the two countries.

As we have seen, it had long been in Henry's mind to effect a marriage between his daughter Margaret and the King of Scots, and the events of the last few years must have convinced him that in this union lay the main hope of a stable peace between the two kingdoms. The caution of Henry and the susceptibilities of James rendered the nego-   1499
tiations somewhat dilatory. On the 12th of

---

[1] Rymer, XII. 673; *Rot. Scotiae*, II. 532.

July, 1499, the truce was renewed at Stirling; and on
September 11th of the same year Henry appointed Fox, bishop
of Durham, to negotiate the marriage The
next year saw a further step towards the desired
object. As the prospective bride and bridegroom were within
the forbidden degrees, Henry (July 28) sought a papal
dispensation for their union. In 1501 it was at
length arranged that commissioners representing
both countries should meet in London, in November of that
year. Before the commissioners met it is recorded that an
interesting discussion took place in the English Council. In
objection to the marriage it was urged that Margaret might
one day inherit the throne of England, which would thus pass
to the King of Scots. In any case, was Henry's reply, this
could never come about, since the larger kingdom must
inevitably absorb the smaller[1].

1500

1501

On January 24, 1502, the marriage-treaty was at length
concluded. For both nations, it may safely be
said, it was the most memorable engagement to
which either of them had yet become a party. It was the first
pacification, as distinguished from a mere truce, which had
been struck between them since the breach of 1332, when
Edward III set at naught the treaty that had been concluded
with Robert Bruce. It was in its results, however, that the
treaty of 1502 was to become so notable an event in British
history; for out of that treaty were to issue in due course the
union of the Crowns and the union of the Legislatures of
England and Scotland. So far as James was personally concerned, however, the marriage brought him no great gain and
no great happiness. In keeping with his miserly temper
Henry made a close bargain in the matter of his daughter's
dowry. From her husband she was to receive an annual
income equal to £2000 sterling or £6000 Scots, and she was

1502

---

[1] Polydore Vergil, XXVI. p. 607, 46.

to bring him only 30,000 angel nobles or £10,000 sterling[1]. Among the causes that were to lead to Flodden, not the least, perhaps, was the friction occasioned by Henry VIII's refusal to give up a portion of his sister's dowry.

On the same day that the marriage compact was signed two other treaties[2] were likewise concluded, which in the light of subsequent events form a strange comment on the futility of human foresight By the one, the two kingdoms were bound to perpetual peace and mutual defence ; by the other, to the preservation of order on their respective frontiers. Yet only eleven years were to elapse before Scotland's greatest disaster, of which England was to be the appointed instrument.

It was not till August of 1503 that Margaret, then in her 15th year, was brought to her adopted country. Conducted by the Earl of Surrey and a long train of knights and nobles, she was met at Lamberton by the Earl of Morton with a similar following of Scottish barons. At Dalkeith she was received by James, when the whole company rode to Edinburgh, now the indisputable capital of the country. On August 7th the marriage took place in the Abbey Church of Holyrood—the event being celebrated by a succession of shows of every description such as the country had never witnessed before. In the "Thistle and the Rose[3]," the official effusion of the chief poet of the time, William Dunbar, we have the lasting memorial of an event charged with significance for the future of Scotland

1503

Till the accession of Henry VIII, six years after the marriage of James and Margaret, there was no serious difference between the two countries ; and during these years

---

[1] Rymer.

[2] On the day following the signing of the treaties, Patrick, Earl of Bothwell, as James's proxy, contracted marriage with Margaret.—Leland, *Collectanea*, IV. 261.

[3] The title of this poem contains the first authentic notice of the thistle as the Scottish badge.

Scotland increased her resources and her prosperity in greater degree than at any former period of her history. In what this development consisted we shall afterwards see. But in other directions, also, there is manifest proof of the activity of the king and of the growing strength of the country. In his relations with foreign countries he was able to exercise an influence, which, however, was probably due to their respective positions rather than to the inherent strength of Scotland. But it was by his vigorous administration of the Highlands and Western Isles that James earned his highest praise as a ruler, and that he made the greatest advance on the work of his predecessors.

We have seen that in January, 1494, the forfeited John, Lord of the Isles, had given in his submission to the government. From James's visit to the Isles in 1493, however, he must have learned that the settlement of the Islands must be a work of time and labour; and from the energy with which he threw himself into it he appears to have enjoyed his task The very year of John's submission showed him how far his work was from being complete. In April he repaired and garrisoned the castle of Tarbet; and repeating his visit in July sought to extend his authority by also garrisoning his castle of Dunaverty in south Kintyre. In this last work, however, he gave mortal offence to Sir John of Isla[1], who considered himself the rightful master of the whole of that district. The audacity of the act that followed gave curious proof of the regard that was paid to the royal authority. Before the very eyes of James, who was now aboard his fleet on the point of return, John of Isla stormed the castle and hung its governor over the walls. At the moment James was powerless; but, before the year closed, John, together with one of his sons and their accomplices, met their end on the Borough Muir of Edinburgh.

The year 1495 saw James once more among his trouble-

---

[1] Sir John of Isla was grandson and representative of Sir Donald of the Isles, surnamed Balloch of Isla.—Gregory, p. 89.

some subjects. With a greater force than on any previous occasion he took up his quarters (May) in Mingarry Castle, Ardnamurchan, where he received the submission of many chieftains, and assumed possession of the Islands of Coll and Tiree[1] On the strength of this extended influence a notable step was taken the following year to introduce order into the whole dominion of the Isles. By a decree of the Lords of Council each head of a clan was made responsible for the serving of summonses on his own vassals[2].

During the years 1496 and 1497 James was mainly occupied with the affair of Perkin Warbeck ; and he had little leisure to attend to the Isles This slackening of rigour had the usual result Alexander of Lochalsh, of whom we have already heard, seized the opportunity of reviving his attempt to restore the ancient lordship As in his previous attempt, he again broke into the district of Ross, where he was defeated by the Mackenzies and Munroes at a spot called Drumchatt. Nor was he more successful in the attempt he next made to raise the Islands. The summary punishment that had overtaken John of Isla and his accomplices must have been fresh in their minds ; and no chieftain was found ready to risk a similar fate. Thus baffled in his ambition, Lochalsh was forced to take refuge in the island of Oransay, where he was surprised and slain by a chieftain favourable to the king

After the treaty of Ayton in 1497 James was once more at liberty to attend to the Isles, and he addressed himself to his task with even greater energy than ever Thrice in 1497 and once in 1498 he visited the Islands in person, and in both years a drastic measure was taken to reduce them to order. By the first of these measures all the charters he had granted during the preceding five years were revoked The second measure was still more decided. Archibald, Earl of Argyle, was appointed Lieutenant of the whole Lordship of the Isles,

---

[1] *Exchequer Rolls*, vol. x. pp. lxiv—lxvi.
[2] *Acta Domin. Concil.* VII. fol 39.

and was commissioned to let them on lease for a term of three years. Still further to break up the power of the native chieftains, large tracts of land were given to such as had supported the royal authority, and notably to the eldest son of the Earl of Huntly, who received an extensive territory in the district of Lochaber, formerly the possession of the Lord of the Isles[1].

The immediate effect of this policy was to drive to desperation a large number of native chiefs who only needed a leader to move them once more to revolt. Such a leader they soon found in Donald, the natural son of that Angus whose exploits have already been recorded. Donald, it will be remembered, had been carried off when a child and placed in the keeping of the Earl of Argyle. By certain devoted adherents he was now (1501) delivered from his prison, and conducted to the island of Lewis, whose lord, Torquil Macleod, took up the cause of Donald with ardour. It was in vain that the government commanded the lord of Lewis to surrender Donald; and the revolt drew to a head. In 1503 the Islanders under their new leader burst into Badenoch, the inhabitants of which were the vassals of the detested Earl of Huntly, and wasted the country with fire and sword. Apparently it was not till the following year that the government took steps to put an end to these fresh troubles. First, in a Parliament which met in March an Act was passed which would have been altogether admirable if those for whose good it was intended had been in a condition to profit by it. For the effective administration of justice among a people "almost gane wilde" two Sheriffs were to be appointed, one of whom was to hold his court in Dingwall, and the other at Tarbert or Lochkilkerran[2]. What was more to the purpose, the whole military array of the kingdom was summoned, and placed under the command of the Earls of Argyle, Huntly, Crawford, the Earl Marischal, and Lord Lovat.

[1] *Exchequer Rolls*, vol. XI. pp. lxv—lxvii
[2] Acts of Parliament, II. 241, 249.

Yet even on this scale three campaigns during three successive years were needed before the revolt was finally quelled and Donald Dhu secured in the castle of Edinburgh. Thenceforward the dominion of the Lords of the Isles gave no further trouble during the remainder of James's reign. As hereditary sheriff of Inverness, Caithness, Ross, and the Northern Hebrides, the Earl of Huntly became responsible for all these districts, while to the Earl of Argyle were entrusted the southern islands with the adjacent mainland. Thus reduced to tranquillity, the Western Highlands and Islands began to share in the general progress of the country, and it is a signal tribute to the justice of James's dealings that none of his subjects followed him with more loyalty to the field of Flodden than the men whose country had so often felt the force of his arm[1].

In the variety and activity of her foreign relations we have abundant proof that Scotland like the other countries of Western Europe had entered on the new time; and it is in this period between the peace of Ayton and the accession of Henry VIII that we find these relations most interesting and suggestive. By a happy chance Scotland possesses a series of documents in this connection which are among the most valuable memorials of the time. These documents consist of the correspondence of James with foreign courts, composed mainly by his secretary Patrick Panter, a native of Montrose[2]. As Panter had studied in the schools of Paris towards the close of the 15th century, he had acquired something of the purity of Latin style which had resulted from the Revival of Learning, so that his letters possess the double interest of being at once the production of a scholar and a man of affairs.

With the Court of Rome James was in close communica-

[1] Gregory, p. 112.

[2] Ruddiman published two volumes of these under the title of *Epistolae Regum Scotorum* (1722, 1724), and Mr Gairdner has printed more of them in his *Letters and Papers of Richard III and Henry VII* (Vol. II.). Many still remain in MS.

tion throughout the whole of his reign, and till his quarrel with the imperious Julius II enjoyed its friendship and favour. His first Parliament, we have seen, despatched to Innocent VIII a justification of the proceedings taken against James III; and the following year there came a papal rescript granting the desired absolution to all who had been concerned in that king's misfortunes. Another favour bestowed by the same pope proved for a time to be of doubtful good for the nation. As has elsewhere been remarked, there was a traditional rivalry between the sees of Glasgow and St Andrews; and the erection of the one into an archbishopric could not be regarded with approval by the bishop of the other. Glasgow had secured a university in emulation of her rival, and she was not likely to be content till she had likewise the distinction of an archi-episcopal see. Her claims were ardently supported by the king[1] and the Estates, and in 1492 she received the coveted honour. If there was rivalry before, there now followed such envying and strife as became a scandal to the nation. So unseemly, indeed, became the doings of the two prelates that Parliament was at length constrained to interfere and to stay their quarrel, by the effectual threat that their rents would be suspended if they did not accept its decision[2].

The dealings of James with Pope Julius II reveal a state of things that forms a significant commentary on the heresies of the Lollards of Kyle. It would appear that there was no Christian country where ecclesiastical scandals had been more flagrant than in Scotland; and though the day of reckoning was fast coming these scandals seemed in every reign to become more cynically regardless of public decency. The story of James IV's disposition of benefices is, in truth, as conclusive regarding his own lack of real moral elevation as it is of the degradation of the Papal See. On the death of Scheves in 1497, the Duke of Ross, James's brother, though

---

[1] James was a canon of Glasgow Cathedral.
[2] Acts of Parl. II. 232.

only twenty-one years of age, was on no ground of fitness appointed to the vacant archbishopric. But when Ross died in 1503 a still more disgraceful transaction followed. To the primacy of all Scotland was chosen a bastard and a minor, in double violation of the canon law. The youthful primate was Alexander Stewart, James's son by his mistress, Marion Boyd, a youth whose early death at Flodden, his association with Erasmus, and his interest in learning, have made him one of the interesting figures in the history of his country. Yet this remarkable arrangement was but one of many of the same character. Thus, on the intercession of James, another of his natural sons, who bore his own name, was appointed to the rich abbey of Dunfermline, his secretary Panter received a dispensation to hold three benefices; and the treasurer, Beaton, received first the bishopric of Galloway, and afterwards that of Glasgow[1]. So excellent a son of the church, nevertheless, did the King of Scots appear to Pope Julius II that in 1507 he presented him with a purple hat and a sword with a gold scabbard, and named him the "Protector of the Christian Religion[2]."

James's relations to another court—the court of Denmark, with which Scotland had made such an excellent bargain in the preceding reign—were more to his own and the national credit. Since the union of Calmar in 1397 Denmark had been united with Norway and Sweden; but the relations of the three countries were never satisfactory, and during the reign of John, the uncle of James IV, they were as unsatisfactory as ever. In addition to his troubles with Norway and Sweden, John like his predecessors had to reckon with the insubordination of the free city of Lubeck, which had a long list of grievances against his government. Beset by his many enemies, John made

---

[1] Gairdner, *Letters, &c.*, vol. II. pp. lxix—lxxi.

[2] The title was granted on the ground that James had shown himself the only peacefully disposed prince in Europe.—Boece, Lives of Bishops of Mortlach and Huntly.

frequent appeals for assistance to his nephew of Scotland, who
to the best of his ability responded with all the good feeling of
a kinsman.   Moreover, as the resources of the Scandinavian
kingdom were on a scale somewhat similar to those of his own,
such assistance as James was able to give was sufficient to turn
the balance in favour of the Danish king.

There was friendship between the two countries from the
beginning of James's reign.   In 1492 an embassy despatched
to Denmark effected a treaty of mutual defence which was
confirmed at Stirling on the 5th of May, 1494 ; and three years
later it was followed by an interchange of privileges in matters
of trade.   But James was to find that his alliance with king
John was likely to be accompanied with some outlay.   In the
years 1501 and 1502 the Swedes were once more asserting
themselves against Denmark, and, in accordance with the late
treaty, James despatched to his uncle's aid two ships of war
and two thousand men with the Earl of Arran as commander.
The result was only the temporary success of John ; for in
1504 James sent the Lyon-king to Denmark to ascertain the
cause of the continued hostilities.   In 1505, however, John at
length succeeded in bringing the Swedes to terms, and apparently without the further assistance of the King of Scots.
But the Swedes were no sooner pacified than the city of
Lübeck (1506) reasserted its old grievances against Denmark ;
and John again made appeal to his nephew for support.   An
embassy from Scotland in 1507 may have had some effect, for
in that year an arrangement was made between John and the
refractory city.   But the arrangement was shortlived.   The
next year there was again misunderstanding between the
Danish king and Lübeck, which succeeded in making common
cause with Sweden against their common enemy.   Still faithful
to his ally, James at different times sent his two best naval
commanders, Robert Barton and Andrew Wood, to his assistance   But with the accession of Henry VIII in 1509 he soon
found himself so fully occupied by his own affairs that he had

neither the power nor the opportunity of giving further effectual aid to Denmark[1]

In James's dealing with another minor potentate, also a kinsman, his character appears in its best light. Since the marriage of his grandfather with Mary of Gueldres, Scotland had always been on friendly relations with the country from which she came; and James IV was able to be of great help to his contemporary, Duke Charles. By one of his acts, indeed, the duke gave great offence to the King of Scots, who spoke his mind with all the frankness of a kinsman and a superior. In 1504 Charles had received into his dominions Edmund de la Pole, Duke of Suffolk, and representative of the House of York, who by his singular conduct had given considerable trouble to Henry VII In a letter of strong expostulation James showed him the folly of his conduct; and called upon him to expel Suffolk from his dominions[2]. Having complied with James's demand in this matter the duke could appeal to him with the better grace on the troubles that now overtook him. Between Philip of Castile, who was also master of the Low Countries, and his father Maximilian, king of the Romans, the Duke of Gueldres was now leading a precarious existence; and against his enemies he could find few friends to support him When he appealed to James to stand by him, however, he received a cordial response. In a letter addressed to Henry VII James told the English king that should he lend his countenance to the action of Philip and Maximilian against Gueldres, he must in that case be prepared for war with Scotland By the date when this letter was written, however,

---

[1] Aarsberetninger fra det Kongelige Geheimearchiv, indeholdende bidrag til dansk Historie af utrykte kilder, Forste Band (Copenhagen, 1852–4); Gairdner, *Letters, &c.*, vol II.; Note on the relations between Scotland and Denmark in the reigns of James IV of Scotland and Hans of Denmark, by Sheriff Mackay (*Works of Dunbar*, Scot. Text Soc., vol. III)

[2] Gairdner, *Letters, &c*, II. 192.

Philip of Castile was dead, and in the new combinations that arose the duke was relieved from the immediate danger of his position[1].

It was through James's family connection with Denmark and Gueldres that he was induced to intervene in their affairs; but in his own interest he was led into entanglements with other countries which throw a further light on the expansion of his kingdom. As will afterwards be noted James was deeply interested in the commercial development of his country, and still more in the creation of a powerful navy. But as other countries were equally eager in these objects, quarrels were bound to arise at a time when maritime law was as imperfectly defined as it was arbitrarily enforced. In his fostering of commerce and the navy, therefore, James was frequently brought into collision with other powers; and to one of these quarrels was in large measure due that breach with England which ended in his overthrow and death. Thus we find him demanding redress from Louis XII for damages done to the persons and goods of three Scottish merchants on the coast of Brittany[2], and on another occasion despatching a threatening letter to the magistrates of Dantzig in behalf of Scottish traders in the Baltic[3] To the summer of 1506 belongs an incident which possesses the double interest of illustrating the spirit of the time and of showing the irresponsible action of these "ocean-warriors" of whom Sir Andrew Wood and the Bartons are the most notable Scottish types. For some time, it appears, the Dutch had been working considerable havoc on the ships of Scottish merchants, and James at length determined that this business should not be all on one side. In this year, as it happened, he completed the building of "ane greit and costly ship"; and it occurred to him that it could not be put to better service than the chastisement of the Dutch. Entrusting the command of this ship to Andrew Barton, he gave

[1] Gairdner, *Letters, &c.*, II. 206.   [2] *Ibid*. p. 202.
[3] Ruddiman, I. 19.

him a free commission to do his best to make accounts even
Barton had already had much practice in work of this kind,
and on this occasion he did not fall below his reputation.
According to the historian who relates the whole affair, Barton
took many ships, and by way of practical illustration of his
success, sent home to the king "certane pipis [casks] with the
heidis of the Hollanders" whom he had slain[1]. Some two
years later Robert Barton, the brother of Andrew, was the hero
in an affair which throws further light on the maritime law of
the period On the representation of certain Portuguese, who
alleged that he had seized one of their ships, Barton was
imprisoned by the magistrates of Campvere (now Veere) in the
island of Walcheren, with the full intention of having him
hanged. Just in time to save his subject, however, a letter
arrived from James, which put Barton's proceedings in such
a satisfactory light that it stayed further proceedings against
him. James's plea is contained in a letter which he wrote
to Maximilian giving an account of the whole affair. About
thirty years before a Portuguese fleet had seized a ship belonging to James III, and commanded by John Barton,
father of Robert. As no amends was made by the Portuguese government, letters of reprisal had been granted to
John Barton and his sons; but it was only by the late act
of his son Robert that compensation had at length been
exacted. So far from being piracy, therefore, that proceeding
was but an exercise of simple justice on the part of James
and his subject[2]

It was ominous for the future of James and his kingdom
that in the last years of Henry VII there were already indications of a coming quarrel Disturbances on the Borders, for
which each party blamed the other, were producing an amount
of friction which only the prudence of the two kings could

---

[1] Leslie, p. 74.
[2] Gairdner, *Letters, &c*, II. 273.

prevent from resulting in an open rupture[1]   One outrage especially roused James's indignation, and in the end was an occasion
of quarrel against England   At a meeting held on the Borders
for the purpose of adjusting grievances, Sir Robert Ker, Warden
of the Middle Marches, and a favourite of James, was murdered
by three Englishmen, named Starhead, Lilburn, and John
Heron Lilburn was given up, but the other two escaped,
and James made complaint that Heron especially was not
secured and punished.   The English king, on his part, had
his grievances against James   For some time past numbers
of Scots, certain of them men of high rank, had been passing
through England, without safe-conducts, on errands which
Henry regarded as highly suspicious   Two of these persons,
the Earl of Arran and his natural brother, Sir Patrick Hamilton,
Henry even saw fit to arrest and to detain through the greater
part of the year 1508[2].   Always cautious, how-

1508

ever, he sought to avert an open breach, and
sent an agent[3] to Scotland to ascertain the mind of James.
This, however, proved to be no easy matter   James parried
every question, and could not be brought to commit himself
for or against the old league with France, which was the main
object of Henry's fears

The English agent had hardly gone when on May 9th an
embassy came from Louis XII with the express purpose of
strengthening the bonds between Scotland and France.   The
ambassador charged with this mission was well fitted to carry
it to a successful conclusion—that Bernard Stewart, lord of
Aubigny, who had come on a similar errand in the reign of
James's father.   Since that time, however, Aubigny had won

---

[1] To the year 1504 belongs the well-known Raid of Eskdale, in which
James and Henry combined to punish the thieves of that district.—
Treasurer's Accounts; Armstrong, *Hist of Liddesdale*, 1 190.

[2] Gairdner, *Memorials of King Henry VII*, p. 105.

[3] Mr Gairdner gives reasons for supposing that this agent was Thomas
Wolsey, afterwards the great cardinal —*Letters, &c*, vol. 1. p lxi

such distinction in the wars of France in Italy, that he now ranked with the first captains in Europe, and was undoubtedly the most distinguished Scotsman then living. Aubigny was a man after James's own heart, and was received in princely fashion; and the poet Dunbar expressed in courtly verse the pride of the nation in their famous countryman. But Aubigny's visit had a melancholy termination. He had been only a month in Scotland when he died; and the result of his mission was conveyed to Louis by the companion of his embassy, the Lord President of the Parliament of Paris[1].

The accession of Henry VIII in 1509 forms the critical division in the reign of James IV. Hitherto James's career had been mainly one of uninterrupted prosperity and success. At home he had speedily put down the revolt at the outset of his reign; he had outdone all his predecessors in reducing to order the Western Highlands and the Isles; and to the country at large he had given a peace and prosperity which it had hardly known before. His nobles, who had given such trouble to preceding kings, were content to be his servants and coun- sellors; and it is a significant proof of his ascendency and independence that from the year 1509 only one Parliament met till the end of his reign[2] In his dealings with other princes he had been as fortunate as in his own kingdom. Henry VII had shown an eager desire to be on friendly terms with him, and had given him his daughter in marriage; suc- cessive popes and kings of France had courted his alliance; and in his direct intervention with other powers he could flatter himself that he had influenced the political conditions of Europe. When Henry VIII, a youth of eighteen, came to the throne, however, James was not long in discovering that he

---

[1] Leslie, p. 77; *Exchequer Rolls*, vol XI. p. lv. As showing James's eagerness to assist France, it may be mentioned that in 1507 he offered a body of 4000 men to Louis XII. Ruddiman, I. 83—85.

[2] The Council held at Twiselhaugh, which will afterwards be referred to, can hardly be regarded as a Parliament.

had a very different person to deal with from Henry VII. With a temper as quick as his own the new English king combined a brutal force and an iron resolution which gave him the advantage over the sensitive and romantic King of Scots.

During the first two years of Henry VIII's reign the relations between the two countries were even more cordial than they had for some time been. On Henry's accession, James sent Forman, bishop of Moray, a name of sinister omen in Scottish history, to convey his congratulations and to arrange for the renewal of existing treaties. As in the beginning of the following year Henry also renewed the English alliance with France there seemed a fair prospect of his remaining on friendly terms with his brother-in-law, James of Scotland. But events soon occurred in European politics which were to set the brothers at mortal defiance, and to make both of them the unhappy instruments of unscrupulous potentates more powerful than themselves.

In 1508 the League of Cambrai had been formed for the despoiling of Venice by the four leading personages in Europe, Pope Julius II, Ferdinand of Aragon, Louis XII of France, and Maximilian of Austria. The confederates, however, soon quarrelled over their spoils, and Julius II was specially wroth at the presence and acquisitions of the French in Italy. To drive them beyond the Alps, therefore, became the grand object of that indefatigable pope; and the formation of the Holy League (October, 1511), which eventually

1511

included Julius himself, Henry VIII, Ferdinand, and Maximilian, promised the speedy fulfilment of his desires.

The King of Scots could not look on with indifference at this gathering of enemies round his ancient ally; and his indignation gradually rose against the English king, of whom, moreover, he had personal reasons to complain. In August, 1511, his favourite captain, Andrew Barton, was slain in a sea-fight in the Downs, with Sir Edmund Howard, Lord Admiral of England, and his two ships, the Lion and the Jenny Perwin, towed into the Thames. When James expostulated against this action done in times of peace, he was told that it did not become kings to quarrel about pirates. Another incident belonging to the same period increased the ill-feeling between the two countries. It will be remembered that only one of the assassins of the Warden, Sir Robert Ker, had been punished for his crime. But it was not the custom of the Borders to leave such deeds unavenged; and Sir Andrew Ker, son of Sir Robert, now charged two of his vassals to give an account of Starhead, who since the beginning of the new reign had come out of his hiding. Starhead was also disposed of, but Heron, the chief assassin, was still at large, and James still bitterly complained that the slayer of a March Warden should not be brought to justice[1].

Yet in the policy he was now following it was not Henry's interest to quarrel with the Scots. Having resolved to take his part in the war against France, he could not with prudence leave James behind him as an active enemy. Accordingly, in November he sent ambassadors to offer compensation to the Scots for past violations of the peace. But there was one point on which James would not give way: till Henry should detach himself from the league against France there could be no satisfactory arrangement between them. In a letter of James to Julius II, dated the 5th of December, we have the full expression of his mind towards England about the close of 1511. If Henry went on as he had been doing, slaying and imprisoning Scottish subjects, war, James declared, could be the only issue[2]. Yet it is clear that at this time James sincerely desired peace; and with the object of effecting a reconciliation between Julius and Louis, he despatched Forman, bishop of Moray, to use his influence on the part of both[3].

As the result of the Holy League, the year 1512 saw the outbreak of hostilities between its various parties and its victims. After brilliant fighting 1512

---

[1] Buchanan.   [2] Ruddiman, I. 122.   [3] *Ibid.* p. 125.

on the part of the French, they were at length driven out
of Italy. Henry VIII, also, plunged into war in such
blundering fashion that he became the scorn of his allies
as well as of his enemies. So far as James was concerned,
however, the year was confined to negotiations with the
leading persons in the great contest. The number of envoys,
indeed, who in succession visited the Scottish Court must have
impressed him with a sense of his own importance. In
February came a papal envoy, Octavian Olearius, with ex-
hortations to James to lend his assistance in maintaining
the peace of Europe. Olearius remained in Scotland for
several months; but the answer he carried back with him could
not have been satisfactory to his master, as James insisted
that the King of England was the chief disturber of the
peace in making war on France and doing all manner of
injuries to himself[1]. In May Lord Dacre and Dr West
came with proposals on the part of Henry to compose all
quarrels and to confirm the existing peace. The two ambassadors were received with all courtesy; but James saw
in their errand only the English king's desire to have his
hands free to deal with France[2]. More successful in his
mission was de la Motte, the French ambassador, who arrived
in the country about the same date as Dacre and West.
On his voyage de la Motte had performed certain exploits
which would not make him less acceptable to James. He
sank three English ships, and brought seven others captive
into Leith. The object of his visit was to urge James to
war with England, and he bore ample promises of help in
money and all military furnishings. The response of James
was rash beyond precedent: he renewed the ancient league
with France not only against England but against every
enemy who should choose to attack France[3].

[1] *Exchequer Rolls*, vol. XIII. p. lxvi.
[2] Leslie, pp. 84-5.
[3] Pinkerton, II. 75, note. In September of this year (1513) Louis

Meanwhile, the relations of Scotland and England were not improving. Both by sea and land there was already virtual war between them. In July of 1512, Robert Barton, the brother of Andrew, took thirteen English prizes ; and the English repaid the Scots with interest. On the Borders, also, deeds of violence were increasing, and neither Government took effective measures to stop them. To add to all this friction, an English expedition was despatched in June to the attack of Guienne; and, though it failed lamentably, it showed once for all that Henry was determined on war with France. Still James delayed to quarrel openly with England ; and even though de la Motte returned in November, bringing a ship of war laden with artillery, powder, and wine, the year closed without the outbreak of hostilities[1].

Though both James and Henry were now convinced that the sword must decide their quarrel, it was the interest of both to postpone hostilities as long as possible.

1513

During the opening months of 1513, therefore, they still continued to interchange civilities. In January James sent Lord Drummond to signify his willingness to overlook all past injuries if Henry would desist from his attempts against France; but the offer was rejected with scorn. Dr West, who was sent by Henry to James in the month of March, was not more successful in effecting an understanding. In his interviews with James and his queen he received equally little satisfaction. He appealed to Margaret, as the sister of one king and the wife of the other, to use her influence in maintaining peace between them. But Margaret was in full sympathy with her husband ; and she had, moreover, a grievance of her own against her brother, who had refused to give up certain jewels which formed part of her inheritance. West's message to James bore that Henry was willing to con-

XII granted letters of naturalization to every Scotsman in France.— *Memoirs of the Alliance between France and Scotland*, p 33.

[1] Leslie, p. 85.

done all past wrongs if James would agree to confirm the perpetual peace. On one condition, only, however, would James accept this proposal : Henry must first undertake to abandon the league against France[1].

To report how things now stood in Scotland Forman was once more despatched to the French Court. In Forman James appears to have placed implicit confidence ; yet there is good reason to believe that Forman was not true to his master. With singular adroitness he had made himself equally acceptable to James's friends and enemies. From England he received the rich priory of Cottingham, from Louis of France the archbishopric of Bourges , and shortly after the death of James Leo X made him Archbishop of St Andrews. For what now followed he must be held in a large degree responsible; and in the next reign he was indeed directly accused of having betrayed his country[2]. To give the final impulse to James, de la Motte returned to Scotland in May, bringing four ships freighted with flour and wine. But what would weigh more with James than any gifts of Louis, there also came from his queen, Anne of Brittany, a special message couched in the spirit of a bygone age of chivalry. Sending him a ring from her own finger, she besought him as her true knight to advance three feet into English ground and strike a blow for her honour[3].

The last friendly letter of James to Henry was written on May 24. James had heard from the French king that there was some talk of a year's truce between him and his enemies; and in the vain hope of the truce being realized he brought the matter before Henry. What Henry meant was

[1] The important parts of West's dispatch are given in Mr Gregory Smith's excellent book, *The Days of James IV*, p. 129.

[2] Ruddiman, I. 209

[3] Pitscottie, it should be said, is our only authority for these statements. A turquoise ring said to have been taken from James's finger, and preserved in the College of Heralds, London, may be the gift of the French queen.

seen some five weeks later, when on the 30th of June he crossed to Calais to the invasion of France. James's course was now clear; and thenceforward nothing availed to turn him aside from his fatal purpose. On the 26th of July he sent the Lyon Herald to Henry with a message which was meant and was understood as a declaration of war; and on the day following he despatched a fleet to the assistance of France, whose commander, the Earl of Arran, wasted his time and strength in an attack on the town of Carrickfergus[1]. But an invasion of England was the enterprise on which all James's thoughts were now bent, and he issued a summons for the whole array of the kingdom to meet him in the third week of August on the Borough Muir of Edinburgh. Through the gloom of the national disaster that followed the incidents of this time easily assumed a mysterious and exaggerated hue; and it is in this light that we may understand the two famous warnings that preceded the march to Flodden. A few days before James joined his army he was worshipping at vespers in the church of Linlithgow when there appeared before him the figure of a man, bareheaded, clad in a long gown, and with a pikestaff in his hand. In solemn tones the stranger warned him against proceeding with his enterprise, and having told his errand "vanished away as he had been a blink of the sun, or a whip of the whirlwind, and could no more be seen[2]." Another intimation portended still more unmistakeably the approaching calamity. When the army had assembled on the Borough Muir and the king was in Holyrood, a voice was heard at midnight from the Market-cross, calling in tones that were heard throughout the city the names of the earls and lords, barons and gentlemen, who within forty days should appear before the master of him who spoke[3].

The war broke out before James began his march. In

---

[1] Sir David Lyndsay's *Squire Meldrum.*

[2] Pitscottie; Buchanan.

[3] Pitscottie.

the beginning of August, Lord Hume[1], now Warden of all
the Marches, entered Northumberland with a force of 6,000 or
7,000 men, and achieved all the work of a successful raid
What had happened so often before, however, now happened
to Hume. Retarded by his booty, he was overtaken by an
English army under Sir William Bulmer, at Milfield, and was
forced to give battle under the most unfavourable conditions.
It was the English archers who decided the day, and Hume
with the loss of all his booty, fled across the border, leaving
behind him many dead and still more prisoners[2]

The news of the Ill Raid, as it came to be called, only
quickened James's desire to tempt fortune on a larger scale
With an army whose numbers[3] are not accurately known he at
length marched to the Border, and crossing the Tweed took
up his position at Twisel on the 22nd of August. Here two
days later he held a council which passed a noteworthy act in
view of the coming campaign. Little thinking of the full
significance of its action, the council ordained that the
heirs of all who fell in the war should be exempted from
the royal dues of wardship, relief, and marriage. Proceeding
to Norham, James captured its castle after a six weeks' siege,
and took in succession those of Etal, Ford, and others in the
same corner of the country. But James's incapacity as a leader
became more evident every day. Wasting his time in these
petty achievements, he was letting slip the opportunity of
striking a really important blow, and specially of taking at
advantage the coveted town of Berwick, then unprepared for a
formidable attack. It was now the month of September, and
since he had crossed the Border, there had never been a fair
day or even hour "but great cold, wind, and wet[4]." For a

---

[1] Alexander, third Lord Hume.

[2] Leslie, Buchanan, Hall, Holinshed.

[3] Polydore Vergil gives the number of the Scots as 60,000 ; Hall as
100,000

[4] Leslie.

feudal host his army had already been long in the field; many had now secured ample booty; and the discomfort from the weather and the want of food told on the spirits of many more As the result of all these causes men deserted in such numbers that it told seriously on the strength of James's arms, and should have urged him to immediate and decisive action According to some accounts, his folly was the more reprehensible for the cause that occasioned it In Ford Castle, which had come into his hands, he is said to have frittered away the hours in trifling with Lady Heron, the chatelaine of the place[1]—an occupation, in truth, more in keeping with the general impression of James's character than the responsibility of a king and a commander.

Meanwhile, the day was approaching when he was to be brought face to face with the adventure he had sought. When Henry VIII sailed for France, he was fully aware that he might count on an invasion of his kingdom by the Scots. Against such a contingency, therefore, he had entrusted his best soldier, the Earl of Surrey—the same who had brought James his bride—with the defence of the country On the news of the preparations of James, Surrey had taken effective steps to discharge his trust. By the first of September, according to his summons, the English army was to meet him at Newcastle and thence to march against the enemy. The foul weather told on Surrey's movements as it had told upon the Scots; but on the 3rd of September he was at Alnwick, when he arranged his order of battle. His numbers were between 30,000 and 40,000; and in their midst was borne the sacred banner of St Cuthbert. Well knowing the character of the Scottish king[2], Surrey despatched a pursuivant with a challenge which was admirably fitted to serve his ends Taunting James with a breach of honour in attacking a kingdom with which he had sworn

---

[1] Pitscottie, Buchanan.   [2] See above pp. 312, 315.

perpetual peace, he defied him to try on the following Friday
"the righteousness of the matter" between them. To sting
James still more effectively, Surrey's son, the Lord Admiral of
England, sent the insolent message that he was there to answer
for the death of the pirate Andrew Barton, at whose fate James
had been so much concerned. Instead of treating these
bravadoes with disdain, James with the irresponsibility of a
knight-errant accepted a challenge which might involve the
fate of his kingdom[1]

Having accepted the gage of battle, James left the neighbourhood of Ford Castle, and crossing to the left bank of the
Till, took up a strong position on the hill of Flodden, an
offshoot of the Cheviots. By Wednesday the 7th, Surrey had
reached Wooler Haugh about ten miles south of the Scottish
camp, and on the left bank of the Till. Between the two armies
lay Milfield Plain, where a few weeks before Lord Hume met with
his disaster in the Ill Raid, and on this ground Surrey proposed
to the Scottish king that they should fight their battle in a fair
field. Rash as he was, however, James was not to be tempted
from the position he had deliberately chosen; and Surrey was
compelled to approach the Scots from another direction.
Whatever may have been the relative number of the two hosts,
Surrey's next movements showed that he was confident in his
superior strength[2]. On Thursday the 8th, he marched northwards on the right bank of the Till, and on the following day
recrossed the river with his main body at Twisel Bridge, the
remainder passing by a ford a little higher up. At Twisel

---

[1] James had on two previous occasions avoided battle with Surrey, so
that he may now have felt himself constrained to accept his challenge

[2] Surrey had learned through his herald the number and condition
of the Scots.

The authorities for the battle, it should be said, are mainly English,
and in several important points are contradictory and incredible. Extracts
from these authorities will be found in Mr Gregory Smith's *The Days of
James IV* (Nutt, 1890.)

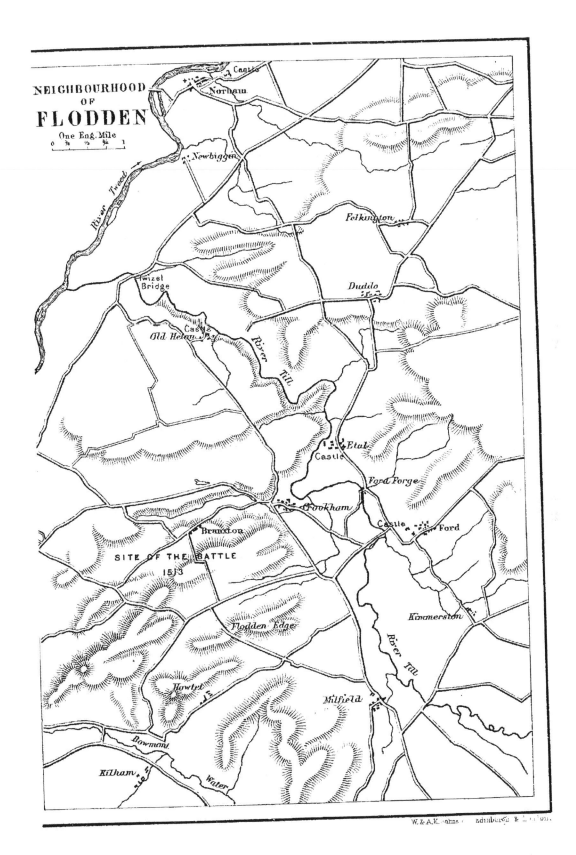

Bridge he was about nine miles north of the Scottish camp ; and, as Friday was the day appointed for the trial of battle, he at once marched southwards towards Flodden A sudden movement of the Scots must have told him that they on their part meant to abide the challenge. Some two miles to the north of Flodden is Branxton Hill, which might have proved advantageous ground for the English army. To prevent its occupation, James, setting fire to his tents, marched under cover of the smoke from the hill of Flodden to the lower eminence, and there awaited the approach of the enemy. When the smoke cleared away, the two hosts found themselves face to face between four and five o'clock in the September afternoon. The hour was late for the work that was before them ; but the day had been fixed and neither side shrank from the contest

The Scots were arranged in four battalions, and before the fight began Surrey made a corresponding disposition. To the left wing of the Scots, which was in two divisions, led respectively by Lords Crawford and Montrose, Huntly and Hume, were opposed two bodies under Lord Howard, Admiral of England, and his brother Sir Edmund Howard ; the Scottish centre, led by the king, faced that of England under Surrey ; and the Scottish right under Lennox and Argyle had for their antagonists the men of Cheshire and Lancashire with Sir Edward Stanley as their leader. Behind the Scottish centre was a reserve force under Bothwell ; while Lord Dacre led a similar detachment in the rear of Surrey. The English army faced southwards, and the Scots looked towards their own country

The fight began on both sides with the play of artillery ; but at the outset the Scottish master of the ordnance was slain[1] ; and his men were speedily driven from their posts

---

[1] This is Hall's statement ; but Robert Borthwick, the Master Gunner of Scotland, was not killed at Flodden. Hall may have meant Henry Lord Sinclair.—*Exchequer Rolls*, Vol. XIII. p. clxiii.

Then with the impatience that had so often cost them dear in the past[1], the whole four divisions of the Scots quitted their advantageous positions and met the enemy on the lower ground. At once the fight became general, but while Surrey from his chariot surveyed the whole field[2], the King of Scots was content to fight like a common soldier. The various fortunes of the day proved how well the two hosts were matched. Huntly and Hume at the head of the Scottish left swept before them the division under Sir Edmund Howard; though for some un-explained reason they brought no aid to their less fortunate countrymen. The other section of the Scottish left suffered heavily under the charge of Lord Howard, and lost its two leaders, Crawford and Montrose. On the Scottish right the day was adverse from the first. Charged by the knights and dis-tressed by the arrows of the men of Lancashire and Cheshire, the Highlanders were driven from the field—their leaders, Lennox and Argyle, being among the slain. Meanwhile, the two centres fought with such equal fortune that neither side could claim the advantage. But, as the evening wore on, the superiority of England became hourly more apparent. James was strengthened by Bothwell's reserve, and he must have been joined by many from the other divisions; but his right wing was gone, and Lords Hume and Huntly did no further service. On the other hand, after having defeated Lennox and Argyle, Stanley, returning from his pursuit of the High-landers, threw himself on the rear of James, who was now beset in front by Surrey, and on the left by Lord Howard and his brother. Thus brought to bay, the flower of the Scottish army closed round their king, and formed a circle which still

---

[1] It is in connection with this warlike impatience of the Scots that Buchanan applies to them the phrase *praefervida ingenia*, which has become hackneyed under the form *perfervidum ingenium Scotorum.—History*, p 321. (Edit. Ruddiman.)

[2] Surrey was in his 70th year. Pitscottie speaks of him as "an old crooked carle lying in a chariot."

remained unbroken though exposed to the onslaught of the whole English strength. As the ground became sodden with blood and the late rains, the Scots took off their shoes to secure a firmer footing ; and the darkness alone put an end to the conflict.   It was only when the morning broke that Surrey discovered that he was master of the field, for during the night the main remnant of the Scots who had fought round their king had quitted their position and were nowhere to be seen

The fight at Flodden[1] was no national disgrace such as Edward II brought upon his country at Bannockburn.   The English "wanted no good will" to follow up their advantage by an invasion of Scotland; but though Surrey learned that the Scots had lost almost all their natural protectors, he had suffered so much that he was unequal to further efforts.   But if Flodden was no national disgrace to Scotland, it was among the greatest of her disasters.   With her king had fallen twelve earls, fourteen lords, an archbishop, a bishop, two abbots, together with knights and gentlemen so numerous that there was scarcely a family of consequence in Scotland that had not occasion to remember the folly of their king.   Yet no bitterness pursued the memory of James, though on at least three distinct occasions he had wantonly imperilled the national existence. His popular gifts, forming so favourable a contrast to the character of his father, and, above all, his gallant death on the field of battle[2], which in the case of a king appealed so powerfully to the imagination of the people[3], atoned for all his shortcomings, and James has always held his place among the favourite kings of his country.

---

[1] By the English it was known as the battle of Branxton. Fortunately in the interests of literature, the Scots chose the name of Flodden.

[2] James's body is said to have been found on the field of battle, and thence conveyed to Berwick and afterwards to London. The Scots, not without some reason, refused to believe in the truth of this.

[3] Hall expresses this feeling.—"O what a noble and triumphant courage was thys, for a kynge to fyghte in a battayl as a meane soldier."

To what extent James deserves the credit of having improved his country, it is difficult to determine. It is to be noted, however, that throughout his whole reign no commanding figure meets us but his own. He was always surrounded by his leading nobles; but none of them played a part on the scale of their predecessors in previous reigns. The Earls of Argyle and Huntly did effective service in the subjugation of the Western Highlands and the Isles; the two families of the Humes and the Hepburns had honours and lands heaped upon them beyond any of their fellow-subjects, and they wielded between them the chief power in the south of Scotland; yet no one of these nobles appears to have aimed at being more than merely powerful subjects. Nevertheless, it is quite in keeping with the "simple wilfulness" of James's character that he should be influenced by astute counsellors, who were skilful enough to conceal their ascendency. Such a counsellor in James's later years was Forman, bishop of Moray, whose promptings emphasized the weakest sides of his nature, and involved him in a policy which had such a tragic result for himself and his country.

In the varied activity of James's reign we have conclusive proof of the general expansion of the national spirit. Legislation, commerce, the administration of justice, intellectual development—in all these there was a forward movement that distinguishes this reign from those that preceded it. So far as James was personally concerned, his highest claim to respect is the improvement of justice throughout the length and breadth of the country. In the case of the Highlands and Islands we have seen how he secured peace and order by their thorough subjugation and the establishment of sheriffdoms and new centres of justice. By giving real effect to the ayres or circuit-courts held by the justiciars James did a further important work. By frequent enactments these courts should have been held twice in the year under the presidency of the king; but, in point of fact, those enactments had in large degree been a dead letter. From the very beginning of his reign, however, James threw himself with zest into the work of these courts. His zeal, indeed, was not wholly due to a disinterested love of justice. In visiting the remotest parts of his kingdom he relieved his morbid unrest of nature, and with these business journeys he combined those pleasures to which he was devoted— hunting, and all manner of festivities being the invariable ac- companiments of each justice-ayre. As, moreover, the fines and escheats imposed by the justiciars made a considerable part of the royal revenues, it is evident that the king had a personal interest in the efficient administration of the law. Of the need of such administration we have notable proof even towards the end of his reign. In 1510 a justice-ayre held at Jedburgh is described by Leslie in the following passage. "The king rode forth from Edinburgh the 8th of November, well accompanied, to the water of Roulle, where he took divers broken men, and brought them to Jedburgh; of whom some were justified[1], and the principals of the troubles came in linen clothes, with naked swords in their hands, and halters about their necks, and put them in the king's will: who were sent to divers castles in ward, with sundry others of that [*sic*] country men also : whereat the Borders were in greater quietness hereafter[2]."

One other memorable step towards the improvement of justice is associated with the name of James. The Court known as the "Session," which had been established by James I, and which James II had endeavoured to reform, had proved to be inefficient. Assembling only for brief periods in different parts of the kingdom, it had been unequal to overtake the business that was brought before it. To remedy this evil the Parliament that met in March 1504 enacted that hence- forth there should be a "Daily Council" chosen by the king, which should sit permanently in Edinburgh, or wherever the

---

[1] Executed.   [2] Leslie, pp. 81—82.

king should make his residence—the new court to have the same powers as that of the "Session." Till it was superseded by the Court of Session in 1532, the "Daily Council" was the supreme court of justice in Scotland.

By his firm government at home and his energetic policy abroad James created the necessary conditions for the development of commerce. But by legislation, also, he did something to encourage the enterprise of his subjects. The debasement of the currency, which had reached its height in the preceding reign, especially called for attention, and, as we have seen, the question was dealt with in successive Parliaments of James. But the best known Act of James for the encouragement of industry was one for the creation of a fishing-fleet. In the intention of those who framed it this Act was to serve a double purpose. Fishing had always been one of the chief industries of Scotland; but owing to the limited number of boats "great innumerable riches" were lost to the country. Moreover, if fishing-boats were more numerous, they would bring employment to "idle men and vagabonds" for "the eschewing of vices and idleness." Accordingly, to meet these two objects the following extraordinary law (May, 1493) was passed. In all towns and burghs boats were to be constructed, the least of which must be of twenty-two tons burthen, and all of them to be ready by the following Shrove-Tuesday. For the manning of these boats the officers of each burgh were to lay hands on all the "stark, idle men" within their bounds, who must either consent to accept this service or be banished from the burgh.

From the beginning of the commercial development of Scotland it was with the Low Countries and specially with Flanders that her transactions had been mainly carried on. It has already been noted how prominently the Flemings come before us in such reigns as those of David I, William the Lyon, and Alexander III. By the marriage of Mary, fifth daughter of James I, to the son of the Lord of Campvere, the intercourse with the Netherlands became still more close. Hitherto the staple of Scotch trade had been the town of Bruges ; but it was now removed to Middelburg in the island of Walcheren, and in the territory of the Lords of Campvere[1]. It was during the reign of James IV, however, that Scotland derived the greatest profit from her connection with the thriving communities of Flanders. Flemings had all along settled freely in Scotland ; but towards the close of the 15th century they came in increasing numbers, bringing with them those handicrafts for which their country was famous. Of the nature and extent of the trade carried on between Scotland and Flanders we have an interesting record in the Ledger of Andrew Halyburton, a Scottish merchant settled at Middelburg from 1492 to 1503[2]. Halyburton held the position of Conservator of the Scots privileges in the Netherlands, whose duties were to look after the "weal" of Scotch traders and as far as lay in his power to save them unnecessary expense in the conduct of their business. From his ledger we learn the articles of export and import that made up the trade of Scotland. The list of exports gives us no exalted notion of the home industries of the country. They are mainly wool, hides, skins, salmon, pearls, and cloth of cheap quality. On the other hand, the commodities brought into the country partly explain the frequent denunciation by the Estates of the luxurious living of certain classes of the people. Among these imports are lawn, holland, cambrics, silk, velvet, taffety, satin, damask, ribbons, gold and silver thread, jewelled rings, and considerable quantities of wine. In this long and close association with Flanders we find adequate evidence of a fact which deserves to be emphasized—that in the true interests of Scotland, Flanders was more valuable to her than France. More picturesque and romantic, the Franco-Scottish alliance had been of doubtful benefit to the smaller country, and the

---

[1] In James IV's reign the staple was removed from Middelburg to Campvere. Gairdner, *Letters, &c.* vol. II. p. lxiii.

[2] The Ledger was edited by Cosmo Innes in 1867.

time was soon to come when it proved an actual hindrance
equally to its religious, its political, and its commercial development.   On the other hand, in more prosaic fashion the
intercourse with Flanders had been productive of unmixed
good in showing the way to an intelligent cultivation of the
natural resources of the country.

On no object was James more ardently bent than on the
creation of a Scottish navy   The idea was not original, for
Robert I had seen that a navy might be made a source of
strength to the country, and had shown a keen interest in the
building and improvement of ships.   But his example had not
been systematically followed by his successors, and it is to
James IV that the credit belongs of seeking to realize Bruce's
project.   In this object, as in others, James was only obeying
the spirit of the age, since naval enterprise was one of the
matters that preoccupied men's minds during the latter part of
the 15th century.   But in this, as in all his undertakings,
James displayed an energy which insured the attainment of his
purpose   Writing to Louis XII in 1506, James tells him that
he had long been engaged in building a fleet for the protection
of his coasts.   He exhausted the timber of his own kingdom
in the construction of ships, and had to apply to Denmark and
France for a further supply—the latter country also providing
him with trained shipwrights.   So successful were his efforts
that his navy at its best comprised 16 large ships and 10
smaller ones.   But the building of the "Great St Michael,"
the largest ship then existing, was James's special pride.
According to Pitscottie, who had his information from her
captain, Robert Barton, and her quarter-master, Sir Andrew
Wood, "she wasted all the woods of Fife" in the building;
she cost £30,000, apart from her artillery; she had a crew of
300 sailors, she had 120 gunners, and 1000 marines.   James
was fortunate, also, in his naval commanders; for Sir Andrew
Wood, the Bartons, father and sons, have taken their place
among the national heroes of Scotland.   But this armament,

which James had created at such labour and expense, shared in the final disaster that overtook his kingdom and himself. Sent to France, under the command of the Earl of Arran, it reached the shores of that country, but what eventually came of it history does not relate. As for the "Great St Michael," it was sold to Louis XII the year after James's death for the sum of 40,000 francs of Tours.

In intellectual expansion as well as in general enterprise the reign of James IV forms an epoch in Scottish history. The famous educational Act of 1496 would of itself indicate the enlightened views of James and his counsellors. According to this act, all barons and freeholders were to send their eldest sons to the schools from the time they were eight or nine years old. At the "grammar schools" they were to remain till they had acquired "perfect Latyn." They were then to proceed to the "schools of art and law," where a curriculum of three years would qualify them to administer law and justice in the parts of the country to which they belonged. By this arrangement, it was stated "that the poor people should have no need to seek our sovereign Lord's principal Auditors for each small injury."

It was at the earnest request of James that in 1495 Pope Alexander VI granted a bull for the foundation of the university of Aberdeen. The fate of the university of Glasgow had not been encouraging; but the new university was more prosperous in its beginnings. It had for its patron William Elphinstone, bishop of Aberdeen, whose foundation of King's College is only one of his many good deeds to his country; and for its first principal, Hector Boece, who with John Major represented the Scottish scholarship of his day. By his wonderful History of Scotland Boece came to stand in a somewhat dubious light with posterity; but he at least succeeded in giving an impress to the new institution which influenced all its future fortunes. At the mother university of St Andrews, also, an advance was made which assured to her the advantage over

her rivals. To its original Pædagogium was added by Prior
Hepburn the College of St Leonard's, which in days fast
coming was to be a stronghold of the new religious teaching
that was to undermine the ancient church.

By the creation of a third university it was now definitively
settled that university development in Scotland was to follow
very different lines from those of England. In Scotland there
was scope for only one university, and had the nation been
satisfied with that of St Andrews, it might have played a part
in Scottish history such as Oxford and Cambridge have played
in the history of England. But the universities of Scotland
have been called to humbler though perhaps not less useful
functions. They have exercised little influence on the social
and political life of the country, but by the non-professional
part of their studies they long filled the place of those secondary schools which it was the desire of Knox to provide.

Not the least distinction of James's reign was the introduction of printing into his kingdom. Brought into England
in 1477, and into Denmark in 1480, it was not till 1507 that
the art was first practised in Scotland. With the intelligent
curiosity that distinguished him, James appears to have realized
the importance of the new invention, and conferred a
monopoly on the two men who introduced it—Walter Chapman and Andrew Millar. The art had not come too soon to
Scotland, for among the other glories of the time was the
appearance of men of learning and genius, whose productions
form part of the national inheritance. To the reign of James
belong the poems of William Dunbar[1] and Gavin Douglas, who
in any age must have been among the first literary figures of
their time. Regarded as historical documents, the poems of
Dunbar are the most vivid representations we possess of the
prevailing tone of the society in which he moved. King,

---

[1] Chapman and Millar printed seven of Dunbar's poems in the first
volume that issued from their press.

queen, courtiers, churchmen, burgesses, all are there depicted with a brutal frankness which in itself reflects the age, and assures us of the essential truth of the portraiture. What is of further historical interest both in Douglas and Dunbar is the blending in them of the Middle Age that had gone and the new age that had come. By their larger view of life and their more direct knowledge of the classical tradition they show that they have been influenced by the revival of letters; while in the moments when they remember the profession to which they both belonged, they fall back on that cloistral attitude towards men and things which is the note of mediæval Christianity. The two Scotsmen who represented the learning of their country, John Major and Hector Boece, typify in striking degree the same contrast between the old order and the new. Born about the same date, and both educated in the schools of Paris, the one is in most respects the antithesis of the other. Boece, like his acquaintance Erasmus, was wholly the scholar of the Renaissance, and by his intellectual interests and the comparative purity of his Latin style, unmistakeably showed his training and his proclivities. Major, on the other hand, was the schoolman pure and simple, and, as a survival of the past, excited the ridicule alike of Rabelais and Melanchthon.

These various evidences of the progress of the nation are fully borne out by the remarkable report on Scotland prepared by the Spanish agent, de Ayala. During his visits in 1496 and 1497 Ayala had ample opportunities of seeing the country for himself; and he assured Ferdinand that he had set down nothing which he did not believe to be true. At the same time, it is evident that he had come under the personal fascination of James, and was disposed to say the best he could of him and his kingdom.

Ayala's estimate of the royal revenues is specially interesting, as it is the most definite and complete we possess, and does not seem to be far from the truth. Even in the most prosperous period of his reign James was in constant straits for money. This was partly due to expensive personal habits, but mainly to his expenditure on artillery and the navy, all of which came from his private purse. At one time, indeed, James seemed about to emulate the ways of Empson and Dudley in order to meet his various expenses. In his desperation he even had recourse to the disused casualty[1] of Recognition, which implied the forfeiture of all estates whose owners could not produce their title-deeds; but the threatening murmurs of his subjects warned him of the dangerous course he was treading[2]. Ayala enumerates six sources of revenue that pertained to the Kings of Scots. From his arable and pasture lands[3], which were let on a three years' lease, James received a rent of 50,000 pounds Scots, or 40,000 ducats; from the customs[4] 25,000 ducats; from the administration of the law 25,000; and from the casualty of ward 20,000. From all benefices in the church the king received their full revenues during vacancies, and one year's reserve on presentation. In addition to his income in money there was supplied in kind such store of fish, meat, poultry, &c., as kept the royal kitchen in abundance in whatever part of his dominion James was pleased to travel[5].

The account which Ayala gives of the general prosperity of the country is not inconsistent with the intimations we receive

---

[1] In Scottish feudal law *casualties* were such emoluments arising to the superior as depended on uncertain events, such as ward, marriage, &c.

[2] Leslie, p. 73.

[3] The counties or earldoms which, either by forfeiture or ward, were in the hands of James IV were Fife, Strathearn, Menteith, Moray, Mar, Ross, Orkney, and Sutherland. In addition to these the shires of Stirling and Linlithgow were crown lands, as also at a later date of James's reign the Earldom of Sutherland. *Exchequer Rolls*, Vol. XI. pp. xciv—cxxxiv.

[4] "While the gross revenue from the customs in the reign of James III amounted on an average to £3300, their yield during the five years now in question [1497—1501] was, as has been seen, only £3106."—*Exchequer Rolls*, Vol. XI. p. lii.

[5] In this reign the practice of letting the customs became usual.—*Ib.* Vol. XII. p. xxxi.

from other sources, which have already been indicated. "The towns and villages," he says, "are populous The houses are good, all built of hewn stone, and provided with excellent doors, glass windows, and a great number of chimneys. All the furniture that is used in Italy, Spain, and France, is to be found in their dwellings It has not been bought in modern times only, but inherited from preceding ages" The character he gives of the people shows that his prepossessions did not blind him to their shortcomings "The people," he writes, "are handsome They like foreigners so much that they dispute with one another as to who shall have and treat a foreigner in his house. They are vain and ostentatious by nature. They spend all they have to keep up appearances. They are as well dressed as it is possible to be in such a country as that in which they live. They are courageous, strong, quick, and agile They are envious (jealous?) to excess." The Scottish women are described in terms which are corroborated by subsequent travellers in Scotland. "The women," he says, "are courteous in the extreme. I mention this because they are really honest, though very bold They are absolute mistresses of their houses, and even of their husbands, in all things concerning the administration of their property, income as well as expenditure. They are very graceful and handsome women. They dress much better than here (England), and especially as regards the head-dress, which is, I think, the handsomest in the world."

In one sentence Ayala sums up the general impression of the country which he had received at once from his own observation and the testimony of those whom he had met; and the sentence may stand as a fairly accurate estimate of the reign of James IV. "There is as great a difference," he says, "between the Scotland of old time and the Scotland of to-day as there is between bad and good[1]."

---

[1] Bergenroth, *Calendar of Spanish Papers*, II, 169—175.

CHAPTER VIII.

JAMES V (1513—1542).

English king	French king
Henry VIII ... 1509—1547.	Francis I ... 1515—1547.

Emperors : Maximilian, Charles V.
Popes : Hadrian VI, Clement VI, Paul III

DURING the reign of James IV the influence of foreign affairs on Scotland had been greater than during any previous period of her history. In still greater degree she was influenced by her foreign relations during the reign of his son and successor, James V. The great European events between 1513 and 1542 were of a nature that could not but directly and profoundly affect the fortunes of Scotland as a member of the Christian community of nations. As will presently be seen, those who successively governed Scotland throughout the reign of James V directed the national councils either in accordance with the promptings of England or France. In religion, the revolt of Luther from Rome, and the assumption by Henry VIII of the headship of the Church in England, bore results in Scotland which eventually led to the ruin of her national Church and the consequent union of her crown and government with those of England. But it was the politics of the continent even more than religion that affected Scotland during the reign of James V. For Scotland, as for the other Christian powers, the absorbing circumstance of the time was the life-long rivalry of the Emperor Charles and Francis I of France. By her traditional alliance with France Scotland came to have a stake in this struggle, which involved her existence as a nation, and absorbed the main energies of her king. The disaster of Solway Moss, which broke the heart of James V and laid the country open to the guile and force of Henry VIII, was as directly the result of the Franco-Scottish alliance as Flodden itself.

Though their natural leaders and the choice of the nation had fallen at Flodden, the Scots had passed through too long and stern a discipline to lose   1513 heart even in such a calamity. Edinburgh, now the acknowledged capital, showed a notable example to the rest of the country. The men of the Border had fallen in such numbers in the late battle that the way was open into the heart of the land, and the capital would naturally be the first object of the enemy's attack. Its provost and other magistrates were among the slain; but those who had been left in charge of the city took instant steps against the threatened danger. In a stern proclamation to the citizens they ordered the women to offer up prayers in the churches, and all the men capable of bearing arms to have their weapons in readiness. For the first time, also, a wall was now constructed round the city, whose remaining fragments testify to the haste and untrained hands of those who built it.

On their parts the queen and the chief men left in the country lost no time in arranging a form of government[1]. Flodden was fought on the 9th   1513 of September, and in the third week of that month the Estates met at Stirling and crowned the infant king[2] (Sept. 21). In a

---

[1] The energy of the queen and her councillors is convincingly proved by the Register of the Acts of the Lords of Council. Some interesting extracts, illustrating the action of the Council after Flodden, will be found in the *Scottish Antiquary* for January, 1898.

[2] *Act. Dom. Con.*

will drawn up before his fatal march James IV had named
his wife as regent in the event of his death ; and his instructions
were now duly carried out—Margaret being appointed guardian
of her son and regent of the kingdom, while with her were
associated as councillors, James Beaton, archbishop of Glasgow,
and the Earls of Huntly, Angus, and Arran   But as things
now stood it was impossible that this arrangement could be
either effectual or permanent.   So many were the causes of
unsettlement, indeed, that the wonder is that after a minority
of fifteen years the kingdom should have come safely through
the trial.   The immediate cause of strife, however, was the
distribution of the benefices of the churchmen who had fallen
at Flodden—the see of St Andrews being the specially coveted
prize of the leading competitors.   When such prizes were
going it was of high importance to the rival candidates and
their supporters who should be the chief person in the country.
From Margaret as regent a certain section of the nobles had
nothing to expect ; and they turned to another personage as
more likely to serve their own interests   This was John, Duke
of Albany, son of that Albany so energetic in the reign of
James III, and heir to the Scottish crown in the event of the
infant king's death[1].

The arrangement at Stirling had not long been made when
a secret message was despatched to Albany in
1513   France, requesting him to come to Scotland and
assume the regency[2].   But Albany, it would appear, was
already acting on his own behalf.   On November 26th a
meeting of the Scottish Estates was specially summoned to
give answer to two ambassadors sent with a message from
Louis XII of France.   The ambassadors, one of whom, the
Sieur de la Bastie, was to have good reason to regret he had

---

[1] Leslie, p. 97 —For the first part of James V's reign Leslie is specially
valuable   Till about the year 1524 he appears to have based his narrative
on contemporary authorities which are lost   After that date he becomes
less detailed and less trustworthy.   [2] *Ibid.*

ever set foot in Scotland, bore two proposals, both of which were accepted "in ane voice" by the assembled barons and churchmen. The one proposal was for the continuance of the old alliance with France, the other that Louis should send Albany to Scotland with men and arms for the defence of the country against England[1]. That the country required such defence had been signally proved during the course of the preceding months; for Lord Dacre, the Warden of the English Marches, had carried devastation into the Middle Scottish March, and was only waiting his opportunity of repeating the same work in the west[2]. At the close of the year 1513, therefore, the prospects of the kingdom were sufficiently gloomy—with divided counsels within and an enemy ready to take advantage of all its misfortunes.

The threatened coming of Albany was now the event to which all parties looked with hope or fear, as their interests dictated. To Henry VIII the   1514
presence of Albany in Scotland would be a source of danger which he could not ignore, since it would mean that Scotland, in greater measure than ever, would be the instrument of France All that Henry could do, therefore, he now did to avert the untoward event He wrote to his sister Margaret, and he wrote to Louis XII, calling upon both to keep Albany in France; while, at the same time, his Warden of the Marches continued to show the Scots what was implied in having the King of England for an enemy The two countries were, in truth, still at open war. In spite of their divisions at home the Scots, it would seem, were able to repay the exploits of Dacre with some effect. In March 1514 they burnt five towns in the East Marches, led a force within two miles of Berwick; and only waited the arrival of Albany, Henry was told, to attempt the recovery of the town[3].

[1] *Acts of Parl. of Scotland*
[2] *State Papers of Henry VIII*, vol. I. part II. pp. 680—703
[3] *Ibid.* p. 763

But whatever strength or cohesion the Scots possessed

1514 was sorely tried by a remarkable proceeding of the regent Margaret. On April 30 she gave birth to a posthumous son; and on August 6 she married the Earl of Angus, who had not yet reached his twentieth year. Her authority had been precarious before; but by this step she at once brought to a head all the rivalries of the leading personages in the country. Against Margaret and Angus were ranged the Lord Chamberlain Hume, one of the most powerful barons in the kingdom; the Earl of Arran, the next heir to the Crown after Albany, and James Beaton, Archbishop of Glasgow and Chancellor of the realm—all of whom were in favour of the coming of Albany. In October came the occasion to which all must have been looking forward, the death of Bishop Elphinstone, who had been accepted as the successor to the vacant see of St Andrews. For the coveted office both parties were ready with their candidates—Angus with his uncle, the poet Gavin Douglas; and the Humes with John Hepburn, Prior of St Andrews. For a time the Humes and their allies had the advantage, and drove Gavin Douglas from the castle of St Andrews, of which he had taken possession with the help of his friends. Nor did the action of the Hume party stop there. At the head of a strong force they compelled the regent to flee from Edinburgh to Stirling, whence she was again brought to Edinburgh, virtually a prisoner in the hands of her enemies. All these events took place in November; and the same month saw the important castle of Dunbar in the hands of the Sieur de la Bastie, as the representative of Albany.

On the 1st of January, 1515, Francis I succeeded Louis

1515 XII on the throne of France; and his accession directly bore on the fortunes of Scotland. The object on which Francis set his thoughts from the beginning was the invasion of Italy; and to carry out this enterprise it was in his interest to be at peace with England. If he were to

---

[1] *State Papers of Henry VIII*, vol. I. part II. pp. 933—939.

be on good terms with England, however, he could not show himself hostile in Scotland, and the question of Albany's passing to that country placed him in an embarrassing dilemma. For the moment it was necessary to have England as a friend; but the past history of France had shown that the old league with Scotland was not to be lightly dropped. As things actually went they could not have happened more favourably to Francis. On May 15 the Scots accepted the pacification which had been arranged between England and France in August of the preceding year, and on the 17th of May Albany entered the harbour of Ayr with a well-manned fleet of eight ships[1].

The task that lay before Albany was one which, with his powers and opportunities, was hopeless from the outset. Since the beginning of the year there 1515 had been no improvement in the relations of the rival factions. In January the Earl of Lennox had seized Dunbarton in the interests of the supporters of Albany; and the Earl of Arran had nearly caught Angus on his way from Glasgow On the other hand, the Pope had interfered in the affairs of St Andrews, and effected a compromise between Angus and the Humes. The see of St Andrews was given to Andrew Forman, whose proceedings in connection with Flodden place him in such a dubious light; Dunkeld was given to Gavin Douglas; and the Abbey of Coldingham to the youngest brother of Hume[2].

In himself Albany was not specially fitted for the work before him As admiral of France and the possessor of large estates in that country, he was 1515 accustomed to a standard of luxurious living he was not likely to find in Scotland. Moreover he could speak neither Scots nor English—a grave defect, since many lords, such as the Chamberlain Hume, whom it was his interest to conciliate,

[1] Leslie, p. 102.
[2] Buchanan.

23—2

were ignorant of French[1]. Yet the prospect before him was such as might have tempted an ambitious man to face even greater difficulties. Between Albany and the Scottish throne there were only two infant princes, and all the other children of James IV had died in infancy. With the aid of Francis, therefore, it was almost a probability that he might one day win the crown for which his father had so desperately gambled.

Albany was received in Edinburgh with the utmost enthusiasm; and at a meeting of the Estates in July (1515) he was proclaimed not only Regent of the kingdom but guardian of the princes—a notable proof of the ascendency of the party that favoured France. The immediate proceedings of Albany showed that he was confident of his strength. He shut up in Blackness Castle Lord Drummond, the grandfather of Angus, on the ground that a year before he had struck the Lyon Herald; and he sent Gavin Douglas, the new bishop of Dunkeld, to the sea-tower of St Andrews. As the history of Scotland had lamentably shown, however, the possession of the heir to the throne was indispensable to the full mastery of the kingdom; and to the attainment of this object Albany now addressed himself. A sinister secret that oozed out materially strengthened his hands: Henry VIII, it came to be known, was plotting for the conveyance to England of the two princes and their mother. In a meeting of the Parliament which still sat in Edinburgh

1515

---

[1] The Earl of Surrey in a letter to Cardinal Wolsey gives the following character of Albany: "By many ways I am advertised that the duke of Albany is a marvellous wilful man, and will believe no man's counsel, but will have his own opinion followed. I am also advertised that he is so passionate, that and he be apart among his familiars, and doth hear anything contrarious to his mind and pleasure, his accustomed manner is to take his bonnet suddenly off his head, and to throw it into the fire, and no man dare take it out, but let it to be brent. My Lord Dacre doth affirm, that at his last being in Scotland he did burn above a dozen bonnets after that manner."—Brewer, *The Reign of Henry VIII*, I. 552.

Albany secured the election of four peers, from whom Margaret was to choose three, to be entrusted with the guardianship of the king and his brother. To Margaret, then at Stirling, his decision was conveyed, but she refused to give up her children, and Albany prepared to secure them by force[1]. On the 4th of August he appeared before Stirling with a body of 7,000 men, when Margaret, seeing further resistance in vain, made an unconditional surrender of herself and her children. To complete Albany's triumph, Margaret with her husband and his brother Sir George Douglas, fled to the Borders, where at Harbottle she gave birth to a daughter, afterwards Lady Lennox, the mother of Darnley. Over another formidable opponent Albany was equally successful. The chamberlain Hume had been among the most eager for the coming of Albany to Scotland; but a quarrel, sedulously fostered by the English warden Dacre, had arisen between them at the beginning. By August the quarrel had gone so far that Hume fortified Fast Castle in defiance of the Regent's authority, and fled to England only on the approach of a force stronger than his own. Induced to give himself up, he was placed in Edinburgh under the charge of Arran; but on October 12th both the gaoler and his prisoner disappeared[2], thus ridding Albany of every powerful person opposed to the interests of France. The capture of Hamilton Castle, the chief fortress of Arran, and the death of the Duke of Rothesay, the younger of the two princes, seemed to complete Albany's good fortune at the close of the year 1515[3].

Albany's triumph, however, was more apparent than real; and during the year 1516 we find him encompassed with difficulties which eventually proved too great for him. In January through the agency of France a

1516

---

[1] It was at Stirling and not at Edinburgh that Margaret's dramatic refusal to give up her children took place.—Brewer, I. 213.

[2] Angus gave himself up to Albany before the close of the year.

[3] Brewer, I. pp. 212—219.

new truce was concluded with England which was to last till
Whitsunday This arrangement came opportunely for Albany,
as in the following month he had to deal with a new revolt
against his authority. The Earl of Arran, who through the
good offices of his mother had made his peace with the Regent, once more broke into rebellion, in alliance with Lennox,
Glencairn and other barons Though they possessed themselves of the castles of Dunbarton and Glasgow, however,
Albany proved too strong for them, and they were forced to
give in their submission. The measure that he now adopted
to conciliate discontented parties was perfectly in keeping with
the past policy of Scotland. He made a generous distribution
of Church benefices among the more powerful and rapacious
families whom it was his interest to conciliate—a proceeding,
says Bishop Leslie, "in which there was greater respect had to
the satisfying to the avarice of the world, nor to the pleasure of
God in promoving of godly men to have used their office
according to their calling[1]." Seeing how things now went in
Scotland, Angus, to the great disgust of Henry VIII[2], parted
company with his wife in England and in conjunction with
Hume was received into favour by Albany—their forfeitures
being removed at a meeting of the Estates in May.

Everything might now have gone well but for the hand of
Henry in the affairs of the Scots. In June a
1516
truce was renewed between the two countries till
Midsummer of 1517, but so long as Albany was in Scotland
Henry could not be content. To a meeting of the Scottish
Estates on July he even sent the imperious demand that, if
they wished to retain his friendship, they must send Albany
home to France This insolent message was resented even by
the lords most favourable to England; and Henry's envoy
was told that Albany would be kept as long as it seemed for

---

[1] Leslie, 106.

[2] "Done like a Scot," was Henry's exclamation on hearing of this act
of Angus.

the good of the country. Nevertheless, Henry effectually contrived to make Albany's position increasingly uncomfortable.
In strict accordance with his instructions, the Warden Dacre
sedulously fomented the dissensions of the Scots nobility, and
could even boast that he had 400 Scots in his pay. The
results of his intrigues were seen in the month of September,
when Lord Hume and his brother were imprisoned on a
charge of treason, and, to the dismay of the nobles who had
been their allies, were publicly executed, and their heads set
on the Tolbooth of Edinburgh.

While England was thus working so mischievously in
Scottish affairs, Albany failed to receive that
support from France which, as events were to   1516
show, was indispensable to the maintenance of his authority.
The straits to which he was reduced seem to be proved by his
proceedings at a meeting of Estates which was held in the
month of November. At his own instance he was declared
the second person in the kingdom, and his step-brother,
Alexander, set aside in his favour[1]. Having thus secured his
position, he next asked permission to visit France, undertaking
to return in the space of six months. Albany's rule had left
much to be desired in the matter of firm and just government;
but his departure would in all probability reduce the country
to chaos. His proposal, therefore, was at first rejected; though
he contrived to gain the concession that in the following April
he should be allowed to carry out his visit.

The leading event of the year 1517 was the departure of
Albany for France on the 7th of June. What
was the predominant motive that led him to   1517
leave Scotland it is difficult to say. He may have been sick of
his life of the last two years; but it is certain that he retained

---

[1] Alexander Stewart was the son of Alexander, Duke of Albany, and
his first wife Catherine Sinclair, daughter of the Earl of Caithness. The
Regent Albany's mother was Agnes of Boulogne, daughter of the Earl of
Boulogne.

an eager interest in Scottish affairs, and that he was able to do
the country a real service by his presence in France. The
arrangements he made before his departure showed his desire
to conciliate England and to create a balance of interest among
the leading personages in Scotland. To gratify Henry the
queen-mother was permitted to return a fortnight after Albany
sailed for France, though it was stipulated that she was to
make no attempt to recover her power. As vice-regents during
his absence he appointed Andrew Forman and James Beaton,
the Archbishops of St Andrews and Glasgow, with the Earls
of Huntly, Argyle, Angus, and Arran. As regards the king, it
was arranged that he should be kept in the castle of Edinburgh
in charge of the Earl Marischal and Lords Borthwick and
Ruthven

On the 26th of August Albany effected an arrangement
with France[1], which must have been acceptable
to the large majority of all ranks of Scotsmen.

1517

At Rouen he concluded a treaty which renewed the ancient
alliance between France and Scotland. By this treaty the two
countries took bonds of mutual aid against all enemies, and
specially against England, and included in the arrangement a
prospective marriage between the King of Scots and a daughter
of Francis I. Yet an event that happened in the autumn
threatened to strain the relations between the two allies.
Before his departure from Scotland Albany had made the
Sieur de la Bastie Warden of the Marches in succession to
Lord Hume. The appointment was one which in itself is
sufficient to show how little Albany knew of the character and
traditions of the country of which he wished to be master. As
the friend and instrument of the man who had sent the late
Warden to death, de la Bastie was marked for destruction by
the unwritten law of the Border. The opportunity was soon
made. Decoyed from his castle of Dunbar, the unfortunate

---

[1] Teulet, *Papiers d'État...relatifs à l Histoire de l'Écosse au* XVIe *Siècle*,
I. 39.

Frenchman was slaughtered in a swamp in the attempt to escape a band of the relentless clients of the Humes. The vice-regents professed to the indignant Francis that they did their best to bring the murderers to justice, and threw the blame on Henry VIII for harbouring the fugitives[1], but it is probably nearer the truth that their conflicting interests effectually sheltered the crime.

Albany had promised that his absence should not extend beyond six months[2]; and if things had gone as he could have wished, he would probably have kept his word. As it was, however, the six months were extended to four years and a half. Thus left to herself, the condition of Scotland was not happy, since throughout the whole period there was no central authority equal to the firm government of the country. Between the houses of Douglas and Hamilton, represented by Angus and Arran, there was a continuous feud which was the frequent occasion of open strife and seriously disturbed the public peace.

The most important event of the year that followed Albany's departure was again the proceeding of the queen-mother. Having convinced herself that her hus- 1518 band Angus was guilty both of neglect and infidelity, she came to regard him with all the intemperate hate of her Tudor nature ; and, contemptuous as her brother of all public decency, she set her heart on a divorce. But Angus was of the first importance to Henry in his policy towards Scotland ; and by dint of browbeating he succeeded in diverting her for a time from her purpose. A reconciliation that followed, however, only intensified Margaret's distaste ; and in her wrath she made overtures to Albany which seriously embarrassed her brother in his dealings with Scotland.

As a real force in the country, indeed, Margaret was of little account, and the struggle for the first place lay between Angus and Arran. The house of Hamilton had not yet

---

[1] Teulet, 1. 8.   [2] Leslie, 108.

embraced its later policy of alliance with France against England, for its present head wavered to the end in his relations to either country. But at this period he on the whole leant to France; and as far as lay in his power endeavoured to hold together the party of Albany. At the present moment, however, the King of France found it his interest to be on friendly terms with England, and he had bound himself to keep Albany at home, and to leave the Scots to themselves[1]. In Scotland, therefore, there was now a coolness towards France, which gave the advantage to Angus over his powerful rival.

In September of 1519 an occasion was given for bringing their quarrels to a head. Besides being one of the vice-regents Arran held the office of Provost of Edinburgh, which greatly strengthened his position in the country. His term of office having expired, however, he was not only refused re-election, but through the influence of the Douglases the gates of the city were shut in his face. Common councils between the vice-regents were thus at an end; and while Arran made his headquarters in Glasgow, Angus retained his hold on the capital. When in the month of December, therefore, ambassadors came from England and France with offers to include Scotland in a truce made between these two countries, there was seen a singular spectacle. In Edinburgh the ambassadors were received by Angus, but as Arran refused to appear, a convention was summoned to meet at Stirling as being neutral ground. At Stirling Arran and his supporters duly appeared, but as Angus did not present himself, the truce was accepted on the authority of a section of the council of the nation[2].

To the year 1520 belongs another encounter between the Hamiltons and the Douglases which is one of the best-known affairs of the kind in Scottish history. At a meeting of the Estates towards the close of April the followers of the two earls found themselves face to

1519

1520

---

[1] Brewer, I. 511.   [2] Leslie, 113-4.

face in the capital. The followers of Arran, however, chanced
to be greatly superior in numbers, and the rumour went that
they intended to take the opportunity of once for all crushing
their enemies According to the story, Gavin Douglas, bishop
of Dunkeld, sought to avert the impending conflict by an
interview with Beaton, archbishop of Glasgow, the ally of the
Hamiltons. Calling his conscience to witness, Beaton pledged
his oath that no mischief was intended, and at the same time
struck his breast by way of emphasis As his hidden mail
rang under the blow, "Your conscience, my lord," exclaimed
Douglas, "is not a good one, for I heard it clatter[1]." The
main street of Edinburgh was soon the scene of a desperate
struggle between the two factions, which resulted in so complete
a triumph for the Douglases that the affair came to be known
as "Clean the Causeway." Arran himself escaped by a ford
through the Nor' Loch, his brother Sir Patrick Hamilton being
slain by Angus's own hand[2].

Such being the state of affairs in Scotland, the only hope of
tranquillity seemed to lie in the return of Albany. But the
probability of this event turned upon issues beyond the control
of Albany's friends in Scotland In the year 1519 Charles of
Spain had been chosen emperor to the lasting chagrin of
Francis I, and that rivalry at once began between them which
for more than a quarter of a century was to distract Western
Europe by diplomacy or war To gain the friendship of
Henry VIII became an important object with both potentates,
and by permitting Albany to return to Scotland Francis would
at once have foreclosed this advantage. Throughout the year
1521, however, the relations between Francis and Henry
became so strained that there was no longer reason why
Albany should not be sent to Scotland to be a thorn in the
side of the English king In more than one embassy the

---

[1] Pitscottie is our only authority for this conversation.

[2] Leslie, Buchanan, and Pitscottie all relate this affair. The year 1520
seems to be the correct date.

Scots had threatened that if their regent were much longer
detained they must be forced to appeal to England to set their
affairs in order.   At length in November 1521, Albany was
permitted to sail and arrived in Scotland on the 19th of that
month[1]

The return of Albany effected an immediate revolution.
Supported by the queen-mother, Archbishop
Beaton[2], and the Earl of Huntly, "the most
powerful baron in the kingdom," he effectually served the
purpose for which he had come—of creating a diversion in
favour of France by occupying the attention of England.   The
provost and other magistrates whom Angus had set up in
Edinburgh were turned out of their offices, and Angus with his
leading supporters fled to the Borders.   In this ill turn of their
affairs the Douglases despatched the bishop of Dunkeld to the
English Court to persuade Henry to come to their assistance.
All that the bishop could do he certainly did; for in a
memorial against the duke he charged him with all the evils
that had occurred in Scotland since the beginning of the reign,
and accused him even of being the murderer of the infant
Duke of Rothesay.   It needed nothing to whet Henry's anger
against Albany; but, at this moment, he was not in a position
to rush into a war with Scotland either for his own sake or the
sake of the Douglases[3].

1521

Albany's policy in Scotland was guided solely by the relations of England to France, and during the year
1522 these relations became such that in August
a great English army crossed the Channel   With the steady
purpose of strengthening the French king, therefore, Albany
proceeded with his measures against English influence in

1522

---

[1] Leslie.

[2] Beaton was now Archbishop Elect of St Andrews. The death
of Forman is assigned to 1522 by Keith; but from one of the Laing
Charters (No. 134) it appears that Forman was dead by April 10, 1521.

[3] Brewer, I. 518 *et seq.*

Scotland. At a meeting of the Estates during January and February his ascendency was clearly proved As on the occasion of Albany's previous sojourn in Scotland, Henry despatched the Clarencieux herald with a menacing demand that Albany should be sent back to France. On appearing before the Estates, however, the envoy was received with "grim and angry look" both of "high and low[1]"; and was told that he had come on an idle errand. As his only formidable enemy, the Earl of Angus, was sent to France in the month of February, it seemed that Albany was now in a position to direct the strength of Scotland at his pleasure. But in spite of all their feuds and self seeking the Scottish lords had really at heart the integrity of their country. In September Albany was able to lead a considerable army towards the Western Border, and to threaten Carlisle. As it happened, the occasion was specially opportune for an invasion of England; but when it came to the point of actually carrying war across the border, even the great earls who had welcomed him to the Regency—Huntly, Argyle, Arran—refused to run the risk of another Flodden in the interests of France The English warden, Dacre, who had his spies everywhere, was well aware of Albany's dilemma, and profited by it accordingly. By the proposal of a month's truce which he had no authority to offer he gave Albany the opportunity of retreating from a position which his refractory nobles must have made every day more difficult[2]. Having thus failed in the chief object of his presence in Scotland, Albany once more sailed for France (October 28)[3] after appointing as a council of regency, Huntly, Argyle, Arran, and a Frenchman named Gouzolles.

Though Albany had gone, the French interest in Scotland was still predominant. Henry VIII would have liked to

---

[1] Brewer, I. 529.

[2] See Dacre's Despatch, Brewer, I. 534.

[3] Leslie (p. 123) erroneously assigns this date to the beginning of March 1523.

establish an influence in Scotland by peaceful measures, and
twice sent the Clarencieux herald with this object.   But
though he was now supported by his sister, the queen-mother,
who had become estranged from Albany during his late visit,
the power of France defeated all his schemes   In November
his envoy offered a truce till the end of the
1523   following February; and on his second mission
in January he proposed a marriage between the Scottish king
and Henry's daughter, the Princess Mary, but both proposals
were rejected by the Council of Regency.   Seeing the Scots
thus bent on war, Henry, or rather his minister Wolsey,
prepared to let them have enough of it.   On February 26 the
Earl of Surrey ("the scourge of the Scots" Henry called him),
son of the victor of Flodden, was appointed lieutenant-general
against the Scots, the East Marches being entrusted to the
Marquis of Dorset, and the Western to the veteran Dacre.
The Scots were in no state to offer a successful defence of their
country.   They were themselves but half-hearted in the war
against England; and the King of France failed to redeem his
promise of sending them efficient aid.   From April to September,
therefore, the Borders were subjected to a succession of raids
which appear to have surpassed all previous expeditions of
the kind in the thoroughness of their work   In April Surrey
laid waste Teviotdale and the Merse; in June Dacre wrought
similar havoc on Kelso and its neighbourhood, and on the 30th
of August Wolsey was in a position to write that in these districts
"there is left neither house, fortress, village, tree, cattle, corn,
or other succour for man[1]."   A third expedition in September
was attended by incidents which proved that the Scots had
lost none of the resolution with which they had faced their
enemy in times past.   With a force of 9000 men the Earl of
Surrey marched against Jedburgh, which was so flourishing a
town, he tells us, that it had twice as many houses as Berwick.
At every step he was harassed by the Scots, who fought with

[1] Brewer, I. 543.

such daring that the English commander describes them as "the boldest men and the hottest that ever I saw any nation." Surrey, however, succeeded in his object of giving the town to the flames, though he had to report the loss of 800 horses as the result of a stampede created by the Scots who hung upon his army[1].

But all these terrible doings were of no avail, for on the very day of the burning of Jedburgh Albany once more landed in the unhappy kingdom. 1523 On this occasion he brought men and supplies sufficient to be formidable if directed with skill and good fortune; and he lost no time in turning them to account. With a great army of Scots in addition to his foreign auxiliaries he marched towards the East Border at the end of October. As described by George Buchanan, who was present as a volunteer, the expedition was unlucky from the beginning. The season was one of unusual severity; and when Albany came to the Border the barons again, as in the previous year, refused to march out of their own country. From the north bank of the Tweed, however, he directed his artillery against the castle of Wark; but though the cannonade was seconded by a spirited attack of the French auxiliaries, after two days' siege the place still remained defiant. In all these circumstances Albany found but one course open to him. With a mutinous army, in the worst winter weather, and with Surrey threatening him from Berwick, there was little prospect of any worthy achievement, and he accordingly disbanded his army and returned to Edinburgh. This signal failure seems to have convinced him that his career in Scotland was at an end. In a meeting of the Estates held in November it was decreed that his French troops should be at once sent home; and without their support he could have no hope of fulfilling the chief end of his sojourn in the country. After a few months of fruitless negotiations with England, therefore, Albany left Scotland on the 20th of May[2], and on this

---

[1] *State Papers of Henry VIII*, IV. 46-7.   [2] Buchanan.

occasion never to return.   His management of Scottish affairs
had not been attended by good fortune; yet he may be said to
have saved Scotland from English ascendency at a period
when it might have been dangerous to the independence of
the country, and it is an interesting fact that the Scottish
historians most nearly his contemporaries, Protestant as well as
Catholic, speak kindly of the Gallicised Scot who came to the
country in the hour of need that followed the disaster of
Flodden.

Now that Albany was gone Henry VIII found his opportunity for decisively interfering in the councils of Scotland;
and it is perhaps from this moment that we may date the
beginning of a distinct party favourable to an English as
opposed to a French alliance.   From the days of the first
Stewarts there had been frequent treasonable intercourse
between Scottish nobles and the successive kings of England;
but an English party with specific aims had never existed till
the years that immediately followed the final departure of the
Regent Albany.

But though Albany was out of the country he had left
both a party and leaders behind him.   Dunbar
1524   Castle, "the key of Scotland," as it had been
called, was in the hands of Gouzolles, and remained in his
possession for twelve years longer.   Above all the French
interest was upheld by James Beaton, now Archbishop of
St Andrews, as well as Chancellor of the kingdom, who in
policy and craft showed himself no unworthy antagonist of
Wolsey himself.   If he were to gain his ends in Scotland,
indeed, Wolsey realized that by some means or other Beaton
must be got out of the way; and he devised a plan which was
simplicity itself.   It was to propose a conference on the
Borders at which Beaton should be one of the Scottish representatives; but from which he should be quietly conveyed to
England till Wolsey's purposes were fulfilled.   But Beaton was
not to be caught in the snare, and shutting himself up in his

sea-tower of St Andrews he wove his schemes in safety[1]. An unexpected coalition, however, was to put him in the power of his enemies. Within two months after the departure of Albany the Earl of Arran entered into a confederation with the queen-mother which effected a revolution in the country. By the present state of affairs a hopeful prospect had been opened up for Arran. Albany was gone, Angus was in France, and in the beginning of the year the great Earl of Huntly had died and left as his heir a boy of ten. As Arran came next to Albany in nearness to the throne, therefore, it was even a probability that he or one of his house should one day be King of Scots; and with this object before him he now threw in his lot with England. On the 26th of July the queen-mother in concert with Arran brought her son, then twelve years old, from Stirling to Edinburgh, and with the approval of many of the leading men in the country had him "erected" or proclaimed *de facto* King of Scots. A guard of 200 men was sent by Henry for the defence of his nephew; and with the aid of this force Margaret was further enabled to strengthen her position. Having decoyed the chancellor Beaton to Edinburgh, she shut him up in the castle, and kept him there till the state of his health made his release a necessity[2].

The party of England thus appeared to have triumphed; and further measures were taken to secure its permanent ascendency. Bribes were distributed **1524** to useful persons; spies were set to work even in the king's palace; two ambassadors, Dr Magnus and Roger Ratcliffe, were sent to the Scottish court to further English interests, and in September a truce of three months was concluded between the two countries. But the wandering affections of Margaret were again to disturb all combinations. She now cast her fancy on Henry Stewart, second son of Lord Evandale; and though he was a mere youth raised him to the

---

[1] *State Papers of Henry VIII*, vol. IV.
[2] *Ibid.*

office of Lord Treasurer. Her passions were further compli-
cated by the arrival of her husband Angus in Scotland in spite
of her vehement protestations to Wolsey and her brother
Henry But in the absence of Albany Angus saw his opportunity; and incited and counselled by his brother Sir George
Douglas, entered on a course of action which was to raise his
house to the greatest eminence it had reached at any period of
its history, but which was eventually to prove the cause of its
irremediable ruin.

Margaret did all that lay in her power to exclude her
husband from authority; but the house of
1524   Douglas had always been popular, and Angus
found himself strong enough to attempt even desperate
measures. In November while the Estates were sitting in
Edinburgh, Angus and Lennox with a great following broke
into the city at four in the morning. By means of the ordnance in the castle, however, Margaret compelled him to
withdraw from the city without accomplishing his object of
securing the person of the king. But it soon appeared that in
the absence of Albany Angus was the first person in the
country. At a meeting of the Estates in Feb-
1525   ruary of the following year a council of eight
was chosen to take charge of the king and to manage the
affairs of the country. In the divided interests of these
councillors Angus found his opportunity, and he gradually
made himself virtual master of the kingdom The course of
European events throughout the year 1525 brought further
strength to Angus. On March 31st the King of France was
defeated and taken prisoner at the battle of Pavia, an event
which was attended by a double result for Scotland. It
foreclosed any speedy help to those who favoured Albany, and
who were thus forced to cultivate a more friendly attitude
towards England. Moreover, the disaster to France caused a
change in the policy of England herself. It had been the
aim of Wolsey's diplomacy to hold the balance between

the emperor and Francis, and now that France was in a
state of humiliation, he made such friendly overtures to that
country that an alliance was concluded on the 30th of August
In these circumstances it was hopeless for the French party to
maintain their old attitude towards England. They had still
the support of public feeling, indeed, as was unmistakably
shown by the treatment of the English envoy Magnus in the
capital The women, he wrote to Wolsey, cursed him in the
streets and abused him as the cause of the bad harvest[1]. But
events were too strong for mere sentiment, and on the 10th of
October a three years' truce was arranged with England.

Angus's two chief opponents were Margaret and the Earl of
Arran, for in the course of the year 1526 archbishop Beaton gave proofs that he was now   1526
working in the interests of England[2]. As for Margaret, her
hatred to Angus had carried her so far that she actually
received bribes to use her influence in favour of the French
alliance. But her ridiculous conduct had deprived her of all
influence in the country; and an event of this year led even
Arran to abandon her cause. In a meeting of the Estates
held in June it was decreed that since the king was now
fourteen years old he should be allowed to enter on his
prerogatives This arrangement was solely the work of Angus,
who, having taken care to have the king in his hands, became,
like the Boyds and the Livingstones of a previous age, the
master of the country. Unsupported by Margaret and Beaton,
therefore, Arran found it his interest to work in common with
Angus and to play a secondary part in the kingdom. Yet the
Douglases had to hold their own against many and powerful
enemies, chief among whom was the Earl of Lennox, a noble-
man of high character and accomplishments and a special
friend of the young king. Twice in the course of this year
Lennox made the attempt to deliver James from a constraint

---

[1] *State Papers of Henry VIII*, vol. IV part I. p. 746.
[2] *Ibid* p. 904

24—2

from which he himself longed to be freed. In July Angus led
an expedition to the Borders accompanied by the king, Lord
Hume, and other barons, and while near Melrose was attacked
by Walter Scott, laird of Buccleuch, a retainer of Lennox.
The victory was stiffly contested, but in the end Buccleuch
was worsted, and the king was brought to Edinburgh by the
followers of Angus. A still more determined effort was made
by Lennox in person, and proved fatal to himself. In the
beginning of September he led a strong force from Stirling
with the intention of rescuing the king in Edinburgh, but was
met at Linlithgow by the Hamiltons under Arran. It had
been the intention of Angus to join arms with Arran; but
among other causes of delay the king had feigned illness to
retard the march of the Douglases. Seeing the king's evident
motive, Sir George Douglas passionately exclaimed that he
would see him torn in pieces rather than that he should escape
their hands—a speech which James never forgave and which
must in some measure palliate his unrelenting hostility to the
whole Douglas name. Meanwhile, the Hamiltons and the
men of Lennox had already joined battle, and with such
advantage to the former that the arrival of Angus only completed the victory. Lennox himself was among the slain, and
was mourned by James at once as his special friend and as the
only person who had the power and the will to deliver him
from durance which had become intolerable.

The power of Angus was now supreme, and at a meeting
of Estates in November he secured his position by extensive
forfeitures of his enemies, and the liberal distribution of offices
and benefices among his friends. When on
1527
March 11, 1527[1], Margaret at length succeeded
in divorcing him, and immediately afterwards married Henry
Stewart, it made no change in his position. This was, indeed,
the period, when in the well-known words of Pitscottie, none
durst strive with a Douglas, nor yet a Douglas's man. It was

---

[1] *Wigton Papers* (Misc. of Mait. Club), vol. II. part II. p. 368.

by no special force of mind and character that Douglas had attained the place he now held, but simply through family influence and the interested support of England. " Angus is gentle and hardy," wrote the English envoy Magnus, " but wants wit[1]", and his failure to maintain order was probably as much due to want of power as want of good will. Six times he led expeditions against the clan of the Armstrongs, whose turbulent doings were continually embroiling the country with England, and on each occasion was baffled in his attempts to chastise them[2].

The last months of Angus's ascendency were signalized by an action which was the work of archbishop Beaton rather than himself. In February 1528 Patrick Hamilton, the protomartyr of the Scottish Reformation, was burned at St Andrews for heresy. Since the year 1494, when the thirty Lollards of Kyle were brought before James IV, we have heard nothing of the spread of opinions contrary to the teaching of the Church. But since that date Luther had rent Christendom in twain; and his doctrines had speedily found their way into Scotland. By 1525 Lutheran writings were so numerous in the country that an Act of Parliament was passed in that year prohibiting their importation under the severest penalties attached to heresy. But it was the teaching and death of Hamilton that, according to John Knox, decisively marked the beginning of the Reformation in Scotland. From this moment the new opinions spread with a rapidity which seriously alarmed the leaders of the Church; and the impending religious revolution in England was to drive them into a policy which eventually proved their destruction.

In June of 1528 came the ruin of the Douglases—apparently as sudden as it was overwhelming. Under circumstances of which we have no

1528

1528

---

[1] *State Papers of Henry VIII*, vol. IV. part II. p. 1244.

[2] Armstrong, *History of Liddesdale*, p. 253.

certain knowledge[1] the king escaped from their hands and
made his way to Stirling Castle, which was then in the keeping
of those unfriendly to Angus.   As had happened in the case
of the Livingstones and the Boyds, the Douglases by the loss
of the king were at once reduced to impotence   The leading
nobles and churchmen flocked to James at Stirling ; and by
the beginning of July he was in a position to march on Edinburgh and to occupy the town, whence he was able to direct
his efforts against the fallen clan   James was only in his 17th
year, but he had the precocity of his race, and possessed many
of the qualities that make kings popular.   As described by
Buchanan, who had resided at his court, he had a handsome
countenance and was of middle height and strongly and
gracefully formed.   His eyes, we are further told by bishop
Leslie, were grey and keen, and he never forgot a face he had
once marked.   Owing to the conditions of his upbringing he
was almost illiterate.   It is said that at the age of twelve he
could not read an English letter without assistance[2], and even
in manhood he could speak very little French[3].   On the other
hand his natural parts were good, and it is noted of him that
he came to possess a perfect acquaintance with the laws and
institutions of his kingdom[4].

The first object of James was the humiliation of the
Douglases, whom he henceforth pursued with
1528   an   inveteracy   of   hate   which   affected   the
national policy, and was one day to recoil on his own head
From Stirling he had issued a proclamation banishing them
beyond the Spey, and forbidding any member of the family
to approach within six miles of his person ; yet with all his

[1] Pitscottie tells the story in great detail ; but Mr M'Neill has pointed
out that as far at least as the Exchequer Rolls go they tend to discredit
Pitscottie (vol. XV p liv)

[2] *State Papers of Henry VIII*, vol. IV. part I. p 1232.

[3] Teulet, I p. 124

[4] Buchanan.

efforts it was not till November that he was able to drive Angus and his dangerous brother from the country. In a packed meeting of the Estates held in September a decree of forfeiture was passed on Angus and all his kin; and during the remainder of the autumn James strove to put the decree into execution. In October he took possession of Coldingham, but was compelled to withdraw in haste by a force led by Angus himself. In an attempt to take the stronghold of Tantallon he was equally unsuccessful, being compelled to abandon the siege and to withdraw to Edinburgh. But as in previous contests between the Douglases and the Crown, time told in favour of lawful authority; and before the close of November Angus was forced to seek safety in England

At the period when James V became master of his kingdom new adjustments were taking place in European politics which affected the whole subsequent course of his reign. In 1526 Francis I had been restored to his own kingdom, and his deliverance was immediately followed by the Holy League, directed against the Emperor by Clement V, Francis, Henry VIII, and the Republic of Venice. In 1527 Christian Europe was horror-stricken at the sack of Rome by the troops of Charles, the immediate consequence being a straiter league against him, in which Francis and Henry took the leading part. When the government of the country passed into James's own hands, therefore, his foreign policy was marked out for him. He knew that the fall of Angus, as the representative of English interests in Scotland, could not but be unwelcome to Henry, and that he might count on his mischievous interference in the affairs of his kingdom. But in the present relations of England and France a quarrel with Henry was out of the question, and on December 1528, a peace of five years was concluded at Berwick between the two countries.

1528

Within his own dominions James had certainly ample

scope for all the vigour and prudence he might possess.
On the Borders and in the Highlands and Islands there
was equal unrest and insubordination; and in the interests
of the whole country it was indispensable that good order
should be restored in these districts.   James addressed himself to his task with all the energy of his father, but apparently
not with equal prudence.   On the Borders it was especially
the Armstrongs of Liddesdale who had made themselves conspicuous by their defiance of the authority of James and Henry
alike.   In 1526 they were seeking to possess themselves of the
Debateable Land; in 1527 they were harbouring English
fugitives in spite of the protests of Henry's ministers; and in
the beginning of 1529 they were able to boast that they had
burned 52 parish churches in Scotland, besides much damage
done in England, adding insult to injury by affirming that
they "would not be ordered either by Scotland or England[1]."
As these are the representations of their enemies, they probably
contain an element of exaggeration; but after every abatement
the conduct of the Armstrongs had been such as to call for
summary dealing in the interest of the public peace.   Accordingly in the summer of 1529 James proceeded to the Border,
and with the assistance of Lord Bothwell apparently succeeded
in quieting the unruly districts of Liddesdale and the Middle
March.   Before the close of the year, however, the men of
Liddesdale were again at their old work of invading England.
More vigorous measures, it was evident, must be taken with
men who thus set at naught the authority of their sovereign;
and James prepared to take them.   In the conviction that the
evildoers were abetted by certain of the Border chieftains, he
placed in ward Lords Bothwell and Hume and the lairds
Maxwell, Johnston, Buccleuch, and six others,
and about the end of June (1530) he once more

1530

---

[1] *State Papers of Henry VIII*, vol. IV. part II. p. 1060, p. 1540;
Ibid. part III. pp. 2327–8.

led an expedition to the Border[1].   As the theme of one of the
most famous of Scots ballads, this expedition of James is
among the best known incidents of his reign ; yet no accurate
details of his proceedings have come down to us.   By means
which have not been satisfactorily explained, John Armstrong,
laird of Gilnockie, the most notorious of his clan, with forty-
eight of his comrades fell into the hands of James, who
straightway hanged them on the nearest trees.   If there was
any treachery in the affair it would seem that, so far as the
evidence goes, it must lie at the door of Lord Maxwell or
Armstrong's own brother[2].   That the punishment itself was
fully deserved the evidence of state papers leaves us in no
manner of doubt.   James deemed his authority now so
fully assured that he relieved from ward all the border chiefs
with the exception of Bothwell.   Yet time was to show that
the rigour of his action was not wholly in the interest of
Scotland.   By his stern dealing he weakened the strength of
those who were the natural defenders of the country against
England, and when his own hour of trouble came he learned
to his cost how far he had alienated the affections of so
important a body of his subjects.

The condition of the Highlands and Islands next claimed
the attention of James.   We have seen that at the close of the
reign of his father these districts were so thoroughly pacified
and reconciled to the Crown that none of his subjects followed
James IV more willingly to Flodden than the island chiefs.
But the state of things that followed his death was too strong a
temptation for "the wicked blood of the isles."   The chiefs
had hardly returned to their homes when they set up as Lord
of the Isles Sir Donald of Lochalsh, son of that Alexander of
Lochalsh who had given the government so much trouble in
the days of James IV.   The old story was again repeated.
Donald and his supporters laid violent hands on the persons

---

[1] Armstrong's *Liddesdale, etc.*, pp. 270 *et seq.*
[2] Pitcairn, *Criminal Trials*, vol. I. part I. p. *245; Leslie, p. 143.

and possessions of all who opposed them, Colin, third Earl of Argyle, was entrusted with the same task that had been assigned to his father; and lieutenants were appointed for the defence of the mainland. In 1515 the Regent Albany made liberal offers to certain of the island chiefs, who deserted Donald in such numbers that he was forced to make his peace with the government. But Albany's own difficulties presented an opportunity to Donald which he could not let pass In-cited by the agents of Henry VIII, he entered into communi-cations with Lord Hume which were cut short by that noble-man's execution in 1516. Yet Donald did not desist from his efforts to gain the object of his ambition, and it was not till his death in 1519 that the islands were reduced to tolerable order. Under the lieutenancy of Argyle this state of things continued till the year 1527, when two sensational events gave rise to fresh strife and confusion. Maclean of Dowart had married the aunt of Argyle; and from motives which can only be con-jectured had determined to get rid of her[1]. As the most effectual means of accomplishing his end he exposed her on a rock over which the sea flowed at full tide. The lady was rescued; but such an outrage could not be passed over in the Scotland of the 16th century, and Maclean, while on a visit to Edinburgh, was murdered in his bed by his wife's brother, Sir John Campbell of Calder. To avenge their chief the Macleans at once took up arms; and it was at this juncture that James became master of his own person and king in reality.

Uniting their arms with the clan Donald of Isla, the Macleans began reprisals on the partizans of Argyle; but their leaders soon saw that their action was desperate. By concilia-tions and threats the revolt was checked; and Alexander, the chief of Isla, was led by the kindness and tact of James to become the steady supporter of the Crown. The policy of

---

[1] According to the authors of *The Clan Donald*, Maclean had con-ceived a violent passion for the daughter of one of his vassals.—I. 336.

James, indeed, was that of his father—to attract his wild subjects by direct intercourse with those whose influence was greatest with them. But in carrying out this policy he lacked the prudence which distinguished his father. The power of the Earls of Argyle in the Islands had become such that it was deemed dangerous to the Crown; and in 1531 James saw fit to throw Archibald, the fourth earl, into prison, and to deprive him of all his powers in the Islands—thus adding another to the long list of nobles who were to exact a stern reckoning from him at a later day. As far as the Islands were concerned, however, the results were all that could be desired. Their chiefs, as a body, became law-abiding subjects, and by frequent visits to their homes James succeeded in gaining their affections in as great degree as his father[1].

By the close of 1532 all the forces were in full working which were to result in the disastrous end of the reign of James V—his alienation from his nobles, his close union with his clergy, and his antagonism to Henry VIII. In 1530 died the Earl of Arran, who, now that Angus was no longer his rival, would probably have stood by James in his preference for France before England[2]. Of several other nobles James had already made secret or open foes. By his harsh treatment of Bothwell and Argyle he had rendered them equivocal subjects; and James's natural brother the Earl of Moray, with the Earl of Crawford, was equally disposed to play the traitor should the opportunity come. The conduct of Bothwell affords conclusive proof of the dangerous path that James was treading. In December 1531 Bothwell held a secret conference with the Earl of Northumberland in which he made some astounding communications. He was willing, he said, both to become Henry's subject and to aid him in his wars against Scotland.

---

[1] Gregory, *History of the Western Highlands and Isles*, pp. 114—143.

[2] On his deathbed Arran is said to have twice or thrice sent the singular message to James that Angus was the only lord true to him.—*State Papers of Henry VIII*, vol. IV. part III. p. 2833.

with a thousand gentlemen and six thousand commons. Such, he added, was the disposition of certain nobles towards James, that he had no hesitation in promising that Henry could be crowned King of Scots within a brief space in the capital itself.

The five years' peace with England which had been concluded in December 1528 had not yet expired; but since that date momentous events had been happening in that country which inevitably led to increasing friction with the King of Scots. Henry's desire for a divorce from Catharine of Aragon had successively led to the fall of Wolsey, to his breach with Rome, and his assumption of the Headship of the Church of England. In these revolutionary changes it was more necessary than ever that Henry should be either master of Scotland or in good relations with its king. But James never appears to have had any real doubt as to the course he should pursue. On the part of his subjects at large there was no disposition to follow the example of England. His own position, also, hardly left him an alternative. Alienated as he was from many of his most powerful nobles, he depended for support on his clergy, who had never been richer or more influential than now. Moreover, James had inherited a devotion to the Church which in any case would have deterred him from following in the steps of his uncle; and though he both taxed its revenues and denounced its shortcomings, he remained to the end its faithful son.

In 1532 James performed a notable act of which more will be said hereafter—the foundation of the College

1532

of Justice. It is with its bearing on the general policy of James, however, that we are here concerned. To meet the expenses of the new foundation he imposed a tax on ecclesiastical benefices which gave deep offence to his clergy, and so embarrassing became his position that in October of this year it was reported to Henry that James was afraid to raise a large army lest it should turn against himself[1]. Yet

[1] *State Papers of Henry VIII*, vol. VI. Oct. 22.

everything seemed to show that a large army would soon be
needed. The peace between the two countries still nominally
continued; but on a small scale they were virtually at war.
Twice in this year large detachments of Islanders passed over
to Ireland, not without the cognisance of James, to give trouble
to the English government in that country. In the autumn
mutual raids began which at another time would inevitably
have led to a declaration of war. In November Northumberland penetrated into Lothian, and was able to report that he
had not left "one peel, gentleman's house, nor grange, unburnt
or destroyed[1]." Nor were the Scots behind in the same work,
since besides smaller raids, it is recorded that 3000 of them
made their way into England, and returned laden with booty.
These doings went on into the year 1533; but
still neither country was prepared to proclaim 1533
open hostilities—a fact of which we have the adequate explanation in the relations of both parties to France. France at this
moment was on friendly terms with Henry; and, therefore, was
not disposed to annoy him by lending support to the King of
Scots. Through the action of the French king, indeed, a
temporary reconciliation was at length effected between James
and Henry. In May, 1533, commissioners from both countries
met at Newcastle with the object of arranging a truce.
Strangely enough it was on the part of the Scots that the chief
difficulty was raised. In the course of the late raids the
English had seized "certain old houses and vaults[2]," known
as Caw Mills, which the Scots maintained lay within their
country. So pertinacious were their representatives that at
length in October the English commissioners gave way, and a
truce was concluded for the space of twelve months. A more
durable arrangement followed the next year, when on the 12th
of May a peace was concluded which was to last
till the death of one of the two kings. As a 1534

---

[1] *State Papers of Henry VIII*, vol. VI. p. 680.

[2] *Ibid.* p. 335.

further token of good will Henry in the course of the same
year sent to James the Order of the Garter by Lord William
Howard, brother of the Duke of Norfolk—an honour which
Charles V and Francis followed up by sending him the Orders
of the Golden Fleece and of St Michael[1].

The two countries being now on this friendly footing, Henry
was bent on drawing the bands still closer.
Isolated as he now stood in Christendom, it
was of the first importance that he should bring James to the
same way of thinking in religion as himself. But of such a
result there was now less likelihood than ever. In August of
1534 James had burnt three heretics in deference to the wishes
of the clergy; and a step which he took in July of 1535
implied the probability of further divergence from the wishes of
Henry. The question of the marriage of their king was now
one of pressing urgency for the whole Scottish people. Among
several matches an alliance with Henry's daughter Mary,
afterwards queen of England, had most seriously engaged the
minds of the councillors of both kings. But James now
decisively put this alliance aside by a formal offer of marriage to
Marie de Bourbon, daughter of Charles de Vendôme. As the
negotiations were somewhat protracted, however, Henry in the
month of October despatched his chaplain, Dr William Barlow,
to bring his eloquence to bear on the King of Scots. The object
of Barlow's mission was to persuade James to follow his uncle's
example and to break with Rome; and in furtherance of this
end to propose what had been suggested by Howard in the
previous year, that James should pay a visit to England when
all matters might be amicably discussed by the two kings.
James expressed his willingness to visit his uncle; but on the
point of religion he was not to be moved, and Barlow had to
return with an evil report of James's subservience to his council,
which was mainly composed of "the pope's pestilent creatures,

1535

[1] Francis did not send his order till April, 1536.—Bapst, *Les Mariages
de Jacques V* (1889), p. 273, note.

and very limbs of the devil." Even now Henry did not abandon all hope of his nephew; and in the beginning of 1536 he sent back Barlow accompanied by Lord William Howard—the one being entrusted with spiritual and the other with temporal matters. This errand had no more success than the first, and an unfortunate coincidence confounded the eloquence of Barlow. In the midst of an oration in which he was denouncing the errors of Rome, there came such a violent thunderstorm that James devoutly crossed himself, and exclaimed that he did not know what frightened him most—the thunder or Barlow's blasphemy[1].

1536

The marriage-treaty with Marie de Vendôme was signed on the 29th March, 1536; and in spite of his imperfect knowledge of French James determined to meet his betrothed in person. Accordingly, on the 24th of July, in company with Sir James Hamilton of Finnart (of whom we shall presently hear more) and a hundred knights, he set sail for France, but was driven back on Galloway by storms and contrary winds. On the 1st of September he set sail again; but on this occasion with a much more brilliant following, as it comprised the Earls of Argyle, Rothes, and young Arran, the Lords Fleming and Maxwell, and so many other attendants that they freighted seven ships. Having reached Dieppe, he at once proceeded to St Quentin[2] in Picardy, where Marie de Vendôme was then residing. A grievous disenchantment awaited him, for the lady we are told, was "bossue et contrefaicte." So great was his disillusion, indeed, that James at once set himself to break off the match and to project another. From the beginning of his reign there had been proposals for his marriage with Madeleine, the third daughter of the French king, and this arrangement he now ardently took up. The consent of Francis was soon gained,

1536

---

[1] *State Papers of Henry VIII*, vol. IX. p. 172.
[2] Not to Vendôme as is usually stated.—Bapst, 289.

his only objection being the delicate health of the intended bride. On the 6th of November the marriage compact was signed; and on the first day of 1537 the union was celebrated with becoming splendour in the Church of Notre-Dame, at Paris. One other act signalized James's sojourn in France. While at Rouen, in April, he attained his full majority of twenty-five, and in imitation of his predecessors he revoked all grants that had been made during his minority. After an absence of nearly nine months James landed at Leith on the 19th of May, accompanied by his bride and a brilliant following, among whom was Pierre de Ronsard, then in his thirteenth year and destined to be the first poet of his day in France.

1537

James's visit to France was a turning-point in his reign. By the close alliance he had now formed with that country he was thrown into more emphatic opposition to England than ever; and he had, moreover, brought home from his visit a conception of the royal prerogative as well as expensive tastes which were alien to the traditions of his own kingdom. Through his entanglements with England and his troubles at home the four years and four months that remained to him were to strain him to the utmost; and the collapse of his body and mind in the prime of his life is convincing proof that he was unequal to the position in which he found himself.

To the year of his return belongs a succession of untoward events that must have seriously marred his happiness On the 7th of July, within two months of her arrival in Scotland, Madeleine of France died, to the sincere sorrow of James and his people. The conduct of his mother, also, was again creating a scandal in the country. She had grown weary of her youthful husband, Henry Stewart, now Lord Methven, and was seeking a divorce with a view to reuniting herself with the discarded Angus. Two other events which are wrapt in some mystery seem to show at once the growth of a suspicious temper in James and the existence of a

1537

dangerous feeling against his rule. These were the execution of the Master of Forbes and Lady Glammis on the 14th and 19th of July respectively Both of these persons were related to the exiled Angus—Lady Glammis being his sister, and Forbes his brother-in-law. The trial of Forbes came first—the crimes laid to his charge being that he had the "abominable imagination" of shooting the king in Aberdeen , and had stirred up "treasonable sedition" in the king's host when in service against England at Jedburgh The high rank and great personal beauty of Lady Glammis made her case still more memorable. That she was considered a dangerous person is proved by the fact that she had thrice already been brought to trial on serious charges. The crime for which she was now condemned was the seeking of the king's death by poison and of plotting in favour of her brothers, the Earl of Angus and Sir George Douglas, and the sentence, duly carried out, was that she should be burned on the Castle Hill of Edinburgh[1]. Of the justice of these sentences it is impossible to speak with certainty, as the materials in both cases are at once meagre and contradictory. Yet there are circumstances that must dispose us to believe that both deserved their fate. Their family connections and their previous history make it more than probable that they were concerned in malpractices against the State. Moreover, since the day that Angus had been driven from Scotland he had never ceased to plot the overthrow of James and his own recovery of the great position he had lost At the period, also, when Forbes and Lady Glammis suffered the last extremity of the law, Angus and his brother were specially active in their treasonable efforts, and were among the main causes of the hostilities between the two kings which were to end so disastrously for James.

During the remainder of James's reign the absorbing interest of the country was his policy with regard to England. That war must come sooner or later became every day more

---

[1] Pitcairn, I pp. *183—*197.

apparent. The traditional enmity of the two countries was
now intensified by differences of religion, and occasions of strife
were indefinitely multiplied. During James's absence in France
Henry had taken the opportunity of informing himself of the
state of public feeling in Scotland regarding its king. Ralph
Sadler, a name associated with Scotland for the next half
century, paid his first visit to the country with that object; and
he had been followed by a spy, named Henry Ray, who had
pursued the same end by different means. No sooner had
James returned than Henry found a cause of quarrel that
eventually led to the outbreak of hostilities. As the result of
Henry's religious policy many of his Catholic subjects had
sought safety in Scotland; and he complained to James that
he was guilty of a breach of amity in not giving them up
Another protest he made was less reasonable, and showed what
was his real motive in all his dealings with the Scottish king
He insisted with a pertinacity which could only raise suspicion
of his ultimate intentions that James should receive Angus and
reinstate him in his former dignities   To such a demand it
was not likely that James would ever listen, since the appearance of Angus in the country must inevitably lead to complications within and without which would not lessen the difficulties
of his position

Accordingly James steadily pursued the policy which he
had followed from the beginning; and a step
which he took in the year 1537 still further
widened the breach between him and Henry. The month
following the death of Madeleine, James had sent David
Beaton, nephew of James Beaton, and afterwards the great
cardinal, on an important mission to France. His errand
was ostensibly to report the death of Madeleine, but its main
object was to find another wife for James in France. The
mission was completely successful; and on the
10th of June, 1538, the new bride landed at
Crail in Fife The lady was the eldest daughter of the Duke

of Guise, Marie de Lorraine, and widow of the Duc de Longueville, who by her character, her talent, and above all by her family connections, was to play a part in the country of her adoption which places her among the great personages of Scottish history

As her subsequent career was to show, Mary of Lorraine was in the fullest sympathy with the policy which James had hitherto followed As a daughter of France she was an absolutist in politics, a fervent Catholic, and the enemy of England Prudent as she was and with a natural aptitude for affairs, she could not fail to exercise a powerful influence on her impulsive and passionate husband, and his last years would seem to show that he was not altogether his own master. At the close of the year of her arrival James proceeded in his ill-judged course of alienating his great nobles. He deprived Bothwell of the lordship of Liddesdale, and took possession of certain lands belonging to his natural brother, the Earl of Moray, and to the young Earl of Huntly In September 1539 the queen was reinforced by an ally whose fidelity to their common interests was to give him an evil name in the traditions of his country and was eventually to bring him to an end which is one of the tragedies of its history. In that month David Beaton succeeded his uncle in the see of St Andrews[1], and was then enabled to display on a wider field that talent and worldly ambition of which he had already given unmistakeable proof. His accession to this new office was signalized by proceedings which in his case cannot be set down to the pure and fervent zeal of an apostolic faith. The burning of heretics in 1534 had not been followed by the extinction of false doctrine; and it now became necessary to make a few more examples At the close of 1539 and the beginning of 1540, as we are told by Buchanan, who himself escaped chastisement only by the special favour of James, there was great activity against heretics. Many suspected of Lutheranism, he

---

[1] He had been made Cardinal in December 1538.

says, "were seized towards the end of February (1540); five were burned; nine recanted; and many were exiled." Yet while the Church was taking these energetic steps in its self-defence, its own shortcomings were the jest of the people. At Linlithgow on the Feast of Epiphany 1540, Lyndsay's "Satire of the Three Estates" was played before the King and Court. As the main object of that satire is to hold up to ridicule and detestation the ignorance and grossness of the clergy, the performance was certainly a strange comment on the contemporary dealings with those who had lifted up their voices in advocacy of a purer religion and more responsible teachers

The ascendency of Beaton as the known enemy of England and the new religion quickened the desire of Henry for a better understanding with the King of Scots. At this period it seemed that a contingency long dreaded by Henry was at length about to be realized. In 1539 a league of the Catholic Powers against the heretic England appeared to be taking shape, and though eventually it came to nothing through the rivalries of the powers themselves, the warning was sufficiently disquieting. To suppress Beaton, therefore, and to bring James over to his side became the pressing object of Henry's policy. Accordingly, he once more despatched Sadler to the Scottish Court with many counsels and suggestions to its king. To discredit Beaton Sadler bore with him certain intercepted letters, which, had James been so disposed, might have given him a handle against his great subject. As an inducement for James to accept the friendship of Henry, Sadler pointed out to him that only the life of Prince Edward stood between him and the English throne. With regard to religion Sadler showed him that by following the example of his uncle he would find an abounding source of revenue in the confiscation of the goods of the Church[1]. But all Sadler's eloquence was in vain.

1540

---

[1] It was on this occasion that Sadler expressed his master's disdainful

Whatever might be James's private desires and opinions, the whole course of his conduct had tended to throw him on the support of the clergy, as opposed to the nobles. A remarkable statement by Sadler, which is borne out by other evidence, is a notable proof of the opposition that existed between James and his leading barons The clergy, Sadler wrote, had presented to the king a list of three hundred and sixty nobles and barons who might be deprived of their estates on a charge of heresy[1].

To the summer of this year belongs an interesting episode of James's reign. In the year 1539 there had been a fresh revolt in the Isles under one **1540** Donald Gorme, which had threatened to attain formidable proportions, but which had been closed by the death of its leader in battle. To punish those who had been engaged in this revolt and to pacify the disturbed districts James now took a decisive measure On the 29th of May he set out on the circumnavigation of his kingdom with a fleet of twelve ships well-equipped with artillery, and accompanied by Cardinal Beaton and the Earls of Huntly and Arran. The result of the voyage was triumphant Disaffected chiefs were seized, those friendly to the Crown were rewarded, and garrisons were placed in suspected districts. Finally, at a meeting of the Estates held in December the Lordship of the Isles together with North and South Kintyre were annexed inalienably to the Crown[2].

surprise that James should seek to add to his income by sheep-rearing and "other mean ways" Henry had forgotten that his own ancestor Edward III was known as the "royal wool-merchant."

[1] Sadler, *State Papers* (1809), I. 94. Sadler had his information from Arran Knox, who also mentions the scroll (*Works*, I. 81, 82, 84), probably had the story from the same source

[2] Gregory, 143-9. The voyage is commemorated by a tract entitled "The Navigation of King James V round Scotland, the Orkney Isles, and the Hebrides or Western Islands," drawn up by Nicholas d'Arfeville, cosmographer of Henry II of France.

Meanwhile the difficulties of James's position were closing round him In the Parliament of December 1540 he confirmed the revocation of all grants made during his minority—an act, which however just, was certainly impolitic in view of his existing relations with England. Another sensational proceeding in August of the same year was likewise of questionable prudence On a somewhat doubtful charge of treason he put to death Sir James Hamilton of Finnart, known as the "Bastard of Arran," who in spite of his crimes and unscrupulous character had hitherto enjoyed his confidence. To the disaffection caused by the revocation of grants was thus added an offence to the house of Hamilton, which was never noted for its forgiving spirit. It would seem, indeed, that James's many anxieties had already induced symptoms of that mental and physical collapse which was to cut him off in the prime of his life. In the visions of the night, we are told, he was beset by the image of Hamilton, who with ghastly gesture announced his approaching doom.

A terrible domestic calamity befell James in the following year. Two infant sons, who had been the fruit **1541** of his marriage with Mary of Lorraine, died within three days of each other, thus leaving the kingdom once more without an heir. Possibly to divert their thoughts from their sorrow James and his queen in this same year made an interesting progress through the country, attended by their leading nobles. At Perth they were received "honourably with triumph." But it was their visit to Aberdeen that made the greatest impression on their subjects. Here for fifteen days they were entertained by the town and the university with a succession of plays, disputations, and orations "in Greek, Latin, and other languages," which last entertainment could not have greatly edified either James or his consort Returning south by way of Dundee, where great preparations were made for them, they passed to Falkland, and closed their progress at Edinburgh

In the summer of 1541 Cardinal Beaton was out of Scotland, and the King of England once more seized
the opportunity of seeking an understanding
with James.   The sagacious Sadler was again his envoy , and his main errand was to bring about Henry's long-desired object of meeting his nephew   The meeting of kings had been somewhat frequent of late years.   Charles V had visited England, and had even trusted himself with his great enemy Francis , and Henry himself had gone to France and held interviews with its king Against the wish of his counsellors the bishops James consented to meet Henry at York in the month of September ; and Henry duly appeared at the appointed time and place   To Henry's indignation James failed to keep his engagement.   When it came to the point James's advisers had dissuaded him from an interview, which might have been attended with results fatal at once to their ascendency and to the Roman Church in Scotland.   When, in October, Margaret Tudor died at the castle of Methven, it seemed as if the last link of friendship between the two countries had at length been snapped

Yet open war did not come for a few months longer, and there was again talk of an interview between
the two kings in January, 1542 What might
have been the result of this interview between the two kings it would be difficult to say ; but in the case of James, as in the case of his father, it was France that was mainly responsible for the strife that now arose between England and Scotland   At this moment the King of France was at feud with Henry : and he expressed the decided wish that there should be no interview.   Bound as he now was to France, James could not disobey this request ; and thus out of deference to her ancient ally he led the country straight to the disaster of Solway Moss, as James IV for a similar reason had led it to Flodden.   Thus thwarted in the hope of an interview, Henry was prepared to take somewhat desperate measures to reach his ends.   It was suggested to him that James might be seized in his own

country and conveyed across the Border ; and the suggestion appeared such an excellent one that Henry submitted it to his Council, which fortunately took a more correct view of the law of nations than their master.

It was Henry who took the first step towards open hostilities. In the month of August Sir Robert Bowes, accompanied by the Earl of Angus and his brother, Sir George Douglas, led a force of 3,000 men into Teviotdale ; but the result was not encouraging. At Haddon-rig, just across the Scottish Border, they were attacked by the Earl of Huntly, who gained such a decisive victory that an immediate invasion of England seemed the natural consequence. Negotiations followed in which Henry took a higher tone than ever ; but James was not to be moved from his resolution to put France first and England second in his foreign relations , and so long as this was the case Henry could not be satisfied He accordingly prepared for an invasion of Scotland on a scale that threatened to be formidable. To the Duke of Norfolk, "the Scourge of the Scots" (son of the victor of Flodden), he entrusted the charge of the expedition. No formal declaration of war was made[1] ; but in a lengthy manifesto Henry endeavoured to justify his proceeding[2]. In the tone of a much-injured and long-suffering superior, Henry in this curious document boldly reasserted the old claim of suzerainty, and enumerated his many grievances at the hands of his contumacious vassal. Norfolk's achievements, however, did not come up to his master's expectations He burnt Roxburgh and Kelso and about twenty villages ; but his army was badly victualled, and he had a watchful foe constantly on his skirts His instructions had been that he should make his way to the capital , but with the above exploits he had to rest satisfied and his retreat closely bordered on a flight[3].

---

[1] *Hamilton Papers* (1890), vol. i. p xxviii, note

[2] Henry's manifesto is given in Hall, pp 846—856 (Ed. 1809).

[3] *Hamilton Papers*, vol. i pp. xxix—xxxii.

But it was in the state of Scotland itself that Henry was to find the most effectual furtherance of his desires.

On the news of Norfolk's invasion James had   1542
assembled a force of 36,000 men, and marched to Fala Moor to give the enemy battle. When he found that Norfolk had retired he would fain have followed him into England, but his nobles refused to cross the Border Their reasons were the old ones which they had placed before the Regent Albany. The war was in the interest of France and not of Scotland; and should the king come to harm there was no heir to succeed him, and the country would be in the same case as after Flodden. Deeply mortified, James was forced to disband his army without striking a blow in revenge for the insult that had been offered to his kingdom.

Backed as he was by the great churchmen, however, he had little difficulty in raising another force, and within a month a body of at least 10,000 men were on their way to the Western Border. To divert the attention of the English warden Arran and Beaton were to make a feint of attacking the opposite March. On the night of the 23rd of November the army that was meant to do serious business lodged in two divisions at Langholm and Morton Kirk. An hour and a-half before day-break they had crossed the Esk and were busy at the usual work of a border raid[1]. Their coming, however, was not unexpected; and the English deputy-warden, Sir Thomas Wharton, issued from Carlisle, and having collected a force of some 3,000 men disputed their further progress. Between the water of Leven and the Esk the two armies came face to face, and it was at this moment that the confusion must have arisen in

---

[1] The following account of the affair at Solway Moss is based on three Despatches in the Hamilton Papers, and materially differs from the traditional narratives.— Vol. I. pp. lxxxiii—lxxxvi, 307—308, 317—319. A plan of the ground is given in the *Transactions* of the Cumberland and Westmoreland Antiquarian and Archæological Society for 1886, Art. XXVI.

the host of the Scots which was to make the day the most disgraceful in their military annals[1].   For reasons unexplained James had not accompanied his army but had remained at Lochmaben to await the result of the invasion[2]   What is still more inexplicable, the army had proceeded thus far without a responsible commander   Now that the enemy was before them, however, Sir Oliver Sinclair[3] announced that he held the king's commission appointing him to this charge.   Of Sinclair we know little beyond the fact that he had accompanied James to France, had been made governor of Tantallon Castle, and had received other marks of royal favour   The manner in which Sinclair's announcement was received showed how great was the breach between James and his nobility.   The great barons who were present refused to accept Sinclair as their leader, and the whole host became immediately a disorganised mass   Yet the nobles showed no craven spirit before the enemy.   Dismounting from their horses, they endeavoured to infuse their own spirit into their followers   But the dissensions of their leaders had broken their confidence ; and the Scots were gradually driven back before a force hardly a quarter of their own.   But in the position in which they then stood retreat was desperate.   Their only means of crossing the Esk was a narrow ford near the hill of Arthuret, and beyond the ford was the Solway Moss from which the disastrous day has taken its name   As they crowded to the ford all order was lost , and the English leaders had them at their discretion. The result of the day is conclusive proof of the hopeless panic that had beset the Scots   Twenty only were slain ; many were

---

[1] The writer of one of the English despatches says that the Scots were "in a maze"

[2] If the expedition had proved successful James was to have followed it into England

[3] He was the son of Sir Oliver Sinclair of Roslin, the eldest son by second marriage of William, last Earl of Orkney.—*Genealogie of the Santeclaires of Rosslyn*, by Father Richard Augustin Hay (Thomas Stevenson, Edin., 1835)

drowned, and twelve hundred taken prisoners, among whom were two earls, five barons, and above five hundred lairds and gentlemen[1].

It is the concurrent testimony of the early Scottish historians that the tidings of Solway Moss cut off the last hope of James, and was the immediate occasion of his premature and pathetic death.   His misfortunes of the last few years had all converged to one end.   The loss of his children, the miscarriage of his desires at Fala Moor, and the late ignominious overthrow, tended alike to foreclose the policy to which willingly or un-willingly he had committed himself since he had become a responsible sovereign   With England hostile, his most power-ful subjects alienated, and France a dubious ally, a greater spirit than that of James might well have abandoned hope ; and beaten down by his successive disasters James succumbed to his evil fortunes   From Lochmaben, where he received the news of his broken host, he proceeded to Edinburgh, and thence to his favourite palace of Falkland.   A fresh untoward incident stung him to the quick.   A few days after Solway Moss the Somerset Herald was murdered by two English fugitives in Scotland, and James was accused of being party to the crime.   But James's account with earth was soon to be closed.   On the 6th of December he took to his bed ; and the record of his last days shows that he knew his work was done. As his mind ran on late events, he was heard constantly to mutter the name of his friend and favourite Sinclair[2], who, with the royal standard in his keeping, had been taken in the fatal battle   On the 8th the news was brought that a daughter, afterwards Mary of Scotland, had been born to him.   But the

---

[1] The points in which this account of Solway Moss differs from that hitherto given are mainly these —the precise place of the engagement, the numbers of the English (usually given as a few hundreds), and the behaviour of the Scottish barons.

[2] A letter of Sir George Douglas confirms the testimony of Knox to James's sorrow for the loss of Sinclair.—*Hamilton Papers*, I 338

news gave him no comfort; and in words that are variously reported, he exclaimed that the Crown had come to his house by a woman and would pass from it by a woman. On the 14th of December he passed away at the age of thirty years and eight months[1].

The course and conclusion of James's reign are the sufficient comment on his capacity as a ruler; but his portrait is incomplete without a reference to the image of him that dwelt in the minds of his people. Of all Scottish kings except Robert I, James V would appear to have been the most popular. The very designations under which his subjects spoke of him attest the general affection with which he was regarded. He was "the king of the Commons," "the Gaber-lunzie king," "the Red Tod [Fox]." Like his father he had an inherent love of justice, and the special gift of adapting himself to all ranks of his people. It was his habit to assume various disguises and to mingle freely with his subjects with the double purpose of ascertaining their wishes and of gratifying his own love of adventure. As to these popular qualities he added notable skill and courage in the use of his weapons, he thus possessed in special degree the gifts that have perpetuated the image of certain kings in the memory of their people.

In administration and legislation, in commercial and intellectual development, the reign of James V falls far behind that of his father. While James IV played a part of some importance in relation to other countries, neither the opportunities nor the abilities of his son put it in his power to exert a similar influence. The state in which James V left his kingdom, also, seems the sufficient proof that he did not possess the administrative capacity of his father. Following his father's methods, he succeeded in pacifying the Isles; but in his dealings with

---

[1] This is the correct date, as is determined by a special note on the margin of the "Liber Emptorum," preserved in the Register House, Edinburgh.

the Borders he signally failed to conciliate those who were the permanent cause of trouble. Moreover, while James IV by his firmness and tact drew his nobility closer to him every year, his successor alienated the same body to a degree that recalls the times of James III.

The one memorable legislative act of James V was the foundation of the College of Justice in 1532. We have seen the gradual movement towards an efficient tribunal from the reign of James I. The "Session," established by that king and reformed by James II, had been transformed into the "Daily Council" by James IV. The distinctive feature of the Daily Council was that it should sit permanently in Edinburgh, or wherever the king should make his residence. But this judicial body did not fulfil the aims and expectations of its founders, and the College of Justice was framed with the view of correcting its shortcomings—being a development of the Daily Council, modelled largely on the Parliament of Paris[1], but with modifications suggested by the institutions of other countries. As in the case of the Daily Council its jurisdiction was limited to civil actions, and its decrees were to have the same effect as those of the Lords of the Session. It was to be composed of fourteen persons, seven lay, and seven spiritual, and a president who should always be a churchman—the entire body being virtually the nominees of the Crown. By two other provisions the influence of the Crown was further secured in the new court. The Lord Chancellor might take the place of the president when he pleased, and the king at his discretion might add three or four members to the permanent body. The new court may have been constructed with the best intentions, but it did not for many a day realize them. From an Act of Parliament passed in the last year of James's reign we gather that "wrangous judges" were still a grievance to the

---

[1] In the "Transactions of the Franco-Scottish Society" (Scottish Branch) Sheriff Mackay has written an interesting paper on the relations between the College of Justice and the Parliament of Paris.

country; and we learn from Buchanan that in his time the court became an instrument of tyrannical injustice from which there was no appeal.

The Parliaments that met in 1535 and 1540 passed a series of minor Acts, certain of which may serve to show the preoccupations of the time. The planting of woods, forests, and hedges is once more insisted upon[1]; every landed man is commanded to possess at least one hagbut; hostelries are to be set up in every burgh, and the price of their commodities fixed at the beginning of each year; no man is to sell cattle or sheep to any Englishman, nor to send victual or salt to England, no person is to be chosen provost, baillie or alderman of a burgh except "honest and substantious burgesses," and no earl, lord or baron is to trouble the burgh adjoining his land, in the army of Scotland no one is to be mounted except the great barons, and every parish is to choose a captain of its fencible men. The Parliament of 1542 passed certain Acts which give us further interesting glimpses into the time. One of these was "for the reparation and mending of the deformities of the town of Edinburgh" and another decreed that thenceforward all Acts of Parliament should be printed so that none of the king's subjects might plead ignorance of the laws of the land. More significant, in view of what lay in the near future, was the legislation regarding the state of the Church, in this Parliament of the last year of James V. In spite of all the burnings of heretics, their dreaded opinions still spread apace; and if the evil was to be checked, drastic legislation was urgently necessary. What is remarkable, however, is that in an Act for the reforming of kirks and kirkmen it is specified that "the unhonesty, and misrule of kirkmen, both in wit, knowledge and manners," are the chief causes of their being "lychtlyit and contempnit."

---

[1] According to John Major it was owing to their short and precarious leases that the small tenant-farmers did not plant trees or hedges.—Lib. I. Cap. v.

The reign of James V was not distinguished by the intellectual activity that so remarkably characterized that of his father, yet it was not without its eminent men of letters Gavin Douglas lived into this reign, but his literary activity belongs to that of James IV, Hector Boece died in 1536, and John Major about 1550, and both, by their works and their teaching, were ornaments of their time. But the distinctive literary productions of the reign of James V were the works of John Bellenden and Sir David Lyndsay. As the translator of Hector Boece and Livy Bellenden exhibited qualities as a writer which afford interesting proof of the influence of the revival of learning on the cultured mind of Scotland. In the highly artificial structure of his sentences and the studied care of his diction we may trace the direct effects of the new ideas regarding the classical writers on vernacular literature. The name and influence of Lyndsay doubtless appear far greater to us than to his contemporaries. His most biting satires on Church and State were but the licensed common-places which the Church had all along permitted in those public exhibitions with which they had amused the people. That the clergy could look on amused at such an exhibition as that of the Satire of the Three Estates seems to show that they had little fear of its really injuring them with the people. Whatever may have been Lyndsay's influence in hastening the Reformation, however, his writings are at least invaluable documents for the history of his time. He was instructed both by reading and travel; as an attendant on the king and by his subsequent connection with the Court he had excellent opportunities of becoming acquainted with the movement of affairs in Church and State, and as a country gentleman he was thoroughly conversant with the general condition of the people. It gives the greater historical value to his work that it is conceived and produced in the spirit of the reformer rather than of the poet; and the result is that he has registered a multitude of details regarding the lives, customs, and manners of all classes of his

fellow-countrymen which render him the best exponent of his
time.

The reign of James V marks the close of a period in
Scottish history. The distinctive characteristic of the period
that had closed had been the struggle between the Crown and
the barons—a struggle, as we have seen, that had been carried
on with varying success by either party. During the weak rule
of Robert II and Robert III the Crown was forced to make
the best terms it could with its powerful subjects; able though
James I had proved himself, his rashness and rapacity wrought
his own tragic end and the temporary ruin of his cause;
James II and James IV, in circumstances as difficult as those
of any other kings of their house, proved that by firmness and
tact even the most formidable barons could be converted into
good subjects; while James III by his weakness and folly
turned against him all classes of his people. When James V
became an actual king he had to deal with conditions which
were unknown to his predecessors. The death of so many of
the chief nobles at Flodden threw the main responsibility of
the government into the hands of the clergy; and for various
reasons James was led to maintain their predominance. In
his preference of France to England he was supported by the
clergy but opposed by most of his barons; and the progress of
events confirmed him in the policy he had adopted from the
first. His two French marriages widened the breach between
him and his nobles, and made him still more dependent on
the Church. The quarrel of Henry VIII with Rome had
likewise an influence on Scotland which cannot be measured
by any accumulation of details—the example of England being,
in truth, a great fact that touched men's minds at a thousand
points, and influenced them unconsciously to themselves. By
the close of the reign of James V two alternative courses lay
clearly before the nation, and the fact that these alternatives
had arisen distinguishes that reign from those that went before
it. The course that commended itself to James and his

ecclesiastical advisers was the continuance of the traditional policy of alliance with France and fidelity to Rome. To an increasing number of the laity, both nobles and commons, however, the wiser course seemed to be to throw in their lot with England as a policy dictated by nature herself. Ambition and self-seeking in the case of both parties obscured the issues that had thus been opened up ; but these issues were such as could not be put aside, and the overthrow of Mary Stewart at Langside, twenty-six years after Solway Moss, gave the definitive victory to Protestantism and the English alliance.

BIBLIOGRAPHY.

This Bibliography contains a list of the Authorities on which the present volume is mainly based.

A. GENERAL.

Acts of Parliament of Scotland (from 1124), Record Series.

National MSS. of Scotland (from 1094), Record Series.

Exchequer Rolls of Scotland (from 1264), Record Series.

Register of the Great Seal of Scotland (from 1306), Record Series.

Rotuli Scotiæ (from 1291), Record Series.

James Anderson, *Diplomata Scotiæ* (1094—1412).

Ancient Laws and Customs of the Burghs of Scotland (from 1124), Scottish Burgh Record Society.

Unpublished Charters in Register House, Edinburgh (from Malcolm IV).

The Laing Collection of Charters (Edinburgh University Library).

Calendar of Documents relating to Scotland (from 1272), Record Series.

Rymer, *Fœdera* (from 1100).

The Historians of Scotland (consisting of 10 volumes, and comprising the Chronicles of Fordun, Wyntoun, the Book of Pluscardyn, &c).

John Major, *A History of Greater Britain*, Scottish History Society.

George Buchanan, *Rerum Scoticarum Historia* (translated by James Aikman, 1827).

Bishop Leslie, *De Origine, Moribus, et Rebus gestis Scotorum, libri decem* (translated by Father James Dalrymple, Scottish Text Society).

Bishop Leslie, *The History of Scotland from the Death of King James I to the year* 1561, Bannatyne Club.

Robert Lindsay, of Pitscottie, *The History of Scotland* (from 1437 to 1604).

Lord Hailes, *Annals of Scotland* (1057—1370).

Pinkerton, *History of Scotland from the Accession of the House of Stuart to that of Mary*.

Gregory, *History of the Western Highlands and Isles of Scotland* (1836).

Patrick Fraser Tytler, *The History of Scotland from the Accession of Alexander III to the Union*

Hill Burton, *The History of Scotland from Agricola's Invasion* ——

E. W. Robertson, *Early Kings of Scotland* (to 1285).

Skene, *Celtic Scotland* (to death of Alexander III)

Cosmo Innes, *Scotland in the Middle Ages.*

    „   „   *Sketches of Early Scotch History.*

    „   „   *Scotch Legal Antiquities.*

John Mackintosh, *History of Civilization in Scotland.*

Duke of Argyll, *Scotland as it was, and as it is.*

Cochrane-Patrick, *Mediæval Scotland.*

Hume Brown, *Early Travellers in Scotland* (from 1295).

    „   „   *Scotland before* 1700 *from Contemporary Documents.*

The Clan Donald, by the Rev. A. Macdonald, minister of Killearnan, and the Rev. A. Macdonald, minister of Kintarlity, Inverness, 1896.

Theiner, *Vetera Monumenta Hibernorum et Scotorum, &c.* (1216—1547), Romæ, 1864.

Statuta Ecclesiæ Scoticanæ (edited by Joseph Robertson).

Origines Parochiales Scotiæ, 3 vols, Bannatyne Club.

Cunningham, *The Church History of Scotland from the Commencement of the Christian Era to the Present Century*, 2 vols.

Grub, *An Ecclesiastical History of Scotland*, 4 vols.

Bellesheim, *History of the Catholic Church in Scotland*, 4 vols (translated by Hunter Blair).

The Church of Scotland, edited by Herbert Story, D.D, F.S A.

Stephen, *History of the Scottish Church*, David Douglas, 1896.

B. SPECIAL.

BOOK I. *THE BEGINNINGS OF SCOTLAND.*

Tacitus, *Life of Agricola.*

Ptolemy, *Geography* (Book II)

Dio Cassius (Book LXXVI).

Lives of Hadrian, Antoninus Pius, Commodus, and Severus (Scriptores Historiæ Augustæ).

Bede, *Ecclesiastical History* (ed. Plummer).

Camden, *Britannia.*

＞ Sir Robert Sibbald, *Historical Inquiries concerning Roman Monuments and Antiquities, &c.* (1707).

Alexander Gordon, *Itinerarium Septentrionale; or, a Journey thro' most of the Counties of Scotland, &c.* (1726).

John Horsley, *Britannia Romana, or the Roman Antiquities of Britain, in three books* (1732).

William Roy, *Military Antiquities of the Romans in Britain* (1793).

Robert Stuart, *Caledonia; a descriptive account of the Roman Antiquities in Scotland* (1845).

Chalmers, *Caledonia,* 3 vols. 1807–24.

Christison, *Early Fortifications in Scotland; moats, camps, and forts* (1898).

Rhys, *Celtic Britain* (2nd ed).

Adamnan, *Life of St Columba* (ed. Reeves, Fowler)

Anglo-Saxon Chronicle, Record Series.

Chronicle of the Picts and Scots, Record Series.

Collectanea de Rebus Albanicis, Iona Club.—(In this work Dr W. F. Skene has collected from the Irish Annals and the Norse Sagas the various passages dealing with the early history of Scotland.)

The Historical Works of Symeon of Durham, Record Series.

War of the Gaedhil with the Gaill, or the Invasions of Ireland by the Danes and other Norsemen, Record Series.

Book of Deer, Spalding Club (edited by Dr John Stuart).

Father Innes, *Critical Essay on the Ancient Inhabitants of Scotland* (In the series of the Historians of Scotland.)

Reeves, *The Culdees of the British Islands.*

Joseph Anderson, *Scotland in Early Christian Times,* David Douglas.

Dowden, *The Celtic Church in Scotland.*

BOOK II. *THE CONSOLIDATION OF SCOTLAND.*

The Anglo-Saxon Chronicle ⎫
Chronicle of the Picts and Scots ⎪
Symeon of Durham ⎬ as above.
Collectanea de Rebus Albanicis ⎪
Book of Deer ⎭

Chronicle of Melrose, Bannatyne Club.

Chartulary of St Andrews, Bannatyne Club.

Marianus Scotus, *Chronicon universale a Creatione Mundi &c. usque ad annum Christi* 1083

Ailred, *De Bello Standardi* (see Sir Roger Twysden's *Historiæ Anglicanæ scriptores decem*)

John and Richard of Hexham, *Historia de gestis regis Stephani et de Bello Standardi* (see Twysden)

Turgot, *Life of St Margaret, Queen of Scotland* (translated by William Forbes-Leith, S J., 1884)

Henry of Huntingdon, *De Gestis regum Angliæ* (translated and edited by Thomas Forester, Bohn's Antiquarian Library).

William of Newburgh, *Historia sive Chronica rerum Anglicarum* (translation by the Rev. Joseph Stevenson). Church Historians of England.

Ordericus Vitalis, *Historia Ecclesiastica* (Duchesne, *Historiæ Normannorum Scriptores antiqui*).

Willelmi monachi Malmesburiensis de Regum gestis Anglorum, libri v; et Historiæ novellæ, Record Series

Chronicle of Holyrood, Bannatyne Club

Chronicle of Man (ed P. E Munch, Christiania, 1860).

Chronica Magistri Rogeri de Houedene, Record Series.

Gesta Regis Henrici Secundi Benedicti Abbatis, Chronicle of the Reigns of Henry II and Richard I, 1169—1192, known under the name of Benedict of Peterborough, Record Series

Matthæi Parisiensis, Monachi Sancti Albani, Chronica Majora, Vols II—VI (1216—1259), Record Series.

Matthæi Parisiensis Historia Anglorum, sive, ut vulgo dicitur, Historia Minor (1067—1253), Record Series.

Radulfi de Diceto Decani Lundoniensis Opera Historica. The Historical Books of Master Ralph de Diceto, Dean of London, Record Series.

Chronicle of Lanercost, Bannatyne Club.

During the period covered by Book II, public and private charters begin to throw light on the general history of the country.

A list of printed and unprinted Chartularies will be found in Cosmo Innes's *Lectures on Scotch Legal Antiquities*, pp. 190—193.

BOOK III *THE STRUGGLE WITH ENGLAND.*

Documents and Records illustrating the History of Scotland, and Transactions between Scotland and England (edited by Sir Francis Palgrave), Record Series.

Documents illustrative of the History of Scotland from the Death of King Alexander III to the Accession of Robert Bruce (edited by the Rev. Joseph Stevenson), Record Series.

Chronica Monasterii S. Albani —(1) Thomæ Walsingham Historia (1272—1422) (2) Wilhelmi Rishanger, Chronica et Annales (1259—1307), Record Series.

Scotland in 1298.—Documents relating to the Campaigns of Edward the First in that year, &c. (edited by Henry Gough) (Gardner, Paisley, 1888)

Papers relating to Sir William Wallace, Maitland Club.

Sir Thomas Grey, *Scalacronica*, Maitland Club.

Ragman Rolls, Maitland Club.

Chronica Rogeri de Wendover, sive, Flores Historiarum, Record Series.

Nicholas Trivet, *Annales sex Regum Angliæ* (from Stephen to Edward I).

Chronica Monasterii de Melsa ab anno 1150 usque ad annum 1406, Record Series.

Bartholomæi de Cotton, Monachi Norwicensis, Historia Anglicana (449—1298), Record Series.

Annales Monastici —Vol IV. Annales Prioratus de Wigornia (to 1377), Record Series.

Chronicle of Henry Knighton, Canon of Leicester, Record Series, and in Twysden

Chronicle of the Reigns of Edward I and Edward II, Record Series.

A Collection of Political Poems and Songs relating to English History from the Accession of Edward III to the reign of Henry VIII, Record Series

Chronicle of Adam Murimuth, with the Chronicle of Robert of Avesbury, Record Series.

Calendar of Entries in the Papal Registers, illustrating the History of Great Britain and Ireland (edited by W. H Bliss), Record Series, Vols. I and II, 1198—1342.

Robertson, *Index of Charters* (1798)

Ayloffe, *Calendar of Ancient Charters* (1772)

Barbour's *Bruce*, Scottish Text Society

Blind Harry's *Wallace*, Scottish Text Society.

Hill Burton, *The Scot Abroad.*

Francisque-Michel, *Les Écossais en France, et les Français en Écosse*, Vol. I.

Sir Herbert Maxwell, *Robert the Bruce and the Struggle for Scottish Independence*, Heroes of the Nations, Putnam's Sons.

BOOK IV. *THE CROWN AND THE BARONS*

Thomas of Walsingham } as above
Henry Knighton

Extracta e Chronicis Scotiæ, Abbotsford Club

Register of Moray, Bannatyne Club

Jean Chartier, *Chronique de Charles VI.*

Continuation of Bower's *Scotichronicon*, Pinkerton, I, 514—516

Law's MS, in Library of University of Edinburgh, A. C., c. 26.

Letters and Papers illustrative of the Wars of the English in France during the Reign of Henry the Sixth, King of England (edited by the Rev Joseph Stevenson), Record Series

Chronicle at end of Wyntoun (given in Pinkerton, Vol. I, pp. 502 *et seq*)

Ferrerius's Continuation of Hector Boece's History of Scotland (ed. Paris, 1574)

Paston Letters (edited by James Gairdner)

Letters and Papers illustrative of the Reigns of Richard III and Henry VII, Record Series (edited by James Gairdner)

Drummond of Hawthornden, *History of the Five Jameses;* and Ruddiman, *Epistolæ Regum Scotorum* (Edinb. 1722).

Memorials of Henry the Seventh : Bernardi Andreæ Tholosatis Vita Regis Henrici Septimi ; necnon alia quædam ad eundem Regem spectantia, Record Series (edited by James Gairdner)

Accounts of the Lord High Treasurer of Scotland, Vol I (1473—1498), Record Series (edited by Thomas Dickson).

Calendar of Letters, Despatches, and State Papers, relating to the Negotiations between England and Spain, preserved in the Archives at Simancas, Record Series (edited by G. A. Bergenroth and Don Pascual de Gayangos).

Calendar of State Papers and Manuscripts, relating to English Affairs, preserved in the Archives of Venice (Vols I—V, 1202—1554), Record Series (edited by Rawdon Brown).

Acta Dominorum Concilii (MS. in the General Register House Edinburgh).

Original Letters, illustrative of English History (edited by Henry
　　Ellis, London, 1825).

Calendar of Letters and Papers, Foreign and Domestic, of the
　　Reign of Henry VIII, Record Series, Vols. I—XV (1509—1540),
　　(edited by J. S. Brewer and James Gairdner).

The Ledger of Andrew Halyburton, Record Series (edited by
　　Cosmo Innes).

Leland, *Collectanea*, Vol IV.

Inventaire Chronol. des Documents relatifs à l'Histoire d'Écosse,
　　Abbotsford Club

Aarsberetninger fra det kongelige Geheimarchiv, indeholdende
　　Bidrag til dansk Historie af utrykte Kilder, Förste Bind
　　(Copenhagen, 1852)

Polydore Vergil, *Historia Anglica*

Edward Hall, *The Union of the Two Noble and Illustre Famelies
　　of Lancaster and Yorke* (1548).

Acts of the Lords Auditors of Causes and Complaints (1466—1494),
　　Record Series (edited by Thomas Thomson).

Acts of the Lords of Council in Civil Causes (1478—1495), Record
　　Series (edited by Thomas Thomson).

Teulet, *Papiers d'État relatifs à l'Histoire de l'Écosse au* XVIᵉ
　　Siècle, Tome I, Bannatyne Club.

A Diurnal of Remarkable Occurrents that have passed within the
　　country of Scotland since the Death of King James the Fourth
　　till the year MDLXXV, Bannatyne Club.

The Hamilton Papers. Letters and Papers illustrating the Political
　　Relations of England and Scotland in the XVIth century,
　　Vol. I (1532—1543), Record Series (edited by Joseph Bain).

Criminal Trials in Scotland, from A D. MCCCCLXXXVIII to A.D.
　　MDCXXIV, Maitland Club, by Robert Pitcairn.

Wigton Papers, Miscellany of Maitland Club.

The State Papers and Letters of Sir Ralph Sadler (Edinburgh,
　　1809)

Jusserand, *The Romance of a King's [James I's] Life*, Fisher
　　Unwin, 1896.

Gregory Smith, *The Days of James IV*, David Nutt, 1890.

Edmond Bapst, *Les Mariages de Jacques V*, Paris, 1889.

CAMBRIDGE. PRINTED BY J. AND C. F. CLAY, AT THE UNIVERSITY PRESS.